Oliver St John Gogarty was described by
Sir Charles Petrie as 'the work of a
modern Boswell' and his biography of
Brendan Behan also received high praise.
As a playwright he has had much success
with verse plays written in the Noh form,
accompanied by music and dance, which
have been performed at the Dublin
International Theatre Festival and off
Broadway. He has performed his one-
man show on Brendan Behan in Britain,
Europe and the United States. He has
had three books of verse published.

He was a noted sportsman, winning the
Irish Pole Vault title while he was still a
schoolboy and, at the same time, playing
first-class rugby. Two years later he won
the British Universities Welter-weight
Boxing Championship.

Ulick O'Connor was called to the Irish
Bar in 1951 and practised as a barrister
for fifteen years. He is also a member of
the Board of Directors of the Abbey
Theatre, Dublin.

Author photograph by James G. Maguire

Ulick O'Connor is a biographer,
playwright and poet. His biography of

Celtic Dawn

A Portrait of the
Irish Literary Renaissance

Ulick O'Connor

TOWN
HOUSE
DUBLIN

dback in 1984 by Hamish Hamilton
Pu   k in 1985 by Black Swan
Rep   erbac n 1991 by Black Swan

This edition published in 1999 by
Town House and Country House
Trinity House, Charleston Rd
Ranelagh, Dublin 6

ISBN: 1-86059-064-0

A CIP catalogue record for this book is available from the
British Library

Printed by Caledonian International Book Manufacturing,
Glasgow, Scotland

Cover:

A Girl Reading in Fitzwilliam Square
by Mainie Jellett, Private Collection, Dublin
By kind permission of the Jellet Trust

Contents

Illustrations

Author's Note

This book is the portrait of a period. It may be said that not enough emphasis has been given to one character while another occupies too prominent a position in the foreground. My answer is that I have placed them as they fit the portrait. The fury which ardent admirers may feel when they find a favourite in shadow – or, indeed, not represented at all – may be compared to that of those musketeers in Captain Franz Banning Cocq's militia who complained that they had been relegated to the background in Rembrandt's famous painting *The Night Watch*. But Rembrandt was not attempting conventional portraiture – he was seeking to represent the excitement and agitation he sensed from the scene before him. I have tried to convey the energy and elation of an era on Europe's last island, during which significant literature was produced. It was perhaps the last in a series of renaissances which flourished in different countries since the Italian one in the fourteenth century. To capture the essence of that era through the characters of those who created it is the purpose of this book.

Acknowledgments

I would like to thank Christopher Sinclair-Stevenson who provided the early inspiration for this book.

I would like to record my deep gratitude to Liam Galligan and Joseph Boggan of Reindear Shipping Limited for their patronage in enabling me to write it. I am grateful to the Ireland Fund who gave me a grant when it was needed. William Marx helped me generously by way of the Irish Institute. Tony O'Reilly was always helpful and encouraging. Tom Keating was also a benefactor. In the preparation of this edition I was grateful for the patronage of Denis O'Brien.

I was fortunate in the later stages to have the assistance of a superb researcher, Alan Sweetman, whose enthusiasm, industry, knowledge and attention to detail were invaluable. To my typists, Yvonne Pym, Eve Mooney, Vivien Cosgrave and Lynn Kemp much thanks is due.

Sean White kindly let me see his unpublished thesis on Standish O'Grady and was helpful in other ways. Sean Ó Luing put useful papers at my disposal. Brendan Ó Cathaoir helped with research. Gerry O'Flaherty was unsparing in his proof reading and in lending his advice on the manuscript at different stages. Monk and Winifred Gibbon read the manuscript and offered many helpful suggestions. Picture research was conducted with great skill by Jeanne Marie Finlay and Michael O'Brien of the O'Brien Press.

Julian Evans was most helpful as editor and, with the gentlest of hints, often steered me in the right direction when inspiration was failing.

I wrote this book in a variety of places, including Morocco and Malta, and I am grateful to the Tourist Boards of these countries for their facilities.

I was given assistance by many people in this work, but I should like to acknowledge the following in particular: Dr Robert Becker; Dr Francis Byrne; Dr James Flannery; Conal Gogan; Dr John Kelly (St John's College, Oxford); the late J.M. Kerrigan; Ciarán Mac an Ailí; Tomás Mac Anna; Tadgh McGlinchey, Jr; Ciarán Mac Mathúna; Augustine Martin; Joe Molloy; Peter Morrisroe; the Librarian and Staff of the National Library, in particular Brian McKenna and Peadar Mac Mathúna; Dr Eoin O'Brien; Michael O'Connell; Dr Donnchadh Ó Corráin; Micheál Ó hAodha; Seán Ó Luing; Chris O'Neill; Vincent O'Neill; Sheila Richards; Douglas Sealey; the late Arthur Shields; Dr Trevor West.

My grateful thanks are also due to the following individuals and oranisations for permission to quote from work still in copyright: BBC Publications for the talk with Gogarty in *Irish Literary Portraits* by W.R. Rodgers; Jonathan Cape Ltd for material from *Portrait of the Artist as a Young Man* and *Chamber Music*; William Collins, Sons & Co. Ltd for material from *Cities, Islands and Towns* by Arthur Symons; the Society of Authors on behalf of the Shaw Estate for material from *John Bull's Other Island* by George Bernard Shaw; the Society of Authors as the literary representative of the Masefield Estate for material from John Masefield's *Memories of Yeats*; Miss D.E. Collins for material from G.K. Chesterton's *Autobiography*; the Society of Authors as the literary representative of the James Joyce Estate for material from a speech by Joyce from 'The Day of the Rabblement', from *Stephen Hero*, from a letter by Joyce to Ibsen, and for 'Tilly' from *Pomes Pennyeach* and a limerick about Lady Gregory; Sean MacBride, SC, for a speech by Maud Gonne; McGibbon & Kee for material from *It Isn't this Time of Year at All* by Oliver St John Gogarty; Michael Yeats and Macmillan London Ltd for extensive material from W.B. Yeats's *Collected Poems*, *Collected Plays*, *Collected Letters* and *Autobiographies*; Penguin Books Ltd for material from *I Claud* by Claud Cockburn; Douglas Sealey for material from *Love Songs of Connacht* by Douglas Hyde, and from speeches, letters and diaries of Hyde; and Southern Illinois University Press for material from *Holloway Diaries* edited by Robert Hogan and Michael O'Neill.

Prologue

Coming to live in Ireland can have a disturbing effect on the newcomer. Bernard Shaw put it down to the climate which he maintained

> will stamp an immigrant more deeply and durably in two years apparently than the English climate will in two hundred.

As early as 1368 the English were worried by the problem of colonists who had gone native. Whole families of Norman overlords were speaking Gaelic, wearing Irish dress, patronising native music and becoming indistinguishable from the race they had been instructed to colonise. Statutes (Edward II, 125) were enacted to prevent by force of law this assimilation, but the process continued nevertheless. 'Lord how quickly doth that country alter men's natures,' wrote Edmund Spenser in 1596, noting with disapproval how the colonists seemed to have become even more stubborn and disobedient than the natives. Cromwell made an attempt to solve the matter by transplanting the native Irish to Connacht so as to allow those newcomers of English descent who replaced them to retain their identity without contact with the indigenous race. The promulgation of the Penal Laws in 1704 was designed, as the Chancellor of the Exchequer said at the time, to demonstrate that

> the system did not presume an Irish Catholic to exist except for the purpose of punishment.

Despite these strenuous efforts to separate the two

13

classes, both continued to show that they shared more in common than that they differed.

In 1782 an Irish Parliament entirely composed of Protestant representatives declared itself empowered to enact laws independently of the English Parliament. These manifestations of patriotism, clearly demonstrated in public declamation, so alarmed the English that eighteen years later they abolished the Dublin Parliament altogether and transported its representatives to Westminster.

But the Statutes of Kilkenny, the Penal Code, and the Act of Union, were all unavailing against the assimilating qualities of the island, and throughout the nineteenth century, though the country was now governed directly from England, it could be seen that a personality was emerging on the island, neither Anglo-Irish nor native-Irish but a blend of both. The new Irishman was in the process of being born just as the new Englishman had come into being three centuries before, a fusion of the different elements on the island.

In July 1958 I attended the funeral service of Lennox Robinson, a Director of the Abbey Theatre, Dublin and one of its early successful playwrights. The service was held in St Patrick's Cathedral in the heart of Dublin. St Patrick's is the showplace of the Anglo-Irish, a splendid building with soaring Gothic vaults and a baptismal font in which it is said a Scandinavian king of Dublin was baptised.

The service was indistinguishable from an Anglican one. The anthem was Greene's 'Lord Let Me Know Mine End' and the voices of the choir swirled upwards against the ribbed vaults, in the soaring and receding echo of Anglican chant.

On the walls of the Cathedral hung the flags of regiments who had distinguished themselves in the service of Empire. Beneath were inscribed the names of the many battles in which generations of Anglo-Irish had fought to build up England's power across the globe. But the voice of the Dean who read the lesson was unmistakeably Irish, and so were the faces of those who filled the pews. As the Catholic friends of Lennox Robinson had been prohibited by their Archbishop from taking part in the service, it could fairly be said that the majority of people there represented the Protestant Irish. But that these were Irish and not English there was no doubt, though the head of their church had been an English queen.

Then there was the Latin inscription on the wall on the right-hand side of the church: *Hic depositum est corpus Jonathan Swift . . . ubi saeva indignatio ulterius cor lacerare nequit.*

Here lies the body of Jonathan Swift . . . where savage indignation can no longer lacerate his heart.

It was from the epitaph of a one-time Dean of the Cathedral. What Englishman, wishing to discriminate himself for posterity, would have chosen such words? They have in them the fury of the Gaelic poets contemporary with Swift, who railed with similar savagery against the downfall of their chieftains. That Swift was in tune with the native condition we know from at least one Irish translation that he made, and from his friendship with musicians and poets of the alternative culture. His fury against English misrule in Ireland, expressed in imagery so fantastic that it rivalled the wildest extremes of the Gaelic satirists, so captivated his fellow citizens that he became a hero of the Dublin working class, and was carried on their shoulders to and from the very cathedral which represented the religion of those who were engaged in suppressing the Gaelic nation.

Near St Patrick's Cathedral, in College Green, stands the statue of Henry Grattan. Like Swift he was an Anglo-Irishman born in Dublin. But with the rise in 1782 of a parliament which claimed to make its own laws he had become within the context of the time an Irish patriot. His speech at the inauguration of that parliament would become a hymn of nationalism recited round the firesides of nationalist Ireland in the nineteenth century.

I will never be satisfied as long as the meanest cottager in Ireland has a link of the British chain clanking to his rags; he may be naked, he shall not be in iron; . . . and though great men should apostatize yet the cause will live; . . . the immortal fire shall outlast the organ which conveyed it, and the breath of liberty like the words of the holy man will not die with the prophet, but survive him.

Grattan had absorbed the personality of the race as Swift had. His oratory had poetic elements that belonged to the Celtic imagination rather than the tradition of Pitt and Fox. When, after the Act of Union, he was elected for Malton and rose to make his maiden speech in the House of Commons, the members laughingly greeted him by clapping their hands to the beat of his measured oratory. But they were dealing with someone who came from a people whose gift was the spoken word. It was not difficult for him to introduce a counterpoint rhythm which put their clapping out of joint. Again and again he varied his rhetorical beat till the jeering subsided, and the House listened spellbound for four hours. This was the imposition of a new sound in a foreign chamber and behind it beat the muffled cadences of the Gaelic nation.

Grattan's statue faces Trinity College where he had been a student. In 1833, thirteen years after his death, a young man named Thomas Davis entered the College. It was an auspicious time for a Protestant with nationalist leanings, because with the relaxation of the penal laws Catholics were for the first time allowed to become students there. Young men who had grown up in the Anglo-Irish tradition and those who came from a native background now mixed together on equal terms. This mingling of two breeds was to accelerate the process that had already been at work subconsciously in the national mind. With two young Catholics, John Blake Dillon a barrister and Charles Gavan Duffy a solicitor, Davis founded *The Nation* newspaper, in which they set down their philosophy of an Ireland looking to the ancient race as the primary source of their inspiration, but absorbing the elements as well of the later peoples who had arrived on the island.

The Great Famine of 1845–1848 retarded the process. Davis himself died in 1845. But a year later another leader was born who was to mirror in his personality the various characteristics of the different elements in the new Ireland.

Charles Stewart Parnell became Leader of the Irish Party in 1880. He was a Wicklow landlord whose grandfather on his paternal side had been a Minister in Grattan's Parliament.

As a parliamentarian Parnell was cold, methodical, masterful. In opposition at different periods to Disraeli, Gladstone, Salisbury he excelled each of them in tactics. He perceived that the alliance between the three main forces in the country – revolutionary republicanism, land agitation and the middle class parliamentary movement – could bring into being a party that would be a force in parliament without whose help no English party could govern. Though he succeeded in winning the revolutionary movement to his side, so subtle was the stance he adopted that his enemies, though they tried, found it impossible to bring about his downfall by allying him with extremist doctrines. His personality changed constantly, alternating between the cunning peasant and the aloof aristocrat, the hot-headed Celt and the calculating Saxon, and his rhetoric embraced both the revolutionary language of the hillside men and the measured phrases of parliamentary pleading.

Parnell was the first of the ruling caste to speak for the whole nation in a constitutional crusade. He epitomised the new Irishman and sent waves of regeneration through the people that hastened the process of the recognition of the national being. It was the exhilaration and elation of this period that excited the imagination of writers and artists and, as in the case of the Elizabethan age, led to the creation of significant literature.

Part One

1   The Gentry

Land is the reward of the colonist. In Ireland it had frequently been taken from the original owners and parcelled out to newcomers who at first had no links with the dispossessed.

At the beginning of the eighteenth century, although Irish Catholics formed three-quarters of the population they owned only five per cent of the land. They were excluded from the professions and public service and could not enter Parliament. The penal code which deprived them of these rights was, in the words of the historian Lecky, intended to 'make them poor and keep them poor – degrade them into a servile class'. The Act of Union finally encapsulated Ireland as a colony, quenching an embryo local parliament and ensuring that the country be run by two men, a Viceroy and a Chief Secretary. Under them a permanent Under Secretary, Lord Chancellor and an Attorney-General functioned. As the King's representative the Viceroy had nominal power. But as a member of the Cabinet the Chief Secretary answered questions on Ireland in the House, and was responsible for the drafting of Irish bills so that it was in his hands effective power lay. The permanent civil service was largely English. The aim of Dublin Castle, which functioned as the centre of Government, was to remodel the Irish character until the native population became a part of the imperial structure that included Scotland and Wales.

That this system of imposed government was ruinous had become notorious by the middle of the nineteenth century.

The Great Famine of 1845–48 had underlined the ineffectiveness of the Government when faced with catastrophe. A failure of the potato crop, the chief diet of the rural population, was met not with adequate schemes of relief, but with the frenzied application of laissez-faire economic doctrines, the result of which was effectively to halve the Irish population. In 1845 the population had been 8.5 million. By 1848 it was 4 million. Two million had died of starvation and disease, two million had emigrated on famine boats. Even before the Famine the German traveller Kohl had thought that the conditions of the Irish peasant had made 'even the poorest of the Letts, Estonians and Finlanders, dwell and live very respectably'. Thackeray had been horrified by the vast hordes of beggars he came across everywhere on his travels and Carlyle, who visited the West of Ireland in 1846, thought it might be better to shoot the workers rather than create employment and have them survive in a sub-human state.

But the revival of the potato crop in 1848 did not end the horror. To survive many had had to spend their savings and were unable to pay rent. Many landlords showed themselves merciless. Between 1849 and 1853, 316,000 people were evicted from cottage and cabin and put on the roadside. Some survived by digging holes in the bogs, roofing them with peat and existing as troglodytes.

The landlords who drew vast monies from multitudes of pitiful tenants suffered no such deprivations. Against the desolate landscape of untilled fields, brown bogs and ruined cabins, reared the image of the big house. Here were lavish hospitality, dinners, balls, hunts. This privileged class entertained one another as they had done before the Famine. No expense had been spared in erecting their great mansions; Cassels, James Gandon, Ivory, Wyatt, had come to Ireland to build for this extravagant but discerning ruling class. Their houses were filled with paintings and furniture acquired on travels in Europe or brought back from foreign countries while in the service of Empire.

After the Union a number of them spent the greater

part of the year in London, renting out their town houses in Dublin. Those who stayed behind did 'the season' from January to March in Dublin, when the Viceregal court sat in Dublin Castle and the young girls from country houses took residence in the city in the hope of acquiring husbands at the great balls and entertainments.

Between the majority of landlords and tenants there was virtually no contact. From time to time violence erupted. Moonlighters, Ribbonmen, Peep-O-Day Boys, conducted campaigns of cattle maiming, house burnings, even assassination against those whom they regarded as representatives of a system that oppressed them.

But despite these barriers – which had grown from one nation's desire to subdue another – other forces were at work of a more subtle nature, which were to bring the two classes to a stage where a section of them would recognise a common identity. In each century for a brief period the barriers had been breached which had held the two communities apart. This time they would be demolished in the deluge.

Three members of the landed gentry would act as precursors of the change that would take place. Their names were Standish O'Grady, Douglas Hyde and Charles Stewart Parnell: the discoveries in Irish literature of the first two would mould the course of the literary movement; and the third would act as a catalyst in the national metamorphosis. In a country house in the West of Ireland in the winter of 1870 a young Irish barrister found himself with nothing to do. An Atlantic gale was blowing outside and, unlike the warm subtropical Bantry Bay further south from which Standish O'Grady had come, once the rain blew from the sea in Galway there was no question of venturing out. Standish O'Grady was the grand-nephew of the Lord Chief Baron, Viscount Guillamore, and also of one of Nelson's captains, Admiral Hayes O'Grady. His uncle had fought at Waterloo with distinction and become a general.

O'Grady's father was a minor landlord who was also Rector of Bearhaven in County Cork. Standish himself sometimes collected rents during his vacations as Revising Barrister for Belfast; he also contributed to English and Irish journals and newspapers through which, like many young barristers, he supplemented his meagre income at the Bar.

In appearance he was much more like what was known as the native-Irish than the landlord class. He had dark hair and brilliant white skin, a roguish eye and a musical Cork accent. He carried himself well (he had been a champion hockey player at Trinity College) and was of medium height and well built.

As he watched the rain beating the windows, Standish O'Grady noticed a set of books on the table nearby. They were O'Halloran's *History of Ireland* in three volumes. Now at Trinity College, Dublin, O'Grady had never been made aware that Ireland had a history. Not a hint had been uttered by pastor or master. More bored than curious, he took up the books and began to read them. After the first few pages his excitement grew. What ancestral memories welled up in him we know not, but the reading of these three volumes changed his life. He learnt now for the first time that Ireland had a culture which went back five hundred years before the birth of Christ, and which was as clearly identifiable as that of the Greeks or Egyptians. For the next ten years he was to devote himself to producing in popular form this history 'drawing its life from the soil as a natural growth', and publishing it in 1880.

In the Royal Irish Academy he discovered the original manuscript translations of the tales and sagas he had read about in O'Halloran's history, which had been collected by the scholar Eugene O'Curry. Such a collection put him on solid ground as he began to create his style which would represent for his reader the vigour and originality of the history he was writing about.

It was not, of course, history in the real sense of the word. More accurately it could be described as the record of a high culture which had existed from about 500 BC and which had been handed down in oral form through the Bardic Sagas. It was not until the eleventh century that they had been first transcribed.

The chief manuscript document was the Táin. Here were told the tales of the heroes against a background of kingly wars, as Homer had told his in the *Odyssey*, and the unknown narrator in the *Nibelungenlied*. As the Greek and German tales had Ulysses and Siegfried for heroes, so the Irish had Cuchulain. He is the authentic heroic figure, god-born with the 'hero light' which plays about his head when danger threatens: cunning, devious, outrageously brave and a destroyer of his enemies, whether by the help of the gods or his own skill at war. Cuchulain's deeds in the services of Conor, King of Ulster and the Knights of the Red Branch at Eamhain Macha are retold in the Táin along with the saga tales of Deirdre and the Sons of Usna.

I desire [wrote O'Grady in a pamphlet which preceded the publication of his history] to make this heroic period once again a portion of the imagination of the country and its chief characters as familiar to the minds of the people as they once were.

How well he succeeded can be seen from the tributes by the writers who followed him in the Irish literary revival.

Whatever is Irish in me he kindled to life [Yeats would write later] to him every Irish imaginative writer owes a portion of his soul.

For George Russell (AE) Tennyson's Knights of the Round Table were tepid compared with the figures created by O'Grady.

It was the memory of a race which rose up within me as I read, and I felt exalted as one who learns he is among the children of kings.

O'Grady was a fervent believer in the Union. In December 1881 he organised a convention of landlords to resist the proposed implementation of the Gladstone Land Acts, which would transfer minimal rights to tenants. He was not a nationalist in the political sense of the word. But he had discerned a sense of nationhood between himself and the other community in the country. He could speak of 'our common ancestry' and take pride in the pre-Christian Gael 'who communicated arts and sciences to the Greeks rather than received from them'.

The reading of those ancient manuscripts illuminated that part of his consciousness which up to that time had remained unaware of any other identity but that of a settler living in a hostile community.

Born in 1860 Douglas Hyde, like Standish O'Grady, was a rector's son. Like O'Grady too he was of landed gentry stock. His ancestors were Elizabethan planters from Berkshire who had received land grants in County Cork where they built a splendid mansion, Castle Hyde. He would remark in later years that his first ancestor in Ireland was a friend of the Earl of Leicester, a favourite of Queen Elizabeth. Hyde was brought up in Frenchpark, County Roscommon at Ratra Rectory, a mile from the mansion of another kinsman, Lord de Freyne.

Hyde used to say later that he learnt Irish as a young boy 'because it was a fine and worthy tongue'; but for a rector's son to learn the language of the peasantry was in those days as likely as a white planter in Africa interesting himself in the native culture. That was the way the Irish gentry tended to look on the peasantry – as white negroes. In fact Lord Salisbury had implied as much when, campaigning against Home Rule, he had used the phrase: 'You would not confide free representative institutions to Hottentots.'

One of the factors in bringing Hyde in contact with the native Irish culture was that he had not been sent to school as a boy but had been educated at home. A splendid shot with a natural eye, and a flexible wrist on the river, he had spent much of his early youth in the company of gillies and labourers. They spoke Irish among themselves, and young Douglas with his ear for language began laboriously to learn the tongue he heard around him. First of all he wrote it out phonetically. Then with the use of an Irish Bible he learnt the Gaelic script so that he could read and transcribe accurately. With this key to the tongue of the people he made an exciting discovery: that the peasantry in northern Connacht were rich in bardic culture, legend and folklore. They would tell him around the cottage fire, as he rested after a day's fowling, tales that went back before the time of Christ, or recite poems that had the ring of courtly verse about them. The revelation of this sunken culture had a dramatic effect on this young man. He recognised that the people his class despised were in possession of a culture thousands of years old and which had survived in the oral tradition of the cottages despite many attempts to exterminate it. This discovery aroused in young Hyde deeply anti-English feelings. His diaries have many verses written in Irish, calling down his 'dreadful curse on the island of the Saxon red with blood', and summoning Irishmen to free their country 'by rising and drawing their blades like men'. But though secretly he cherished these treasonable sentiments they did not prevent young Douglas from leading the typical life of a Roscommon gentleman. He played cricket, went to tennis parties, attended county balls where he was much admired for his good looks – dark watchful eyes and high, almost Slavonic, cheekbones. In his anti-English poems Hyde was not striking out against his own breed but against the exploitation of another class of Irishman under foreign rule, and at the manner in which an imposed system had prevented the two classes in Ireland from mutual participation in each other's culture.

As Douglas became more fluent in Irish he collected more and more folklore and poetry. When he was seventeen he picked up 'Mo Bhrón ar an bhFairrge' from an old woman living in a cabin in the middle of a bog, and translated it into English, little thinking that twenty years later it would be in the Oxford Book of English Verse.

My grief on the sea,
  How the waves of it roll!
For they heave between me
  And the love of my soul!

Abandoned, forsaken,
  To grief and to care,
Will the sea ever waken
  Relief from despair?

My grief, and my trouble!
  Would he and I were
In the province of Leinster,
  Or county of Clare.

Were I and my darling –
  O, heart-bitter wound! –
On board of the ship
  For America bound.

On a green bed of rushes
  All last night I lay,
And I flung it abroad
  With the heat of the day.

And my love came behind me –
  He came from the South;
His breast to my bosom,
  His mouth to my mouth.

This was a folk poem, but Hyde had also come across poetry which had survived from an era when the king of each province kept court bards trained in a tradition of courtly verse. He had a remarkable gift as a translator and was able to render into English the complicated internal assonance and rhyme of this courtly verse, while at the same time keeping to the metre and meaning of the original, as he has done in 'Ni bhFág Mise Bás

28

Duit', which he took down at the elbow of a scyther working in the fields, who recited it in Irish for him.

For thee I shall not die,
Woman high of fame and name;
Foolish men thou mayest slay
I and they are not the same.

Why should I expire
For the fire of any eye,
Slender waist of swan-like limb,
Is't for them that I should die?

The round breasts, the fresh skin,
Cheeks crimson, hair so long and rich;
Indeed, indeed, I shall not die,
Please God, not I, for any such.

The golden hair, the forehead thin,
The chaste mien, the gracious ease,
The rounded heel, the languid tone,
Fools alone find death from these.

Thy sharp wit, thy perfect calm,
Thy thin palm like foam of sea;
Thy white neck, thy blue eye,
I shall not die for thee.

Woman, graceful as the swan,
A wise man did nurture me,
Little palm, white neck, bright eye,
I shall not die for ye.

Douglas's father, the Reverend Arthur Hyde, wanted his son to take orders and come back as a parson to Roscommon and use his knowledge of the native language to recruit peasants for the Protestant faith. Douglas was revolted by the idea, and had many dreadful scenes with 'the Governor' before he finally agreed at the age of twenty-one to study Divinity at Trinity but without consenting to take orders at the completion of his College career. In fact, though he was to complete his Divinity studies in four years, taking many honours on the way, he went on to study Law, taking out his Doctorate in 1888.

His years in Trinity convinced Douglas that the Irish language might be a bond 'to weld together the Irish nation'. He was to write a monumental *Literary History of Ireland*, tracing the course of literature in Gaelic from 500 BC to the nineteenth century. He would also be largely responsible for the founding of the Gaelic League, whose purpose was to preserve the Irish language and which was to have enormous social and political implications for the evolution of Irish society between 1893 and 1922.

But Douglas Hyde's major contribution to the literary movement was his translation of folk poetry and religious songs which he had collected in Connacht and which he took down from the lips of the peasant people or traced with Sherlock Holmes-like tenacity in ageing manuscripts, some of which were discovered in cottages and stables in the West.

It was through the prose translations of Hyde's 'Love Songs of Connacht', 'Songs Ascribed to Raftery' and 'Religious Songs of Connacht' published between 1890 and 1894 that Yeats, Lady Gregory and Synge would find a key to native Irish culture, and recognise that here was material which could be used as the foundation for an original movement in literature.

In April 1875 a young Irish landlord took his seat in the House of Commons. He was extremely good-looking with magnetic eyes. Frank Harris thought him 'by far the handsomest man I had ever seen in the House of Commons – the noble profile, the great height, the strange blazing eyes, the thin white face'.

Charles Stewart Parnell was from Avondale, County Wicklow but he had been elected for County Meath in the Home Rule interest by 1771 votes to 912.

In speech and bearing Parnell seemed a typical product of public school and Cambridge. But the House was soon to learn that he harboured very different sentiments from the standard product of his class in Ireland. Within a few days of taking his seat he told the Members, 'Ireland is not a geographical figment, she is a nation.' And some months later when he was accused, in relation to the three Fenian prisoners executed in Manchester for the killing of Constable Brett, of apologising for murder, he replied coldly, 'I do not believe, and I never shall believe that any murder was committed in Manchester.'

Though in many respects Parnell had the typical background of the Anglo-Irish gentry, there was one key difference between himself and his fellow landlords – his mother was an American. Her name before her marriage to John Parnell of Avondale had been Delia Stewart, and she was the daughter of an admiral in the American Navy who had carried out so many daring exploits against the English that he was known as 'Old Ironsides'. Delia Stewart Parnell used to say:

> My grandfather fought against the English during the War of Independence in 1812 and I suppose the Parnells had no great love for the English either. Sir John Parnell fought against the Union and gave up office for Ireland, and Sir Henry was always on the Irish side against England. It was natural, then, for Charles to hold the views he does. But it's not the English people that the Parnells have disliked, it is the English dominion.

At his mother's town house in Dublin as a young man Parnell had met American Civil War veterans who had come over to take part in the Fenian rising. At convivial dinners he had joined in choruses of anti-English songs and listened to speeches which would have been regarded as treasonable if they had been heard by spies of Dublin Castle. His sisters Anna and Fanny were rabid nationalists. Anna had thrown a rose into the dock at the trial of the dynamitard O'Donovan Rossa in 1870; Fanny was the author of a poem which was recited at national gatherings throughout the country and which began:

31

Shall mine eyes behold thy glory, O my country?
Shall mine eyes behold thy glory?
Or shall the darkness close around them ere the
   sunblaze
Break at last upon thy story?

Soon after he had entered the House of Commons Parnell became aware of a small hunch-backed Irish member who dressed in a bright sealskin waistcoat and who wore wellington boots under trousers that were cut short. It would have been difficult not to notice Joseph Biggar, the Member for Belfast, for he spent a large part of his waking hours in Parliament holding up the business of the House. Biggar had discovered the possibilities of the American tactic of filibustering and was determined to apply it to the mother of parliaments in the absence of any interest by the government in improving conditions in his native land. 'Mr Biggar,' wrote the *London World* of 5 March 1876, 'brings the manner of his store into the illustrious assembly and his manner even for a Belfast store is very bad. When he rises to address the House as he did at least ten times last night, the air is heavy with the odour of kippered herring.'

Parnell was quick to spot the effectiveness of Biggar's tactics and to join with him in the policy of obstruction. There could hardly have been two less likely allies than the leprechaun-like Member for Belfast and the tall, aristocratic Member for Meath, but working in tandem in the Commons they made a perfect combination.

That a member of the landlord class should adopt the tactics of shopkeepers shocked *The Times*, who resented the House of Commons 'being sent to school by a few ignorant Irishmen'.

Parnell's reply to criticisms of this sort infuriated his opponents even more. 'The first thing you've got to do with an Englishman on the Irish question,' he told the *Freeman's Journal*, 'is to shock him, then you can reason with him right enough.' On 31 July 1877 he, Biggar and a few colleagues kept the House in continual session from

4 p.m. on Monday to 6.30 p.m. on Tuesday to pass the South African Bill, the longest session so far in the history of Parliament.

Obstruction policies were not acceptable to the gentlemanly leader of the Irish Party, Isaac Butt. But Parnell knew what he was doing: within two years he had gained control of the Party and Butt had been deposed. Once elected Parnell set out to make the Irish Party what Lord Curzon later described as 'the most formidable political combination that has been seen in our time'. He was helped in his objective by the land agitation which had begun in 1877 in County Mayo. This was led by an organiser of genius, Michael Davitt, whose family had been evicted from their cottage in County Mayo in 1851 and who had emigrated to Lancashire where Davitt had grown up. Educated by Quakers, Davitt had nevertheless at an early age become involved in revolutionary activity and served ten years' penal servitude (after being convicted on charges of possession of dynamite) before being released in 1876. Shortly afterwards Davitt had returned to Ireland where he organised the Mayo Land League which was the first combination in these islands to use passive resistance as a means to change unjust land legislation. The formula used by the Land League was to refuse to pay rents which were deemed unjust, and to boycott those who accepted the land from which a tenant had been evicted. The evicted tenants were rehoused and reimbursed from a public fund. As the landlords up to this time had exercised feudal authority over their tenants, such organised resistance was a direct challenge to their power. With the threat of a repeat of the Great Famine of 1845 (the value of the potato crop fell from 14.7 million pounds in 1876 to 6.7 in 1879) the Land League swept Ireland. Mass meetings of farmers on horseback and frieze-coated peasants took place throughout the country and made reform of the land laws a national issue.

Parnell quickly recognised the power of the League.

He also perceived, with the acute political insight which was to characterise his career, that the other element necessary to consolidate his constitutional campaign was the physical force movement, at that time in the hands of the Irish Republican Brotherhood. If he could get the Land League and the 'hillside men' on his side he could forge a political weapon in Parliament that could make it impossible for Conservatives or Liberals to rule without the help of the Irish members.

By the time Parnell became Leader of the Party in May 1880 he had persuaded the Irish Republican Brotherhood to support him and to put forward nominees for Westminster. Michael Davitt had thrown the weight of the Land League behind him. Then Gladstone unwittingly canonised Parnell. He placed him and ten other leaders in prison in October 1881 and left them there for six months. From his cell Parnell virtually took control of the country and forced the Government to release him without conditions the following May. The author of the Coercion Act under which he had been imprisoned, W.E. Foster, resigned as Chief Secretary, but before he did made an acknowledgement of Parnell's power:

> I think we may remember what a Tudor King said to a great Irishman in former times. 'If all Ireland cannot govern the Earl of Kildare, then let the Earl of Kildare govern Ireland' ... in like manner, if all England cannot govern the Honourable Member for Cork then let us acknowledge that he is the greatest power in Ireland today.

Foster's prophecy proved correct. By 1885 Parnell had ousted Gladstone on the issue of the Coercion Acts, replaced him by Salisbury and six months later removed Salisbury, to replace him with Gladstone once more. By this time Parnell held the balance of power in Westminster with eighty-six Nationalist members returned at the election. Gladstone, now converted to the principle of Home Rule for Ireland, went to the country in 1886 on the issue, but lost the election to the

Conservatives. From Parnell's view the result was irrelevant, as it was clear that from now on no matter what party was in power the Irish question would dominate Parliament. Egypt, Sudan, India faded into insignificance beside this *damnosa hereditas* of British politics.

Parnell reached the height of his power in 1888 when, after being accused by *The Times* of conspiring in the assassination of Lord Frederick Cavendish and Under-Secretary Burke, he was vindicated by a Commission appointed by Parliament. When the House rose to cheer him after his name was cleared, he refused to acknowledge their congratulations. 'What would they have said if I'd lost?' was all he would say to a fellow MP.

Parnell played a dual role that captured the emerging personality of his people. To many he appeared cold and unapproachable. Once in the House of Commons he remained calm and white-faced during the course of a savage attack on him. Afterwards a friend noticed his hands, and saw that the palms were blood-stained where the nails had bitten into them. It was this controlled passion which had enabled him to dominate Parliament, but would not have worked with the revolutionaries and land agitators whom he had to control in his own Party. There he allowed the other side of his personality to surface. At revolutionary gatherings in Paris or New York he joined in the singing of rebel songs and the anti-English talk that dominated many of the evenings, allowing the landlord part of his personality to subside, while that side of him which derived from his contact with the people took over. He who was held by his enemies to be a cold Anglo-Saxon pragmatist had a decided mystical element in his character. 'I should never have burnt the witches of old,' he once told his fellow MP William O'Brien. 'Macbeth's mistake was not in consulting the witches but only in believing the portion that pleased him in their advice. You never know in what strange quarters knowledge may be hidden. The foolishness of The Cross was the breathlife of Christianity.'

Another time he talked about science never being

worthwhile until it proved itself by getting 'outside this little world to support life in a new atmosphere so that a voyage to the planets or even to the stars won't be much more difficult than that of Columbus'. By some process of insight inexplicable in terms of his upbringing, he seemed to understand the symbols that derived from the primitive beliefs of the people and used to point out that as the great mystics like St John of the Cross and St Francis all required woman helpers to further their plans, so young men would never have sacrificed themselves for Ireland had they not pictured her as a woman, which made the risks worth taking.

His dual nature, Anglo-Saxon pragmatism allied with a Celtic mystical streak, defined the image of the new Irishman that Yeats, AE, Hyde and O'Grady had discerned on an instinctive level. Poised for power at the end of the second last decade of the century, Parnell generated an energy that fuelled the elation unleashed in the national being.

2   Country House Culture

From three great country houses in Connacht would
come three of the four people who were to create the
Irish Literary Theatre which was the foundation of the
literary renaissance. These were Coole Park, Moore
Hall and Tulira Castle. Lady Augusta Gregory was not
born at Coole, but she was to make it a gathering place
for poets and playwrights and artists. George Moore's
family had lived at Moore Hall for generations. Edward
Martyn, who lived in Tulira, came from a Norman family
who had arrived in Ireland in the twelfth century. What
was the background of these unusual landlords of mixed
racial origin who were to inaugurate one of the important literary movements of the century?

Lady Gregory was born Isabella Augusta Persse in
1852, four years after the end of the Great Famine. Hers
was a large family, eighteen in all, of whom Augusta
was the fourteenth, the last girl though with four
younger brothers. The Persses lived at Roxborough in
East Galway, on a 6,000-acre estate. It was so large that
four masons were continuously at work repairing the
demesne walls. Roxborough had its own smithy, saw
mills, carpentry, coach and dairy shops.

The family were of Cromwellian origin and low
church. Augusta had a strict upbringing. She was not
allowed to read Shakespeare or Scott till she was
eighteen. At the end of each day there was a strict
examination of conscience: 'what sin have I committed
in thought, word or deed?' Her mother believed that all
Papists were damned, and encouraged the girls to

promote conversions among the tenantry. Once there was an embarrassing scene when a Persse sister pulled the arm of a child in the direction of a Bible tent, while a priest pulled another arm in the opposite direction. Augusta must have been of an independent frame of mind even as a young girl, for though she gave in to her mother on most matters she would never join in proselytism of any kind.

She had had, unlike the rest of the family, a Catholic nurse. Before she came to Roxborough Mary Sheridan had been employed in the household of Hamilton Rowan, the pardoned rebel of the 1798 insurrection. She used to tell the little girl tales of the rebellion and how she had herself talked with people who had been in a theatre when the French landed at Killala in 1798 and could recall how the audience stood up and cheered at the news. This gave Augusta an interest in Irish history which the rest of the family would have derided. She used to slip into a shop in Gort and, hardly able to see over the top of the counter, would hand in her sixpences to buy rebel literature.

'I look to Miss Augusta to buy all my Fenian books,' the shopkeeper would whisper to his friends.

The girls were educated by governesses. As soon as they came of age they were given a season in Dublin to find husbands. Augusta never did have a season. Her mother obviously envisaged her role as that of housekeeper at Roxborough. It was clear that she had a gift for getting things done. When she found that the local shopkeepers were overcharging, she opened a shop herself and sold at competitive prices to make them reduce their rates. Her 'Temperance Tent' was famous in the county. She would erect this on fair days so that the cattlemen could have a first-class meal after the fair – but without alcohol. (It does not seem to have occurred to the Persses that their opposition to their tenants' drinking was hardly consistent with drawing lavish profits from the family-owned distillery in Galway.) Augusta was known for visiting the sick but, unlike her sisters, without attempting to change their religion. One incident indicates the practical bent of mind that was to be a feature of her character later on. She found a girl dying in a windowless cabin. Nothing could be done for the poor creature, who was far gone in consumption. Augusta brought along the estate carpenter to put in a window.

'It must be always good to let in light,' she said, and the sick girl slipped out of life with the changing skies and the waving trees in her perspective, instead of the dark walls of a cabin.

Daring her mother's displeasure, Augusta had become a secret reader. When one brother brought home George Herbert's verse, won as a school prize, she smuggled the book up to her room and read it from cover to cover. She learnt to read Dante in the original, by comparing the Italian with the French translation she had brought to her. When at last she was allowed to read Shakespeare she learnt whole plays off by heart by propping the collected works up in front of her mirror and memorising the lines as she dressed in the mornings. Later she would recite them to herself as she went on her daily walks.

Slieve Echte, a range of hills behind Roxborough, was her place of escape. From here she looked down on the Burren with its limestone labyrinth inlaid with flowers and the distant Atlantic crashing beyond. Sometimes a deer would break through the heather, or a snipe rise from a pool that seemed on fire in the sunset, and she would experience an emotion that she would only identify in later life, 'the desire to express the perfect'.

Augusta had to conceal from the male side of the family any tendency she might have had of expressing the artistic side of her nature. The Persse house was a man's one, shooting, fishing, riding to hounds. The 'Seven Brothers' as the Persse boys were known, were safe in the neighbourhood despite the family's unpopularity, because 'had one been killed the other's would have run down and shot the assassin'. Their feats on horseback over the formidable Galway stone walls had passed into legend. One of them turned a hose on guests when he had been thrown out of a hunt ball. Another, when there was a threat to his life, walked into a public house and put a bullet through each number of the clock. These brothers were half barbarian without culture, who belonged to the eighteenth century where their daring and indifference might have brought them recognition in some colonial adventure. But the old feudal system was in the process of breaking up and the Persse boys had to stay at home now to guard the estates. They had grown up in the countryside and they had the necessities of life around them in the mountains, woods, and pasture of their vast demesne. One of them did go to Dublin to study at Trinity College, but he spent his time collecting street ballads which he could never be persuaded to publish.

At twenty-seven years of age Augusta was still unmarried. She was small, perhaps a little plain, but with large, intelligent brown eyes ('she had the most limpid beautiful brown eyes I have ever seen,' a friend recalled) and a well-shaped sensuous mouth. She spoke in the accent of her class, but with a certain curious impediment which gave her conversation a homely touch. She used to say 'dis' and 'dat' and this inability to pronounce 'th' gave an impression of a lisp. But once she got into conversation these defects were forgotten and she could enthrall listeners with her talk about the countryside and about literature and art, when there was company that might show an interest. The trouble was that such company was rare at Roxborough.

So Augusta was delighted one day when, at a cricket match there, she met Sir William Gregory who had just retired as Governor of Ceylon and who was so taken with her talk that he spent the whole afternoon with her. For her it was an experience to find someone who spoke several languages and had a feeling for literature and art.

On his part he was struck by this attractive girl who

was so obviously out of place among her uncouth family. They wondered indeed what the ex-Governor of Ceylon was doing spending the afternoon with their bookworm sister.

Later that month Sir William dropped a hint at dinner in a neighbour's house that he would like to meet the young Persse girl again and she and he met once more at a dinner there. After this it was not considered improper for Sir William to invite her and her brother Richard to dine and stay the night at Coole, the Gregory estate which was seven miles from Roxborough. This visit was a success, but the Persse brothers were still sceptical about their sister's chances. Even when Sir William let it be known that he had left her in his will a choice of six books from his magnificent library, no one in Roxborough thought that he had more than a fatherly interest in the young girl. Once when a brother, back from a shoot at Coole, brought her a book which Sir William had sent her, he handed it to her with a sarcastic remark which indicated that the family did not really consider that their sister could enjoy reading.

Then for some winters she went to Cannes with her mother, to nurse her brother Richard who had consumption. There she met Sir William again, whom it was quite clear now had grown fond of her. On the day she was leaving he called to the hotel three times.

Back at Roxborough she received a letter in the post which contained a proposal of marriage. Augusta joyfully accepted, recognising that life as a drudge for her brothers at Roxborough was over and that she would henceforth live in an atmosphere where learning and culture were valued and not derided. Curiously enough, the brothers were also delighted at the news. Though they would lose a housekeeper the marriage meant that the shooting between Coole and Roxborough would run together. They had been disappointed when a younger sister failed to catch Edward Martyn of Tulira (seven miles away) because if she had it would have meant that they could have shot the whole countryside without a break.

Sir William Gregory had been at Harrow with Trollope. Later at Oxford he acquired a reputation as an Irish rake with his betting exploits. When he was twenty-two he won £5,000 on the Derby. In 1842 he entered Parliament as a Conservative for the Dublin constituency. He sold his stables in 1855 and two years later was elected as a Liberal Member of Parliament for Galway. From then on life would be full for him. He bought old masters for the house at Coole. He became a trustee of the National Gallery and Chairman of the Committee to reform the British Museum. In 1871 he was made a Privy Councillor and in 1872 obtained the Governorship of Ceylon. No doubt his family connections had helped his quick promotion once he had shown that his addiction to the turf was at an end. His grandfather had been Under Secretary for Ireland and an ancestor had been Chairman of the East India Company.

He was sixty-two and she was twenty-eight. They were married in Dublin in St Matthias's Church on 4 March 1880 and left immediately afterwards for the wedding journey which was to be an extensive tour of Rome, Athens and Constantinople. It was at Rome that Augusta had her 'first real dinner party' at the British Embassy, where the Gregorys were invited to meet the Crown Princess of Russia and the Princess Royal.

When they arrived back at Coole Augusta was able to take a close look at the house where she was to spend the rest of her life. It was a pleasant Georgian dwelling house, unexceptional architecturally except for a drawing room and dining room with great bow windows. Behind were seven magnificent woods, all with different names and in contrast to the plain exterior of the house the inside was hung with the lavish collections of several generations of Gregorys.

In such an atmosphere with the congenial company of a literary husband Augusta's temperament blossomed. For the next thirteen years of her life she would travel to many countries and spend much time in London among leading statesmen, writers and painters of the period.

She would visit India, Egypt, Turkey, Ceylon. Back in London she would entertain with some style in the Gregorys' London house in St George's Place.

In 1881–82 the Gregorys spent the winter in Cairo. This visit was to give Augusta her first involvement in politics and to result in her meeting with a most unusual Englishman who was to be an important influence on her life.

Colonel Ahmed Arabi, a former private in the Khedive's army, had led a mutiny against what he considered was the corruption of the Turkish pashas who administered Egypt. Arabi had been put under arrest when the Gregorys arrived, and Sir William became interested in his case as soon as he heard of it. He was convinced that had there been better treatment of the Egyptian officers in the army and more attempt to involve Egyptians in local government the revolt would not have taken place. He wrote a long letter to *The Times* defending Arabi's position and outlining some of the absurdities of the case.

The letter was read by an Englishman living at Heliopolis, near Cairo. This was Wilfrid Blunt, a cousin of the Duke of Rutland, whom Gregory had last seen in a Madrid bull ring attired in a toreador costume, an unusual attire for an attaché at the English Legation, as Blunt at that time was. After Blunt had left the Diplomatic Corps he had become a poet, explorer and breeder of Arab horses. At the time he met Sir William he was living in an Arab tent with his wife, Lady Anne, both of them dressed in flowing Bedouin robes. Blunt and his wife were delighted to find someone who shared their views on Egyptian politics, especially a person of Sir William's influence. They invited the Gregorys to their tent where they dined in an incense-filled atmosphere along with three Arab sheiks. The result of this meeting was that the Blunts and Gregorys decided to work together for Arabi's cause. Later Blunt was to write to Augusta:

You talk of having your political education in Egypt and so too do I with you. For before that eventful year of 1882 I had never played a public part of any kind or written so much as a letter to *The Times* with my name to it, and we made our education over it.

She set to work with him immediately on the project and helped him to translate Dante's lines (on the good deed that helped Provanszano Salvali) to insert in his letter of appeal to *The Times*.

When she returned to England Lady Gregory continued her campaign for Arabi. She wrote a long article in *The Times*, 'Arabi and His Household' which, according to the *St James's Gazette*, 'made every woman in England Arabi's friend' and was published later as a pamphlet.

Now, however, Arabi mounted guns on the forts overlooking Alexandria and challenged the Khedive's authority. The English fleet under Sir Beauchamp Seymour bombarded the town for ten and a half hours and Arabi was defeated and captured by Sir Garnet Wolsley's forces at Tel-el-Kebir in August 1882.

It became imperative for the Gregorys and Blunts to act swiftly if Arabi was to be saved. They organised a lawyer for his trial and collected funds to pay for his defence, with the result that the death sentence which had been passed on him for treason was commuted. He was banished to Dar-es-Salaam where Sir William was able to ensure that he was generously treated. Lady Gregory did not let the matter rest there, however. In 1886, when she and Sir William were visiting his old colony of Ceylon, she went to see Arabi who had been transferred there and reported to Wilfred Blunt that he was looking well and had not dissipated himself with drink as had been suggested by his enemies. In the same year when they stayed with the Viceroy, Lord Dufferin at New Delhi, she used the occasion to promote Arabi's cause. Her pleas resulted in Arabi's allowance being raised and his eventual release in 1891. This prolonged campaign was typical of Augusta's tenacity. When she took the bit between her teeth she was not likely to stop until she got what she wanted. Arabi never forgot how much he owed her. On a picture of Arabi which Lady Gregory kept in her dining room all her life was written, 'From Arabi the Egyptian: I present my picture to Lady Gregory as a souvenir to preserve friendship.'

During the time she had worked with Wilfrid Blunt in Cairo Augusta had fallen under the spell of this fascinating Englishman. His good looks impressed her and she delighted in the fact that they were 'a positive annoyance to his enemies'. When Lord Houghton sneered to her 'the fellow knows he has a handsome head and he wants it to be seen on Temple Bar', she must have smiled secretly. She had seen more than she should of that handsome head.

Working closely together and finding themselves often alone, by the nature of their campaign, Augusta and Wilfrid had become lovers. Blunt was a notorious womaniser and it was not unpredictable that he should have set his cap at the young, recently-married wife whom he felt was being kept too much in the background by her elderly husband who was greeted everywhere with the reverence due to a former colonial governor. Augusta had a strong sensuous side to her nature and she was swept off her feet by Blunt's vigorous courtship. Looking back on the relationship in later life when she herself had become an ardent advocate of freedom from English rule in her own country, Augusta concluded that the fact that Blunt 'lived his life for freedom' had been one of the factors in their coming together, besides his dashing personality and good looks. She thought him one of Plutarch's men and later recalled:

He has never given up his right of protest against injustice in Egypt and elsewhere, denouncing the floggings and hangings of the villagers of Denshawi in 1905 – calling out against the hanging of Dingra, the Hindu political assassin in 1909; against the Italian massacres of Arabs in Tripoli in 1911; against the hanging of Roger Casement in 1916, and against the

45

lawyers' arguments used in the British Cabinet to urge and justify the late war. An unusual and gallant record for a Sussex gentleman of many acres, of inherited wealth and ease.

Blunt justified his liaison by asserting 'that the passionate element in our intercourse at this time proved a source of inspiration and of strength. It was under this influence that I was able to carry on the hardest public battle of my life, the rescuing of Arabi from the vengeance of his enemies – she working with me and advising and encouraging.'

Blunt remained in Cairo while Augusta went back to London with Sir William who, whether he knew what had occurred between the pair or not, spoke highly of Blunt, praising him for the manner in which he had fought Arabi's case 'almost single-handed'.

From now on Augusta was to enjoy the life that was available to the wife of a former colonial governor in this period of the Empire. The Dufferins in India, the Layards in Constantinople, the Duffs in Madras: visits to these friends of her husband enabled Augusta to make friendships, some of which were to last throughout her lifetime. Enid Layard, wife of the Ambassador to Turkey, Sir Henry Layard, became her special friend. Lady Layard had set up a hospital for the sick in Vienna. She involved herself in her husband's work and set down the Cyprus Treaty in her own handwriting. (It was to Sir Henry that the French writer Bosquet had said at Balaclava: 'c'est magnifique, mais ce n'est pas la guerre'.)

When she visited Enid Layard at Constantinople, Augusta and her friend would spend the morning rummaging in the bazaars and then in the afternoon cross the bay, bringing a kettle with them to make tea on the shores of the Bosphorus. It was Enid, herself the daughter of Lady Charlotte Guest the translator of the Welsh legends, who gave Augusta her first typewriter. Did she see in her friend a future translator of legends?

In London Sir William was absorbed in his work at the

National Gallery and the British Museum. Augusta kept an autographed fan on which she collected the names of people she met around this time. W.E. Gladstone, Lord Tennyson, J. McNeill Whistler, Randolph Churchill, Sir Arthur Sullivan, Sir John Millais, Redvers Buller, G.M. Trevelyan, are some of the names that appear on it. She had made a special friend of Sir Frederick Burton, Director of the National Gallery. One day Augusta had accompanied a group which was being taken around the gallery by Sir Frederick. When they stopped before a painting of Mary Magdalene and someone said that 'she did not look altogether repentant', Augusta piped up from the back of the crowd, 'perhaps she did not grow quite good all at once'. She thought that Sir Frederick looked closely at her as she said this and her instinct was right. He had noted what she had said and from then on they became firm friends. She discovered he came from Clare and had been a friend of Thomas Davis, the patriot of the 1840s who was editor of *The Nation*. Sir Frederick had actually designed the frontispiece of *Sons of the Nation*, a book of rebel songs edited by Davis. As he was a strong Unionist Lady Gregory would tease him about this. But he would reply, 'Poor dear Davis, I could never refuse him anything.' Burton's paintings at the time when Lady Gregory met him were much sought after: 'Venetian Lady', 'The Turret Stair', 'The Arran Fisherman's Drowned Child' being three examples.

Henry James was another friend who used to come to her Sunday evenings. She felt an immediate kinship with him. 'Perhaps England was not really my country,' she would say, 'any more than his.'

He was the only one of her visitors who used to greet her little fairhaired son Robert with a kiss. She found him a comfortable person to talk to, although she often felt he was taking mental notes of certain things she said, to be used later in his novels. Once she chided him for having left one of his heroines upon the doorstep without giving more information about her, and he

47

replied, 'That is life, that is just how we find that we have parted with so many we have known – on a doorstep.'

In her diary Augusta records a good deal of anti-Gladstone comment at her table. At a dinner in St George's Square someone said to Lady Cooke, 'You must confess Gladstone is a Heaven-sent statesman,' and her ladyship replied, 'I hope it will be a long time before Heaven is in the family way again.' Another person at the table came up with the comment, 'I wish he were cut into cat's meat,' and somebody replied, 'Don't say that, he would poison the cats.' Gladstone was an enthusiastic convert to the cause of Home Rule for Ireland and the Irish landed classes held him in contempt. But what was even more frightening than the prospect of Home Rule was the fact that landless men in the country, encouraged by the atmosphere of freedom that seemed to be in the air, were organising in pursuance of their rights.

And young Mr Parnell, instead of condemning these dangerous activities, was actually encouraging them in the House and proposing to have Fenians and rebels stand for parliament.

East Galway, where the Gregorys' house Coole was, was one of the areas most affected. 'The landlord shooting season has set in with great briskness in my county,' Sir William Gregory wrote to Sir Henry Layard in October 1881, after he had returned from London. A few months later his neighbour, Walter J. Bourke of Gort, was shot at and killed by five assassins who had concealed themselves behind a stone wall and fired at his trap as he passed by. Bourke was a particularly bad landlord who had evicted a tenant and replaced him by one of his own choice. The newcomer had received the following letter which Bourke had repudiated with a sneer:

Raftery, if you dare attempt to work the farm of the boycotted Bourkes or even look over the wall at it you can be sure of Dempsey or Doherty's doom – do not think the tyrant Bourke will make me afraid like the Mayo men: believe me faithfully to be,

Captain Moonlight.

The following week another of the Gregorys' neighbours, John Henry Blake, was shot dead outside Loughrea, a town about six miles away from the Gregorys' home at Coole.

At Roxborough the Persses were living in a virtual state of siege. Groups of soldiers were encamped on the estate to protect the household, while Augusta's brother Algernon could only walk around the property with five soldiers guarding him. Wherever he went in the countryside he carried a loaded revolver. Few of the neighbouring landlords could leave their property without a guard.

Coole, however, was free from harassment because 'the Gregorys had always been good landlords'. As a young man Sir William had proposed in Parliament that the land should be in the people's hands and had declared himself in favour of Catholic emancipation. But only a small section of his class shared his view. The rest were caught in a system which they had made no effort to end and were now reaping the whirlwind.

Wilfrid Blunt, having exhausted the cause of Egyptian nationalism, now felt himself impelled by the tide of events in Ireland to take a hand in the fight for freedom there. Full of enthusiasm he came over in the winter of 1886 to campaign for the Land League and promptly landed himself in jail after a speech delivered at Woodford in County Galway. Lady Gregory was not in Ireland at the time but she sent a Persse cousin who was a magistrate to see Blunt, and the two of them talked for some hours about horses, relieving the tedium for a while at least for the aristocratic prisoner. After his release Blunt gave Augusta a piece of tarred rope that it had been part of his duties as a prisoner to unravel and which she would use as a bookmark for the rest of her life.

Blunt recognised that the Gregorys were good land-lords and he wrote to Augusta to say he was glad she got her rents, but advising her not to let her agent 'play tricks with the tenants'. One can see from her letters to him that she was anxious to show him that she was growing in political awareness of the situation in the country. In July 1886 she wrote to him with some pride that a tenant had mistaken her for the priest's sister, and on finding out the mistake said, 'Aren't we very happy to have such a plain lady?' meaning that the tenants thought her without airs or graces.

Then again she told him in June 1888 that some alleged moonlighter had called out to his brother at the door of Galway jail after a Star Chamber-style inquiry, 'Get Lady Gregory to help us.'

When Blunt published his collection of prison poems In Vinculis written in 1888, it was to Augusta he sent the proofs. 'Shall I not be doing some notable service to the Unionist cause by mutilating them,' she wrote back to him, jestingly. But he trusted her implicitly, so that the set of poems finally appeared before the public proof-read by Lady Gregory. His long anti-imperial poem 'The Wind in the Whirlwind' she transcribed for him in her neat hand and it is impossible to think that she should not have been influenced in some manner by the savage denuncia-tion of Empire that ran through it.

But Blunt knew his own limitations in the field of Irish politics and encouraged Augusta to involve herself in the injustices of the country because 'an Englishman cannot be of the same use Irishmen themselves could and my turn has not yet come'. It would be some time before Augusta Gregory would devote herself to the improvement of her country's condition, but it was through her relationship with this generous Englishman that she was brought more quickly to the realisation of the need for reform.

Though most of the other estates in the county were in turmoil in these years, the fact that Coole at least was exempt left Augusta free to enjoy her life as mistress of a country estate.

We can imagine that it was in the library that Augusta found herself most at home. She was a born writer who as yet had found no outlet for her talent. The Arabi pamphlet, a few articles in newspapers were the extent of her published work. In the library she could read as she had never done before, spending every minute of her spare time there. Organising the household at Coole was not difficult for her after her years of apprenticeship at Roxborough. Soon she had the Coole estate running as smoothly as she had done at home. People liked the new mistress with her attentive air, her readiness to share their misfortunes and her interest in local customs. To get herself better acquainted with the people Augusta attempted to learn Irish and studied an Irish grammar with an ambition to become proficient in the language.

Her son Robert was born in 1881 and from that time on she had absorbed herself in his upbringing. As he grew up he spent his holiday at Coole and the rest of the year at his prep school, then at Harrow. The Gregorys did not take the boy on their journeys to India and Egypt, so that he had not seen a great deal of his father before Sir William died in 1892 after a visit to Ceylon. He was seventy-four. Robert was away at school on the night his father died. He noticed the candle at his bedside behaving strangely. 'If it falls and goes out my father will die,' he said to himself.

After the funeral Augusta put on widow's weeds. She would wear them for the rest of her life.

She was forty, and though mistress of Coole till her son's majority, she was not a rich woman. She immediately thought of increasing her income by writing. Wilfrid Blunt recommended her to Margot Tennant, who was starting a new weekly, as a political writer. This came to nothing as the magazine did not get off the ground. Augusta then set herself to the editing of her husband's autobiography which she had induced him to set down before his death: 'for Robert's sake, a good name is better than riches and no mean part of the heritage of a son.'

She worked on it during the first year after Sir William's death and then sent the manuscript to John Murray. He liked it and agreed to publish it, if she would have it gone through by someone else. He suggested Sir Henry Layard (an eminently suitable choice for Lady Gregory) and on 16 October 1894 the book arrived at her little flat in Queen Anne's Mansions, London. When it was published on the 23 October she had her first experience of the thrill of publication.

Awoke early and flew to *The Times*, was relieved to find a review in; rather a dull and unappreciative one, but still in a good place. Then in the reading room I found F. Lawley's enthusiastic article in *The Telegraph*; a fairly good one in *The Morning Post*, and one in *The Daily News* giving plenty of quotations. And at Murray's I had got *The Standard* notice which had come out and all are kind, and none have discovered the mistakes in Greek and elsewhere. So I felt a load roll off me, I should have taken it to heart so terribly if the book had fallen flat. Now it has had its good start, and must stand or fall by its own merits. I also have nice letters from the houses I have sent it to, and the Murrays are most amiable.

She spent the next few days going round the bookshops to find out how the book was selling, and was delighted to hear from a friend that there was a notice in the libraries which said 'this book being in great demand, it is to be returned as soon as possible'.

She had sold the house at St George's Place and taken rooms at Queen Anne Mansions near Enid Layard who now lived in Queen Anne Street. Sometimes she would go out to stay with the Layards at their palazzo in Venice. There one evening she had heard Robert Browning read his own poems and he wrote out a poem for her, 'All that I know of a certain star'. He warned her that she would not make money from poetry but she was determined to turn her pen to writing in some way that would bring in an income. On a later occasion Queen

Alexandra and the Empress of Russia came to lunch with the Layards. Afterwards Augusta seems to have been quite naughty, mimicking the royal guests and making fun of their German accents.

She spent as much time as she could in London in the hope of getting writing commissions. She had discovered at Coole a collection of letters to and from the Under Secretary who had been her husband's grandfather, and persuaded a publisher to commission a selection on the strength of Sir William's autobiography. The task of editing and selecting the letters was to occupy her over the next four years. She set about it with her usual energy. In order to understand the background to the letters, many of which had been written during O'Connell's campaign for Catholic emancipation, she made a careful study of the history of the period.

Once she had got her commission under way she began to spend more time at Coole. She was delighted that the drawing rooms looked so well with their new acquisitions from St George's Place. But there may have been an implicit criticism of Sir William's taste in her observation that 'all the rubbish was put away'.

She worked hard preserving fruit from the garden, gooseberries, strawberries and raspberries for school treats, and for Robert when he would come from Harrow with his friends. Planting trees in the beautifully wooded Coole was to be one of her chief delights to the end of her life. In winter she planted larch and silver spruce, evergreen oak, and hoped that the rabbits would not uproot them. The trees, she would say, became her companions and their enemies hers. Later when she would become disheartened at some unfair criticism of her enterprises, she would work off her anger by hacking away with a little hatchet at the clinging vine which was threatening her beloved trees.

She continued the practice she had begun at Roxborough of taking a personal interest in her tenants. In her journal she noted:

I have read in Stanley's life of 'the loneliness of the selfish man'. I must try to avoid that, and am likely to do so for already the poor are at my door. Little K. has knitted a petticoat, a moth-trap, but I had to buy it at a fancy price, her brothers and sisters being down with the measles; old Davy Boland has died, his wife and children all away in America and the burial falls on me. F.'s children are said to be left destitute, and Curtain, W'.s old Kinvara bailiff, writes from the workhouse hospital for help.

Thus she was in 1896, before her momentous meeting with Yeats at Duras near Coole, a widow of forty-four years of age who had travelled widely, met many notable figures in literature and politics. It was clear that she had a gift for organisation. She possessed a remarkable tenacity and once started on a project would not under any circumstances relent until she had it completed. She had a keen sense of humour and a feeling for words. Her encounters with Arabi Bey and Wilfred Blunt had sharpened her sense of freedom and given her a sympathy for the oppressed. But there was little hint of the creative power that was latent in her. It needed a catalyst to release it, to ally it with her organisational abilities, for her to become one of the most remarkable women of the century in the arts.

Moore Hall stands on the edge of a lake at Ballyglass, County Mayo. The lake, Lough Carra, is of an extraordinary hue, emerald green, which seems to lend its colour to the landscape around it. There is no area which does not partake of this mysterious green in some way – a green which if you watch it long enough drains the energy and acts as a delicious impediment to action – save the hills beyond with their dips and curves. They are blue enough, perhaps, though the pink heather shows through the blue in places as the clouds come and go, changing the colour every few minutes. The house built in 1794 by a Moore who had made a fortune in Alicante, was three stories with a Venetian window and an imperial Doric portico. Above this was a triple window framed by fluted pilasters. The façade still stands and the effect is massive, as if the building had been erected in stern counterpart to the lethargy engendered by the lake which lies at the foot of its lawns.

The Moores had been in the west of Ireland for some hundreds of years and claimed descent from Sir Thomas More. They had intermarried with Catholic and Protestant, but when George Moore was born in February 1852 were currently in a Catholic phase, a matter which was to be of some concern to the eldest son in his later years.

George Henry Moore, the novelist's father, after a youth and early manhood devoted to raising horses, had settled down and become Member of Parliament for Mayo. Horrified by the devastation of the Famine, he had decided to enter politics to see if he could improve the lot of the Mayo peasants. By degrees he had become so extreme in his views that The Times, after one particular speech, called for his arrest. He was frequently spoken of as a future Leader of the Home Rule Party.

George Henry Moore owned 12,000 acres, was a good landlord and popular among his tenants. They took a particular pride in his racing successes, for he had restored his stables some years after he had entered Parliament. At the back of Moore Hall the huge racing stables were flanked by a private racecourse modelled on Aintree's Grand National course; it was said that when Croagh Patrick won the Stewards Cup at Goodwood the estate did not recover from the celebrations for a week.

As a little boy George's favourite question had been, 'Do you think when I'm big I'll ride at Aintree?' He rode gallops every morning, read the Racing Calendar, the Stud Book, the latest betting, and was determined to be a successful steeplechase rider. He knew the pedigree of every horse in England before he was fifteen and much of his spare time was spent at the stables gossiping with the jockeys and stable boys about his favourite pastime. It is no wonder in later years that he would be fascinated by the writings of Turgenev, for there is something akin to the Russian experience about this great mansion in the middle of a deserted Irish landscape, utterly absorbed in gambling.

George was being educated at home, for a brief period at Oscott College, Staffordshire had proved a failure. Triumphalist theology and bad food determined him to get out of the place at any cost, and one Easter he arrived home and announced that he had been expelled for spelling the name of his Saviour as 'Jeasus'.

Afterwards his father found out that George had scandalised the Reverend President by declaring that he no longer believed in confession and compounded the offence by adding, 'Dr Northcote, you did not always believe in confession yourself.' The little lad had somehow found out that the President had at one time been a Protestant and had joined the Church only when his wife had died.

Though young George was badly educated in the formal sense, he had managed to absorb some knowledge of literature and painting from his father who was well read, and used to take him round the National Gallery when they visited London.

Perhaps he took him too often to the galleries because one day George told him he wanted to take up painting as a profession. His father had sent him to a London crammer to study for the Army exam, but he spent more time with his cousin Jim Brown, who had exhibited in the Royal Academy, than he did studying to be a soldier. Even though the elder Moore was not unsympathetic to the artist's life he was keenly aware of the indiscretions of his own youth when he had twice nearly gambled his fortune away. He had resolved on a safe career for his son and it seemed that George would have to wait until he came into his inheritance before he could follow the career of his choice.

When George was eighteen the problem resolved

itself. His father died suddenly of a heart attack. George Henry Moore was only forty-eight at the time of his death. He had an immense popular following and if he had become Leader of the Irish Party he would have been acceptable to the extremists who up to then had boycotted Parliament. It was even said that if a revolution were to break out that George Henry Moore would not have been averse to taking part. At his funeral at Kiltoome, where the family vault was situated, a nationalistic young priest delivered the panegyric:

> Woe, woe is Ireland. George Henry Moore is gone. The pall of death has fallen on her most gifted and devoted son. Oh, my country, now mayest thou weep – weep scalding tears from your million eyes until their very fountains are dried up. Long years of mourning after today art thou widowed indeed. . . .

It is important to remember George Henry Moore's position in Irish politics, as his son for the next twenty years of his life was to endeavour to separate himself from his native background. Not in reaction to his father's commitment, but because he feared becoming involved in national politics might distract him from his chief purpose in life, to become an artist.

George loved his father, who combined Victorian sternness with a sympathetic understanding of the original side of his son's character. But the young man was frank enough to admit to himself the bright side of the catastrophe. He would have no need to wait now to have enough money to live the life he wanted. Those 12,000 acres would give him the necessary security. 'I loved my father; and yet my soul has said, "I am glad". . . . My father's death freed me and I sprang up like a loosened bough to the light'. He had recognised his true nature – that of the artist who will place his art above family, religion or race.

But his mother and his guardian would not agree to George going away immediately – he wanted to take himself to Paris – and though he had come into a considerable amount of money he would have to wait until he was twenty-one to use it as he wished.

Meanwhile he attended classes in London, studied art with his cousin, led the life of a man about town and went back and forth to Moore Hall. All the time he was waiting for the day when he would be twenty-one. On 24 February 1873 he was all set to go. He left for Paris, bringing with him a valet, as he thought an Irish gentleman should.

Moore took up residence in the Hotel Russie at the corner of the rue Drouot and the boulevard des Italiens. Nearby was Monsieur Jullian's Academy of Painting where Moore enrolled as a pupil. He paid the Professor forty francs and in order to find out as much as he could about Paris life, frequently asked him out to dinner and the theatre.

Alas, art held no future for him. He turned out to have no talent as a painter. He has told us in his *Confessions* that one night he sat down and wept bitter tears when the truth dawned on him. All was not lost. If he could not be a painter he might become a poet instead. But here he seemed to have even fewer gifts than he had shown with palette and brush. We have the evidence for it in his book of verse *Pagan Poems* which has survived. Dreadful lines like 'Beyond the weak hour's hopeless horoscope' and 'Fair were the dreadful days of old' abound in the slim volume.

However, Moore had certain social talents. People liked him. This was to be his salvation. For he learnt by ear, and it was in the company of the literary and artistic figures of Paris in this golden age that he found the inspiration that would enable him to begin his career as a writer of original prose.

Villiers de l'Isle Adam swept round the cafés from midnight till dawn wrapped in his great cloak, talking the plots of his novels out in public as his entourage paid for meals and drink. Soon Moore had become one of his following, eagerly absorbing the conversation of this extraordinary man. He would sit entranced as Villiers discoursed on his scheme to create an automaton which would be an improvement on a real woman – or tell how he was writing a story about a house for suicides which would provide a choice of exits including crucifixion, for those who, tired of being men, wanted to become gods.

For years Villiers had worked on a single book. His most notable work, the symbolist play *Axel*, was not produced until after his death because of interminable revision. 'My words are weighed on scales made of spiders' webs,' he used to tell George. His Irish acolyte would note this advice and apply it to his own work. It was Villiers who introduced him to Mallarmé and at the symbolist poet's Tuesday evenings with a few friends sitting beside the fire Moore first experienced the cut and thrust of French literary conversation.

Mallarmé mentioned Moore's name to Manet, and one evening the young writer was sitting in the Nouvelle Athènes when the great painter approached him. Moore was so flustered that he pretended to be correcting proofs. But when Manet asked him if the noise of the café did not distract him, he managed to stutter out: 'No, but you do, so like you are to your paintings.'

He was struck by Manet's finely-cut face, aquiline nose and strong chin and his elegant clothes. When Manet asked him to come to his studio to sit for him, Moore was delighted. Moore's hair was light coloured at the crown and he watched with admiration as the painter brought out the blonde gold on the canvas, painting yellow ochre on top of yellow ochre which according to Moore's training at the atelier should have resulted in a dirty grey. But Manet painted by instinct, Moore noted, and 'matched the tints without premeditation'. (He was not at all pleased with the finished portrait which became known as 'Le Noyé repêché' – 'the drowned man fished out'. Manet's comment when he heard of Moore's disapproval was: 'Is it my fault if Moore has the look of a broken egg yolk . . . or if the sides of his face are not aligned?') Indeed Moore was by Paris standards an unusual sitter, an oddity even with his long neck and sloping shoulders, his chin too small for his high-browed forehead, and his pale yellow hair the colour of daffodils. But he had found out how to amuse the French with his pose of a golden-haired fop and his amusing use of their language to shock and astonish, though Theodore Duret (the historian of the impressionists) has recalled that Moore liked to emphasise his social status and would never become familiar with those 'whom he thought to be below his rank as an Irish landlord'.

Now Moore became an accepted figure in the cafés and salons, finding himself accepted in company with Mendès, Degas ('a man of yellowish temperament in a suit of pepper and salt'), Renoir, Sisley, the Goncourts. He longed to meet Zola and one day after Manet in fun had persuaded the young Irishman to dress up as a Paris workman for the Bal d'Assommoir, he was introduced by the painter to the realist writer. Zola greeted him coldly, but Manet persuaded Moore to go out to Médan to meet him in his house, where they got on famously together. Moore felt he had made a friend, though he was a trifle dubious of the numerous Japanese paintings on the walls depicting 'furious fornications', which he thought rather overdid the naturalistic message.

As an aspiring writer Moore had specially designed a set of rooms for himself in one of the old houses in the rue de la Tour des Dames in Montmartre. The walls were covered with cloth, dark green and golden in colour with fluttering jades imprinted on it. A cardinal red canopy hung from the centre of the drawing room to give the appearance of a tent and a terracotta faun seemed to leap about in the scarlet gloom. Another room had a Buddhist altar, a statue of Apollo and a bust of Shelley. Huge censers burned incense and there were great church candlesticks and palms.

In a corner was something which looked liked rolled-up rubber tubes. Sometimes it moved and a visitor would recognise it as a python. Moore called the beast 'Jack' and fed it every month with a live guinea pig while his kinsman and fellow painter Lewis Hawkins, who shared the flat with him, would play the *Vexilla Regis* on the organ.

> The little beast struggles and squeaks, the snake's black bead-like eyes are fixed. How superb are the oscillations: now he strikes him and with what exquisite gourmandise he lubricates and swallows.

As Moore had not read widely, each new book became for him a divinity. When he had worshipped enough he would lay it aside and commence at another shrine. One day he heard someone talk of *Mademoiselle de Maupin* and immediately went down the quays and purchased a second-hand copy. The book swept him off his feet. The androgynous transposition which Gautier arranges in his novel, where sex was switched with a swiftness that took Moore's breath away aroused a sensual awareness that he had never received from any other form of art. Reading Shelley had removed from him the burden of belief in Christianity, now Gautier's book gave him a belief in the divinity of the flesh.

> I cried *Ave* to it all, lust, cruelty, slavery, and would have held down my thumbs in the Coliseum that a hundred gladiators might die and wash me free of my Christian soul with their blood.

Zola had shown him the possibility of a new art which would be based on science, in opposition to the imagination of the old world and would embrace every aspect of life. But Moore recognised that Zola lacked style and this he found in Flaubert, who became his exemplar till he discovered (probably by ear) that style in the English language had made a leap forward with Walter Pater, who from then on became his model. He never, however, became an apostle of scientific narration and would jeer at the Goncourts who had pioneered the naturalist method 'for not recognising the necessity of allowing the artistic stomach to do its work in its mysterious fashion'.

Then one day, dressed in his Japanese gown entertaining a lady friend in his apartment, he received a letter from his uncle telling him that the Moore estates in County Mayo were in trouble because of the land agitation. George wrote back an indignant letter, asking was the refusal of the tenants to pay rent 'a result of the new communism'? But he was practical enough to recognise that his carefree existence in Paris was endangered. After travelling to London to discuss his affairs with his uncle he decided to dispose of his apartment in Paris and sell his effects.

In the summer of 1880 he returned to Ireland.

At first he inclined to the belief that the estates had been mismanaged by his cousin Joe Blake. But when he had taken a tour of his lands he discovered this was not so. The Land League had given the peasants new status. The harvest of 1879 had been almost as bad as the famine years and with that memory in their minds the peasants were determined not to pay the landlord a rent and leave themselves without the means of buying food the following year. It was more likely that Joe Blake, who also owned land, had been too absorbed with his own difficulties to supervise George's affairs properly. They parted equably when Moore acquired a new agent. In October 1880 he set out to inspect his 12,000 acres. Some of the countryside depressed him, waterlogged plains where tenants were trying to grow a few potatoes at five shillings an acre. He witnessed an eviction from a cottage 'which seemed like a rat's nest built on the edge of a cess pool', noticed how many of the cabins were built of loose stones without a bush or tree to protect them from the Atlantic wind, and passed a dwelling place that struck him as having passed the farthest limit of human degradation:

Into the bank formed by the cutting of the peat a few poles have been thrust, and on these poles sods of earth have been laid, the front and sides are partly built up with soft black mud. And in this foul den a woman has brought up five children, and in the

62

swamp a few potatoes are cultivated, but the potato crop has failed this year and the family are living on the yellow meal the parish authorities allow them. They are boiling it now in the black iron pot, and will probably eat it out of the pot, for the hut contains nothing but the pot and the straw on which the family sleep. The man in a torn shirt looking like a wild beast is climbing out of the bog hole.

This spectacle of the countryside was not typical of the land which Moore owned, for the Moores had always been good landlords and the tradition of the family had included not only George Henry Moore's labours on behalf of the people in Parliament, but a John Moore who had assumed the title of President of the Republic of Connacht when the French invading army had landed at Killala in 1798. Nevertheless, George found it heartrending to go back to Moore Hall and noticed how quickly the estate had fallen into disrepair since he had lived there as a boy – the great wide path of the racecourse which meandered in and out of the woods and fields, overgrown and useless. On an untended lawn in front of the house a solitary peacock shrieked morosely for its hen.

The tenants came up to negotiate with him but were not impressed when he hinted to them that if they persisted in non-payment of rent he would sell Moore Hall to an Englishman who would be unlikely to be as generous as the Moore family had been. He hated them as they countered his suggestions with roguish jeers: 'Oho, still if you did we'd make him wear the green in earnest – make an Irishman of him for ever.'

However, he did reduce the rent, and money, though in smaller amounts, began to flow again. It was impossible to go back to Paris. But he was determined more than ever to follow an artist's career – though he had decided to become a writer rather than a painter. Perhaps if he lived frugally he could make a career in London. Encouraged by the sale of a forest on his estate he set out for London in the spring of 1881.

He settled in Cecil Street in the Strand, and started to work on novels as well as writing poems. Soon it became clear that his poetic career was not being taken seriously by the literary set, so he settled down to writing prose, which he would maintain throughout his life was a much more difficult medium than verse. His first novel *A Modern Lover*, which deals with the corrupting effect of the friendship of three women on an artist who then uses them to establish his fame, was a critical success. It was well reviewed in the *Spectator* and the *Fortnightly Review* and hailed as setting a new trend in the English novel. But the circulating libraries, afraid of its author's association with Zola, refused to handle it and Moore's hopes of making money out of the book were dashed.

It was quite different with his second novel *A Mummer's Wife*, published in 1884. This tale about a working-class woman from a Staffordshire pottery town who elopes with an actor went into three editions in the first month of its publication. It was reviewed by every newspaper and literary magazine and *The Pall Mall* carried on a controversy on '*la question* George Moore' for weeks.

Moore had persuaded Zola to write the preface of the French edition which showed where he believed the inspiration of his book had come from. His ambition, he used to say, was to become Zola's offshoot in England, '*d'être enfin un ricochet de Zola en Angleterre*'.

A Mummer's Wife was the first successful attempt in English to adapt the French naturalistic technique to an English background. The asthmatic fits of Kate Ede's husband Dick Lennox are described with a scientific accuracy which no English novelist would have thought necessary at that time. When Kate Ede vomits in the cab over her dress and the velvet seat, Moore spares no detail in his description. Inhibitions which would have held back contemporary novelists meant nothing to him, schooled in the French tradition. To furnish himself with information about the life of an acting troupe he had toured for a while with a friend of his brother Augustus, who conducted a company that played a translation of *Les Cloches des Cornevilles* around the provinces. Moore had also spent some months in Hanley in Staffordshire to get the atmosphere of a pottery town. The life of the poor in the potteries is drawn with great skill, and the descriptions of the countryside outside the industrial town are masterly. Yet with all his naturalistic technique Moore could not have succeeded with his second novel without his marvellous sense of atmosphere and prose style.

> At the bottom of the valley, right before her eyes, the white gables of Bucknell Rectory, hidden amid masses of trees, glittered now and then in an entangled beam that flickered between chimneys, across brick-banked squares of water darkened by brick walls. Behind Bucknell were more desolate plains full of pits, brick and smoke; and beyond Bucknell an endless tide of hills rolled upwards and onwards. The American tariff had not yet come into operation, and every wheel was turning, every oven baking; and through a drifting veil of smoke, the sloping sides of the hills with all their fields could be seen sleeping under great shadows, or basking in the light. A deluge of rays fell upon them, defining every angle of Watley Rocks and floating over the grass-lands of Standon, all shape becoming lost in a huge embrasure filled with the almost imperceptible outlines of the Wever Hills. And these vast slopes which formed the background of every street were the theatre of all Kate's travels before life's struggles began. It amused her to remember that when she played about the black cinders of the hillsides she used to stop to watch the sunlight flash along the far-away green spaces, and in her thoughts connected them with the marvels she read of in her books of fairy tales.

But the insight into character is also remarkable. The gradual disintegration of the personality of the girl thrown from her respectable working-class background into the hurly-burly of touring life and the dependence on her rough good-natured husband are portrayed with a faithfulness that only an artist writing within the severe restraints of the naturalist school could have achieved.

With one sweep of the arm she cleared the mantelboard, and the mirror came in for a tremendous blow as she advanced round the table brandishing her weapon; but, heedless of the shattered glass, she followed in pursuit of Dick, who continued to defend himself dextrously with a chair. And it is difficult to say how long this combat might have lasted if Dick's attention had not been interrupted by the view of the landlady's face at the door; and so touched was he by the woman's dismay when she looked upon her broken furniture, that he forgot to guard himself from the poker. Kate took advantage of the occasion and whirled the weapon round her head. He saw it descending in time, and half warded off the blow; but it came down with awful force on the forearm, and glancing off, inflicted a severe scalp wound. The landlady screamed 'Murder!' and Dick, seeing that matters had come to a crisis, closed in upon his wife and undeterred by yells and struggles, pinioned her and forced her into a chair.

'Oh, dear! Oh, dear! You're all bleeding, sir,' cried the landlady: 'she has nearly killed you.'

'Never mind me. But what are we to do? I think she has gone mad this time.'

'That's what I think,' said the landlady, trying to make herself heard above Kate's shrieks.

'Well, then, go and fetch a doctor, and let's hear what he has to say. . . .'

'Yes, yes, I'll run at once.'

'You'd better,' yelled the mad woman after her. 'I'll give it to you.'

'Let me go, will you?'

But Dick never ceased his hold of her, and the blood,

66

dripping upon her, trickled in large drops into her ears, and down into her neck and bosom.

'You're spitting on me, you beast! You filthy beast! I'll pay you out for this.' Then, she perceived that it was blood; the intonation of her voice changed, and in terror she screamed, 'Murder! Murder! He's murdering me! Is there no one here to save me?'

In the winter of 1884 Moore left London and came back to Ireland, determined to write a novel about the power of Dublin Castle over the life of the country. It was from the Castle that political power was exercised throughout the country and he wanted to depict the corrupting influence of the administration even on the very class whose privilege it was meant to uphold. He was shocked at the 'horrible system of terror' to which young girls were subjected, the 'muslin martyrs' who were sent up each year from the country by their families in the hope of getting husbands during the season at the Viceroy's mock court; if they did not succeed, they could consider themselves lucky to find at home in the neighbourhood a dispensary doctor or a police inspector. Being himself a landed gentleman, Moore was able to gain admission to the social scene in Dublin during the season and have himself invited to the balls at Dublin Castle. He borrowed the necessary court dress but had to buy the 'velvets' which he later re-sold at a profit, an indication that he had no intention of joining any social group except for the purpose of clinical observation.

A Drama in Muslin gives a vivid picture of a threatened society with the distant drums of the dispossessed throbbing in the background. That Moore was capable of seeing the true economic situation of the country through the imperial sham, is shown by his observation that the national income derived from the peasantry, apart from a few distilleries and breweries in Dublin.

In Ireland every chicken eaten, every glass of champagne drunk, every silk dress trailed in the street,

67

every rose worn at a ball comes straight out of the peasant's cabin.

During his stay in Dublin he went down from time to time to stay at Moore Hall. While there he greatly enjoyed visiting his cousin Edward Martyn who lived at Tulira Castle, about fifty miles away in County Galway. Edward came from a wealthy County Galway family who had settled in the west in the eleventh century. They traced their descent from an Oliver Martyn who had come to Ireland with the Norman Baron Strongbow. The Martyns were in the unique position of having had an Act of Parliament passed to enable them to retain their land. As Catholics they would have been subject to the savage Penal Laws enacted in the reign of Queen Anne to restrict the right of their co-religionists to own land, but because of some ancestor who had been merciful to Protestants during the Jacobite Wars an Act had been passed exempting them from these laws. The result was that at the end of the nineteenth century the Martyns owned extensive estates in two counties as well as house property in Galway city. Thus, when Edward's father died – the boy was eight – he was left a considerable fortune. As boys he and his cousin George had been close friends. They used to spend the winter together in London where their parents had houses in Alfred Place and Onslow Square. It is an indication that Edward shared something of his cousin's desire to shock that as little lads they would delight in baiting their neighbours by playing croquet in Onslow Square on Sundays, a pastime acceptable to Catholics but not to the stern Sabbatarians who would arrive in force in top hats to eject them.

Edward had been at Beaumont and Oxford and was in many ways a typical Galway landlord. He rode to hounds, was a good shot and served on the Galway Grand Jury. Though a Catholic, he had no sympathy with Home Rule and he was noted for his severity in dealing with malicious injury claims. His agent had been fired at during one of the Land League agitations.

But his manner of living was decidedly eccentric. Though the owner of a magnificent Gothic castle, he lived in a cell-like room with a bare bed and a college mattress. In the centre of the dining room of his Castle was a table designed after Dürer and six oak stools with knife-like edges. A high canonical chair stood near the window with a reading stand in front of it. Here Edward would read the Latin poets, the lives of St Augustine and St John Chrysostom. In the evenings he would go out to the great hall of the Castle and play on the harmonium motets from the polyphonic composers, Palestrina, Vittoria, Orlando di Lasso.

It was his mother who had persuaded him to rebuild the old Queen Anne building with its fifteenth-century tower. She had hoped this would encourage him to marry and settle down. Edward threw himself enthusiastically into the re-building, brought Ashlin the architect from Dublin to superintend the work, and John Diblee Crace to do the staircase and stained glass windows. William Scott designed the baldachin in the private chapel.

The result was magnificent. A castellated house of two stories with a porch, tower and battlements on which there were splendid gargoyles greeted the visitor. Inside they would find the splendour of the Gothic revival enhanced by the owner's stamp. There are fireplaces like Bavarian schlosses with clocks set into their sloping roofs, and between the rooms the Great Hall soars up through marble arches like something out of a Wagnerian set. Everywhere is Edward's monogram indicating how much of himself he had put into the construction of his masterpiece.

But when it was finished his eccentricity asserted itself. He refused to sleep in the new castle, but retired to his Norman keep with its bare room and primitive sanitary facilities. Henceforth he would keep his house for the entertainment of his friends, but live for himself the life of an ascetic in a private cell.

This was his way of telling his mother he did not want

69

to marry. She had dominated him from his youth and he maintained that he had no desire to hand over now to another woman 'walking after her and carrying her parasol and shade'.

Edward was a natural celibate who took colour from self-denial and admired the poetry of the troubadours based on ideal love. He used to say that he had much in common with his Crusader ancestors, and would have rejoiced to hear hymns of thanksgiving on returning from battle against the Saracens sung by basses, tenors, altos – held by a divine boy's voice for four bars, high up in the cupola.

Yet he would not become a priest, maintaining that no one had less a vocation than he. Moore was obviously quoting from a conversation with Edward when he makes John Norton say in *Celibates*:

> My attitude is this. There is a mystery. No one denies that. An explanation is necessary, and I accept the explanation offered by the Roman Catholic Church. I obey Her in all her instruction for the regulation of life; I shirk nothing. I omit nothing; I allow nothing to come between me and my religion. Whatever the Church says I believe, and so all responsibility is removed from me. But this is an attitude of mind that you as a Protestant cannot sympathise with.

Edward had once told his cousin that if he had not been a Catholic he would have 'gone to pieces'. By this he meant that he could survive only by an unquestioning acceptance of church law. His Jesuit schooling had given him a motive for a scheduled existence – fear of hell. To remain unmarried was safe. If he relaxed his celibate code there was no knowing what hidden emotions could be unleashed.

Edward's ambition was to be a writer and he had a well-stocked library, which included the works of Swift, Landor, Browning, Tennyson, Pater, Rossetti, Dickens, Thackeray, Fielding, Poe, Gautier, Flaubert and the Restoration dramatists. But his accursed scruples, product of an anxiety complex, had interfered with his progress here. A lengthy poem which he had composed on the friendship between Phidias and Pericles was burnt because he thought it had unsound implications. It was not that Edward placed the august nakedness of the gods below the ascetic message of the Christian image. But he felt some rivalry between the twisted form on the crucifix and the radiant Apollo – and as always throughout his life the first won.

His one completed prose work, *Morgante the Lessor*, a satire on society after Rabelais which was published in London, demonstrated that Edward had not the gift of converting indignation into art and it was dismissed by the critics.

After this he became even more scrupulous and discovering that volumes in his library by Descartes, Montaigne and Pascal were on the church's Index of forbidden books, he had his bishop write to Rome for permission to retain them.

It would be wrong to regard Edward as a pious dolt. He was intelligent and sensitive and, when he could emancipate himself from religious prejudice, capable of good writing, as he would later demonstrate. He had an excellent eye for painting and a natural ear for music, and was to found a school for stained glass as well as a polyphonic choir in later years. Edward was encouraged in his literary efforts by his cousin Count Florimond de Basterot. The Count lived ten miles away in a villa at an inlet in the sea at Duras. De Basterot came from an old French family who had settled in Ireland after the French Revolution (marrying into the Lynch family, Galway wine merchants), but who kept their estates in France, from which they derived their income. The land on which the Persses had built Roxborough and on which Sir William Gregory's ancestor had built Coole had been purchased from the de Basterots who at one time owned large estates in East Galway.

The Count wintered in Rome and Paris but in the

summer months returned to Duras where he had created a sort of continental salon, inviting his friends Maurice Barrès, Guy de Maupassant and Paul Bourget to stay with him. It was in this company that Edward's taste for literature grew, and that he conceived the ambition to be a writer.

He began to invite friends from England to stay in the Gothic mansion and the fame of his excellent table, the hunting and shooting on his land, made Tulira talked of in London. He had come down from Oxford without taking a degree, but he had made enough friends to form a jolly group whenever he wished to put together a house party on his estate.

Now in the winter of 1883 he was delighted to see his cousin George. The two of them would talk literature and art late into the night. Despite his scruples Edward was prepared to put up with George's anti-clerical jibes and outrageous comments in order to avail himself of literary conversation. Edward's mother, a pious woman, was not particularly enthusiastic about her son's friendship with the cousin. But she must have hoped that in some way he would try to break down Edward's misogyny. Yet curiously Moore the woman lover made no attempt to involve Edward with the opposite sex. He accepted his cousin's eccentricity as part of his original temperament and he delighted in it as a writer will who has sensed excellent material for his notebooks.

Back in England Moore accepted an invitation to stay with his friend Colvill Bridger whom he had met when he was studying at Gurles Army crammer. The Bridgers were squires with an estate at Shoreham in Sussex and Moore fell in love with the place as soon as he saw it. Mrs Bridger, Colvill's mother, was entertained and amused by the writer, and the two flaxen-haired sisters took him out to balls and dinners. The extraordinary thing was that the son of an Irish patriot who had led a Bohemian existence on the Paris left bank now found himself fascinated by the lifestyle of the English gentry. Every Sunday George went to church in top hat and umbrella and sang Anglican hymns with the enthusiasm of a convert. The village green, the church spires, the red tiles of the farm houses, the smocks of the peasants, filled him with intense emotion when he thought of them and 'the noble Saxon heart full of love of truth and freedom'. With his own upbringing as a country gentleman, Moore had no difficulty in partaking to the full of the life at Shoreham. He could ride, shoot, fish, play a good game of tennis. Once when he was out hunting he took a fall, and his friends were impressed that evening when his boot was found to be full of blood though he had not complained of his injury and had continued to hunt through the day.

This love affair with 'dear sweet Protestant England' is not easy to explain. Perhaps it was that after the individuality of French society, the contented, disciplined life of an English squire at the height of Victorian prosperity proved irresistible to him. Maybe the calm of the English countryside with its yeoman farmers and centuries of tradition contrasted with the unsettled countryside of his native Mayo with its multitude of cabins divided by stone walls.

Whatever the reason, his enthusiasm for this new life engendered in him an extreme dislike of his own country. The Land Acts of 1881 had begun the dissolution of the power of the Irish landlords and Moore had worked himself into a fury at this legislation which threatened his existence as a writer. When he published *Parnell and His Island* in 1886 (a collection of essays about Ireland) it was full of ferocious denunciation. 'Ireland is a bog,' he wrote in the introduction, 'and the aborigines are a degenerate race, short, squat little men with low foreheads and wide jaws.'

He poured out his contempt on the peasants who were threatening his income:

Never was an Irish peasant known to spend a penny of his newly-acquired fortune in improving his house and relegating the pig to a sty. The planting of a few flowers would relieve the intolerable bleakness of his

73

cottage. He spends his share of the money in the public house, his wife and daughters spend theirs on hideous millinery, dreadful hats with ostrich feathers and shaped as mantles, and tea and eggs for breakfast.

Indeed, he became almost maniacal in his desire to dissociate himself from his own people:

> When I look Ireland in the face, the face I've known since I was a little child, I find myself obliged to admit the existence of a race hatred – a hatred as intense and as fierce as that which closes the ferret's teeth on the rat's throat.

The land campaign filled him with fury, as he saw the Irish peasant undermining the Saxon 'who had created the greatest empire the world has ever known'. He abused Parnell for having created a party subsidised by 'American potboys and chambermaids who now hold the destiny of the British Empire'.

Fifteen years later Moore would launch a similar attack on the same British Empire and eulogise in its place the Irish people. He never openly retracted his earlier statements and seemed unaware of the incongruity between them and what he later said.

Moore never exercised any guidance upon himself. He let himself be as he was. As Max Beerbohm wrote:

> He was content to look on at himself, sometimes rather disparagingly, always with absolute detachment. While he swam he looked on from the bank and never when he sank did he offer himself a helping hand.

His autobiography, *Confessions of a Young Man*, finally established Moore. The public had wanted to know what the author of *The Mummer's Wife* and *A Drama in Muslin* was like. Now he told them and created the legend of himself through his autobiography. He had set out to shock and he succeeded. Christ was described in the book as 'the pale Socialist of Galilee', and Moore proclaimed a new order.

I hate Him and deny His Divinity. His Divinity is falling. It is evanescent in the sight of the goal He dreamed – again He is denied by His disciples. Poor fallen God.

Of course Swinburne had said much the same thing in verse. But this was in prose and could be quoted in the newspapers. It could have landed Moore in trouble but he got away with it. He was, after all, only thirty-six and his excesses were looked on as the outpourings of one of the younger generation. His having lived in Paris helped: an associate of Manet, Degas, Zola, Anatole France, Leconte de Lisle could be forgiven such views.

The prose of *Confessions of a Young Man* demonstrated the direction that Moore's style was taking. He had learned from Flaubert the need for dignity of language. In the prose of Walter Pater he had discovered how style could be used in a modern idiom in the English language. Now Moore was to recreate the English novel twice over, with *Esther Waters* in 1894 and in 1905 with *The Lake*. To the first he brought the naturalist technique, to the second that of the symbolist. But had he not developed a prose style as perfect as he did, he could never have succeeded in becoming one of the important writers of his time.

Confessions of a Young Man established his reputation. Soon he had become the recognised authority on the French impressionists. He could claim to have introduced the new painting to the English public, and his book *Modern Painters* when it appeared in 1893 became immediately a bible for those interested in art.

In the world of theatre he also had considerable influence. He had been a devotee of Antoine's tiny Théâtre Libre in Paris, where a former clerk from a gas company had courageously presented the new drama of Ibsen and Strindberg to a select public. In London Moore collaborated with J.T. Grein in the founding of the

Independent Theatre, which was the first English drama society to put Shaw and Ibsen on the stage. Moore used his position as a critic to promote Grein's project and lashed out at what he regarded as conventional stupidities in the London theatre. Beerbohm Tree, for instance, had received a good deal of attention for introducing a real fountain into the production of *A Midsummer Night's Dream* but the comment he drew from Moore was 'when I want to hear a tap drip I go to the scullery'.

He attacked the audiences, 'the older inhabitants of the villa forgetting the seriousness of life in imbecile stories', and campaigned vigorously for the new theatre.

His own play *Strike at Arlingford* was produced in 1893 at the Opéra Comique in the Strand, and received good notices. William Archer preferred it to Shaw's *Widowers' Houses*, a misjudgement, but it shows that the immediate impact of the play was not inconsiderable. It dealt with a miner's strike and should have had the support of the socialists. But the Fabians disliked it, maintaining that it did not distinguish correctly between trade unionism and socialism. What emerges from Moore's stage instructions is that his stage management and use of lighting were well in advance of his time. This experience was to be of importance when he came to direct the first play of the Irish Literary Theatre eight years later.

Meanwhile he was excited about his next novel. 'Duchesses', he told a friend about this time, 'everybody writes about them. My next book is about a servant girl.' It had not been done before. But Moore was determined that the principles of the naturalistic school should be explored to the full.

Eight years before, when he had first come to London, he had lived in a lodging house kept by an avaricious landlady and his chief diversion had been long conversations with a servant maid, Emma, a pale overworked girl with red hair who had that dull honesty which was sought after by employers. Moore thought Emma's honesty was 'essentially English' and he used her as a model for his *Esther Waters*. Recalling his memories of the racing world where horses were bred, he set the scene in a country house against a rural background of English life such as he had come to know from his visits to the Bridgers at Shoreham.

Esther Waters is a girl who, instead of having her illegitimate child adopted, brings him up in the appalling conditions of the time. Moore skilfully shapes the girl's character so that the reader can sense its strength, without the piety which was assumed essential to the Victorian idea of goodness. The racing scenes are, as might be expected, superbly sketched, but Moore was particularly proud of his depiction of Derby Day. 'Thirty or forty pages, no racing, only the sweat and boom of the crowd – the great Cockney holiday.'

Esther Waters sealed Moore's reputation. 'Q' in the *Spectator* called it 'the best book of its kind in the English language'. Twenty-five thousand copies were sold in a year and a postcard from Gladstone approving of the book enabled Moore to break down the prejudices of the circulating libraries and have his books accepted. This was a significant breakthrough, as he had fought a tenacious battle against the right of the libraries to act as censors. He was even more pleased when he learned that a young nurse, strongly influenced by reading *Esther Waters*, had opened a home for unmarried mothers in London.

Moore was now very much a figure in London artistic circles. There was a touch of the Frenchman in his dress: high-heeled shoes, small top hat at an angle, a malacca cane. He had a high wide forehead with blue eyes and striking pale yellow hair. His skin was unlined like a child's and of an extraordinary pallor, absolutely white. The shoulders drooped drastically to a neat well-made body, but his shapely hands seemed too small for his lean, sinewy arms, hardened from the use of the reins on the racecourse. It was an unusual face, but what struck an observant newcomer were his eyes, 'sheer clear-water blue'. Sometimes they would look vacant, but if something caught his interest they could become the eyes of a hawk. Even in repose though, there was always a look of querulousness on his face, the uneasy curiosity of the artist. He used his hands in conversation like a Frenchman, waving like fins at his side if he was deprecating something that he had heard, or flying up to heaven in real or simulated expostulation. When he had said something which he knew would have a shocking effect the hands would fall to his side followed by a slow laugh, 'K H K, K H K, K H K'.

His conversation was unpredictable. He brought the French habit of frank conversation on sexual matters into polite circles in London and his scatology shocked even Oscar Wilde. An example of his talk in this vein is caught by Vincent O'Sullivan with whom he was discussing *Esther Waters*:

> My book is about a servant girl. There is nothing pretty or namby pamby about her. After reading all about the purity and ideal beauty of 'ladies' and the respect due them by men that you find in Meredith and Bourget and Henry James, think of any 'lady' you may chance to be in love with when she goes to the water closet, pulls up her skirt and wipes her backside. That is what all the idealism about women comes down to in the end. When you share the same room with a woman in an hotel, if it is only for two or three days, you are bound to see her physical habits, and they are not a bit poetical. Bourget shuts his eyes to that. He doesn't see his Duchesses have the same physical needs as a charwoman.

The subject of women seemed dominant in his conversation. Shaw remembered an occasion when Moore spoke of being driven out of the house by a woman who threw a lamp at him. Yeats tells of Moore coming into a room and throwing himself on a couch and saying, 'I wish that woman would wash.' He conducted his affairs as Oscar Wilde had said he conducted his education, in public, and while he and Pearl Craigie the novelist were lovers, he talked so much about her that the ensuing gossip probably deterred Lord Curzon from marrying her. He had no hesitation about describing their quarrels to a room full of people:

> Once she and I were walking in the Green Park.
> 'There is nothing more cruel than lust,' she said.
> 'There is,' I said.
> 'What is that?'
> 'Vanity.' And I let her go a step or two ahead and gave her a kick on the behind.

His greatest love was Maud Burke of San Francisco, who married Sir Bache Cunard but who remained on and off throughout Moore's life his closest woman friend. To her daughter Nancy he once said:

> I am penetrated through and through by an intelligent, passionate, dreaming interest in sex, going much deeper than the mere rutting instinct. I am turned to woman as a plant does to the light as unconsciously, breathing them through every pore and my writings are but the exhalations that follow the inspirations.

It was hard to know if his gaffes were intended or not; when they aroused a roar of laughter he would look round in simple wonderment. 'What is the joke? Tell me the joke. If there is a joke let me share it with you.'

Once in the company of his painter friends Sickert, Tonks and Steer, he announced suddenly: 'I have been told that Michelangelo carved the David from a block of marble that had been improperly quarried. Now if anyone gave me a block of marble that had been improperly quarried I could no more carve the David – than I could fly.' Then the hands flying up from his sides, the mischievous look of the little boy in the face, and the inevitable 'what is the joke?'

After the success of *Esther Waters* he could become

savagely dismissive of rival writers. 'Hardy the villager, Conrad the sailor, Henry James the eunuch' were some of his sneers. 'Meredith's *Tragic Comedians* struts and screams like a cockatoo,' he said one night, and infuriated by the excessive praise which *Far from the Madding Crowd* aroused, he once announced loudly at a tea party that 'Hardy is one of George Eliot's miscarriages'.

Now he renewed his friendship with his cousin Edward Martyn. Edward had taken up rooms in Pump Court in the Temple, discovered for him by Sir William Geary, his barrister friend from his Oxford days. George found it an admirable place to talk the night away after he had laid down his pen. Besides, he was fond of Edward and it was an opportunity to enjoy his company. Mrs Martyn had forbidden Moore to come to Tulira after she had detected a resemblance between the character of the priest who spat on the carpet in *A Drama in Muslin* and the local parish priest of Ardrahan.

Edward would hear Siegfried's motif from *The Ring* whistled below his window and would then open the door to admit his cousin. Presently the churchwardens would come out, while George would talk about his latest novel and Edward about his playwriting ambitions. Superficially they seemed miles apart. Edward the ascetic, George the sensualist. But they both loved music and art and above all they shared a sense of the ludicrous. No matter how outrageous George might become, a hearty burst of laughter from both of them could end their differences.

Edward had had a conversion during this London period. One night he had gone to Ibsen's *Little Eyolf* and come back transfigured by 'its exquisite music trembling in my heart' and 'wishing to be alone so that the exultation should not be interrupted'. He would find in *Rosmersholm* and *The Master Builder* the effect of a symphony, and profound knowledge of the human heart and character. Since Ibsen's works were shocking to the Victorian conscience it is an indication of how the artistic side of Edward's temperament came to the surface where the theatre was concerned so that he should see only the imaginative side to these plays, and dismiss as irrelevant the elements which seemed hostile to religion. From now on the chief purpose of his life would be to write plays in emulation of the master.

The first play Edward had completed under the spur of his new enthusiasm was *The Heather Field*. The main character is a West of Ireland landlord, Carden Tyrell, who is facing financial ruin in the administration of his estates. He will not surrender to what he regards as unfair demands by his tenants. Instead he devotes his energy to reclaiming a vast tract of mountain which has been overrun by wild heather. His friends warn him that he is squandering his fortune; his wife (who represents in Edward's mind the materialism and lack of idealism in women) does everything to frustrate his plans. Finally when he raises a new mortgage that bankrupts the estate, she alleges that he has gone mad and tries to have him certified as a lunatic. In the end Tyrell, obsessed with his grand plan and wracked with anxiety, does go out of his mind. In the last scene of the play his little son comes in with a bunch of wild heather buds, which shows that heather has again broken out on the mountain in spite of Carden Tyrell's labours. He, however, is past caring and is happy in contemplation of his dream, indifferent as to whether it will be fulfilled or not.

George Moore wrote an enthusiastic preface to *The Heather Field* when it was published by Duckworth, in the course of which he observed: 'The hero Carden Tyrell is the first appearance of humanity in the English prose drama of today.' This makes a strong claim for the play. But *The Heather Field* is effective drama, and in the context of the London theatre of the nineties was in advance of its time.

Each summer Edward and George set out for Bayreuth for the Wagner season and on the way visited the famous cathedral towns, Cologne, Munich, Frankfurt, to indulge

Edward's love of polyphonic music and Gothic architecture. It is hard to believe that Moore at the age of thirty-six had not yet discerned the difference between Gothic and Norman until Edward explained it to him in Frankfurt, but Moore himself has set this down in his memoirs. On the train (travelling second-class because Edward, though rich, was frugal in his habits) the two Irish landlords would sit, Edward whistling the motifs from the operas to acquaint his cousin with the score before they began their two weeks of music.

However, though they delighted in each other's company they were constantly bickering with each other. Edward could take Moore's sexual jibes with a certain amount of amusement but he could not stand his 'blasphemy'. The relationship between the two was almost like husband and wife as Moore made continual thrusts in an attempt to pierce Edward's religious armour. Once Edward insisted on staying in a lodging instead of a villa in Bayreuth, on the grounds that he wanted an omelette for his breakfast; but Moore suspected that his real reason was that he wanted to be near a church so that he could go to daily Mass. When George sneered at him that he 'needed his magician at his elbow' Edward lost his temper completely and did not speak to his cousin for a week. The situation wasn't improved when Moore remarked in Edward's hearing that his cousin 'runs after his soul like a dog after his tail and lets go when he catches it'.

On the way home they would always stay in Paris when George would renew his acquaintance with his artistic friends; afterwards Edward would trot along the quays, happily picking out scores by polyphonic composers with George marching querulously behind. While Edward had introduced George to Wagner, Moore brought him to the work of the impressionist painters. When they had been in Munich Moore had been surprised to find that Edward rejoiced in the nudes of Cranach because of their 'aesthetic perfection', remarking that he would only disapprove of such displays of naked flesh 'in a photographer's studio'. Now he was to find that Edward's misogyny also failed to assert itself when it came to the ballet girls of Degas and the naked flesh of Manet. Degas had impressed Edward when Moore introduced them by saying 'cynicism is the only sublimity', a concept which seemed close enough to his own ascetic outlook. He brought three Degas paintings back to Tulira, also a Monet and an Utamora. If Edward had seen a young girl at a hunt ball lift her skirt he would have gone crimson with embarrassment; but the naked girls of Degas' paintings were different, because they were art.

Edward once told Yeats that the majority of souls were lost through sex, and Yeats was later to write in an unpublished section of his diary, that this remark suggested in Martyn 'an always-resisted homosexuality'. Moore came to the same conclusion after he had remarked to Edward that he seemed to think sexual intercourse between men more natural than between women, and Edward had replied, 'Well, at any rate it's not so disgusting.'

But celibacy does not necessarily imply latent homosexuality. It is possible to suppress heterosexual feelings, as well as homosexual ones. Having decided not to marry because of his fear of being dominated by the opposite sex, Edward's pious Catholic beliefs would not have permitted him to take a mistress. His solution was to suppress altogether the sexual urge.

Moore makes much in *Celibates* of Edward's alter ego John Norton's visions of 'Christ amid His white millions of youths, beautifully singing saints, gold curls and gold aureoles, lifted throats'. Well; Edward Martyn did found a choir and did compose a sonnet to a choirboy with the lines:

Yet thy boy memory
Fair haired and white will flutter to the sky
A beauty among the children of the stars.

83

He also wrote a play in which the hero is haunted for life by the image of a beautiful boy he had seen drowned at sea. But it may have been precisely because Edward was not homosexual that he could allow himself to contemplate boyish beauty on an aesthetic level, without feeling that he was transgressing his Church's moral code. Moore, in any case, knew very little of the pederast mind. He talked to Nancy Cunard of those 'horrid practices' and threw up his hands in horror at Wilde's case, declaring it 'against nature'.

'Think of two men calling each other "darling" as I'm told some of them do.'
'Oh no, my dear Nancy, it does not bear thinking about'.

Yet though they differed in outlook, Edward and George shared an upbringing which made them more susceptible to continental influences than their English counterparts would have been. Their Catholicism joined them to the cultures of France and Italy to which the Irish Catholic gentry had always looked for inspiration. Edward used to say that when returning to England from the continent it always seemed to him 'like entering a comparatively half-civilised country'. Perhaps it may have been these visits to the continent with his cousin that gave Edward his first interest in Irish nationalism. He would claim himself that it was his reading of Lecky's *History of Ireland in the Eighteenth Century* that brought home to him the injustices of England toward his native land. It is possible that one of the effects of his admiration for Ibsen had been to open his mind to the spectacle of injustice. Whatever it was, the conservative Unionist landlord of ten years before had, by 1892, become a fervent nationalist and a supporter of Gaelic culture.

Edward, for the present, was installed in Pump Court with his ambition to be a playwright. George Moore, at forty, had become a leader of the avant garde in London, though it would be difficult to define his social position.

Looked on in some circles as a notorious Bohemian he was nevertheless a member of Boodles in St James's Street, where he would arrive to lunch with his manuscripts tied together with a string. He spent his weekends at country houses and in winter rode to hounds. He was also a member of the Hogarth Club. There his friends were Wilson Steer, D.S. McColl, William Rothenstein. He had repudiated his master Zola 'because of his lack of style' though he had not forgotten how touched he was when he visited him after criticising him in his autobiography, and Zola's magnanimous comment was: 'Children devour their fathers. That is a rule of nature.' These days Moore was better pleased when people referred to Kate Ede in *The Mummer's Wife* as 'the Madame Bovary of the Potteries', for Flaubert had replaced Zola as his exemplar.

With all his vagaries and feeling one thing alone counted for Moore – his writing. He wrote to a nun, a cousin, who was worried about his absence of belief:

> You dream of God, I of art. I am perfectly happy with art. It fills my life from one end to the other.

3 Dublin Ferment

These were the changes that were taking place among the landed gentry in the countryside in the 1880s. Though twenty years later the city was to be the centre of the literary renaissance, at this time there was a wider gap there between the native and the Anglo-Irish classes than there was in the rural areas. Social divisions were consolidated by the political divisions of a city firmly in the grip of a colonial administration.

Dublin was the second city of the Empire and architecturally one of the most beautiful in Europe. It had been laid out in the eighteenth century: most of its public buildings had been erected at a time of a revival of patriotism under the Irish Parliament of 1782. Apart from St Petersburg, Dublin was the only European capital that retained the classical idiom throughout. Its squares were its high glory with huge cliff-like mansions in rose-red brick, carved in proportion to the width of the street below, so that a feeling of harmony prevailed in the dancing marine light between them and the sky. A circle of hills surrounded the city and the architects built to catch vistas of green and purple at the end of wide streets.

It would be incorrect to call the outlying areas suburbs in the conventional sense. There is none of the geometric consistency that elsewhere blights nineteenth-century suburban building. On boulevards a mile long each house can have a distinctive design. Some will be diminished representations of the stately town houses in the great squares further in. Others will show elegant front doors opening above long flights of steps with a basement below. Victorian innovations there are – fenestration, keystone heads above the doorway, rope moulding: but all the time there is the evidence of a tradition held in the grip of a classical idiom. Like all cities Dublin was subject to penetration from the provinces, but the architectural tradition survived in the hands of local architects and craftsmen who were not to be turned from their vision by the flamboyant demands of the newly rich.

The city lay on the edge of a huge bay with forty miles of beaches around it, one of which Bernard Shaw, who had lived above it, declared to be more beautiful than Naples. Shaw went so far as to maintain that the scenery 'infected' the architecture and that the beauty of Kingstown railway station where he boarded the train to the city 'would be impossible in England'.

It was an imperial city where the pageantry of empire was daily enacted. At eleven o'clock each morning a detachment of troops left Portobello Barracks and marched to the Bank of Ireland. When the King's representative, Lord Spencer, passed through the city in his carriage, he was escorted by the Royal Hussars. In the Phoenix Park, a vast green area near the centre of the city, there were regular military ceremonies in which the regiments paraded, followed by cavalry squadrons that charged by at full gallop.

From parts of the city could be seen rearing up between the buildings monuments more than a hundred feet high to commemorate the victories of British admirals and generals. The streets were alive with military panoply, jaunty Royal Dublin Fusiliers with their crimson tunics and silk-edged Scots caps with streaming black ribbons, blue tunicked Hussars, Lancers with their black plumes nodding back and forward over their steel helmets.

Dublin had its social season from January to March. During this period dinner parties were held each week in Dublin Castle; and on Tuesdays and Thursdays there were dances in the Throne Room, at which the soldiers wore mess kit and civilians ordinary evening dress. In between were levees for bench and bar at which private citizens attended in black velvet suits. More colourful were the Deputy Lieutenants in uniform of scarlet coatee with silver lace and band of shamrocks, and the Privy Councillors with blue coatees buttoned up to the throat with gold embroidery in front, and silk stockings.

The main events of the season were the two State Balls and the Saint Patrick's Day Ball. At the Castle drawing room the Lord Lieutenant in maroon-coloured breeches, amid a cathedral-like atmosphere of twisted candelabra and marble columns, would exercise a last furtive survival of the *droit de seigneur*, and bestow a kiss on each girl presented to him. As he stood on a dais he was surrounded by his court: first there was a semi-circle of red coats, then a private secretary, a military private secretary and assistant undersecretary, the gentlemen-in-waiting, the master of the horse, the dean of the chapel royal, the chamberlain, the general usher, the state steward.

Such panoply was conceived visibly to demonstrate the presence of an imperial administration in a city which was largely hostile to it. For Dublin was a city of the colon. The Protestant ruling class controlled the banks, the civil service, the major industries, though they numbered themselves only one in five of the population. As privilege obtained at all levels clerical jobs in the civil service were not awarded on a competitive basis, and it was impossible for a Catholic to get an appointment. Protestant workers were assured of what jobs were available, while Catholic ones remained idle. The middle class on the whole existed in a world that was a 'little England'. Their children were taught to look on Catholics as a different class – even to speak French with an English accent so as to show contempt for foreigners. There were areas of the city, Rathmines for instance, where they had, in an attempt to imitate the English upper class, refined their accent to an extent that they were unable to understand English actors who came to play on the Dublin stage. One lady who grew up in Rathmines at the turn of the century remembers it as 'resembling a wax museum, lifelike but inanimate models of English people'.

The Church of Ireland, to which the majority of the ruling class belonged, was high in doctrine but low in ritual. A candle lit in church could be looked on with suspicion. A whiff of Rome and a parson might lose his flock. Some indeed, finding even in this established church remnants of Roman ritual, had created exclusive sects from whence they could contemplate the damnation of Catholics with even more certainty than from the evangelical Protestant position.

This ruling class was a frugal hardy breed, who believed in physical exercise. Sport was valued; it was healthy in an uncertain climate and helped to discipline wayward elements in the Irish character. The Fitzwilliam Lawn Tennis Club, founded in 1877, competed with the All England Club for the honour of being the first tennis club in the world. Trinity College Rugby Club is the second oldest in existence. Swimming in the cold green waters of Dublin Bay all the year round was not uncommon for young men. Marathon walks in the nearby Dublin hills at weekends were popular among all ages.

Behind this façade of power existed a sullen, dissatisfied working class who cherished memories of the two rebellions against Castle rule, that had taken place in the city in living memory. Their heroes were Robert Emmet, Wolfe Tone, Lord Edward Fitzgerald, handsome young Protestant idealists who had led forays against English rule. Memories of Lord Edward driving through the city in his carriage with his head cropped in defiance of fashion to show sympathy with the Paris Directory, of Wolfe Tone's death in his cell rather than accept the ignominy of the gallows, of Robert Emmet's last speech from the dock, were handed down from generation to generation and kept alive in the oral tradition of the city.

Bold Robert Emmet the darling of Erin,
Bold Robert Emmet he died with a smile,
Farewell companions both loyal and devoted,
I lay down my life for the Emerald Isle.

From this submerged class would come the impulse
which inspired the last rebellion three decades later,
and which would result in the eventual abolition of
Castle rule.

This was the Dublin to which John Butler Yeats
returned in 1881. He was a rector's son and derived a
small income from land in Kildare. John B. Yeats had
been called to the Bar in 1866. But finding life as a
barrister impossible to reconcile with his determination
to become an artist, he had ceased practice three years
later and brought his wife and family to live in London
intending to make his living with brush and palette.
There he had studied under Poynter at the Academy
School, and had impressed Browning and Rossetti with
his paintings and designs. But he was given no commissions and failed to show at the Royal Academy.

In 1880 the land war temporarily annihilatd the
Yeats' income from land and he decided to bring his
family back to Ireland. He had been one of a brilliant
group at Trinity which had included Edward Dowden,
Alfred Percival Graves (Robert Graves's father) and
John Todhunter the doctor-poet, and he hoped that his
friends would help to get him commissions, outside his
own family connections.

He settled down in Howth, a rhododendron-filled
peninsula, about nine miles from the city, and came in
every day on the train to his studio at 7 St Stephen's
Green. John B. Yeats had married Susan Pollexfen, the
daughter of a well-known Sligo merchant and ship-
owner, in 1863 and they had four children, two sons and
two daughters. The eldest boy was William, who now
transferred from the Godolphin School in London to the
High School in Dublin.

Each day the boy and father used to go in on the train
and breakfast in the studio. After that Willie would go

on to school, which was only a quarter of a mile away in Harcourt Street. Though he had spent the first years of his life in England, Willie had become very much an Irish boy. His holidays had been spent in his mother's town of Sligo, and he had early fallen in love with the Irish countryside and its people, and recognised it as part of his heritage. Besides, his father had constantly stressed the family's Irishness while they were in London.

'The Dublin definition of a gentleman is someone not wholly concerned with getting on in life,' John B. Yeats used to say when the children talked of the success of the parents of their playmates. In Ireland personality had counted more than the discipline and law that the Anglo-Saxon middle-class families looked up to, and their father derided the English fetish of 'character', telling Willie that the hearty fights between the boys at school was simply another example of English absurdity. He would often compare the two countries in terms of Greece and Rome: 'Ireland is like ancient Athens where all were such talkers and disputants. England is like ancient Rome with its legions and cohorts and dull business of conquering the world.' And John Butler was fond of a saying of their grandfather which he used to repeat at table to give his children confidence in an alien environment: 'the Anglo-Irish are socially the equals, and the superiors of most.'

Willie had acquired his father's stance of agnosticism and sceptical positivism. John B. Yeats took his political philosophy from John Stuart Mill and his scientific attitude to life from Darwin and Comte. Such notions were not popular at the High School. Willie's attempts to convince certain masters of their descent from the duck-billed platypus and his discourses on natural selection, holding a daisy in his hand to illustrate his point, aroused anger and dislike in the headmaster, William Wilkins. But young Yeats was excellent at maths and his good looks ensured that his classmates regarded him with a certain envy. 'Graceful, impetuous, his arms swinging in long curved gestures, his eyes flashing as he brushed the long black hair back from his white fore-head,' is how a contemporary remembered him.

Wilkins was furious when the head boy of the school, Charles Johnston, fell under Yeats's spell. Johnston was a handsome boy, a dandy, and number one in Ireland in every examination he entered for. But Yeats believed his mind was parched by excessive study and succeeded in weaning him towards a different world by lending him A.P. Sinnett's *Esoteric Buddhism*.

For Willie too had had a conversion. In reacting from his father's positivism and the fashionable scientific attack on religion, he had reached out to the world of the imagination and the spirit to satisfy his thirst for truth. From now until the end of his life he would seek to apply the same analytical principles to the world of the spirit as his father would apply to the material one. Together Willie and Charlie Johnston would go down to the Natural History Museum in Merrion Square and, pressing their hands over the crystals in the glass cases, convince themselves they felt Odic forces flowing from them.

Johnston's father was furious with his son. He was the Orange Member of Parliament for Ballinakellig and had foreseen a brilliant academic career for the boy who was now turning into an eccentric. Worse was to follow, for Charlie's sister Georgie and his brother Lewis followed suit and opened a vegetarian restaurant in Dame Street where, dressed in flowing costumes, they presided over gatherings of long-haired young men in mustard-coloured tweeds. They were all members of Willie's and Charlie's Hermetic Society founded to study Eastern religions and esoteric subjects, and which met once a month in a room in Adelaide Road.

Meanwhile John B. Yeats, convinced that Willie was concentrating too much on exams and 'getting on', decided to take him away from the High School. He entered the boy in the Metropolitan School of Art in Kildare Street with the idea that everyone should train in art at some time or other. Secretly he was impressed with some of Willie's verse and hoped that he might turn out to be an artist of another sort. This was how it happened. Within a year or so Willie, deciding that his bent was for poetry not painting, had determined on a literary career.

Now he cultivated a limp in imitation of Hamlet and used to gaze abstractedly at his reflection in shop windows to see if his scarlet loose-knotted tie was blowing in the wind in the manner of Byron. Policemen seeing him walking through the city, a gangling figure reciting verse and swinging his arms wildly, would eye him suspiciously, but after a while they decided it was the 'porthry' that was disturbing his head, and left him alone. He often spent his days in the back of his father's studio, cleaning brushes and palettes in between writing poetry. He would read his verse to young writers who came in or read their own out to them, beating time with his hands and chanting with his head on one side. One visitor, the young poetess Katherine Tynan, gave him chlorodyne lozenges for a bad cough. Absent-mindedly he ate the lot in one go and slept for thirty hours.

His father was one of the great talkers of Dublin and spouted interminably as he painted, advancing towards the canvas in great strides and then standing back to survey the effect of what he had done. In the same sentence he had been known to discuss the second part of Faust, the Hesperian Apples, and the relationship of villainy to genius. One of the themes which he expounded was that a successful pirate might as easily have been a great creative artist because of his high positive force, and he was delighted when Willie from the other end of the studio supplied him with an apt phrase to cap his thesis.

'Transmutation of energy.'

'Precisely it. Make a cup of tea.'

Charlie Johnston had gone over to London in order to meet Madam Blavatsky and come back to Dublin to found a branch of the Theosophical Society there. The

Bengali Brahmin, Mohini Chatterjee, was brought over and stayed in the rooms of the only member who lived outside home (the others all lived with their parents), and from him they learned how to approach the Upanishads and the Bhagavad Gita.

One friend who had refused to join the Hermetic Society was sufficiently impressed by Mohini to take up theosophy. This was George Russell, whom Yeats had met at the School of Art.

Russell was an unusual young man. Like Yeats he was six feet tall, he had shaggy brown hair and deep blue dreamy eyes. A clerk by day, he studied art in the evenings and excited Yeats's envy by the images he was able to bring up on the canvas. Sometimes as he was drawing the model a figure of St John would intrude itself. At other times he would try to depict the evolution of human forms within God's mind. When someone remarked that the aura he gave his figures resembled the headdress of the American Indian, Russell admitted that this was so, but maintained that the Indians having visionary gifts saw a similar aura which they represented in the feathered hats their chiefs wore.

Such a person was bound to appeal to Yeats and they became close friends. Russell now told him how when he was sixteen and a schoolboy at Rathmines School, a bleak institution for middle-class boys down the road from the High School, he had become aware of a mysterious quickening of the imagination, and visions which he believed came from another world began to overwhelm him. As he came out of school and looked to the left, he would see the tall hills of Dublin brooding down on the city through the houses and public buildings. Now what had been for him up to then 'a far flash of blue on the horizon' became a place where he could visit at the weekends for spiritual refreshment. To the breathless Yeats he told of visions he had seen there: an airship steered by a young man with black hair blown back from his forehead that passed so close he could have stretched out his hand and touched it; or on another occasion a youth whose body was shot through with sun fire and about whose golden head flew a fiery plumage of singing birds and whom later he would recognise as Aengus, the Irish god of love. Were these visions, the two young men wondered, the memory of some ancient civilisation, or the results of a universal consciousness which each man possessed and which could reveal itself in certain circumstances?

Yeats introduced Russell to Charlie Johnston and the three used to tramp up the hills early on Sunday mornings. One of the advantages of Dublin was that the hills could be reached in forty minutes or so. There in the shadow of Kilmashogue, which Russell had told them was a sacred mountain, they would await visions in a shrine where Druids had worshipped 1,500 years before. Later they came to believe that the Hindu and Irish deities were related and that Bo Derg, Aengus, Mananan, whom they would learn of from O'Grady's books, were manifestations of a universal hierarchy of spiritual beings.

> On such a day as this [Johnston wrote ten years later] rejoicing in the sunlight, we lay on our backs in the grass, and, looking up into the blue, tried to think ourselves into that new world which we had suddenly discovered ourselves to inhabit. For we had caught the word, handed down with silent laughter through the ages, that we ourselves are the inventors of the game of life, the kings of this most excellent universe: that there is no sorrow, but fancy weaves it; that we already are, and always were, though we had forgotten it, within the doors of life.
>
> That young enthusiasm and hourly joy of living was one of old destiny's gracious presents, a brightness to remember when storms gathered round us, as they did many a time in the years since: there was a gaiety and lightness in the air then, a delight of new discovery, that I do not think we shall find again.

Russell was not always an easy person to get on with. He had eccentric habits which made unusual demands on his friends, one of which was to demand that they accompany him to Kill-o'-the-Grange graveyard on Sundays and listen to him read his verses, usually against the competition of a howling wind. Once he called on a friend for the usual ramble and was surprised when he found that it was Christmas Day, a date which had no place in his esoteric calendar. He was too kindly a young man to dislike his parents, but his links with the family were not close. One day he and a friend passed someone in the street to whom Russell gave a nod. 'That's my brother,' he remarked, 'he's too fat.'

The Yeats family and the Russells lived quite near each other. In fact before they met, the Yeats' maid had noticed an abstracted young man passing the house on the way to work and had christened him 'the strayed angel'. Now, late in the evenings when the family had gone to bed Russell would drop in and talk to Willie until the small hours. Lily and Lolly, the two young Yeats sisters, had already had their troubles with their brother's obsession with poetry, as he used to drone like a bee round the fire when at work. 'Now Willie stop composing,' they would say and he would be put in the kitchen till the mood passed. Now, trying to sleep upstairs while their brother and Russell went at it together they comforted themselves with the idea that the two were trying to disincarnate themselves and if they were lucky they might witness the result.

J.B. Yeats did not approve of his son's friendship with Russell. His dislike of religion was so strong that he thought Russell might steer Willie towards a mystical rather than a scientific approach. 'A saint maybe, but reared in Portadown,' he would remark, referring to the philistine northern industrial centre near where Russell had been reared.

On certain weekends Russell and Willie would walk out to Katherine Tynan who lived in Clondalkin, a

Douglas Hyde (standing) with A. P. Graves, the author and father of Robert Graves

Standish O'Grady reading on the lawn at Killiney, 1894

Charles Stewart Parnell, as he was at the height of his power

SEARCHING FOR POTATOES IN A STUBBLE FIELD.

The plight of the peasants during the Great Famine, as seen by the *Illustrated London News*

Coole Park in 1890

Moore Hall, home of George Moore

The magnificent south front of Tulira Castle, rebuilt by Edward Martyn

The Norman Tower of Tulira, to which Martyn would retire

Lady Gregory in a photograph taken at the time of her marriage in 1880

Wilfrid Scawen Blunt in the early 1880s

Emile Zola, one of George Moore's earliest
and strongest inspirations

George Moore in an early photograph. He would have been in his mid-twenties, fresh from his artistic awakening in Paris

Edward Martyn painted by Sarah Purser. Though cousins, he and Moore could not have been greater opposites

country village about five miles from Rathmines. Her father was a substantial farmer and she had achieved some recognition as a poetess, her first book having been praised by Alice Meynell and Christina Rossetti. There was plenty of good food to be had at the Tynan table and the young men would recite their verse after Katherine had given readings of her own. She remembered Willie as 'beautiful to look at with his dark face touched with vivid colouring, the night-black hair, the large eyes'. Russell was for her 'a shy, unashamed boy with benignity and genius shining from him'. She asked him to design an angel as an illustration for one of her books and when he showed it to her it had peacock's feathers on the arms, and smaller ones on the feet. He explained to her that the reason for this was that the motor power of angels lies not in their shoulder wings, but in the backs of their arms and feet.

Sometimes Willie would stay until morning and the only way for him to get home would be on the milk cart which was going to the market. As it reached the main streets he could be seen among the milk cans talking energetically to the driver who he discovered had occult powers; wholly engrossed he would fail to notice the people in the fashionable streets who were looking up in astonishment at the spectacle of the young poet with waving arms lecturing the milkman.

Russell believed that if he allowed himself to be guided by the spirit he would be directed towards his ancestral home. Once he lay awake at night seeking a name for a painting he had done of a being conceived in the Divine Mind. Next day he heard the word 'aeon' whispered to him, and two weeks later opened a book in the National Library where that word was the first that caught his eye. It was the word the gnostics had given the first beings separated from the Deity, and it related to the vision he had had when he had done the painting which inspired the word. From now on he would sign his poems and paintings 'AE' in tribute to the belief that language had a universal origin, in the spiritual entities perceived by primitive man.

By allowing himself to be guided where the spirit willed

he seemed to meet the sort of people that Johnston and Yeats longed to, but never could. Once he came over the hill, the Two Rock, to where his friends were lying on the grass, to tell them he had met an old man on top of the mountain who had said, 'God owns the heavens but He covets the world.'

One Sunday in a spirit of mystical fervour Russell went to Bray, the seaside resort near Dublin, and standing on the esplanade held forth to the passers by. He told them that the earth beneath them was as sacred as that of Judea and that the Golden Age was about them if they would but claim it: that there is a reservoir in which earth memories are preserved, and with which those that partake of the imagination can come in touch. 'All men bear within them,' he said with burning eyes, 'their own divinity, and it needs some adventure of the spirit, some gesture against materialism for each man to gain his inheritance.'

One wonders what the respectable middle-aged couples strolling on the esplanade, the men in their straw hats and blazers, the women in their veils and gowns so tight fitting that they had the appearance of being upholstered, must have thought of this strange young man.

He did succeed in impressing at least one passer by. By chance Standish O'Grady happened to be among the audience and he went back to his wife and told her with wonder in his voice, 'I heard today on the esplanade a young man glorifying the ancient gods of Ireland.' O'Grady recognised that the ancient world he had rediscovered in his volumes of history was becoming part of the imagination of the new generation, and like any author was delighted to find that his work was having its effect.

Despite the fact that the division between Anglo-Irish and native-Irish had been prolonged by political divisions, there had always been an interest in Gaelic culture among a small section of the former. A young Anglo-Irish lady, Charlotte Brooke, was the first to translate the sagas into a sort of 'village-green' English in 1771 and Henry Flood, the great orator of the Protestant Parliament, had left £50,000 in 1781 to endow a Chair of Irish in Trinity College. The Royal Irish Academy, founded in 1784, had encouraged scholarly work in the collection and study of Irish manuscripts and George Petrie, William Stokes and Edward Bunting were among those who had preserved and taken care to rescue literature, poetry, music and history which might otherwise have been swallowed up in the Great Famine.

In 1837 Thomas Larcom, a Scotsman, was appointed Chief of the Ordnance Survey in Ireland. Son of the Governor of Malta, he turned out to have, in addition to a dedication to describing place names and transcribing geography, a sensitive feeling for literature. He employed two scholars, John O'Donovan and Eugene O'Curry, the latter a one-time clerk in a lunatic asylum, to do a major part of the survey. The result was that in addition to the normal reports required by his Department, a vast amount of folklore, saga literature and poetry collected from the people's lips poured in from these industrious surveyors. O'Donovan's reports alone filled one hundred volumes and O'Curry, by the opportunity allowed him through Larcom's discretion, managed to save for posterity oral accounts of the saga period that would undoubtedly have vanished with the Famine. These collections of O'Curry's later formed the basis for an address on 'Early Irish Literature' which he gave in 1856 as Professor of History in Newman's short-lived Catholic University in St Stephen's Green. It was thus through an Englishman and a Scotsman that an important section of Irish historical culture was saved from extinction.

Among the professional classes in Dublin were some who also took an interest in the folklore and antiquity of the country. One of these was Oscar Wilde's father, the surgeon Sir William Wilde. Wilde spoke Irish like a native and made some important early contributions to folklore which he collected from peasants in the west

99

where he had grown up at Moytura, County Mayo. No doubt his O'Flaherty ancestry gave him a sympathy towards the native culture. It was said that when he was offered presents of butter and fowl by peasants in return for medical assistance he would often ask that a piece of poetry or folklore be recited instead.

The woman he married, Francesca Elgee, was also a well-known collector of folklore. Her *Ancient Legends of Ireland* was much praised and widely read and contains some of the most beautiful folk tales in existence. She had as a young girl been known throughout Ireland as an aristocratic rebel, who had written the article for which Charles Gavan Duffy had been convicted of sedition when he published it in *The Nation*. Francesca had stood up in the body of the court and shouted, 'I wrote it, my lord', but no action had been taken against her. Under the name of Speranza she wrote patriotic ballads about the Fenians and English misrule, like *The Famine Year* which was recited round firesides throughout the country.

Weary men, what reap ye? – 'Golden corn for the stranger.'
What sow ye? – 'Human corses that await for the Avenger.'
Fainting forms, all hunger-stricken, what see you in the offing?
'Stately ships to bear our food away amid the stranger's scoffing.'
There's a proud array of soldiers – what do they round your door?
'They guard our master's granaries from the thin hands of the poor.'

Marriage to Sir William had tamed Speranza's political fervour but she continued her interest in folklore for the rest of her life.

John B. Yeats knew the Wildes well and often dined in their Merrion Square house. When he sent his wife to Sir William to have her eyes attended to she was told to leave things as they were; but the surgeon did remind her to ask her uncle Thomas when he was going to send the fishing rod he had promised. Sir William had a name as a lecher and it is interesting, in view of his son Oscar's subsequent development, that his wife may have not have been exactly a puritan in sexual matters either. John B. Yeats remembered his mother telling him that she had heard from the wife of Isaac Butt, the Leader of the Home Rule Party, that she had found Francesca *in flagrante delicto* with Butt some time before marriage to Sir William.

The interest in Irish culture exemplified by the Wildes and some members of the professional classes would have been anathema in Trinity College, the main university in the country which stood right in the centre of Dublin. This is a splendid institution into which you can slip away from the main streets and, passing under the handsome portico, emerge with the tall pillars of Chambers' Examination Hall and the Chapel confronting each other from opposite sides of a cobbled square, flanked by the stern façade of Cassel's Dining Hall and the fine bulk of Burgh's Library.

Founded in the sixteenth century by Queen Elizabeth, it had become an educational establishment for the perpetuation of a ruling class. From time to time a rebel or two had emerged from its halls. But its conformity had been the measure of its success, and Trinity had cut itself off from any communication with Gaelic Ireland. In the eighties it was reaching the height of its academic fame. Among the dons were George Francis Fitzgerald who combined with Lorentz to formulate the principle on which the theory of relativity is based. The Professor of Latin, Palmer, was, according to A.E. Housman, the greatest Latinist of his time, and Henry Macran, Head of the Philosophy Faculty, was the leading Hegelian in Europe. The historians. J.B. Bury and William Hartpole Lecky were also on the staff. Then there was J.P. Mahaffy who had tutored Oscar Wilde ('my first and last teacher in the art of conversation') and who had excelled in so many subjects – Egyptology, Greek, history, music, as well as being an international cricketer and a first-class shot – that Henry Jackson the Cambridge scholar remarked of him that his very versatility prevented him getting the recognition he should have had. People felt that so much knowledge could not reside in one man, whereas 'he had done so much work in four branches of learning as would earn him a European reputation in any one of them'.

Edward Dowden, the Professor of English, had established a world reputation before he was thirty. At the age of twenty-four he had become the first Professor of English in the English-speaking world when Trinity created the post in 1876. Eight years later he produced *Shakespeare – His Mind and Art* which made his name. This was followed by biographies of Goethe and Shelley. Dowden's poetry was published and much admired in London literary magazines. Because of his extreme good looks he had a large following among fashionable young ladies in Dublin.

Yet for Dowden the Irish language was the speech of barbarians, and the culture which O'Grady and Hyde were re-discovering was that of a race of marauders, rebels and bogmen. Dowden refused to take part in the centenary of the poet Thomas Moore in 1879, on the grounds that Moore's work was of no special significance, and over-rated in his own country. He used to beg his friend, the poet Aubrey de Vere, to steer away from Irish heroic subjects and concentrate on an English hero like Thomas à Becket. In later life when it could have been thought that he might have become more flexible, he told a friend, 'I'm infinitely glad that I spent my early enthusiasm on Wordsworth, Spencer and Shakespeare and not on anything Ireland ever produced.'

Such an attitude was typical of the Trinity establishment at the time. 'Do you seriously maintain,' said Dr Brinkley, the Professor of Ancient Literature, to Douglas Hyde on one occasion, 'that there exists the slightest evidence to prove that the Irish had any acquaintance with the art of civilisation anterior to the coming of the English?'

Mahaffy thought that Gaelic literature was nonsense and Dr Atkinson, Professor of Sanskrit (who did understand Gaelic), used to declare that it would be difficult to find a book in Irish in which there was not some passage so silly or indecent 'as to give you a shock from which you would not recover for the rest of your life'.

Why should such men have shut themselves off from the culture that existed outside their gates? It must be remembered that the function of the university was to maintain a privileged class. To admit that the other Ireland had a culture which could be compared to that of Greece or Rome would be to undermine the principle on which the dons' security was based. Their exemplars were across the water, their sister colleges Oxford and Cambridge. There was their real home and not Ireland, which as far as the majority were concerned might have been a lost island in the Atlantic.

John B. Yeats summed up the prevailing attitude in his old university when he said, 'Trinity has always turned away from Irish aspirations to that of England and the Viceregal Lodge. From the first it set itself against any national hope and insulted the national soul.' Despite these differences, John B. Yeats's closest friend at Trinity had been Edward Dowden. Dowden had been an early champion of Whitman when that poet's works were banned in Trinity as godless and secular, and John B. Yeats had held out hope for his friend because of this. He believed that Dowden had a poet's soul and begged him to 'give in to his nature'. But Dowden was a born conservative and gradually became immured in the Trinity tradition till, in the younger Yeats's description of him, 'he withered in the barren soil of Unionism'.

Nevertheless, when Willie was growing up his father's friendship with Dowden proved invaluable. There was an agreeable Sunday evening at Dowden's elegant house, 'Winstead' in Temple Road, about a quarter of an hour from where the Yeats lived; and after a pleasant walk down the tree-lined road with magnificent late Georgian houses belonging to higher Castle officials and successful surgeons and barristers on either side, father and son would climb the stone steps to the professor's drawing room. There they would hear excellent conversation from dons and writers and they could enjoy what Willie called 'the decencies of Anglo-Irish life' as well as an excellent meal.

But presently the elder Yeats began to feel a gap growing between himself and Dowden. It began when he had asked his friend to get him rooms in Trinity so that he could live alone for a while in order to paint some special portraits. This was not difficult for a don in Dowden's position to organise, and John B. Yeats was soon installed. But it turned out that an agnostic and free thinker was unacceptable to the more conservative element in the university and the painter was asked to leave. Dowden refused to make any protest, afraid that he would compromise his position.

J.B. Yeats was no ordinary artist and Dowden, his close friend, must have realised this. Later Henry Lamb was to describe him as 'by far the greatest portrait painter that Ireland has produced' and Robert Henri was to say 'John B. Yeats is the greatest portrait painter of the Victorian era'. That Dowden should have accepted the official view as against the artist's indicated the direction in which he was going. One day he told John B. Yeats a story that horrified him. He had been asked to dine by the Archbishop of Dublin to meet the poet Tennyson. Just as the meal started Dowden had excused himself, by saying that he had tickets for the opera and would have to leave. J.B. Yeats diagnosed this as 'the pose of an Irishman trying to be an Englishman and overdoing the part'. He recognised that the friend of his youth had become ensnared by the establishment. And from then on their paths diverged.

One night Willie Yeats was speaking at the Contemporary Club in Grafton Street. This had been founded by a Trinity graduate, Hubert Oldham, and it was said of the

104

members that the only thing they had in common was that they drew breath. As Yeats was in the habit of saying, harsh argument which had gone out of fashion in London was still the manner of conversation in Dublin. The kind of abuse which was hurled at meetings rather horrified visiting speakers like William Morris when they came over to address the club.

Young Willie, frightfully nervous at first, had developed his oratorical gifts in the cut and thrust of this debating club. Stephen Gwynn remembers noting that 'we were all convinced that young Yeats was going to be a better poet than we had yet seen in Ireland – and the interesting thing is that this was not out of personal liking'. A frequent attender at the Contemporary Club's meetings was the Fenian John O'Leary, who had some time before been released on ticket of leave after serving a sentence of penal servitude for treason. O'Leary was convinced that the great misfortune of Ireland in the nineteenth century was that she had never produced a great poet. One night he remarked to Stephen Gwynn, the biographer and later MP: 'Young Yeats is the only person in this room who will ever be reckoned a genius.'

O'Leary had been born into a well-off family who owned property in Tipperary town. As a young man he had taken part in the rebellion of 1848, but escaped arrest. After that he studied medicine in Queen's College, Cork, before going to Paris to walk the wards of the hospitals. On the boat going over he had met an American art student named James McNeill Whistler, whom he liked so much that they decided to room together in the Hôtel Corneille. Their fellow-lodgers included Swinburne and John Poynter the painter, and since George Du Maurier soon became part of their set, O'Leary spent as much time absorbing art and literature as he did studying medicine.

When he returned to Ireland he renewed his interest in revolutionary politics and became a leading member of the Fenian organisation, dedicated to freeing Ireland by physical force. He put his literary interest to good use when he became editor of the Fenian paper called *The Irish People*. But he was arrested on a charge of sedition in 1865 and sentenced to fifteen years' penal servitude.

Released after eight years but forbidden to return to Ireland, he resumed his old life in Paris. During these thirteen years of exile he became a well-known figure among the revolutionaries from different parts of Europe, who filled the cafés in those post-Commune years. O'Leary was a striking-looking man with a long head, falcon nose and great burning eyes, deeply set; and his noble appearance, added to his reputation of having suffered stoically the horrors of imperialism, brought him a wide circle of acquaintances. Kropotkin became a friend and he counted Turgenev among his literary companions.

When he returned to Ireland in 1885 on ticket of leave O'Leary took rooms in Leinster road, Rathmines, Dublin. He had a small income from house property in Tipperary and did no regular work. He lived very much according to his Paris routine, spending the morning writing letters, cutting clippings from papers to send to his friends, and covering postcards with interminable comments which sometimes finished up around the stamp. He spent his afternoons fishing in the bookshops, but his evenings were given over to people who would drop in to see him. His rooms had become a meeting place for young poets, writers and revolutionaries. Katherine Tynan, Douglas Hyde and the poet T.W. Rolleston were among the regular visitors. Tea was served by his sister Ellen who was thought to resemble Christina Rossetti, with her eyes set wide under her brow and her large eyelids.

O'Leary believed that a political revolution would not succeed without a cultural revival. When his instinct told him on that evening in the Contemporary Club that here was the great poet Ireland awaited, he determined at all costs to get young Yeats along to his evenings. He succeeded and in a short time the two had become close friends. Yeats was fascinated by this Irish patriot who rejected most of nineteenth-century Irish poetry because it was bad literature. Propaganda had no interest for him. It was the awakening of the national soul that concerned him. O'Leary steered Yeats towards the poets who had translated from Irish, Callanan, Walsh, O'Curry, that he might devise a new rhythm that had not yet come into English. Above all he encouraged him to read the works of Sir Samuel Ferguson who had put into verse the same sagas and tales that O'Grady had written in prose.

It was O'Leary's moral force that captivated Yeats. The old man would never abuse his English jailers, though he had an impaired digestion as a result of his treatment in prison and had to live mainly on milk and biscuits. 'Why should I complain,' he said, 'I was in the hands of my enemies.' And when a politician who had gone on hunger strike in Mullingar railed about his predicament, O'Leary's comment was that 'there are some things a man should not do to save a country, one is to cry in public'. He had long dismissed the Church as a possible ally in the fight for freedom and used to say: 'My religion is the old Persian one – to pull the bow and tell the truth.' He admired Parnell because 'of the man's character', but would only follow him in so far as he went for Irish freedom and no more.

Yeats was the only one of O'Leary's friends permitted to interrupt his morning routine. He loved to go along at that time, because he would get the old revolutionary by himself and enjoy his energetic conversation without interruption. He would often arrive to find O'Leary with his glass of milk beside him reading his favourite book, Turgenev's *Torrents of Spring*.

Sometimes O'Leary would talk of his days in Paris, how he had met Whistler on his first day there and how both of them had decided to room together in the Hôtel Corneille. The last letter he got from the painter came from a fashionable address in Chelsea after Whistler had moved to London and become famous. In it he begged O'Leary to call, saying, 'I have been hoping you'd walk in every morning and expected you in vain.' O'Leary would chuckle as he explained to Yeats that the reason he could not call at the time was because a warrant was out for his arrest. One of the people Whistler had wanted him to meet was their former Paris acquaintance John Poynter, later President of the Royal Academy.

He would talk to Yeats of Russian and French literature and discuss his favourite English writers with him too. He admired Swinburne but begged his protégé not to overload his verse with Anglo-Saxon phrasing as he considered Swinburne had done. He would purr with delight as he read some exquisite passage from Pater and then remark that it revealed the decadence of the English who were entombing themselves in a dead language.

O'Leary was on the Supreme Council of the Irish Republican Brotherhood (the secret militant revolutionary group) and enrolled Yeats in the movement, with which in one way or another he was to remain associated all his life. (As late as 1937 he would write to Ethel Mannin that he was 'an Irish nationalist of the school of O'Leary'.)

From now on, Yeats would be regarded by the IRB as 'their man' in the literary movement. It was to bring him in contact with men engaged in dangerous conspiracies and involve him in activities which, while they indulged his love of secrecy, also gave him an insight into elements of the national being that he could never otherwise have become aware of.

O'Leary used to say: 'Davis wants to convert thousands, but I want two or three', and he would name Yeats, Rolleston and Taylor as his choice. These last two were among the group who used to meet at O'Leary's evenings. T.W. Rolleston was the son of a County Court judge and a brilliant graduate of Trinity. He had translated Whitman into German and was the first to introduce Turgenev to English readers when he published him in the *Dublin University Review*, of which he was editor from 1885 to 1886. He was an extremely handsome young man and Yeats used to tell how shop girls would turn in the street as he passed and murmur that here was the successor to Thomas Davis, so powerful was the magnetism of his personality. He too was enrolled by O'Leary in the revolutionary movement and was looked upon as a standard bearer of the new culture.

Rolleston belonged to that small band who have written one poem, and that immortal. His 'The Dead at Clonmacnoise' has featured in numerous anthologies including the Oxford Book of English Verse. But though he published other volumes of verse, there was not a hint of a line of poetry among them, nothing with the thrust and surge of his one success.

> In a quiet water'd land, a land of roses,
>   Stands Saint Kieran's city fair;
> And the warriors of Erin in their famous generations
>   Slumber there.
>
> There beneath the dewy hillside sleep the noblest
>   Of the clan of Conn,
> Each below his stone with name in branching Ogham
>   And the sacred knot thereon. . . .
>
> Many and many a son of Conn the Hundred-Fighter
>   In the red earth lies at rest;
> Many a blue eye of Clan Colman the turf covers,
>   Many a swan-white breast.

John F. Taylor was a barrister of bohemian tastes, famous for defending lost causes. He was a difficult personality but his jury speeches, like those of Isaac Butt and Seymour Bushe, were read and recited in the pubs and around the firesides of the cottages in the countryside. His most famous peroration in the defence of the Irish language is quoted with some alterations by James Joyce in *Ulysses* and Yeats repeats the same speech, also altered, in his autobiography.

109

Taylor never took to Yeats. But though he was put off by the barrister's shabbiness and awkward appearance, Yeats never forgot his powers of oratory which convinced him of 'how great might be the effect of verse spoken by a man almost rhythm-drunk'.

Of the three it was Yeats who was to prove O'Leary's best pupil. Rolleston would fade out of national affairs after some years and Taylor adopted a familiar Irish stance of wallowing in failure, before fading into obscurity. But to Yeats, the connection with O'Leary was of vital importance. 'To him I owe all I have set my hand to,' he wrote later in recognition of the role the old revolutionary had played in his life.

O'Leary lent him money to help him continue with his poetry, arranged the publication of his first book of verse and acquainted him with writers and folklorists, which enabled Yeats to publish two substantial anthologies *Fairy and Folk Tales of the Irish Peasantry* (1888) and *Representative Irish Tales* (1891). To an extent O'Leary began to take the place of his father in Willie's life. John B. Yeats was never to lose the influence he had on his son in his vocation as an artist. He considered it his function to see that Willie fulfilled what he considered to be his purpose in life. The very force of the father's opinion, his lack of tact, often produced a violent reaction between him and his son. Once in an argument over John Ruskin, his father actually broke the glass of a picture over Willie's head. On another occasion, in the middle of a fierce dispute, Yeats senior got so carried away that he asked Willie upstairs to fight him. When Willie replied that he could not fight his father, this extraordinary parent replied, 'Why not?' With his stoicism, his calm persuasion, O'Leary was the antithesis of John Butler Yeats. Willie came to love him as a father. J.B. Yeats was not in the least jealous of O'Leary's influence. In the material sense he had been a hopeless parent. What he had to pass on to his children, his belief in the superiority of the artist's stance, could only be done through inference and example, and he was determined that Willie and Jack (who would become a painter of the top rank) should retain their special receptivity to this. After that he allowed them the freedom he demanded for himself.

Yeats had published his first verse in the *Dublin University Review* before he had met O'Leary. His play *The Island of Statues*, written in Arcadian mode, was accepted after a successful reading in Trinity College. Later *Mosada*, a long poem with Spanish setting, was reprinted in a limited edition, after it had appeared in the *Review*. But Yeats's early long poems were often derivative, with obvious debts to Wordsworth, Shelley and Spenser, and relying to some extent on archaisms. Some of his short poems too were second-rate, like the aptly named 'The Fairy Pedant':

> Afár from our lawn and our levee
> O sister of sorrowful gaze
> Where the roses in scarlet are heavy
> And dream of the end of their days.
>
> Come away, while the moon's in the woodland,
> We'll dance and then feast in a dairy,
> Though youngest of all in our good band,
> You're wasting away, little fairy.

But from this period on a new quality creeps into his work. With his uncanny ear for rhythm he began to pick up metres that were not in the English tradition but which had grown out of the structure of verse in the Irish language. A long couplet of Ferguson with its gapped rhythms could give him a lead:

> My bitter woe it is, love that we are not far away
> In Cashel town, though the bare deal board were our
>   marriage bed this day.

Or Callanan's:

> My bed was the ground, my roof the greenwood above
> And the wealth that I sought – one far kind glance
>   from my love.

111

Ferguson's use of saga material in his lyric poem 'Deirdre and Conor' turned Yeats back for the first time to the rich material that lay around the countryside he had spent his boyhood in.

> When I was a child I had only to climb the hill behind the house to see the long blue ragged hills flowing along the southern horizon. What beauty was lost to me, what depth of emotion is still perhaps lacking in me, because nobody told me, not even the merchant captains who knew everything, that Cruachan of the Enchantments lay behind those long blue ragged hills.

These new discoveries made Yeats impatient with the intransigence of the Trinity set, who had set themselves against the development of Irish culture. He got a chance to launch an attack on those whom he now considered his enemies when O'Leary's hero Sir Samuel Ferguson died in 1886. In an extraordinary article published in the *Dublin University Review*, Yeats lashed out at what he called 'the West Britons' for their neglect of Ferguson and maintained that the greatest of the poet's faculties were killed long ago by indifference. Yeats considered Ferguson 'the greatest poet Ireland has produced, because the most central and the most Celtic'. He compared what he called 'Tennyson's Girton girls in their old costumes of dead chivalry's' unfavourably with Ferguson's heroic 'Deirdre' and alleged that the 'admirable but altogether trivial Edward Gosse was portable and pretty' when set beside the Irish poet, and even accused Matthew Arnold of plagiarism in 'Sohrab and Rustum'. But the real brunt of his attack he kept for Edward Dowden, whom he accused of being false to his country:

> It is a question whether the most distinguished of our critics, Professor Dowden, would not only have more consulted the interests of his country but more also in the long run his own dignity and reputation which are dear to all Irishmen, if he had devoted some of those elaborate pages which he spent on the much bewritten

112

George Eliot, to a man like the subject of this article.

Yeats continued:

> If Sir Samuel Ferguson had written to the glory of that from a moral point of view more than dubious achievement British civilisation, the critics probably including Professor Dowden, would have taken care of his reputation.

In his last paragraph the young critic made it clear that he was cutting the link with Dowden.

> I do not appeal to the professorial classes who, in Ireland, at least appear at no time to have thought of the affairs of their country till they first feared for their emoluments – nor do I appeal to the shoddy society of 'West Britonism' – but to those young men clustered here and there throughout our land whom the emotion of patriotism has lifted into that world of self-dispassion in which heroic deeds are possible and heroic poetry credible.

Dowden was livid. The attack undermined the principles on which he had based his aesthetic outlook – that Ireland had no worthwhile culture, and that his future both as a writer and a critic lay with an English public. Enthroned as a panjandrum in his palace, he chose to regard Yeats's attack as a personal one despite his friendship with the poet's father. There were no more pleasant breakfasts for Yeats at 'Winstead' or delightful dinner parties where he could enjoy the 'decencies of Anglo-Irish life'.

This pattern was one which Yeats was to follow throughout his life. For an artistic principle he would fight to the death. He had an appalling temper, and on occasions when he was defied his whole body would be shaken by fits of the most uncontrollable rage. But he learned to harness his anger as he matured and desired to influence the course of affairs. In later years he would hold his temper in reserve, to unleash it in defence of some writer or principle, when it would attain majestic force, the outburst having been carefully planned in advance.

In Trinity College one night Yeats met Douglas Hyde. At first he took him to be of peasant stock with his high cheekbones, flat deep-set brown eyes and jet black hair. He was surprised to find that Hyde was a rector's son from the west of Ireland who had had a country gentleman's upbringing. But Yeats and Hyde soon stopped discussing shooting and fishing when the poet discovered that Hyde's real passion in life was folklore. It must have seemed a sort of miracle to Yeats that a rector's son would not only collect stories of fairies and heroes from the peasants, but would speak their language as well. Yeats listened enchanted while Hyde told him how he had discovered in a cottage in Roscommon a manuscript black with dirt and reeking with turf smoke but worn away at the corners with constant reading, and how it had contained the two thousand-year-old story of 'The Death of Cuchulain' as well as tales of Ossian. Around the blazing log fires in winter nights Hyde had heard of Diarmuid O Duibhne who had eloped with Grania leaving Finn with his coat of hairy skin, of the speckled bull with the movable horn, the enchanted cat of Rathcroghan, and other wild outpourings of the bardic imagination still alive on the people's tongues. When he found that Yeats shared his enthusiasm for folklore, he told him how to draw tales out of the storytellers, not interrupting them in the beginning or asking them to write theirs down; but after he had given them a glass of whiskey and tobacco, to listen carefully until the tale was over and then ask permission the second time to use a pencil and paper so that the storyteller would not be put off his theme and something irretrievable lost.

Hyde, though, was dispirited because so much of the culture was dying as the people who knew Irish were getting fewer and fewer and the children were growing up as English speakers. He had known one storyteller in Roscommon, Sean Cunningham, who had been taught thousands of poems from ancient manuscripts as a boy. But he had been sent to a national or 'English' school and had a stick hung round his neck and a notch put in it for every word of Irish he spoke at home and a beating administered at school next day according to the number of notches.

Hyde and Yeats became close friends for a while and if his quarrel with Dowden closed one gate for Yeats into Trinity, Hyde opened another. Though there could have been little sympathy for his Irish interests, Hyde's extraordinary scholarship had already made an impact on the university. He had won gold medals in Greek, German, Latin and Modern Literature and was to take a double doctorate in Divinity and Law. When he started Latin lectures his pronunciation was noted by his professor to be different from the other students, and it was suggested that he must have learnt it on the Continent. 'No,' replied Hyde blandly, 'but I have modelled my pronunciation on the Irish.' Another student dazzled by his linguistic ability, said to him:

'You know a lot of languages, Hyde, how many do you know, English, Latin, Greek, Hebrew, German and French I suppose?'

'Yes, and I can read Italian, but the language I know best is Irish.'

'Irish. Do you know Irish?'

'Yes, I dream in Irish.'

Yeats would slip in off the crowded street if he had some free time and make for Hyde's rooms for a cup of tea or glass of whiskey and a chat. Hyde's diary of 4 December 1886 records: 'Yeats came to me this afternoon and we spent three hours together, criticising our poems to each other.' And on 18 December there is this note: 'Great discussion with Yeats on historical drama'.

They did not always agree. For instance, Hyde had reservations about the authenticity of the folk tales collected by Oscar Wilde's mother, Lady Wilde. He maintained she didn't know Irish and he had found it

115

hard to discover which was folk and which was Lady Wilde. Yeats on the other hand thought Lady Wilde's collections were so good that it did not matter either way.

Sometimes it seemed Yeats could be too abstract for Hyde's scientifically trained mind. 'Yeats was at Dowden's tonight. I was bored to death by his blather,' runs in Hyde's diary for 28 January.

Hyde was to be a sort of miracle for Yeats. He finally pulled back the curtain on the scene which had been half-revealed by Standish O'Grady, and which had stood between the Anglo-Irish and the ancient culture. O'Grady had rediscovered the sagas and O'Leary had put Yeats in touch with translations from the Irish by experts like Callanan and Walsh and Ferguson. But in Hyde Yeats found somebody who in his daily life was rescuing the treasure trove out of which Yeats believed a new literature might be made. When he edited his own collection of folk tales in 1888, selecting them from various authors, Crofton Croker, Lady Wilde, Ferguson, William Carleton, Yeats noted in the preface: 'Douglas Hyde is most to be trusted of all. . . . Others see a phase of Irish life; he understands all of its elements.'

Yeats's instinct as usual was right and it was from Hyde he was to derive his first real insight into the inherent nature of native Gaelic culture.

4   London Interval

In 1887 J.B. Yeats took his family to London. They settled
in Bedford Park, a new garden city for artists where
rents were low. The Yeats were dreadfully poor at this
time. Sometimes the sisters were down to twopence a
day for the housekeeping, and had to obtain credit from
shopkeepers. The elder Yeats was torn between the
desire to see his son make his mark as a writer and his
fear that he would lose 'mental liberty'. When Willie
declined a job on the Manchester *Courier* his father,
instead of being disappointed, was relieved. 'You've
taken a great weight off my mind', he told his son. The
quality of the conversation at the Yeats' Bedford Park
home may have helped to compensate for their dire
financial circumstances. G.K. Chesterton, who visited
them, recalled that Willie was, perhaps, the 'best talker
I ever met except his old father'.

> Among twenty other qualities, J.B. Yeats had that
> very rare but very real thing, entirely spontaneous
> style. . . . A long and elaborately balanced sentence,
> with dependent clauses alternative or antithetical,
> would flow out of such talkers with every word falling
> into its place, quite as immediately and innocently as
> most people would say it was a fine day or a funny
> business in the papers. I can still remember old Yeats
> . . . saying in an offhand way . . . 'Mr Joseph Cham-
> berlain has the character, as he has the face, of the
> shrewish woman who ruins her husband by her
> extravagance; and Lord Salisbury has the character,
> as he has the face, of the man who is so ruined.' That

style, or swift construction of a complicated sentence, was the sign of a lucidity now largely lost.

Although he was unable to assist his son financially J.B. Yeats was able to introduce Willie to a number of writers and poets who could help him make his way in the London literary world. Oscar Wilde, though he was then at the height of his fame, was not difficult to get in touch with because their families had known one another in Dublin. Oscar proved a good friend to the young poet and later reviewed his first book of poems in the *Pall Mall Gazette*. Willie was invited to Christmas dinner at Oscar's house. But he made the mistake of trying to tell a story about a giant to one of Wilde's little sons, who ran screaming out of the nursery, terrified with the realistic descriptions. To Yeats Wilde seemed to be trying to live a deliberately cultivated life. Even the way he sat at table with his wife and children suggested an artistic composition. The furniture in the dining room was in white, except for a diamond-shaped piece of red cloth in the table centre, and a red-shaded lamp hanging above. Yeats was fascinated by his new friend's conversational gifts. Even more so than Yeats *père*, Oscar spoke in sentences so perfectly constructed that they seemed to have been composed the night before. Enchanted as he was with Wilde, the practical side of Yeats was disturbed by Oscar's preoccupation with arts 'that do not survive the death of the body'. His merchant blood reacted against his friend's habit of late rising and sleeping away his life. When Oscar said to him, 'We Irish are too poetical to be poets, we are a nation of brilliant failures, but we are the greatest talkers since the Greeks', it seemed to Yeats only too accurate an assessment of the national failing. He, in reaction to such futility, wanted to channel that brilliant talk into a literature that would lift the people out of their torpor. He never forgot his debt to Wilde though, and later when Oscar's conviction in the courts began his downfalls it was Yeats who secured many letters appealing for clemency on his behalf.

Yeats was fascinated to find how much Irish culture had survived in the Wilde household. His father Sir William had taken Oscar on long visits to the west of Ireland when he was a little boy; and now the poet used to sing his own children to sleep with Gaelic lullabies and would tell them wonderful tales of Irish lakes where great carp lay on the bottom who would come to the surface and talk only if summoned in the native language. Oscar had met many of the rebels of the '48 rebellion at his mother's table, including Smith O'Brien and John Mitchel, and he talked to Yeats enthusiastically of them. In fact, part of Oscar's success in the United States in addition to posing as Bunthorne and wearing knee breeches and carrying a lily, was that the Irish-Americans hailed him as a hero because he was Speranza's son, the author of the patriotic ballads which were often sung at their political meetings. He varied his lectures to suit his audience, and when, in San Francisco, speaking to a group of Irish organisations, he said, 'The Saxon took our land from us and left us desolate. We took their language and added new beauties to it', his audience stood up and cheered.

Lady Wilde had come to London after her husband's death and presided over a rather seedy salon which she held in a house in Chelsea. 'I want to live in some high place, Primrose Hill or Highgate, because I was an eagle in my youth,' she told Yeats grandly when he arrived there at Oscar's invitation. As a boy Yeats had been an admirer of Lady Wilde's patriotic poetry. Though wary of the authenticity of her folk tales, he had included some of them in his *Fairy and Folk Tales of the Irish Peasantry*. At her afternoons the two talked expertly on fairies and Yeats was delighted to hear her declare one night that the Irish fairies came of ancient Persian race, but they had acquired the attributes of the soft climate of Ireland. Oscar attended regularly and seemed to work in tandem with his mother, answering her questions as if they had prepared the dialogue beforehand.

119

'Here is Miss Hanna Lynch, a young Irish genius.'

'But Mama, are not young Irish geniuses as plentiful as blackberries on the trees?'

At these afternoons Lady Wilde used to keep the blinds down to exclude the light, and considered it bad form to ask the time. Heavily made up, she seemed at times as if she was a character in one of her son's plays.

Shaw once said of Wilde that he was 'at root a very Irish Irishman and as such at home nowhere else but in Dublin'. One can imagine how Yeats, learning of Oscar's early Gaelic involvement, would have liked to recruit him for his movement. But Oscar had left Dublin before Parnell and the stirring of the imagination. He had thought of remaining there and discussed the matter with his friend Count Plunkett. But the lure of London led him to the mailboat. It was the literary centre of the English-speaking world at the time and Dublin was a backwater. After his release from prison Oscar must have considered returning to Dublin. By then the pot had begun to boil. He would have sensed the beginning of a movement which would feed his creative appetite. Had he not earlier hinted at a Celtic Renaissance as mighty as that of the cities of Italy? But the thought of the scandal his return would cause must have made him reluctant to come to Dublin again. After all, even his mentor Mahaffy had refused to sign a petition asking for his release. As it was he took the boat to Calais in 1897. There three years later he died in Paris, exactly eighteen months after the first presentation of the Irish Literary Theatre at the Antient Concert Rooms in Dublin.

One day in June 1889 she arrived on the doorstep at Bedford Park. John O'Leary had sent her, she said. To Yeats she seemed like a being from another world. Her complexion was 'like apple blossom ... luminous like that of a blossom through which the light falls'. Lolly didn't like the way she smiled on everyone 'with a royal smile'; Lily noticed disapprovingly that she was wearing slippers. But their brother was mesmerised by this statuesque girl who told them her name was Maud Gonne. She took Willie to dine that evening and they spent the following eight evenings together. Yeats couldn't get her out of his mind. He discovered that despite her voice – she spoke with a Dublin Castle voice and not in the easy-going Dublin drawl of the Yeats family – and manner, which suggested an aristocratic background, Maud Gonne was an Irish revolutionary. O'Leary had directed her energy to the cause of Ireland and she had become a legendary figure in the west, organising the peasants to resist evictions, setting up soup kitchens and temporary camps for those who had been unhoused, and on one occasion putting weedkiller in an unpleasant bailiff's soup in an attempt to polish him off. Country people reached out to touch the hem of her coat as if to draw strength from her. She left Ireland for Paris, where she edited a propaganda magazine, *L'Irlande Libre*, which detailed British injustices in Ireland and which was sent free to French, English and American newspapers. She lectured in Paris, Amsterdam, Brussels and her great beauty and histrionic ability drew large audiences wherever she went. On one of her revolutionary missions she had travelled to Moscow with secret documents sewn into the hem of her dress and a revolver in her bag. There she met Wyckham Steed of the *Review of Reviews* who described her as 'one of the most beautiful women in the world'.

Her early years had been spent in quite a different atmosphere. Her father had been brigade-major of the cavalry in Dublin, and she had grown up insulated from the life of ordinary people. When a new Lord Lieutenant would arrive in Dulbin and drive through the city streets amid royal pageantry, Maud and her sister would cheer from the windows of the Kildare Street Club, the gathering place of the ruling class. She had been presented at court where the Prince of Wales, hearing that his son had failed adequately to appreciate her beauty, had brought her to the Royal dais with the remark, 'Get out you young fool, how could you say things like that to a beautiful woman like this?' It was said that Kitchener of Khartoum, not noted for his interest in the opposite sex, had proposed to her. But Maud had no ambitions for social success. She had turned away from a life of hunt balls and riding to hounds, and had decided to dedicate herself to the dispossessed. The combination of beauty, breeding and rebellion proved irresistible to Yeats. 'From this time the troubling of my life began,' he wrote shortly after meeting her. Though Maud obviously liked him, Yeats sensed a barrier between them. He was not to know till ten years later that she had another lover, Lucien Millevoye, a French journalist and politician by whom she had a child in 1891. No matter how long she would remain away on revolutionary activities, she always went back to Paris and her Lucien.

Driven nearly mad by her indifference, Yeats seized on every opportunity to plead his cause. Once he hurried to Dublin to confide that he had a dream that he had seen her and himself as brother and sister in the Arabian desert centuries before. Maud, who was a believer in the occult, was impressed by this, but now she told him that she could never marry him and that henceforth it would be a spiritual friendship between them. Disheartened, Yeats managed to persuade her to spend a few days at Howth with him, lying on the grassy hills of this peninsula outside Dublin and watching the gulls float below while he recited his verses to her.

> I would that we were, my beloved, white birds on the
>   foam of the sea
> We tire of the flame of the meteor before it can fade
>   and flee:
> And the flame of the blue star of twilight, hung low on
>   the rim of the sky,
> Has awaked in our hearts, my beloved, a sadness that
>   may not die.

He pestered her with poems from then on. She was not impressed, though he wrote one of the most beautiful poems in the language for her.

122

When you are old and grey and full of sleep,
And nodding by the fire, take down this book,
And slowly read, and dream of the soft look
Your eyes had once, and of their shadows deep;

How many loved your moments of glad grace,
And loved your beauty with love false or true,
But one man loved the pilgrim soul in you,
And loved the sorrows of your changing face;

And bending down beside the glowing bars,
Murmur, a little sadly, how Love fled
And paced upon the mountains overhead
And hid his face amid a crowd of stars.

He paid frequent visits to her in Dublin where they
became a familiar pair, the statuesque girl and her poet
with his long lock of black hair falling on his forehead,
his lordly pose in temporary abeyance as he followed
attentively at her heels.

When she changed flats (as she frequently did) Willie
was her willing slave in transporting her numerous pets
to the new premises. She had many birds, and he would
walk behind her carrying the cages, loudly declaiming
over the birdsong while her pet marmoset nestled at her
neck. Yeats was not hostile to the birdsong (after all did
not Aengus the Irish god of love have a halo of birds
about his head?), but he had a decided dislike of the
marmoset, whom Maud would use as a confidant, just as
the poet was winning an argument, by talking to the
clinging rodent as if it were a human being.

Willie introduced her to Madam Blavatsky whom she
rather liked for her down-to-earth American commonsense. 'Flapdoodle, that is nothing to do with theosophy,'
Madam said to Maud's delight when she told her of the
theosophists in the Dublin Lodge who disapproved of her
anti-eviction campaign in the west.

Together Maud and Willie experienced Blake-like
visions. She would lie on a green couch in his room in
Woburn Buildings surrounded by candlesticks and, with
a bowl of water between them, would go into a trance.

She never could decide whether these visions were transferred from Willie's mind to hers or whether they had come out of some shared subconscious.

He was to write plays and poems for her, make her the touchstone of his inspiration, but Maud would remain resolute in her refusal to become his lover. When he complained that she made life unbearable for him, she replied with a sweet smile, 'You are making beautiful poetry out of what you call your unhappiness and you are happy in that.' Twenty years after he met her he could still shake and tremble from memory of her.

And what of her that took
All till my youth was gone
With scarce a pitying look?
How could I praise that one?
When day begins to break
I count my good and bad,
Being wakeful for her sake,
Remembering what she had,
What eagle look still shows,
While up from my heart's root
So great a sweetness flows
I shake from head to foot.

5   Death of a Chieftain

For too long Parnell had interfered with the course of Empire. A ferocious libel in *The Times* had failed to shift him. But if his private life could be exploited in the public press this constant sore on the neck of the kingdom might be got rid of. For Parnell was vulnerable. He had been living with a woman for nine years and had two children by her. If her husband could be persuaded to withdraw the tacit consent that he had given to the affair and take action in the divorce courts, might not the wrath of the Irish hierarchy descend on this Protestant landlord?

It was thus it happened. The Irish Party divided, as one member put it, 'in the stench of the divorce court', and the weapon which Parnell had forged to take on the English in their own Parliament was now withdrawn from him.

In a gambler's throw he refused to resign the leadership. Between 1890 and 1891 he contested three by-elections in Ireland and at one of them, in Castlecomer, they threw quicklime in his eyes. Yet in many places he had unexpected support. The Fenians came out on his side. Gratefully, Parnell promised them that if constitutional means failed he would not be above accompanying them on another road. He told the election crowds that he was not just the Leader of the Irish Party, but the 'leader of the Irish nation'.

The mask of aloofness began to slip. 'What will you do, Mr Parnell,' a newspaperman asked, 'if you're the only member of your Party returned in the next Parliament?'

125

'Then I shall be sure of being a Party whose integrity will not be sapped,' he replied with a smile. Then Dublin still supported him. When he came back after the party had split, hundreds of thousands of people met him in the streets with torchlight processions and bands. He had spoken at the Rotunda and the crowd had moaned with delight to hear him again. After the meeting, learning that the party paper *United Ireland* had been taken over by anti-Parnellites, Parnell himself went along to the premises to evict the editor. Seizing a crowbar he smashed in the door of the building and, having gained entry, reappeared in the opening of a second-storey window. His hair was dishevelled, his coat was covered in dust, and his eyes burned with tigerish anger as he spoke to the spellbound crowd: 'I rely on Dublin. Dublin is true. What Dublin says today Ireland will say tomorrow.' It was the cry of the Jacobin to the mob. But Parnell's prophecy went unfulfilled. Ireland did not follow Dublin and his three candidates were beaten in their by-elections. The last one he campaigned in with his arm in a sling. His health gave way in an unprecedented bad autumn and he died on 6 October 1891 at Brighton.

On the early morning before his funeral the wind howled and the rain lashed down as the boat from Holyhead berthed in the darkness at Kingstown Pier. Immense crowds met the coffin and escorted it into the city – a steady march of feet and the bands rising over the noise of the storm. Yeats had gone to the pier that morning to meet Maud Gonne, not knowing that the coffin was on the same ship with her. He noticed the low moan of the rain-sodden crowd as the coffin was carried off the ship, and the muttered curses against Parnell's opponents.

The funeral was the biggest ever seen in Dublin, greater even than that of O'Connell. Five hundred young Gaelic athletes with hurling sticks kept the crowd back. The Lord Mayor's carriage was first, then a carriage with John O'Leary and James Stephens, the two Fenians, and Cipriani the Italian patriot and follower of Garibaldi. It was the Fenian tribute to an Irish patriot whom they felt had been betrayed by England. O'Leary had supported Parnell in the last year, not because he felt that the country's salvation lay in parliamentary agitation, but 'because of the character of the man'. At the City Hall great black wings of crêpe swung out from the portico like the wings of death. Then the procession moved through the packed silent streets to Glasnevin, where Parnell was buried according to the solemn ritual of the Church of Ireland. A woman screamed as the coffin was lowered into the grave, and Katherine Tynan saw at that moment 'the most glorious meteor sail across the clear space of the heavens and fall suddenly'. Maud Gonne, always on the lookout for portents, saw it too. 'A rift in the leaden sky had parted the clouds and a light falling was seen. Life out of death, life out of death eternally.'

Yeats wrote a poem which was published the day before the funeral in *United Ireland*.

> The man is gone who gathered ye unweary
> Through the long bitter way.

His presence would live on.

> Mourn and then onward there is no returning.
> He guides ye from the womb
> His memory now is a tall pillar burning
> Before us in the tomb.

Later, in rather better verse, he would see Parnell in the tradition of his caste:

> Through Jonathan Swift's dark grove he passed, and there
>   Plucked bitter wisdom that enriched his blood.

A nine-year-old Dubliner also composed a poem to the dead leader. James Joyce, whose father was a dedicated supporter of 'the chief', wrote a pamphlet, 'Et tu Healy'. The title was a reference to Tim Healy MP, whom the

127

Parnellites had accused of stabbing Parnell in the back. Joyce's verses, which may not have been all that inferior to Yeats's own lines on Parnell, were privately printed by the father who afterwards used to boast that he sent a copy to the Pope. The only extant lines are quoted by Stanislaus Joyce in his memoir of his brother:

> His quaint perched eyrie on the crags of time
> Where the rude din of this century
> Can trouble him no more.

The boy Joyce was at the Jesuit-run Belvedere College where he was known as 'Gussie' Joyce. He seems to have had at nine years of age the beginnings of the retentive memory he showed later on, for he was able to recall twenty-five years afterwards the effect of Parnell's death on the Joyce family's Christmas dinner in 1891. The account appears in his autobiographical novel *A Portrait of the Artist* where his father appears as Mr Dedalus, his Fenian friend as Mr Casey and his governess Aunt as Dante. (The aunt's curious name probably derives from the Munster habit of eliding the definite article with the following word, so that the words 'the Auntie' would have sounded like 'th' auntie', which a precocious little boy might have turned into 'Dante'.)

> 'Let him remember too,' cried Mr Casey to her from across the table, 'the language with which the priests and the priests' pawns broke Parnell's heart and hounded him into his grave. Let him remember that too when he grows up.'
>
> 'Sons of bitches,' cried Mr Dedalus. 'When he was down they turned on him to betray him and rend him like rats in a sewer. Low lived dogs! And they look it! By Christ, they look it!'
>
> 'They behaved rightly,' cried Dante. 'They obeyed their bishops and their priests. Honour to them. . . .'
>
> Dante bent across the table and cried to Mr Casey.
>
> 'Right, right. They were always right! God and morality and religion come first.'

Mrs Dedalus, seeing her excitement, said to her: 'Mrs Riordan, don't excite yourself answering them.'

'God and religion before everything!' Dante cried. 'God and religion before the world.'

Mr Casey raised his clenched fist and brought it down on the table with a crash.

'Very well then,' he shouted hoarsely, 'if it comes to that, no God for Ireland.'

'John, John,' cried Mr Dedalus, seizing his guest by the coat sleeve. . . .

Mr Casey, freeing his arms from his holders, suddenly bowed his head on his hands with a sob of pain.

'Poor Parnell,' he cried loudly. 'My dead king!'

He sobbed loudly and bitterly.

Stephen, raising his terror-stricken face, saw that his father's eyes were full of tears.

There were many including Yeats who held that an originating cause of the literary renaissance was the turning of the people, in disillusion at the death of Parnell, from Parliamentary politics to a preoccupation with imaginative activity. But it was the energy unleashed by Parnell's messianic influence which was the real source of the renaissance. He had fused in his own personality the characteristics of two cultures and had dared to call himself the 'leader of the Irish nation' – not the Anglo-Irish or the Gaelic Irish, but the Irish nation. The force he generated ebbed with his passing, but lingered in the national being, to be regenerated by those who followed him; and there was no modern Irishman of note who did not in some way owe a portion of himself to the influence of this extraordinary figure.

Standish O'Grady, who had opposed Parnell politically, felt that his death was full of portents for the people, like the passing of St Columba in the eighth century which had been accompanied by similar phenomena.

I state a fact – it was witnessed by thousands. While his followers were committing Charles Parnell's remains to the earth, the sky was bright with strange lights and flames. Only a coincidence possibly, and yet persons not superstitious have maintained that there is some mysterious sympathy between the human soul and the elements, and that storm, and other elemental disturbances, have too often succeeded or accompanied great battles to be regarded as fortuitous.

It was not unexpected that O'Grady would look on Parnell in the context of a hero. As author of *The Story of Ireland* the country for him was peopled with such figures. But he did believe that integration with England rather than separation was the solution to Ireland's problem. For he felt that the Irish aristocracy, through their manifest superiority of eloquence and pen, were the natural leaders of the United Kingdom and that their position, as a ruling class shouldering up a colony, had demoralised them and diverted them from their proper function.

Early on he had foreseen that the fabric of the society he had belonged to would rip apart. In 1881, the year after he had published his first influential book, he had convened a landlords' convention in the Rotunda in Dublin with the purpose of awakening his fellow landlords to their exploitation by England. His utopian plan was to unite them and the workers against the forces of capital. Ireland, he maintained, had been grossly overtaxed since the Union and the only explanation for the docility of their leader class was that they were mesmerised by 'something that called itself the King but which was in fact mercantile greed'.

While Parnell was in Westminster undermining the structure of the Empire, O'Grady back home was raging against his fellow landlords for not supporting it and renewing it in their own likeness. In passages which Yeats said became 'so famous that men would repeat them to themselves like poets' rhymes' he lashed the Irish landed classes.

Straight down – is it not so? Velocity increasing – can you doubt it? The faces not friendly and voices – they multiply, don't they? The air – is it not a little darker than when I last addressed you? The precipice – surely you see it now? Yes, it is quite so; and yet, for all, here you sit tobogganing and steering straight – the sorriest and most ovine set of men that the encircling sun looks down upon today. Alas! I believe there never will be, as I know there never has been within the cycle of recorded things, an aristocracy so rotten in its seeming strength, so recreant, resourceless, and stupid in the day of trial, so degenerate, outworn and effete. You have outlived your day.

He begged his fellow landlords not to cut themselves off from the native tradition but to assert their individuality as Irishmen, as he had done in his study of Irish culture.

At Ireland and all things Irish you girded till, like the doomed suitors, you are forced to laugh with foreign jaws as this beggar nation, ragged and mendicant, whose substance you devoured and whose house dishonoured, springs like the revealed demi-god of yore upon the threshold and twangs the new-strung bow. It sings, sweetly, does it not? Like the swallow. And yet in this Irish history, whose monuments have rotted under your care or accumulated like a mountain of wastepaper, lay for you the key of safety had you but known it, and secrets more precious than equipped armies, or favouring laws, or any Imperial countenance.

When the Childers Report appeared in 1896 and disclosed that Ireland had been overtaxed to the tune of 250 million pounds, O'Grady felt that his arguments had proved themselves. He made a last plea to all parties to come together to obtain restitution. But Standish O'Grady was primarily a writer, a catalyst, capable of articulating the secret feelings of his generation, but not of organising a political campaign. From the turn of the century onwards his influence declined, and his eccentricity took the form of acknowledging, in the columns of the paper he edited, gifts of geese and fowl that had been sent to him by admirers.

With his interest in the occult it was natural that Yeats should seek out Madam Blavatsky and her Theosophical Society in London.

He found much among the London theosophists to confirm his own research in Dublin. His belief in the unity of being was strengthened by their formula that the seven notes of the musical scale related to the seven colours of the planet and each organ of the body had its celestial correspondent. Yeats thought Madam 'a sort of old Irish peasant woman with an air of humour and audacious powers – a female Dr Johnson' and was convinced of her powers. But he was not prepared to accept as Holy Writ, as Madam's other followers did, all that she claimed for her group.

Now he began to conduct sessions in which certain claims of theosophist belief were tested against scientific formulae. Madam inferred that her word did not require elucidation through a test tube or weighing scales and expressed her disapproval. After the writing of a critical article Yeats resigned from the society. In revenge she informed him that the shaving of his beard would bring disaster in the matter of his health and, when this did not occur, foretold some other misfortune.

Yeats quickly found an alternative outlook for his occult interests – a group of Christian cabbalists who called themselves the Order of the Golden Dawn. Their leader was a Cockney who had assumed the name of McGregor Mathers. His London upbringing did not deter Mathers from striding through the streets in Highland dress with a knife in both stockings, yelling out, 'I feel like a walking flame.' As he believed the man had psychic powers, Yeats was prepared to ignore this exhibitionism. He was thrilled once when on a journey to Mather's house he smelled incense in the railway carriage he was in, and attributed this to the nature of the journey he was taking. Another day a student of Mathers' showed him his chest covered in scratches – the night before he had dreamt he was fighting a cat. Yeats recalled a pamphlet on Japanese art he had read as a schoolboy in Dublin, which described the panels in a temple from which the painted horses had slipped out one night to return in the morning to the temple wall, 'still wet but trembling in stillness'.

Yeats studied magic with the scientific detachment with which as a boy he had investigated the relationship of flowers and animals to evolution. For him magic offered a formula by which he could attain something the scientific revolution had failed to provide – an understanding of the mystical side of his nature. He had long since discounted the myth that alchemy was concerned with turning common metal into gold, and recognised that those medieval seekers after truth who had their origins in the philosophers of Alexandria were seeking a universal transmutation of being into an imperishable substance. The Rosicrucian doctrine on which the Golden Dawn cult was based seemed to Yeats an ideal blend between the essential truths of Christianity and paganism – the Rose, symbol of beauty impressed upon the Cross the Rood of Time, the Celtic gods entwined with universal deities.

> Far-off, most secret, and inviolate Rose,
> Enfold me in my hour of hours; where those
> Who sought thee in the Holy Sepulchre,
> Or in the wine-vat, dwell beyond the stir
> And tumult of defeated dreams; and deep
> Among pale eyelids, heavy with the sleep
> Men have named beauty.

He set down his views on his esoteric activities in a

letter to O'Leary who had apparently complained that it was not dignified for a member of the Irish Republican Brotherhood to be running round with Cockney magicians.

Now as to magic. It is surely absurd to hold me 'weak' or otherwise because I chose to persist in a study which I decided deliberately four or five years ago to make, next to my poetry, the most important pursuit of my life. Whether it be, or be not, bad for my health can only be decided by one who knows what magic is and not at all by an amateur. The probable explanation however of your somewhat testy postcard is that you were out at Bedford Park and heard my father discoursing about my magical pursuits out of the immense depths of his ignorance as to everything that I am doing and thinking. The mystical life is the centre of all that I do and all that I think and all that I write. It holds to my work the same relation that the philosophy of Godwin held to the work of Shelley and I have always considered myself a voice of what I believe to be a greater renaissance – the revolt of the soul against the intellect – now beginning in the world.

In the Order of the Golden Dawn Yeats encountered two women who were to be important to him later on. One was Florence Farr, a young actress of spirit and independence who associated herself with various artistic projects in London. She was an 'emancipated' woman, free with her favours, and according to Shaw, whose lover she was, by 1894 her 'Leporello list' totalled fourteen names.

With her personal beauty and excellent voice for verse, it was inevitable that she would gravitate towards the young Irish poet. In later years she was to act in his plays and declaim his verses to a psaltery.

Ann Horniman, the rather plain-looking daughter of a Manchester tea merchant, was a blue stocking who wore bloomers, rode a man's bicycle and on her own had crossed the Alps from Italy to Munich. She had asserted her independence early on and at seventeen had acquired her own suite of rooms and smoked cigarettes. Throughout her life she was to combine rigid views on the arts with indifferent luck, but as this usually coincided with investments of large parts of her personal fortune she was bound to bring off some winners. She was to finance Yeats's first play and later purchase him a theatre in Dublin which would become world-famous.

In 1889 Yeats had published his first book of poetry, *The Wanderings of Oisin and Other Poems*. The publication was made possible by John O'Leary who carried subscription sheets round with him and pre-sold the edition before publication. The book contains poems Yeats would include in the collected edition of his poetry like 'The Ballad of Moll Magee' and 'The Stolen Child'. This last poem has echoes of William Allingham's 'The Fairies'. But Yeats showed that he could break the jingle when the image came up in front of his eyes in a way that Allingham never could have done:

> Away with us he's going,
> The solemn-eyed:
> He'll hear no more the lowing
> Of the calves on the warm hillside
> Or the kettle on the hob
> Sing peace into his breast,
> Or see the brown mice bob
> Round and round the oatmeal-chest.
> For he comes, the human child,
> To the waters and the wild
> With a faery, hand in hand,
> From a world more full of weeping than he can understand.

The title poem of the book was a long narrative one which tells how Oisin, son of Finn, went to the land of youth, lured by a fairy princess Niamh. Returning to Ireland after 300 years he found that the land had become Christianised under St Patrick and that the famous band of his youth had been forgotten. One day, leaning from his horse to lift a stone that the puny folk of the Christian age could not move, his stirrup broke and as he fell to the earth, his prolonged youth left him and he became an old man before the astonished eyes of the saint.

> The rest you have heard of, O croziered man; how, when divided the girth,
> I fell on the path, and the horse went away like a summer fly;
> And my years three hundred fell on me, and I rose, and walked on the earth,
> A creeping old man, full of sleep, with the spittle on his beard never dry.

There is tinsel in this narrative which Yeats would discard later – 'Hoofs of the pale finndrinny', 'bacchant and mortal' – but the poem, divided somewhat pretentiously into three parts, stands up well and was well received in London, especially among the pre-Raphaelite group.

William Morris was full of praise. 'You write my kind of poetry,' he told Yeats one day, and the young poet was exhilarated, for although he had reservations about Morris's poetry he admired his prose so much that he read it slowly the more to savour it. That his ideas and Morris's on the speaking of verse had much in common he discovered when the old poet came out from a reading of his long poem 'Sigurd the Volsung' fulminating because the verse had been spoken without the rhythm he had spent so much time putting into it. Morris disliked Balzac, Swinburne and Milton, but had as his heroes Dante and Keats – enough for Yeats not to quarrel with him. Yeats became a frequent visitor to Kelmscott House where he would eat supper on Sunday evenings and attend meetings of the Socialist League. Morris's innovations in design of furniture delighted Yeats and he could let his mind roam freely in the high day room with the long unpainted tables of new wood, and paintings by Rossetti and Persian carpets on the wall.

When Yeats's collection of essays *The Celtic Twilight* came out in 1893 it was hailed by the Morris group as an Irish version of the pre-Raphaelite movement. Celticism was fashionable at the time. Matthew Arnold had delivered his famous lectures on Celtic literature not thirty years before in which he had diagnosed the distinctive quality of English literature as 'the fairy dew of that natural magic which is Celtic' and claimed to have discerned in Byron and Shakespeare 'the Titanism of the Celt, his passionate turbulent reaction against the despotism of fact'. There was also the backwash of eighteenth-century enthusiasm over Macpherson's *Ossian* (generally held to be a concoction), which had sufficiently impressed Goethe to induce him to include the song of Selma from Fingal into his Werther's *Leiden* and had dazzled Schiller, as well as making the Abbé Cesarotti's translation of the tales the favourite reading of Napoleon the First. But Yeats's book was something quite different from what the pre-Raphaelites or Macpherson had tried to do. Theirs were paper memories or at best translations from a foreign folk tradition. Yeats wanted to portray a living culture. A labourer would tell him of a local beauty dead fifty years ago: 'the sun or moon never shone on anyone so handsome and her skin was so white that it looked blue and she had two little blushes on her cheeks'; yet another would talk of the poet who had commemorated her: 'he was the greatest poet in Ireland, he could make a song about that bush if he had a chance to stand under it.'

In *The Celtic Twilight* Yeats spoke frankly of astral beings seen on a Sligo beach when a girl he was with summoned them from a sea cave, beings she claimed to have spoken to, as peasant children in France claimed to have conversations with the Virgin. An old lady in Mayo told him she had lost four toes walking in 'the other world' and one day a vision of the hell of the artist came before him:

I saw a quantity of demons of all kinds of shapes, fish-like, serpent-like, ape-like and dog-like – sitting about a black pit such as that of my own hell and looking at the moonlight reflection of the heavens which shone up from the depths of the pit.

William Morris had had to go to Iceland to find remnants of the pre-industrial primitive mind to correspond to his ideal of an unspoilt peasant class. Yeats had it at his doorstep.

One incident hastened the division which was growing between the young and the old poet. Night after night at meetings of the Socialist League Yeats had listened to attacks on religion, which he disapproved of. One night he spoke up 'with all the arrogance of raging youth' and maintained that the revolution could only come with astronomical slowness, 'like the cooling of the sun or the dying of the moon', and that only religion would make the change of heart possible. Though Morris rang the bell Yeats continued his harangue. The second time the bell was rung, he sat down mortally offended. Later Morris tried to excuse himself by saying that he rang the bell to save Yeats, but the poet never came back to the Socialist League after that night.

Though superficially they had much in common, there was a wide gulf between the two men. Morris was a product of Oxford hurly-burly, a ruthless single-stick fighter, a handsome Viking of a man who was known to his friends as 'Topsy' and who when he was not teaching 'cuts and guards' was taking part in soda water siphon battles with them. To the end of his days, even when he wore the blue shirt of the working man, he would use public school phrases like 'you'll have to cut' and talked of 'splendid mokes and mills'. All this was light years away from the primitive Ireland that Yeats was trying to tap as a source for a new movement of the imagination. Morris's Icelandic sagas have a pre-Raphaelite touch – ancient deeds seen through the prism of romance. Yeats escaped this influence by his eventual break with Morris, who had been one of the few men he ever really worshipped. Yeats never forgot Morris however. He would often call to mind the great

138

bearded figure at Kelmscott House holding up a glass of claret to the light and exclaiming, 'why do people fear it is prosaic to get inspiration out of wine? Is it not the sunlight and the sap in the leaves? Are not grapes made by the sunlight and the sap?'

'The Rose', published in 1893, completes the drift from the pre-Raphaelites. Yeats now recognised the sentimental element in some of his earlier verse, and thought of sleeping on a board to exorcise it. The man who 'dreamed of faeryland', but chose instead some prudent years, must undergo a period of renewal in a vault of pagan discontent before he comes to peace.

> He slept under the hill of Lugnagall;
> And might have known at last unhaunted sleep
> Under that cold and vapour-turbaned steep,
> Now that the earth had taken man and all:
> Did not the worms that spired about his bones
> Proclaim with that unwearied, reedy cry
> That God has laid His fingers on the sky,
> That from those fingers glittering summer runs
> Upon the dancer by the dreamless wave.
> Why should those lovers that no lovers miss
> Dream, until God burn Nature with a kiss?
> The man has found no comfort in the grave.

Yeats had decided now that he belonged to the Irish tradition and that his English experience would be used as a prelude to bring into literature his country's voice. He made this clear in 'To Ireland in the Coming Times':

> Know, that I would accounted be
> True brother of a company
> That sang, to sweeten Ireland's wrong,
> Ballad and story, rann and song;
> Nor be I any less of them,
> Because the red-rose-bordered hem
> Of her, whose history began
> Before God made the angelic clan,
> Trails all about the written page.

When Time began to rant and rage
The measure of her flying feet
Made Ireland's heart begin to beat;
And Time bade all his candles flare
To light a measure here and there;
And may the thoughts of Ireland brood
Upon a measured quietude.

Nor may I less be counted one
With Davis, Mangan, Ferguson,
Because, to him who ponders well,
My rhymes more than their rhyming tell
Of things discovered in the deep,
Where only body's laid asleep.
For the elemental creatures go
About my table to and fro,
That hurry from unmeasured mind
To rant and rage in flood and wind;
Yet he who treads in measured ways
May surely barter gaze for gaze.
Man ever journeys on with them
After the red-rose-bordered hem.
Ah, faeries, dancing under the moon,
A Druid land, a Druid tune!

6 Sharing With Shaw

Yeats was now to become involved in a theatrical venture with a fellow Irishman who had been described in 1891 by the *Sunday World* as 'someone that everybody in London knows'. He was in his thirties, tall, white-faced, with auburn hair and a bright red beard. His name was Bernard Shaw and he was an art and music critic, a vegetarian, a Fabian Socialist, and he possessed an incorrigible love of showing off which he put to good effect by lecturing the English on serious subjects, leavening his addresses with outrageous Irish impudence. He used to say it had taken him 'twenty years of studied self-restraint, aided by the natural decay of my faculties, to make myself dull enough to be accepted as a serious person by the British public' – but it was his effervescence and Celtic impishness that held them and made them listen to him as he lectured them in his high-pitched Dublin twang that he used to claim was Augustan classical English, as spoken in the Dublin of his youth. Shaw's hero was Ibsen, whom he worshipped for forcing the respectable classes to stand up 'to his terrible searchlight', and for exposing their guilty secrets and tearing off their disguises.

Shaw had not, so far, had a successful production of his plays. However, a piece of bad luck which John Todhunter, the doctor-playwright friend of J.B. Yeats, encountered, gave him his chance. Todhunter's play *The Comedy of Sighs*, presented in a season at the Avenue Theatre, was howled off the stage. The producer of the season was Florence Farr who was

Shaw's mistress. She asked her lover could he provide a replacement? Shaw went out to the Embankment, sat down on a vacant bench and put a few finishing touches to 'Alps and Balkans', but by the time the play was ready for rehearsal it had been decided to rename it *Arms and the Man*. The curtain-raiser was to be Yeats's *The Land of Heart's Desire* which was his first play to have a production.

Shaw was ten years older than Yeats. He had grown up in a Dublin that was not as Yeats's boyhood had been – dominated by Parnell's personality and the Land League agitation of Michael Davitt – but was hide-bound by the smug provincialism of the Castle administration. Shaw used to say that he was 'the downstart son of a downstart' but, like Yeats, he had relatives who were rentiers and could even claim a baronet cousin.

The ménage he had been raised in had been a dominant factor in the shaping of Shaw's character. His father, an eccentric and alcoholic corn merchant, had settled down in somewhat seedy surroundings in Synge Street, Dublin, after his marriage in 1851. Less than a hundred steps away lived one of the most extraordinary men in the city, George John Lee. He was the illegitimate son of a Clare landowner, Crofton Vandeleur, and later would adopt his father's patronymic as his middle name. His passion was music and he had been determined to present and conduct major musical works in Dublin. To understand better the human voice he had dissected the larynx with the help of an anatomist from the Ledwich School who lived next door and who, obligingly, lent his corpses for Lee's experiments. He seems to have had the artist's instinct for the truth. The advent of the X-ray would confirm Lee's theory about the ascending and descending larynx, in step with high and low notes. And years later, when Shaw looked at a score of *Don Giovanni* annotated by Lee, in which he had removed all the repetitive phrases, he was astonished to find that the conductor was a 'century before his time' in this reform.

The Shaws lived virtually beside Lee for two years

before George Bernard was born, though when his mother, Lucinda Elizabeth, first met the musician is not clear. But when she did meet him she fell completely under his spell. Now, when he presented operas and recitals in Dublin, she became his principal singer and sang Margarite in *Faust*, Lucrezia Borgia in Donizetti's opera of that name, Azucena in *Il Trovatore*, among other parts, always tutored, of course, according to the Lee method.

Lee eventually engulfed the entire Shaw household for they moved a quarter mile or so in towards the city centre, and went to live in his Georgian house at 1 Hatch Street, as well as sharing in the summer a delightful cottage by the sea at Dalkey, about eight miles outside Dublin. One result of this musical environment was that Shaw had been able to whistle before he was twelve music from Handel, Hadyn, Mozart, Beethoven, Rossini, Bellini, Donizetti and Verdi. He would go to concerts which were attended by the Lord Lieutenant, where his mother would be cheered for her singing and personally congratulated by the Lord Lieutenant afterwards. Entertainments in Dublin Castle were now open to him through Lee's influence. There he would have seen Sir William Wilde with his wife, Francesca, and their son, Oscar. Did they notice, one wonders, the tall, seedily dressed youth with his auburn hair split in the middle and a curious mixture of arrogance and hesitation? This last characteristic would have come from not ever knowing exactly where he stood. His father did not seem to give a hoot about moving into Lee's house or Lee's association with Shaw's mother. Sometimes, George Carr Shaw would kick a newspaper in the air, accompanied with a whoop of fury, or run ahead in a brisk sprint when he was out for a walk, to wait for his companion to join him before resuming the conversation. Otherwise, he seemed placid when sober, and quietly melancholy when drunk.

Lee's influence had another effect on Shaw that was as important as the musical one. He influenced him in the way that John O'Leary had done for Yeats, by bringing him into contact with the other Dublin, the Catholic Nationalist one. The Lees were Nationalists and had sheltered Fenians in their home after the rising of '67. Lee would talk of 'national freedom and independence' and 'centuries of oppression' to the young GBS. Through him Shaw discovered that Catholics liked good music as much as Protestants and found an opportunity to meet and mix with Catholic groups, with whom his mother sang, through Lee's introduction. This would have been anathema to George Carr Shaw's people who regarded the barrier between the two communities in Dublin as a guarantee of the status quo. When Lucinda Shaw sang in Catholic churches it would have seemed deliberate treachery to George Carr Shaw and his relatives.

Bernard Shaw was to remain an Irish Nationalist all his life and would make himself extremely unpopular from time to time by espousing the cause of Irish rebels and attempting to explain them to the English in terms of Irish history (he even took his nationalism as far as to refuse to stand or take his hat off for 'God Save the King' until the Irish Free State came into being in 1922). When one remembers that Lee slept with his windows open in all weathers (which Shaw did till he was seventy-nine), disbelieved in the efficacy of the medical profession (which idea Shaw used as a basis for The Doctor's Dilemma) and was a food faddist, forbidding white bread in his house, we can see the extent of his influence on the shaping of the young Shaw's personality.

After Lee had attained his supreme ambition in Dublin to stage a Handel festival there with Tietzens and Agnesi (in 1874) he took himself off to London and conducted his musical activities from a house in Park Lane, where he was now known as George Vandeleur Lee. Shaw's mother followed him within a few days, and George Bernard shook the Dublin dust from his heels three years later and joined his mother in London.

Yeats's father had always been afraid that his son

would lose mental freedom by taking up a regular job, and Shaw seems to have picked up the same idea, maintaining that an artist should let his family go barefoot, his mother drudge for her living, rather than work at anything but his art. 'I did not throw myself into the battle of life,' he used to say, 'I threw my mother.'

After writing five unsuccessful novels, he had turned to the theatre. It seemed an ideal outlet for his political beliefs – he had become by then a determined socialist – if he could master the dramatist's technique. This came quickly enough because, as he modestly declared later, 'I was a born playwright.'

Arms and the Man would be his first critical success. It ran with Yeats's piece for eight weeks and attracted among the audience Oscar Wilde, the Duke of Edinburgh and the Prince of Wales. The Prince of Wales, though, was in bad humour at the end of the performance and left the theatre muttering that 'the fellow is a damned crank' – from his point of view a valid enough comment as the play dealt with the triumph in love of the son of a Swiss hotel owner over a Serbian aristocrat as well as satirising the officer class, and contained an implicit criticism of the system of privilege which assured his Royal Highness's continued reign. When Bluntschli, reading off the list of his possessions inherited from his father's hotel, is asked, 'Are you the emperor of Switzerland?' and replies, 'My rank is the highest known in Switzerland. I am a free citizen', it could have come across the footlights as a whiff of grapeshot to some members of the audience.

Yeats had been in a fever of excitement about the whole affair, having written to O'Leary before the first night:

The whole venture has had to face the most amazing denunciation from the old type of critics. It will give you some notion of the row that is going on when I tell you 'chuckers-out' have been hired for the first night of Shaw. They are to be distributed over the theatre and are to put out all the people who make a row. The whole venture will be history anyway for it is the first contest between the old commercial school of theatrical folk and the new artistic school.

(The 'new artistic school' had, in fact, been underwritten by Yeats's friend from the Order of the Golden Dawn, blue stocking Ann Horniman, who had put up the venture at the request of her fellow member, Florence Farr.) Despite his apprehensions, Yeats's own play was received with as much enthusiasm as Shaw's and he attended every performance. He would stand at the back of the theatre in a black sombrero and long cloak and when the play was over go backstage to 'vex' the players with new lines he had thought up in the meantime.

The Land of Heart's Desire is a simple tale of a young woman about to be married who is lured into the other world by a 'fairy child'. It has some admirable verse passages which work well on the stage.

> When winter sleep is abroad my hair grows thin,
> My feet unsteady. When the leaves awaken
> My mother carries me in her golden arms. . . .
> I'll soon put on my womanhood and marry
> The spirits of wood and water, but who can tell
> When I was born for the first time? I think
> I am much older than the eagle-cock
> And he is the oldest thing under the moon.

Later, Yeats was to tell AE that he thought the verse 'unmanly and an exaggeration of sentimental beauty'. He did himself an injustice. The play shows that Yeats had that rare gift among poets of being able to write dialogue in verse that made an immediate impact on an audience. Old sorcerer that he was, he was even in this child's tale able to evoke a sense of evil. One aspect of The Land of Heart's Desire is a depiction of the conflict between Christian culture and the pagan world – a confrontation between the forces of Nature and man-made religions which had displaced the earth rites.

146

When the child sees the crucifix she screams like any educated vampire, and though the priest believes he can win her to his side without the figure on the cross, he is without power to approach her while the crucifix is not in the room. Besides this whiff of diabolism Yeats had introduced an element into the work which was to play a major part in his development as a dramatist later on when he would attempt to bring verse, dance and music together on the stage. Asked by Florence Farr to write a part for her niece Dorothy Paget, he wrote a dance into the part of the child which proved particularly effective on the first night.

George Moore, at the height of his fame with *Esther Waters*, attended the play during the run but did not think it worth his while to go back and meet the young author – although he would recall the impression that Yeats made on him that night.

> He provoked a violent antipathy as he strode to and forth at the back of the dress circle, a long black cloak drooping from his shoulders, a soft black sombrero on his head, a voluminous black silk tie flowing from his collar, loose black trousers dragging untidily over his long, heavy feet – a man of such excessive appearance that I could not do otherwise – could I? – than to mistake him for an Irish parody of the poetry that I had seen all my life strutting its rhythmic way in the alleys of the Luxembourg Gardens, preening its rhymes by the fountains, excessive in habit and gait. . . .

Moore does not seem to have commented on Shaw's play. They had never been particularly close and Moore had probably not forgotten Shaw's remark when he heard of the success of *A Mummer's Wife*: 'Nonsense, but I know George Moore. He couldn't have written that.'

The other Irish star in the London firmament, Oscar Wilde, had on the other hand followed Shaw's career with interest and had written to him, congratulating him on his successes: 'We are both Celtic and I like to think we are friends. England is the land of intellectual fogs and you have done well to clean the air.' This was especially noble of Oscar as he had not been impressed by Shaw's appearance, noting that his hair resembled 'seaweed' and finding the back of his neck especially bleak, 'long, untenanted, dead white'.

As regards Moore, Oscar had never been well disposed towards him and had reserved for him some of his most barbed remarks: 'Moore has not an enemy in the world, and none of his friends like him', or 'Moore, Moore – ah, yes, he's the fellow who wrote brilliant English until he discovered grammar. I know him so well I haven't spoken to him for ten years.'

The enmity between them could have stemmed from their childhood days when Sir William Wilde used to take Oscar over from their Mayo shooting lodge at Moytura to play with the Moore boys in Moore Hall. Whatever it was, it was curious that Wilde the aesthete looked kindly on Shaw the jaeger-suited jester, while he continued to view with contempt a fellow Irishman who from time to time played the role of a French fop for the English with such brilliance.

The performance of their two plays, side by side, brought to the surface a fundamental difference between Yeats and Shaw in their attitude to literature. Shaw had been away from Dublin while the important changes were taking place which had dominated Yeats's boyhood and early manhood. He had experienced none of the tremors that had run through the national being as a result of Parnell's achievement. O'Grady meant nothing to Shaw as his great book on the bardic period was published two years after Shaw had left for London. What would inspire Yeats a decade later in Dublin life simply did not exist in Shaw's time. 'There was no Gaelic League then,' Shaw wrote, 'nor sense that Ireland had in herself the seed of culture. London was the literary centre for English literature and as the English language was my weapon, there was nothing for it but London.'

Yeats on the other hand had come to London, a fully fledged Irish Nationalist and member of the secret Republican Brotherhood, with his mind turned towards Irish culture by the movement that had gathered force with the advent of Parnell. London would be an interval for him. For Shaw it would be his life and he would use his imaginative gifts in satire and social comment, making a contribution not directly connected with Ireland but nevertheless derived essentially from the same qualities that had impelled Swift or Sheridan. When Shaw claimed that Dublin was 'more modern than Paris or Vienna', that he and Wilde 'were Irish Celts' and that Wilde had made England 'again appear insignificant and himself noble, tragic and superior', he was allying himself to Yeats's outlook in his resistance to London's superiority. He never had the slightest doubt as to where his allegiance lay.

I never think of an Englishman as my countryman. I should as soon think of applying that term to a German. I am an Irishman full of instinctive pity for those of my fellow creatures who are only English. When I say that I am an Irishman I mean that I was born in Ireland and that my native language is the English of Swift and not the unspeakable jargon of mid-nineteenth-century London newspapers.

Despite Shaw's reiteration of his Irishness, Yeats was to retain throughout his life an antipathy to his work. Much later on he would describe Shaw's mind as 'like a flash of lightning that reveals nothing behind the clouds', and maintain that, after seeing Shaw's plays, he used to have nightmares in which he was haunted by a sewing machine that clicked and shone but continued to smile at him. *Arms and the Man* he had listened to both with admiration and hatred: admiration for its energy but hatred for the logical straightness which ignored 'the crooked reality of life'. He could give it no better praise than to describe it as an excellent farce. Perhaps what really enraged Yeats was that he wanted to bring rhythm and style to the stage and here was a work succeeding without either.

Yeats saw himself (as he had said in his letter to O'Leary defending his magical practices) as 'a voice of the revolt of the soul against the intellect'. But to place Shaw in the opposite camp was to do him an injustice. Shaw, as much as Yeats, believed that the poet could replace the priest as an interpreter of the infinite, in an age where a vacuum had been created by the rejection of established religion under the impact of the scientific revolution. Shaw's concept was of a creator perfecting himself in mankind through trial and error which, while it would have differed from Yeats's view of the creation, ought not to have been dismissed as if it was the outburst of a raging atheist. In Shaw's only full-length Irish play, *John Bull's Other Island*, it is the mystic, Fr Keegan, who ultimately triumphs over the pragmatism of the Englishman Broadbent and the mockery of the Irishman Larry Doyle. Shaw has given the latter a speech which shows a decided poetic insight into the nature of the Irish character.

> Here in England, if the life is dull, you can be dull too, and no great harm done. But your wits can't thicken in that soft moist air, on those white springy roads, in those rocks and magenta heather. You've no such colours in the sky, no such lure in the distances, no such sadness in the evenings. Oh, the dreaming! the dreaming! the torturing, heart-scalding, never satisfying dreaming, dreaming, dreaming! No debauchery that ever coarsened and brutalised an Englishman can take the worth and usefulness out of him like that dreaming. An Irishman's imagination never lets him alone, never convinces him, never satisfies him – but it makes him that he can't face reality nor deal with it nor handle it nor conquer it: he can only sneer at them that do, and be 'agreeable to strangers' like a good-for-nothing woman on the streets. It's all dreaming, all imagination. He can't be religious. The inspired Churchman that teaches him the sanctity of life and

the importance of conduct is sent away empty; while the poor village priest that gives him a miracle or a sentimental story of a saint, has cathedrals built for him out of the pennies of the poor. He can't be intelligently political: he dreams of what the Shan Van Vocht said in ninety-eight. If you want to interest him in Ireland you've got to call the unfortunate island Kathleen ni Houlihan and pretend she's a little old woman.

Despite a passage like this Yeats would not grant to Shaw the imagination of the poet. Shaw rather plaintively used to say that had he surrendered to the lure of the Dublin hills that looked down on his native city, he might have become a poet like Yeats; and in a letter to Janet Achurch written in 1896, he told her that he had a growing certainty that he would become a dramatic poet. But to Yeats Shaw was in league with the 'horrible generation that in childhood sucked Ibsen from William Archer's hygienic bottle', and having acquired what amounted to a pathological dislike of Ibsen and the drama of ideas, he dismissed Shaw along with the Norwegian dramatist. Ibsen and Shaw were realists and that was that. One might ask how a poet like Yeats could have missed the symbolism and poetic imagery in Ibsen's last play, *When We Dead Awaken*. The answer would be that almost certainly Yeats never read it. Once he had placed a writer in the box he had made for him, he was not prepared to let him easily escape.

In *A Vision*, published in 1925, he gave his love of categorisation full rein and placed Shaw under what he called 'Phase Twenty-one of the Moon – The Acquisitive Man: Self Analysis: Domination of the Intellect'; Ibsen he did not bother to include at all though he dealt with such writers as Matthew Arnold, Tolstoy, Wells, Dostoyevsky, Galsworthy.

In the autumn of 1894, his nerves in pieces from his treatment by Maud Gonne and finding himself in a financially precarious position, Yeats went to live for some months in Sligo with his uncle, George Pollexfen.

Pollexfen was his mother's brother and had been his father's closest friend when they were at school together in the Isle of Man. He was one of the owners of Middleton & Pollexfen & Co., a shipping and milling business which, since the Middletons and the Pollexfens were related, was regarded by the Yeats children as the family firm.

Despite his poverty (that Christmas he confided to Lolly he had only 'two shillings and a half-penny borrowed'), Yeats would always have these prosperous merchant relatives to fall back on. The sea journey to Ireland, for example, cost him nothing. He travelled on one of the Pollexfen steamers which traded between England and Ireland. Once at Sligo his uncle would put him up and take care of his expenses.

Yeats never reacted against these merchant connections, but on the contrary used the training he got from this side of the family to further his artistic career. As regards his personal accounts, for instance, he showed himself an impeccable book-keeper. If he owed money he knew exactly how much it was and would repay it on time. Late in life he used to say that one of his proudest boasts was that he could read a balance sheet at a glance. Without the sense of order and understanding of the exercise of authority which he got from this merchant connection, Yeats could never have succeeded in the various artistic enterprises he would undertake later.

George Pollexfen, Yeats's uncle, was fifty-two years old when Yeats came to stay with him in 1894. He was unmarried and lived in a spacious home attended by a servant, Mary Battle.

Outwardly Pollexfen was no different from his fellow Sligo merchants with whom he mixed in this prosperous western seaport – a well-known horseman in his youth, a freemason, a regular churchgoer. But this unusual man practised astrology, and put much store in the psychic gifts of his servant. He made an ideal companion for his nephew with whom he used to walk twice each day to Rosses Point, eagerly discussing as he went matters of the mind. They would wander in the sandhills near the seashore some distance from each other and practise transferring images and colours till they became convinced they had developed telepathic powers. At home at night George would work on his astrological chart or discuss with Willie his latest communication from the Order of the Golden Dawn (of which he was what might be termed a country member). Upstairs asleep, the psychic servant, Mary Battle, would occasionally echo their visions in her dreams and come down and tell them in the morning a version of what they had been speculating on the night before. It was this dividing of a dream or vision between two or three people that Yeats was to say gave him one of his first intimations of how a people or nation might become bound together by an interchange among dreams or shadows.

Upstairs in his room Pollexfen kept polished and oiled souvenirs of his youth, stirrup and saddle, which he had used when he rode at point to points throughout the west, riding under the name of Paul Hamilton. On a horse his reserve had seemed to fall from him, and if the beast was wild and needed control, it brought out some quality in the rider which made those who knew him think of him as 'a transfigured being'.

John B. Yeats shrewdly discerned a fey element in his merchant in-laws and would maintain that the Pollexfens were 'full of the materials of poetic thought and feeling.' In a splendid phrase he summed up what he believed his alliance with these Sligo merchants had achieved. 'By marriage with the Pollexfens I have given a tongue to the sea cliffs'. He was able to assess his own side of the family with an equally detached stance, when many years later while living in New York, he received a much needed cheque from Willie: 'It was like a Yeats to send this money and make no fuss about it,' he wrote in his letter of thanks, 'it was like a Pollexfen to have it to send.'

153

Willie, with his nationalist views, was often an embarrassment to his uncle during his six-month sojourn. Once, infuriated at a stage-Irish presentation during a masonic concert in Sligo, he hissed the performer and then, feeling that his hiss had not been heard because of the applause, hissed again to make sure it would have its effect. His uncle defended him later, probably impressed by his nephew's courage in making the protest in the first place.

Though the Pollexfens were very rich it was recognised that no matter how much wealth they acquired, they could never, in Anglo-Irish terms, be 'county'. They belonged to 'trade'. Of course, on grand juries and on similar occasions, they would meet the people of the great houses and would know themselves respected by them. But the conventions of Irish life had 'set up a wall'. We can be sure that if Willie felt slighted (and as a writer he was, unlike his relatives, invited occasionally to 'the big house') he would console himself with recollections of his father's people, the Corbets, with their castle at Sandymount, the Butlers with their connection with the Dukes of Ormonde, a great-uncle who had been Governor of Penang.

These six months in Ireland were for Yeats a return to the magic places of his youth. They renewed the Gaelic side of his personality. Refreshed and with his finances in better shape due to the publication of an edited *Book of Irish Verse* and a collected version of his poems and plays published by Unwin, he returned to London that summer.

The Welsh poet Ernest Rhys had met Yeats when he was editing a series of shilling reprints. Yeats told him he was growing jealous of other poets and believed this could only be remedied if he got to know them and heard them read their works. Rolleston was at the time in London, and after introducing him to Rhys the three decided to found the Rhymers' Club where poets could come to read their own work. They chose a pub frequented by Burke, Goldsmith and Johnson, 'The

Cheshire Cheese', which Rolleston celebrated in a verse:

> I know a home of antique ease
> Within the smoky city's pale,
> A spot wherein the spirit sees
> Old London through a thinner veil.
> The modern world, so stiff and stale,
> You leave behind you, when you please,
> For long clay pipes and great old ale
> And beefsteaks in the Cheshire Cheese.

> Beneath this board Burke's, Goldsmith's knees
> Were often thrust – so runs the tale –
> 'Twas here the Doctor took his ease,
> And wielded speech that, like a flail,
> Threshed out the golden truth: All hail
> Great souls! that met on nights like these,
> Till morning made the candles pale,
> And revellers left the Cheshire Cheese.

The poets met four times a week in an upper room with a sawdust floor and would read their latest work in alphabetical order, which meant that Yeats was the last one to read. Regular members included Lionel Johnson, Ernest Dowson, Arthur Symons, John Davison, Richard Le Gallienne. Francis Thompson was not a member but once read there, while Oscar Wilde would only attend meetings of the group which were not held in a pub.

Yeats never forgot the first time that Lionel Johnson read in his musical voice 'The Statue of King Charles at Charing Cross' and felt afterwards that once heard in this cadence the poem could not have the same effect again. Johnson, educated at Winchester and Oxford and wholly English, liked to persuade himself that he was Irish. His 'Celtic' poems have a gushing quality that contrasts with the precision of his lines when he wrote from his own experience. But these Irish-inspired poems gave him a vogue with the London-Irish and the old Fenian, Dr Mark Ryan, would remark that 'Johnson was only happy in the company of Irishmen'. Ryan evidently knew nothing of the other side of Johnson's life and would have been surprised to know that he had been the leader of a homosexual set at Winchester and had written a poem in praise of sodomy to Oscar Wilde on the publication of *The Picture of Dorian Gray*. He was also, as Yeats discovered, a pathological liar. He had enchanted friends with his account of conversations with Cardinal Newman and Gladstone; and his ability to quote directly from what these famous men had said to him intrigued Yeats. Then Yeats discovered after a check on the dates on which these conversations were said to have occurred that they were falsehoods and that Johnson had been inventing the brilliant phrases he had attributed to politician and cardinal. When found out Johnson merely smiled, and with the face and physique of a fifteen-year-old (he was only five feet in height) he seemed like a naughty boy caught in the act. Presently he began to declare that nothing mattered as he would be dead in ten years, and meanwhile he would live as he wished and borrow half-crowns from his friends. In this at least he was accurate, for in 1902 he fell off a chair in a public house and suffered an injury to his head, and was dead on admission to St Bartholomew's Hospital.

Yeats's other close friend at the Rhymers' was Ernest Dowson, whose work he thought immortal, 'bound that is to outlive the famous novels and plays and learned histories and other discursive things'. Dowson seemed to court doom and wished for an early death. He had become a Catholic and carried a cross in his pocket which he would dip in his drink before he drank. So self-conscious that he had to ask Johnson to read 'Cynara' for him the first night at the Rhymers' Club, he had fallen in love with a waitress and when she had married another, gradually drifted into drink though retaining enough sobriety to write from time to time fine poetry. He became reluctant to wash, his tongue turned orange from smoking, his teeth fell out and he finally died of tuberculosis in 1900 in Dieppe.

Aubrey Beardsley, though not a member of the club, was associated with many who were. He fascinated Yeats when he told him that at six years of age he had seen 'a vision of the bleeding Christ over a mantelpiece'. Yeats would have preferred it if Beardsley had seen a wounded Druid, but he was impressed by someone who had seen a vision of any kind – though he thought Beardsley's Catholicism, like that of Dowson and Johnson, 'deepened despair and multiplied temptation'.

Beardsley, Johnson and Dowson were all Catholics with a mystical bent. Yeats's mysticism took the form of occult practices. Though he had grown up beside Catholic churches in Dublin where the daily ritual included the turning of bread into God, such ceremonies had no attraction for him. Agnostic though his upbringing had been, there was something in his Protestant heritage that steered him away from Catholic ritual. In the pagan past of his country he had found a system which nourished his conviction that invisible gates would open as they had for Blake, Swedenborg and Boehme. He would often get angry with Catholic friends who refused to accept his version of fairy happenings, saying, 'Things like that were once the religion of the world', and later on he would recount with relish AE's reply to a friend who had doubted the tenets of theosophy: 'Like all Irish Catholics you are an atheist at heart.'

Unlike his three friends, Yeats had no capacity for dissipation. The merchant blood of his mother's people had given an order to his life that a stockbroker might have envied. Though with his highly-strung temperament Yeats suffered from bouts of nervous exhaustion and was at times on the verge of collapse, he fought his disabilites with a ferocity which enabled him to live another forty years after his friends of 'the tragic generation' had perished from drink or drugs.

Arthur Symons was the one man in the group besides Yeats who survived this doomed generation and who was to have a significant influence on the poet. As a poet

Symons wrote indifferent poetry and could perpetrate dreadful lines like 'down the dazzling vistas of streets'. But he was a prodigious worker who had translated St John of the Cross, Calderon, Catullus, d'Annunzio and was to make a major contribution to criticism with *The Symbolist Movement in Literature*. Symons travelled a great deal and had a flair for seeking out important writers wherever he went. He could describe conversations with Villiers de l'Isle Adam, boast of meeting Huysmans in Paris in 1890 ('an amused look of contempt and pity for human understanding'), describe Verlaine on the same visit ('like Pan among revelling worshippers'), and had been present at the first night of *Ghosts* in the Théâtre Libre in Paris. It was Symons who introduced Yeats, a poor linguist, to French literature. He persuaded him to go over to see Villiers de l'Isle Adam's *Axel* in Paris, which gave Yeats the concept for *Rosa Alchemica* and which was to have a deep influence on him throughout his life.

> Symons more than any man I know [wrote Yeats] could slip into the mind of another and my thoughts gained in richness and in clearness from his sympathy. Nor shall I ever know how much my practice and my theory owe to the passages that he read to me from Catullus and from Verlaine and Mallarmé.

When Yeats went to Paris it was on Symons's introduction that he met Verlaine of whom he has left an extraordinary and uniquely Yeatsian account.

> Meanwhile his homely middle-aged mistress made the coffee and found the cigarettes. ... A slovenly, ragged man came in, his trousers belted with a piece of rope and an opera-hat upon his head. She drew a box over to the fire, and he sat down, now holding the opera-hat upon his knees, and I think he must have acquired it very lately, for he kept constantly closing and opening it. Verlaine introduced him by saying, 'He is a poor man, but a good fellow, and is so like

Louis XI to look at that we call him Louis XI.' I remember that Verlaine talked of Victor Hugo, who was 'a supreme poet, but a volcano of mud as well as of flame' and of Villiers de l'Isle Adam, who was 'exalté' and wrote excellent French; and of *In Memoriam*, which he had tried to translate and could not. 'Tennyson is too noble, too *anglais*; when he should have been broken-hearted he had many reminiscences. . . . At Verlaine's burial, but a few months after, his mistress quarrelled with a publisher at the graveside as to who owned the sheet by which the body had been covered, and Louis XI stole fourteen umbrellas that he found leaning against a tree in the cemetery.'

(The man with the opera hat is clearly Bibi la Purée, the well-known pimp at the Moulin Rouge who was drawn by Toulouse Lautrec. It was probably from Dowson, who was at the funeral, that Yeats learned the story of 'Louis XI's' coup.)

Well briefed by Symons, when Yeats was in Paris he visited the avantgarde theatres of Lugné Poe and Antoine which were to influence his ideas on the evolution of the drama later on. Re-reading Symons's criticism today it is clear that he, more than any other English critic of his time, was able to discern the developments in the French theatre which would influence techniques over the next fifty years. But in the end Symons's addiction to work drove him out of his head and for two years, 1909–1911, he was a lunatic. Yeats had envied Symons's success with ballet girls and music-hall singers, and put the madness down (with predictable exaggeration) to sexual excess. But it was nothing more than a bad case of manic depression from which Symons recovered to outlive Yeats by four years.

In November 1895 George Russell (AE) had written to Yeats asking him 'to clear out of Arthur Symons's vicinity' and come back to live in Dublin, as it would be better for him 'morally, and as a place to get inspiration'. AE was at this time living a very different life from the young man who had known Yeats at the Art School eight years before. He had abandoned painting and become a clerk in a drapery store, Pims of George's Street. The reason he gave for this sudden change was that painting had undermined his will. He believed he required a routine job which would leave him time to develop ethical and mental disciplines so that he could release the dormant spiritual energy in his nature which would present him with mystical experiences. He practised exercises of retentive memory so that episodes of his past life could be played again and again before the mind's eye like a film. He would concentrate on a geometrical form over a prolonged period to improve his mental processes and make it easier to summon up images that were not preconceived. Even in the gas-lit room where he did his daily accounts he encountered extrasensory experiences which assured him that he was loosing his mind from materialistic manacles. Once pictures began flickering before his eyes, and he found that he was being visited by an image of the shop belonging to the father of one of his fellow clerks who was at that time writing a letter home, and had the same scene in his mind.

In April 1891 AE had joined a commune which had been formed by a Scotsman, Frederick Dick. A fine Georgian house had been purchased by the group in Ely Place, just off St Stephen's Green in the City centre. Here he was to live for seven years, practising as a mystic by night and plying the trade of a clerk by day. There were eight other adepts in the commune, both men and women, some of whom were vegetarians and all of whom lived as celibates. AE was to say later these were the seven happiest years of his life, though his income was so small that he often had to test his shoe leather before setting out for a long walk. He had given up painting, but he did not consider it an intrusion on his mystical life to draw murals on the walls of 3 Ely Place. One of the most notable depicted the soul ascending at nightfall from a hunched-up Blake-like figure towards the Absolute, which AE called 'The Night's Resurrection'.

Charles Johnston had tended to deprecate AE's poetry. 'My dear fellow,' he had said to John Eglinton who had shown him AE's poems, 'you have no idea how many people can write like that'. But another theosophist, Charles Weekes, was fascinated by the poems and decided to publish them himself. He paid for the printing at the Chiswick Press in London. They appeared under the title *Homeward: Songs by the Way* published in 1895 by the Whaley Press. Yeats always thought this was AE's best book, and it contains one of his most memorable poems, 'Immortality'.

We must pass like smoke or live within the spirit's
    fire;
For we can no more than smoke unto the flame return
If our thought has changed to dream, our will unto
    desire,
As smoke we vanish though the fire may burn.

Lights of infinite pity star the grey dusk of our days:
Surely here is soul: with it we have eternal breath:
In the fire of love we live, or pass by many ways,
By unnumbered ways of dream to death.

Two years later AE published *Earth Breath*, which did not as a whole live up to the standard of his first book, but contained the visionary poem 'Refuge':

Twilight, a timid fawn, went glimmering by
    And Night, the dark blue hunter, followed fast,
Ceaseless pursuit and flight were in the sky,
    But the long chase had ceased for us at last.

We watched together while the driven fawn
    Hid in the golden thicket of the day.
We, from whose hearts pursuit and flight were gone,
    Knew on the hunter's breast her refuge lay.

Years later AE would write 'Germinal' with its well-known verse:

In ancient shadows and twilights
   Where childhood had stray'd,
The world's great sorrows were born
   And its heroes were made.
In the lost boyhood of Judas
   Christ was betray'd.

But now the poet was more concerned with what he saw in his imagination than how he would express it. This explains the inconsistencies in many of his poems. Many years later he defended this deficiency to a young poet, F.R. Higgins: 'I only want my images to be like a dim tapestry behind my clear-cut idea and I don't want people to look at my tapestry and not listen to me.'

AE had attuned himself so fully to the mystical world that he believed he could hear the voices of plants. This was the sort of experience that men should strive for: 'We are like frogs at the bottom of a marsh, knowing nothing of the many-coloured earth.' And in May 1896 he wrote to Yeats in great excitement, telling him that the arrival of the figure they had been waiting for was imminent.

The gods have returned to Erin and have centred themselves in the sacred mountains and blow the fires through the country. They have been seen by several in vision, they will awaken the magical instinct everywhere, and the universal heart of the people will turn to the old druidic beliefs. I note through the country the increased faith in faery things. The bells are heard from the mounds and sounding in the hollows of the mountains ... out of Ireland will arise a light to transform many ages and peoples. There is a hurrying of forces and swift things going out and I believe profoundly that a new Avatar is about to appear and in all spheres the forerunners go before him to prepare. It will be one of the kingly Avatars, who is at once ruler of men and magic sage. I had a vision of him some months ago and will know him if he appears.

Yeats, too, was awaiting an apocalyptic event at this time. He had been writing his story *Rosa Alchemica* in which the hero Michael Robartes leads his companion to the shores of the Atlantic on the west of Ireland to visit the temple of the Alchemical Rose. This visit is to herald the return of the old Celtic gods to Ireland, Mananaan, Lu, Dagda, Aengus. The book in which this story appeared was dedicated to AE and later Yeats confided to Lady Gregory that the character of the alchemist was based on Russell:

I too await,
The hour of that great wind of Love and Hate.

7 Dublin Interlude

Yeats had kept up his contact with Ireland through the Irish Literary Society. This had been founded on 28 December 1891 when a group of London Irishmen met in Yeats's father's house in Chiswick. These were journalists and writers living in London at the time who wished to publish work and organise lectures in connection with the national literature. Among them were Rolleston, Todhunter, Stopford Brooke and journalists like W.P. Ryan and D.J. O'Donoghue. Yeats was enthusiastic about the idea and eagerly set about working out details of the organisation. He went over to Ireland and toured the provincial towns to organise for the society. He showed a surprising gift of talking to ordinary people and he was compared by one man to Thomas Davis and by another to Davitt. Naturally reserved, he now found that he delighted in talking to strange people every day. But he considered it a surrender to the chief temptation of the artist – 'creation without toil' – and suggested he had found the happiness that 'Shelley felt when he tied a pamphlet to a fire balloon'.

Travelling the towns, nevertheless, he got his first glimpse of the possibility of a national movement which would bring the local towns people in touch with art and it was through the stage that he felt it could be done. He longed to set up a travelling company for such a purpose and this ambition hastened the writing of the first version of his play *The Countess Cathleen*.

The Irish Literary Society, unhappily, was destined to be broken up by dissension. Sir Charles Gavan Duffy returned from Australia, where he had been Prime Minister of Victoria, and with the aura of Thomas Davis's Young Ireland Movement about him, proved difficult and stubborn when he became President of the Society. Unlike O'Leary he would not reject a book which was badly written if its political content was acceptable. But despite the collapse of the organisation there was a major event with which it was connected which was to have a profound effect not only on the literary movement but on the political future of the country.

On 25 November 1892, under the auspices of the Dublin Branch, the National Literary Society, Douglas Hyde delivered his address on 'The Necessity for De-Anglicising Ireland'. This paper brought together the different processes that had been at work since the publication of O'Grady's *History of Ireland* and the impact of Parnell. 'But you ask', Hyde began,

> why should we wish to make Ireland more Celtic than it is – why should we de-anglicise it at all? I answer because the Irish race is at present in a most anomalous position, imitating England and yet apparently hating it. How can it produce anything good in literature, art or institutions as long as it is actuated by motives so contradictory? Besides, I believe it is our Gaelic past which, though the Irish race does not recognise it just at present, is really at the bottom of the Irish heart, and prevents us becoming citizens of the empire, as I think, can be easily proved. And yet this awful idea of complete anglicisation, which I have here put before you in all its crudity, is and has been making silent inroads upon us for nearly a century. The Irish, of all the nations of Western Europe, escaped the claws of those birds of prey, the Romans. Our antiquities can best throw light upon the pre-Romanised inhabitants of half Europe and – we are our fathers' sons.

Hyde described how the races had blended:

Dane and Norman drawn to the kindly Irish breast issued forth in a generation or two fully Irishised, and more Hibernian than the Hibernians themselves, and even after the Cromwellian plantation of the children of numbers of the English soldiers who settled in the south and midlands, were, after forty years' residence, and after marrying Irish wives, turned into good Irishmen, and unable to speak a word of English, while several Gaelic poets of the last century have, like Father English, the most unmistakeable English names.

Hyde proposed an immediate cure for the decline which he believed was under way. 'In order to de-Anglicise ourselves we must at once arrest the decay of the Irish language.' He suggested a campaign of house-to-house visitations, and awards of medals to families who would guarantee that they spoke Irish among themselves throughout the year. He finished with a word of praise for the 'brave and patriotic men' who had started the Gaelic Athletic Association in order to revive Irish games.

> I consider that the work of the association in reviving our national game of caman (or hurling) and Gaelic football has done more for Ireland than all the speeches of politicans for the last five years.

The place where Hyde gave this address, the Leinster Hall in Molesworth Street, was just behind the fashionable Protestant Church of St Ann in Dawson Street, and among the large attendance were members of well-known ascendancy families, including the Gwynns, Henry French, Miss l'Estrange and Sarah Purser. Hyde would not have seen anything of an anomaly in this. It was to the whole nation he was speaking, assuring them they were one, if they attended to their ancestral heritage.

Though Hyde's doctrine was to an extent revolutionary, he had not cut his roots with his own class. His diary of the summer before he gave his address gives a picture of the life of a country gentleman enjoying the leisure left to his breed in the last decade of the century:

14 July [1891]: A Tennis party at Frenchpark (Lord and Lady de Freyne's). We went and played a good deal.

20 July: Cricket at Frenchpark. Annette and I went ... A fair amount of people there.

21 July: We went to Boyle to finish the tennis. The day turned very wet. I had a bad partner, a lady named Miss Marsh, and I was beaten. A terrible day. Dinner and drinks with Dr Hamilton; home at 9.

27 July: Cricket match at Frenchpark: Castlerea versus the Garrison. I fielded fairly well but got only one or two runs. Lunch at the Big House.

4 August: I spent the night in the hotel and this morning I met Sellors and we had a couple of drinks together. Then I took the train to Foynes, 24 miles from Limerick, and arrived at Ard an Oir, the home of Charlotte Grace O'Brien. She and Miss Spring Rice, the sister of Lord Monteagle, were there, and Stockley and Miss Osbourne came in the afternoon. A very wet day.

The remarkable thing is that Hyde's epoch-making speech was ignored by the Irish daily newspapers. The only one to give it any notice was the *Irish Independent* which devoted an editorial to the event but did not quote from the address. The nationalist weekly, the *United Irishman*, commented the following week on the failure to report the meeting and decried the fact that there is no recognition for an Irish Protestant gentleman when he comes out from amongst his own class and fully identifies himself with the life, language, games and customs of the native population.

Yeats followed this up with a letter in which he said he agreed with every word they had said about the lecture. 'It should be more easy for us,' he continued,

who have in us that wild Celtic blood . . . to translate or retell in English which shall have an indefinable Irish quality of rhythm and style, all that is best in the ancient literature. Mr Hyde and Lady Wilde . . . are setting before us a table spread with strange Gaelic fruits from which an ever growing band of makers of song and story shall draw food for their souls.

Despite the attitude of the press in ignoring Hyde's address at the Leinster Hall, it was to have the most far-reaching result. Out of it was to come what Michael Collins, the Irish revolutionary leader, would later refer to as 'the most significant event in three hundred years of Irish history, the founding of the Gaelic League'.

Previous attempts to revive the language through the Society for the Preservation of the Irish Language and the Gaelic Union had failed, perhaps because they lacked the radical philosophy supplied by Hyde's 'de-anglicisation' speech. Now, after Hyde's address, a young law clerk working in the Four Courts called Eoin MacNeill (the first Catholic to be appointed) found himself carried away by its message. MacNeill, Hyde and another law official, O'Neill Russell, founded the Gaelic League on 31 July 1893, 'to keep the Irish language spoken in Ireland'.

The success of the Gaelic League was phenomenal. Ten years later, there were six hundred branches with a total membership of 50,000. Full-time organisers travelled the countryside establishing new branches. Travelling teachers taught Irish, dancing, folklore, music and organised Irish festivals or *feiseanna*. There were branches in every town or village. In the Irish-speaking districts people were taught to read and write their native language, and in English-speaking districts they were taught to speak it. Books and pamphlets in which poetry, music and modern manuscripts appeared, were published by the League. By 1906 Hyde's fame was so great that he was able to tour the United States and collect £11,000 to finance the League. Nor was this Hyde's only contribution in these years. In the summer of 1893 he published a book which was to have a profound influence on the literary life of Ireland. This was *Love Songs of Connacht*, a collection of Gaelic poetry which he had collected from farmers and labourers in the west of Ireland, as well as copying them out from manuscripts he had discovered. The book was bilingual, the Gaelic appearing on the left page and the English on the right, which enabled readers who had no Irish to follow Hyde on his journeys through the countryside in search of verse. Thus a whole generation was brought in touch with the 'hidden Ireland'.

The distinctive quality of the book lay in the fact that Hyde provided verse translations for most of the poems. Gaelic poetry, with its internal rhyming schemes, alliterations and gapped rhythms, is extremely difficult to render into another language and there had been few successful attempts before Hyde to do so. It was because he was a poet as well as a scholar that he was able to bring into English an uncanny feeling of the quality of Gaelic verse. He also supplied literal prose translations of the poems which he claimed 'courageously, though no doubt ruggedly, reproduced the Irish idioms of the original'. This was a modest claim. Yeats was later to say, 'The prose parts of that book were to me as they were to many others the coming of a new power into literature, . . . one of those 'thrusts of power' which Flaubert has declared to be beyond the reach of conscious art.' Yeats may have been a little jealous of Hyde's genius for rendering one language into another in verse. He continually stressed 'the prose' side of

Hyde's work at the expense of the poetic, and hinted that Hyde wrote too easily in verse, 'all day and without apparent effort'. It is easy to see why for instance Yeats would have liked the literal translation of the first verse of the poem which appears on page 41 of *Love Songs of Connacht*. The prose has a run of its own which conveys perfectly the rhythm of Irish speech in English and which Hyde was the first to set down as accurately as it appears here.

O youth of the bound black hair. With whom I was once together. You went by this way last night. And you did not come in to see me. I thought no harm would be done you, if you were to come and to ask for me, and sure it is your little kiss would give comfort if I were in the midst of a fever

But Yeats, not having a knowledge of Irish, would have failed to recognise how Hyde had caught the rhythms of the original poem perfectly in the first line of his verse translation, 'O ringleted youth of my love', and continued in verse after verse, chained deliciously to the Gaelic original, mounting to the magnificent

I thought, O my love! you were so –
    As the moon is, or sun on a fountain,
And I thought after that you were snow,
    The cold snow on top of the mountain;
And I thought after that, you were more
    Like God's lamp shining to find me,
Or the bright star of knowledge before,
    And the star of knowledge behind me.

Love Songs of Connacht was to set the style of the literary renaissance. The direct translations enabled the writers to get the rhythm of Irish language spoken in English into their ears. Some of them would return to the source by learning Irish, the better to extract it, undistilled, as inspiration for their writing in English. One of Hyde's advantages was his scholarship. He was thus able to trace how the popular poetry he collected from the people derived from a sophisticated lineage which encompassed the sagas of the heroic age, the monkish poetry of the seventh and eighth centuries, and a court tradition of extraordinary ingenuity in the use of alliteration, internal rhyme, assonance and rhythmic disciplines. When the Gaelic aristocracy finally broke up and the court poets went down among the people they continued for a time to write as they had for prince or lady. Hyde claimed that when, eventually, the popular poets had placed behind them the rigid classical metres and dispensed with several thousand words which no one except those trained in schools of poetry understood, their verse became 'probably the most sensuous attempt to convey music in words ever made by man'.

What manner of man was Douglas Hyde? It is certain that his character was a complex one. He had a singular gift for getting things done. He was an ideal leader in a country where people's appetite for dispute was as great as their appetite for food. Hyde shunned controversy, remaining all things to all men while keeping his counsel. He had many roles: poet, actor, scholar, organiser and, later, professor and President of Ireland. For each he had a separate approach which enabled him to move between the eddies and currents of Irish controversy. There was the mask of the common man sitting down at the feet of the peasant, collecting folklore. But the same person could be heartily ashamed of his friends, the Tynan sisters, when he showed them round Trinity, fearful lest his college friends might notice their countrified dresses and 'awful brogues'. He could, with some success, appeal to Unionists as well as Nationalists to join his Gaelic League, without letting them guess the fiercely anti-English sentiments that had inspired much of his student verse. Myles Dillon, Celtic scholar and one of Hyde's pupils, noted in later years the diverse nature of Hyde's character. First, the man who drove from church in a chauffeur-driven car with a fur rug round his knees; then the sportsman who could take down a grouse with a left and a right; and the golfer who got on a train at Harcourt Street with a bag of clubs and attempted to persuade his literary friends to take up the game. He was too, it seems, a ladies' man. From his diaries it would appear that for a while he lost his heart to Maud Gonne. There is a reference to his visiting her twice on the same day in November 1889, and meeting her a third time that evening at the Pan Celtic Society. But he had no more luck than Yeats – though unlike the poet he cut his losses and did not brood for years over his failure. Quite a frisky professor Hyde was later, when it came to attractive girl students. The reserved, remote figure of the Gaelic League years now liked to show off to his students in lectures, acting scenes from his own Gaelic plays, jumping and leaping round like a strolling player, even on occasions in his excitement vanishing out of the door into the gloom beyond. Many thought him a dreamer. He was quite the opposite, a man of action who could assume the dreamer's mask to lead the more indolent of his race towards a goal he had set himself to achieve.

Yeats moved to 18 Woburn Buildings in the spring of 1896. It was to be his London residence for fifteen years. When he first became a tenant there was a cobbler's shop on the ground floor and directly overhead a working man lived with his family. In the attic there was a travelling water-colour painter who sold his wares in the streets.

Soon Yeats had made his own lodgings into an interesting artist's abode. He rented a few more rooms and presently had a front sittingroom and two bedrooms. His housekeeper, Mrs Old, whom he had borrowed from Arthur Symons, but who was later to become a much valued permanent fixture, would be summoned by a gong. The sitting room was papered after William Morris fashion with brown paper and there were brown-beige curtains on the walls. Beside the left window was a picture of Yeats by his father and over the fire a drawing for a poster by Aubrey Beardsley.

Monday evenings in Yeats's rooms became a dropping-in place for members of the London artistic community. Among those who were more less regular visitors at this time were Max Beerbohm, William Rothenstein, Charles Conder, Ricketts and Shannon, Ernest Rhys, Arthur Symons. Gordon Craig recalled to the author the way Yeats would greet visitors of his choice. 'He liked the gesture of opening the door. He would do it with a great sweeping movement of his hand: "Come in Craig." ' Such a welcome was reserved for special guests, for others remember that whoever had come in last would welcome the next person who knocked at the door.

A young poet, John Masefield, who thought Yeats's room the most interesting in London, has left a description of Yeats at one of his evenings in Woburn Buildings:

> Perhaps the first impression was of great personal distinction and of a physical condition not robust. He was pale; he stooped somewhat; and as his eyes gave him much trouble then, he seemed to peer at one. His black hair was worn in a shock, very long. It came down to his brow and over his collar at the back. He had a characteristic way of tossing it back with a shake of the head. One saw at once that he was unlike anyone else in the world. The short-sighted eyes, peering through pince-nez from under the billow of hair, were full of fun and keen intelligence. The expression on his face, when not remote with speculation, was vivid with wit.

Later that evening Yeats recited in that 'wavering ecstatic song' which he used for verse.

> His reading was unlike that of any other man. He stressed the rhythm till it almost became a chant: he went with speed making every beat and dwelling on the vowel.

Yeats warned Masefield never to let a mood go without imprisoning it in verse of some kind, 'for the mood will pass and never return', and told him that the important thing about Beardsley's drawing was that he is 'always sitting in judgment on himself'. Later Masefield learned that Yeats had been quite ill with a cold, but had been unable to contact him to cancel, and had received him as if he were in perfect health.

Thus we see Yeats in 1896. At thirty years of age he had become recognised as an important poet in London literary circles. Already he had been through two movements, the pre-Raphaelite and the fin-de-siècle. He was poised for great work. Not many would have thought that this would be accomplished, in the next decade, not in London but in Dublin.

Part Two

1 Getting Together

At the beginning of August 1896 Edward Martyn invited
Yeats and Arthur Symons to stay with him at Tulira.
Moore was already in residence when they arrived.

Yeats was confused as he drove up the avenue by
what he regarded as the worst inventions of the Gothic
revival, the rebuilt part of Tulira, but admired the
fifteenth-century tower which Edward had tricked his
mother into preserving for himself.

Edward had seemed so countrified to Yeats in London
that he expected to be greeted by a bare-footed servant,
and was mildly surprised when an impeccably dressed
butler opened the door. Edward showed them to their
rooms, saying, 'Take your choice', and was amused to
see Symons's face fall when Yeats suggested that they
flip a coin to decide which room they would take. It was
the dilemma of the Englishman in Ireland, unable to
decide whether he was being laughed at or expected to
join in the fun.

That night after dinner, when Edward dimmed the
lights in the great hall and began to play Palestrina on
his harmonium, it seemed to Yeats as they sat in the
shadows that it might have been a stage set for *Parsifal*.

Next morning Edward took them round the house,
showing them the great stained-glass window in the
hall, commissioned from Aubrey Beardsley, and his
Degas, Corot, Utamora, Monet. Yeats was surprised at
Edward's delight in Beardsley and put it down to
Beardsley's drawings of fat women and children drawn
so as to suggest a foetus, feeding Edward's hatred of life.

He tried to tell himself that two traditions had met in Martyn, 'creating the sterility of the mule', and that Martyn admired Swift, Ibsen and John Chrysostom, because 'their hatred of life made abstinence easy'. But this was facile. Ibsen did not hate life and Swift was anything but ascetic when it came to sex. Edward's was not an easy personality to understand and Yeats was far from doing so. Perhaps it was the combination of the convinced Catholic and the wealthy landlord that baffled him: Yeats could never have encountered such a type in his native Sligo where the landed gentry were uniformly of low church Protestant stock.

Edward's cousin Count Florimond de Basterot arrived while Yeats and Symons were there. De Basterot kept apartments in Rome and Paris, but spent his summers in Ireland.

Presently Symons, who was writing a book on islands, wanted to go to the Aran Islands, thirty miles off the Galway coast and the last piece of land between Ireland and the United States. Edward agreed to arrange the journey, and on 5 August 1896 he, Moore, Yeats and Symons, set out for the largest of the three islands, Inishmore, in a seventeen-ton hooker that had come over from Aran. After they landed they went straight to the Atlantic Hotel, where the landlady had her bedroom in the kitchen and the chairs bowed over backwards when they were sat on. Next day Symons, who as a Cornishman had seen much of the ocean in his lifetime, noted that the sea around Aran 'was not like the sea as I know it on any other coast':

> it has in it more of the twilight. And the sky seems to come down more softly, with more stealthy step, more elusive wings, and the land to come forward with a more hesitating and gradual approach; and the land and sea and sky to mingle more absolutely than on any other coast ... after rain the whole bay burned with blue fire.

He also noticed how time seemed to telescope there.

I have never realised less the slipping of sand through the hour-glass, I have never seemed to see with so remote an impartiality, as in the presence of brief and yet eternal things, the troubling and insignificant accidents of life. I have never believed less in the reality of the visible world, in the importance of all we are most serious about. One seems to wash off the dust of cities, the dust of beliefs, the dust of incredulities.

Their guide was a flaxen-haired forty-year-old with golden curls who dressed in the island garb of flannel waistcoat and trousers, and wore on his feet 'pampooties', hide slippers that gave the wearer a grip on the rocky soil. The women wore red petticoats and shawls which they drew closer about them when strangers passed, as women of the East draw their veils closer about their faces. A few of the islanders spoke English – the rest spoke Irish only.

On the second day they visited a Druid church, after that the ruined church of St Enda who had come to the island in AD 480 and a pre-Christian fort, Dun Aengus, with walls eighteen feet high and thirteen feet thick. This made a deep impression on Symons.

We know from the Bardic writers that a civilisation, similar to that of the Homeric poems, lived on in Ireland almost to the time of the coming of St Patrick; and it was something also of the sensation of Homer – the walls of Troy, the heroes, and that 'face that launched a thousand ships' – and which came to me as we stood upon those unconquerable walls, to which a generation of men had been as a moth's flight and a hundred years as a generation of men.

Yeats had come on the trip with the idea of finding background material for his novel *The Speckled Bird*. It was typical of him that while the others did not succeed in finding an islander who had seen fairies, Yeats was able to root out an old man who had heard them, and who complained that their singing kept him awake. He was buying a flute so that with music he might charm them into giving him some sleep. Another day Yeats arrived back at the hotel with a storyteller who told the others how Satan had tried to equal himself to God, then 'looked in a glass in which God could only look' and as he did that 'hell was made in a minute'.

The fourth day they visited the middle island and on the fifth they intended to go to Inisheer. But the hooker's captain warned them that the weather would make a landing dangerous, since there was no pier on the island and they would have to be brought ashore in currachs.

There is a special significance in the visit of Martyn, Moore and Yeats to the Aran Islands in 1896. Lady Gregory, who with these three was to found the Irish Literary Theatre, visited the islands six months later and Synge, the great folk dramatist of the movement, was to make his first visit within two years. These islands were the last outpost of the culture that was at the root of the literary renaissance. It was almost as if they were acting as a magnet to those who were unconsciously seeking to express the Irish imagination. Here it was concentrated in its purest form in the tales, music, dancing of the people. Their physical appearance, the way they carried themselves, their manner, all suggested the culture they belonged to, so untouched were they by contact with any other.

A storm arose on the way back and the group were unable to land at Galway. Instead they made for Ballyvaughan, County Clare, whence they drove back to Tulira along the Clare coast under 'a sunset of gold fire and white spray'.

Meanwhile, at Tulira Yeats was up to his magic. Believing that his style could become over-ornate if he did not harness the dark portion of his mind – the subconscious – he had decided to invoke lunar powers. Each night he repeated the associations with the moon, the cabbalistic tree of life, the name of the Angelic Order of the planetary sphere. On the ninth night he had

180

his reward. Between sleeping and waking he saw, as in a film, a galloping centaur and a moment later 'a naked woman of incredible beauty standing upon a pedestal and shooting an arrow at a star'.

Delighted with himself as he believed he had conjured up the Goddess Diana, Yeats went down to breakfast where he found that his experiment had overflowed into Arthur Symons's mind. His friend had dreamed too of a beautiful woman, but clothed and without weapons. Symons took Yeats out on the lawn to recite a poem he had written to his dream figure 'To a Woman in Sleep'. The verses may have spoiled Yeats's enthusiasm for Symons's psychic powers, for they are without merit, but as he listened to them he heard an angry voice coming from the breakfast room. It was that of the Count de Basterot, Edward's cousin, who also had been affected by Yeats's unleashing of psychic powers and had felt waves coming over him with such force that he had jumped out of bed and locked the door. Both Edward and he demanded of Yeats what he had been at. The poet explained that he had been invoking the moon, which did not draw an enthusiastic response from the two cousins. As pious Catholics, neither Edward nor the Count could condone pagan practice. When Yeats revealed that he had been doing his invocations in the room above Tulira Chapel where Mass was said daily, there were angry yelps from Edward. Thoughts of blasphemy filled his mind and he trembled lest he might have another visit to the Bishop on his schedule, to obtain a dispensation for having been responsible for witchcraft in the vicinity of the Host.

Despite this encounter with Edward, Yeats greatly enjoyed his stay at Tulira and while he was there had an opportunity to meet the woman who would become his chief partner in the dramatic movement.

Lady Gregory's home at Coole was about four miles from Tulira. She invited Yeats and Symons to tea there one afternoon during this visit. Yeats and Lady Gregory had met in London once or twice previously, but this was

181

the first occasion on which they had an opportunity to make an impression on one another. Symons was quick to notice Lady Gregory's interest in the poet. He said later that 'as soon as her terrible eye fell on him I knew she would keep him and he would be lost to lyrical poetry'. Afterwards Symons would always refer to Lady Gregory as *la Strega* ('the witch') and maintain that she had been a bad influence on Yeats.

A few weeks later, when Symons had gone back to London, Yeats moved out to Coole for a few days to stay with Lady Gregory. She asked him while he was there if he could set her some work for the 'intellectual movement' and he told her 'if you get our books and watch what we are doing you will soon find your work'.

After Yeats had gone back to Dublin Lady Gregory set herself to the task of 'finding her work'. She began to learn Irish and bought herself a copy of O'Growney's primer. When she had worked on the grammar she would go down to Mike the gardener and get him to help her with conversation and pronunciation. One of her proudest moments was when Father O'Growney himself sent her a badge with the words 'Gaelic League' on it. Thus it was through Yeats's direction that Lady Gregory first became involved with the other Ireland. The following year she was to be directly responsible for initiating the appeal which led to the first presentations of the Irish Literary Theatre.

It was a few months after his stay on the Aran Islands that Yeats made a visit to Paris which was to have the greatest possible significance in the emergence of the drama movement. Staying at the Hôtel Corneille, opposite the Odéon theatre, he had learned that there was another Irish writer resident there. Yeats sought him out and discovered that his name was John Millington Synge, that he had grown up in Dublin and had taken a degree in music at Trinity College. Afterwards he had studied in Dresden, intending to become a concert violinist and composer, but decided that he had not the temperament and turned to writing. He hoped, he told Yeats, to translate French poetry and prose – Lôti perhaps – into English. He was interested in Breton culture, he continued, and he had studied Irish as a second subject in Trinity College.

We may imagine the glint that came into Yeats's eyes as he heard this. His ears were still ringing from the Irish he had heard on the enchanted journey he had made with Symons, Martyn and Moore two months earlier. Synge came from landed stock – his family drew their money from lands in Galway – but as Yeats studied him on their first meeting, he must have sensed beneath that reserved exterior – the black hair, the high cheekbones, the slow slightly guttural voice – a passionate spirit that could be stirred by contact with Irish culture. 'Give up Paris and go to the Aran Islands,' he told Synge. 'Live there as one of the people themselves. Express a life that has never found expression.'

What he could have gleaned of Synge's family background would not have encouraged someone less discerning than Yeats to try and involve him in an Irish literary movement. His mother had brought him up in a strictly evangelical household in which the native Irish were regarded with the same amount of enthusiasm that a *pied noir* would have for an Arab. England and the Empire were their perspectives, not Ireland. But Synge had revolted as a young boy against this outlook. First of all, he had rejected the doctrine of eternal damnation of hell-fire. Then, as his interest diminished in 'the kingdom of God', he inclined more towards 'the kingdom of Ireland' and had interested himself in Irish history and the treatment of his country by England. When he went to Trinity, he had studied Irish (one of the very few laymen among the divinity students who took the subject in order to preach in Irish-speaking areas) and he culti-vated an interest in the three thousand-year-old passage graves that were to be found near Dublin and in County Meath, and other archaeological remains. He had reacted with disgust at the family's involvement in heartless evictions in County Wicklow, but nevertheless had accepted that he must take a share of the responsibility. As his mother had pointed out to him, his small private income derived from the rents owned by the Synges.

In Paris he was living a lonely life, being shy by nature and unable to form friendships, especially with women. He was a handsome man, with a strong sexual drive, but his lack of initiative and his puritan upbringing had encouraged those women with whom he had formed any sort of a relationship to look on him with something approaching ridicule, rather as an importunate child. He had had some contact in Paris with the Irish community there – he was friendly with Maud Gonne and had shared rooms with Richard Best, an Irish scholar, but his only real friend there was Stephen McKenna, later to be translator of Plotinus, but who was at that time correspondent for the New York *Herald Tribune*.

We do not know Synge's precise answer to Yeats's somewhat imperious advice to leave Paris and go to Aran. Whether at the time he indicated that he would go there, we cannot say. But less than two years later in May 1898 he did set out for the Aran Islands, determined to fill his notebook with information about the life and speech of the islanders.

Synge's meeting with Yeats was to be of the greatest importance to him. They were both of Anglo-Irish Protestant stock and both had an interest in the mystical side of being. Synge, at one time, had studied St John of the Cross and St Rose of Lima before deciding that Catholic visionaries were too ascetic for his taste and that he preferred to believe in 'one world of a soul, and no flesh and no devil'. The day they met in Paris, he had said wistfully to Yeats that he had wanted to unite stoicism, asceticism and ecstasy. 'Two of them have come together, three never.' Yeats was fascinated with his new acquaintance and, as he came to know him, would regard him as the one among writers he knew in whom the artistic element ran purest. Later, he would write of him:

184

He had that egotism of the man of genius which Nietzsche compares to the egotism of a woman with child. He had, under charming and modest manners, in almost all things of life, a complete absorption in his own dream. I have never heard him praise any writer, living or dead, but some old French farce writer. For him nothing existed but his thought. He claimed nothing for it aloud. He never said any of those self-confident things I am enraged into saying, but one knew that he valued nothing else. He was too confident for self-assertion. I once said to George Moore, 'Synge has always the better of you, for you have brief but ghastly moments during which you admit the existence of other writers: Synge never has.' I do not think he disliked other writers – they did not exist. One did not think of him as an egotist. He was too sympathetic in the ordinary affairs of life, and too simple. In the arts he knows no language but his own. . . .

I have often envied him his absorption as I have envied Verlaine his vice. Can a man of genius make that complete renunciation of the world necessary to the full expression of himself without some vice or some deficiency? You were happy or at least blessed, 'blind old man of Scio's rocky isle'.

In 1897 Yeats was back again at Tulira, forgiven for his experiments of the year before. Edward asked him one afternoon would he care to come on a visit to his cousin, Count de Basterot, whose villa lay in an inlet of the sea about six miles away at Duras? When they arrived Lady Gregory was having tea there. De Basterot had become her one real friend in Galway, being not only well-born but able to talk to her about literature, music and art, and give her the gossip from his literary friends in Paris and Rome. She loved the story of how, when Paul Bourget had come to stay, the Count's valet who brought him from the station had pointed to the Atlantic and said in French, 'There is the sea which washes America and the property of 'sieur le comte.'

When Edward arrived with Yeats it turned out that the Count wanted to have a talk with his cousin about some business matters which were private. Leaving the pair alone, Yeats and Lady Gregory went into the steward's office for a cup of tea. We can see the two of them: the poet with his raven black hair and intense dark eyes and olive skin sitting opposite this small demure lady with her quick mind and eager response to ideas. Did she fall in love with him then? Maybe. Many women had done before. When she found that this heart was already elsewhere she was to work for him in recognition of his greatness as a poet and completely without jealousy.

Yeats told her how he had wanted a theatre in Ireland because politics and the church had created listeners. The intellectual communion he wanted between writer and people could come in this way, as it could not through the novel or verse. Dublin was in the grip of the commercial theatre: English touring companies or local groups performing melodramas on popular national subjects; at best Boucicault with his ear for dialogue. But there was no intellectual commitment as the theatre of Scandinavia had or Lugné Pöe and Antoine in Paris, Grein and Archer in London. His own play *The Countess Cathleen* was ready for production, he told her. He wanted to form a company in London to present it. Edward, in despair of getting his *The Heather Field* produced in an English-speaking milieu, had proposed a German production.

Lady Gregory was thrilled. Here was her chance to work for 'the intellectual movement'. Tentatively she suggested putting on the plays in Ireland. Yeats would at first have dismissed the idea as unworkable. Some years before he had wanted to tour Ireland presenting Irish plays but had been unable to get his project off the ground. But as Lady Gregory explained her plan to him, he with his practical mind would foresee possibilities. As wife of the former Governor of Ceylon she had friends in high places. During her travels and as hostess for Sir William in London she had met many who could help just the sort of project Yeats and Martyn wished to launch: Lord Dufferin the Viceroy of India, Lord Ardilaun; the Duchess of St Alban's; the Lord Chief Justice of Ireland, the Right Honourable Horace Plunkett, William Hartpole Lecky the historian and MP were some of the names she mentioned. Lady Gregory's plan was to hire a theatre in Dublin by public subscription to present the plays. She would subscribe the first £25 and the other subscribers would be asked to guarantee £300 to enable the group to present a season of plays every year for three seasons. By the time Edward and his cousin emerged from their business affairs, Yeats had been converted to the scheme by Lady Gregory's enthusiasm and commonsense approach. The four of them went out on to the lawn as the rain had cleared. It was one of those Irish days when the sun continually breaks through the rainclouds and across the lonely inlet they could see the green-washed mountains changing colour under the drifting clouds. There Yeats explained what Augusta proposed to do. Edward agreed almost immediately and the Irish Literary Theatre was born.

A few days later Edward and Willie came over from Tulira to Coole to draft the letter which would set out their aims to potential subscribers. Lady Gregory had some doubts about the use of the word 'Celtic' in the opening sentence. She thought it a bit vague, but 'Celtic' was fashionable at the time so they decided to use it. (Later when Lady Gregory would be asked what was the meaning of the Celtic movement, she used to reply that 'it was a movement to persuade the Scots to begin buying our books while we continued not to buy theirs'.)

> We propose to have performed in Dublin [the letter began] in the spring of every year, certain Celtic and Irish plays, which whatever be their degree of excellence will be written with a high ambition, and so to build up a Celtic and Irish school of dramatic literature. We hope to find in Ireland an uncorrupted and imaginative audience trained to listen by its passion

for oratory, and believe that our desire to bring upon the stage the deeper thoughts and emotions of Ireland will ensure for us a tolerant welcome, and that freedom to experiment which is not found in theatres in England, and without which no new movement in art or literature can succeed. We will show that Ireland is not the home of buffoonery and of easy sentiment, as it has been represented, but the home of ancient idealism. We are confident of the support of all Irish people, who are weary of misrepresentation, in carrying out a work that is outside all the political questions that divide us.

Yeats was clearly responsible for many of the ideas expressed in the letter. They represented the philosophy he had been expounding for a decade previously. One phrase in the letter is obviously his – 'an uncorrupted and imaginative audience trained to listen by its passion for oratory'. This is a throwback to John F. Taylor and the impression his public speaking had made on Yeats, who recognised it as part of an oratorical tradition that was still demanded in Ireland if a speaker was to touch the popular imagination.

The response to the letter was immediate. Almost all of Lady Gregory's candidates replied with generous guarantees (Lord Dufferin sent his in advance). Unlikely prospects like Mahaffy turned up trumps – even if there was a slight edge in his response.

I am ready to risk £5 for your scheme and hope they may yet play their drama in Irish. It will be as intelligible to the nation as Italian, which we so often hear upon our stage.

Lady Gregory was particularly pleased to hear from Aubrey de Vere, a friend of Wordsworth, whom she had met as a young girl in a neighbour's house. Once she had gone into the hills, in deference to his admiration for Wordsworth, to read the whole of 'The Excursion', and had stayed on the side of Slieve Echte determined to finish it until she saw the sun come behind the Clare Mountains. 'Whatever develops the genius of Ireland,' the old poet wrote,

> must in the most effectual way benefit her; and in Ireland's genius I have long been a strong believer. Circumstances of very various sorts have hitherto tended much to retard the development of that genius; but it cannot fail to make itself recognised before very long, and Ireland will have cause for gratitude to all those who have hastened the coming of that day.

As well as titled subscribers the Irish Nationalist politicians wrote in, and there was an impressive response from John Redmond, William O'Brien and John Dillon. Then an obstacle presented itself. It was found that arising out of an eighteenth-century Act of Parliament it would be illegal in Dublin to present plays in halls other than regular theatres. As theatres like the Gaiety, the Royal and the Queen's were beyond the means of the Irish Literary Theatre, the only hope was that a change in the law would allow them to give their performance in a concert hall or a similar unlicensed building. Lady Gregory immediately set out to mobilise her forces. She wrote to William Lecky, MP who replied agreeably that the Local Government (Ireland) Bill which was going through Parliament at that time might be the best place to have a clause inserted which would enable the Irish Literary Theatre to have its performances. Yeats and Lady Gregory went immediately to London where they spent much time in the lobby of the House talking and writing letters. In the end a subsection was added to Clause 59 which provided that the Lord Lieutenant could authorise, on the application of the County Council, the performance of a stage play or dramatic entertainment in a room or building if the profits (as they would be in the Irish Literary Theatre) were to be devoted to the fine arts. This was exactly the sort of business tangle on which the Irish Literary Theatre could have foundered, had it not been for Lady

Gregory's ingenuity. She had a real flair for taking on the establishment and getting the best out of them. It was her stamina and resolution which more than anything else was to save the Irish Theatre movement in its various crises in later years.

In May 1898 Synge had set out for the Aran Islands. He was to pay five visits there before 1903. He was immediately captivated by the people. They seemed to him to have something of the alienation of the artist in their daily lives which were lived outside the conventions of modern society. Wind, sea and island sky seemed to have played a part in the shaping of their personalities; even their language seemed touched by the intensity of the landscape around them. Daily they fought the sullen fields where the bare rock protruded through the sandy soil and the carnivorous sea which claimed so many of the menfolk, none of whom could swim. They seemed to have found an alliance with the forces of nature which enabled them to accept with stoicism the most tragic episodes in their lives.

After he had installed himself on the most remote of the three islands, Synge wrote:

> With this limestone Inishmaan, I am in love and hear with galling jealousy of the various priests and scholars who have lived here before me. They have grown to me as the former lover of one's mistresses, horrible existences haunting with dressed kisses the lips she presses to your own.

He was captivated by the light which heightened every ripple in the sea and crevice in the cliffs. The men dressed in white tweed waistcoats and flared trousers skipping nimbly across the rocky soil in their cowskin slippers, and the women with their flaming red petticoats and black shawls, seemed almost unreal in this vivid light and provided as much variety for the eye as a picture from the East.

One factor which enabled him to enter into their lives

was that he spoke the same language as the people. By the time he left the island for the last time in 1903, Synge had become fluent in Gaelic. Then too, his fiddle came in useful. Soon he had mastered Irish jigs and reels and slow airs, and he would sit at night near the firelight in the cottages and play his airs for the dancing boys and girls. The complete lack of artificiality in the islands seems to have allowed another side of Synge to surface. Perhaps to overcome his shyness, he had mastered on his own a number of tricks which he could show off when he wanted to. He could, for instance, lift a poker with his bare feet and rake the fire with it. Turning his back towards a key placed on the floor, he could bend down, place his head through his legs and pick it up with his teeth. These sleights delighted the islanders, and, along with his fiddle and his knowledge of their language, he built up an intimacy which shattered the restrictions that might have come from class distinction. They called him 'duine uasal', literally 'noble person'. Soon he had made friends among the islanders who talked to him as freely as they would to their own. He found himself an object of attraction to young girls who would walk with him by the seashore hand in hand, and kiss with him when they had a mind to. He reflected upon one of them in his diaries:

... her face came with me all day among the rocks. She is Madonna-like, yet has a rapt majesty as far from easy exaltation as from the maternal comeliness of Raphael's later style. The expression of her eyes is so overwhelmingly beautiful that I remember no single quality of her.

He was wonder-struck as he heard an illiterate islander on 'a wet rock in the Atlantic' tell him tales that took him to the sunshine of the Arno or the vineyards of Würzburg on the Main, stories that had travelled through Persia and Egypt before being finally collected by Renaissance scholars, but which were still alive on the lips of these people on the last islands of Europe.

We can imagine Synge's excitement as the music of the islanders' speech began to catch his ear. He must have known that if he could set it down in some form and transfer its melody to English, he would have brought a new sound to literature. Later he would be accused of distorting and exaggerating the people's speech. But Synge could have answered that there was not a phrase in his dialogue for which he could not show an equivalent in his notebooks. His characters have often been accused of using poetic images that could not have formed part of a peasant's heritage. But Hyde and Lady Gregory, too, found actual poetry on the lips of the people which found its way into their speech as naturally as a new slang word will achieve popular acceptance. For instance, in *The Playboy of the Western World*, Synge has the hero lament that he is going to lose the girl he loves:

And I after seeing the love light of the star of knowledge shining from her brow. . . .

Synge could turn to Douglas Hyde's *Love Songs of Connacht* and in the poem 'A Ogànaigh an Chúil Cheangailte', collected by Hyde among the reapers, show that there was a similar image:

And I thought after that you were a lamp from God, or that you were the Star of Knowledge going before me and after me.

His critics would later say it was blasphemous to have Christy Mahon say in *The Playboy of the Western World* that he would be so delighted kissing Pegeen's 'puckered lips' that he would:

Feel a sort of pity for the Lord God, is all ages sitting lonesome in His golden chair.

But Lady Gregory had come across a similar image in a song sung throughout Galway, 'Una Bhán':

I'd rather be beside her on the couch ever kissing her, than be sitting in Heaven on a chair of the Trinity.

Dublin Castle

The Viceregal Lodge in Phoenix Park

The Viceregal household at a garden party in 1886

William Butler Yeats as a young man, by
the Victorian photographer Hollyer

George Russell (AE) as a young man, by
John B. Yeats

The young Oscar Wilde

Edward Dowden, Professor of English at Trinity College and at one time Yeats's father's closest friend there

Trinity College at the time of Dowden and Mahaffy

John O'Leary by J. B. Yeats

A view of a section of Woburn Walk
where W. B. Yeats lived
from the mid-1890s

A rare early photograph of Maud Gonne, who arrived on Yeats's doorstep 'like
a being from another world'

W. B. Yeats, by Augustus John

The Silver Spears Mountains round Dublin Bay. Shaw called it more beautiful than the Bay of Naples

A rare photograph of Parnell's funeral procession. It was taken from the steps of the Royal Exchange (now the City Hall) beside Dublin Castle

Parnell's funeral procession in Sackville Street (now O'Connell Street)

T. W. Rolleston at 19

Yeats reading in Rolleston's garden, 1894

Synge's method was to take a number of phrases and orchestrate them so that they acquired a marching rhythm of their own, based on a determined number of stresses which gave the effect on the stage of poetic dialogue, but, since their origins were in living speech, ensured that there were naturalistic overtones. In this way, Synge could use passages of extravagant humour and passion and yet remain not unconvincing to an audience.

It's that you'd surely say if you see him and he after drinking for weeks rising up in the red dawn, or before it maybe, and going out into the yard as naked as an ash tree in the moon of May, and shying clods against the visage of the stars till he'd put the fear of death into the banbhs and the screeching sows,

or (on the lips of the Playboy's father):

Oh, I'm raving with a madness that would fright the world! There was one time I seen ten scarlet divils letting on they'd cork my spirit in a gallon can; and one time I see rats as big as badgers sucking the life blood from the butt of my lug; but I never till this day confused that dribbling idiot with a likely man.

There is a lilt even to his short sentences:

Do you hear them cheering him in the zig zags of the road?

For I'm mounted in the spring tide of the stars of luck!

. . . with a man who killed his father, holding danger from the door.

An example of how Synge could orchestrate ordinary speech into heightened dialogue for the stage can be seen in his note of a conversation he had with one of his closest friends on the island, Mairtin O'Conghile. One day, as they were fishing from the cliffs and arguing about the advantages and disadvantages of remaining a bachelor, the old man said to him:

Listen to what I'm telling you. A man who is not married is not better than an old jackass. He goes into his sister's house and into his brother's house: he eats a bit in this place and bit in another place but he has no home for himself; like an old jackass straying on the rocks.

This became, by the time it was used by Synge in one of his plays, an extended melody with its syllables carefully shaped to suggest the lonesome bleat of an animal astray:

What's a single man, I ask you, eating a bit in one house and drinking a sup in another, and he with no place of his own, like an old braying jackass strayed upon the rocks.

Anglo-Irish dialogue – that is, English spoken by people who had previously spoken Irish – had begun as early as the seventeenth century. It had crept into literature in the work of nineteenth-century novelists who used it, often in its crudest form, for humour and diversion but with no hint of poetry. Synge recognised in it structures that could be used to shape rhythmic dialogue, but this was because, unlike the majority of the novelists, he knew the original Irish from which it derived. He wrote only for himself and not for any social or political need. Whenever he wrote of Wicklow, Kerry or Galway he would listen, as George Moore said, 'like a hare in a gap' for the singular phrase that would light up a sentence, and commit it to his notebook. 'Synge,' Yeats said later, 'was the man that we needed because he is the only man I have ever known incapable of a political thought or a humanitarian purpose. He could walk the roadside all day with some poor man without any desire to do him good, or for any reason except that he liked him.'

It was his passion for slipping away from the city when he was a boy and losing himself in the Dublin and Wicklow hills that had given Synge early on the awareness of the solitary life of the vagabond. He had grown up in a Georgian house on an elegant park only three miles from the city centre. Yet in a thirty-minute walk across the fields, he could be in the company of travelling people, vagabonds, who lived out their lives alone in the mystery of the glens. Not long before, within seven miles of Dublin there had been people who spoke only Irish. It was these Wicklow vagrants who had first introduced him as a boy to the wonder of the wandering life. He thought that their vulnerability to the strange colours in the clouds, the voices that whisper in the dark, the smell of spring and autumnal smoulder had inculcated in them the artistic response to life. He noted that their wit, whether in gratitude or abuse, had a quality which distinguished them from rural beggars in other countries: and he was struck one day by the grandiosity of a man of a hundred and one who had begged by the side of the road with the pride of an emperor. After a day spent in the hills Synge used to return to Orwell Park at the dawn of night, with the smell of hemlock, the silent flight of the moths and the hooting of the owls making the life of the city seem as strange and remote to him as Baghdad or Persepolis.

While the vagabond world did not exist in the Aran Islands as it did in the glens of Wicklow, he was able to recognize in the society there a similar sense of alienation to that which he had encountered in Wicklow as a boy. One had prepared him for the other and from the blend he determined to make his art.

2   Life at Coole

Coole was to become a quick forge and working house of thought for the writers of the renaissance. Lady Gregory early realised her gift as a patron of the arts and made her country house available as a working place for those whom she would invite down. After Yeats's first visit she asked him to bring down AE, whom he had talked about a great deal. The following month the two poets arrived at Gort Station. Lady Gregory was surprised to find AE 'a quiet gentleman, simple and composed'. Yeats had described him to her as resembling Michael Robartes in *Rosa Alchemica* and she expected someone with red hair, fierce eyes and rough clothes as Yeats had described him in his tales 'something between a peasant and a debauchee'. The only streak of wildness he showed was when he told her, 'This life bores me. I am waiting for a higher one.'

The following day she rowed the poets across the lake to show them a cromlech. As they sat in front of it Lady Gregory got the feeling that something was about to happen. Sure enough, moments later, AE saw a purple druid. After this they rowed home. Years later Yeats recalled to her another incident when the three of them had gone to the old castle at Balinamantane and had met an old lady who had seen a ghostly drawbridge over the moat and women looking from the windows. Yeats believed that AE 'hated to be put to see anyone else's ghosts' and his friend had wandered round in a sulk. When Yeats asked him hadn't he seen any ghosts, AE replied 'Oh, yes, I do, but they're a low lot.'

At night Lady Gregory listened to the two poets talking. One evening they discussed Shelley on whom Yeats was writing an essay. AE said that it would 'make people angry to be told he had a meaning because what people go to poetry for is to escape from conviction'. Yeats's reply was that 'Shelley was not a political reformer but a prophet with the eternal vision that is never welcome. But people want reformation not revelation which offers nothing but itself'.

AE did not like Swinburne, 'there is nothing but words, nothing behind, but Wordsworth had faith behind him'. Neither did AE like 'the Water of the Wondrous Isles': he said it was mere decoration, an imitation of Malory. Yeats maintained it was no more a pastiche than Rossetti's work was of early Italian pictures.

Lady Gregory has recorded snatches of Yeats's conversation on these evenings:

Goethe has a great genius occasionally impeded by restive fits of intelligence.

All the churches are in danger and they ought to unite and stand together like cows in a storm.

Turkeys have always a look of being related to the county families, and living on a reduced income.

An important visitor to Coole who helped to further Lady Gregory's interest in Irish culture was Douglas Hyde. She met him one day at Tulira, where she was staying with Edward Martyn, coming up the driveway pushing a bicycle. He had intended to come all the way by train. But he had got out at Craughwell to collect some folklore he knew was in the neighbourhood. Lady Gregory was delighted to meet him and she spent the afternoon showing him a cromlech at Cruagh, and introducing him to one of her Irish-speaking labourers, Foley, who to her delight gave Hyde a new story of the ancient band of warriors, the Fianna. They struck up an instant friendship, Hyde with his alert eye discerning that

197

Augusta would be a useful convert to the Gaelic League, and she seeing him as a valuable teacher in the work she hoped to do for Ireland. She had been learning Irish from O'Growney's grammar and by the following Christmas, when Hyde came to stay, her knowledge of the language had become competent with the help of Norma Borthwick from the London Gaelic League, whom she had over to stay with her. One evening Hyde and Miss Borthwick put on a Punch and Judy show in Irish. Later Lady Gregory used to say half jokingly that she held that 'the beginning of modern Irish drama was in the winter of 1898 at a school fête at Coole when Douglas Hyde and Miss Norma Borthwick acted in Irish in a Punch and Judy show: and the delighted children went back to tell their parents what grand curses Hyde had put on the baby and the policeman – the only character who spoke English.'

Augusta worked earnestly for Hyde, tracing a manuscript he was looking for to a baker's shop in Galway, and bringing one of the local men to him who gave him the original of one of the most famous poems of the revival: by Raftery, celebrating the beauty of a Galway girl, Mary Hynes. Later she found seventeen poems by Raftery from a stone cutter near Killeenan.

Hyde helped to give Augusta confidence in her use of Irish. She would never claim to be a scholar but she read the language well and spoke it competently. The summer after she had met Hyde she was delighted when, at dinner with Lord Morris in Spiddal and hearing Irish disparaged, some sayings were quoted to her and she was able to translate them.

Knowing Irish opened up a whole new world for Augusta. Now she could talk the language to the local people and get them to tell her the old tales. In the Gort workhouse she heard two old women arguing about the merits of two rival poets they had seen and heard in their childhood:

One old woman, who was from Kilchreest, said: 'Raftery hadn't a stim of sight; and he travelled the whole nation; and he was the best poet that ever was, and the best fiddler. It was always at my father's house, opposite the big tree, that he used to stop when he was in Kilchreest. I often saw him; but I didn't take much notice of him then, being a child; it was after that I used to hear so much about him. Though he was blind, he could serve himself with his knife and fork as well as any man with his sight. I remember the way he used to cut the meat – across, like this. Callinan was nothing to him.'

The other old woman, who was from Craughwell, said: 'Callinan was a great deal better than him; and he could make songs in English as well as in Irish; Raftery would run from where Callinan was. And he was a nice respectable man, too, with cows and sheep, and a kind man. He would never put anything that wasn't nice into a poem, and he would never run anyone down; but if you were the worst in the world, he'd make you the best in it; and when his wife lost her beetle, he made a song of fifteen verses about it.'

'Well,' the Kilchreest old woman admitted, 'Raftery would run people down; he was someway bitter; and if he had anything against a person, he'd give him a great lacerating. But there were more for him than for Callinan; some used to say Callinan's songs were too long.'

'I tell you,' said the other, 'Callinan was a nice man and a nice neighbour. Raftery wasn't fit to put beside him. Callinan was a man that would go out of his own back door, and make a poem about the four quarters of the earth. I tell you, you would stand in the snow to listen to Callinan!' But, just then, a bedridden old woman suddenly sat up and began to sing Raftery's 'Bridget Vesach' as long as her breath lasted; so the last word was for him after all.

Augusta had become quite a collector of Raftery's work. She had found his grave at Killeenan and used to go by moonlight to her gamekeeper's cottage to get help in translating the poems from a borrowed manuscript.

One of these summers she went to a 'feis' (a celebration of poems and Irish music) in Craughwell and noted the Aran people who had come in from the islands, the men in their loose flannel jackets and the women in crimson. There was piping and tin whistle playing and now and then little barefoot boys would go up on the platform and sing songs of heartbreak and sorrow.

> A woman with madder-dyed petticoat sang the lament of an emigrant going across the great sea, telling how she got up at daybreak to look at the places she was going to leave, Ballinrobe and the rest; and how she envied the birds that were free of the air, and the beasts that were free of the mountain, and were not forced to go away. Another song that was sung was the Jacobite one, with the refrain that has been put into English – 'Seaghan O'Dwyer a Gleanna, we're worsted in the game!'

Later that night she noticed a crowd round an old man who was making many gestures with his hands and saying 'tha se beo, tha se beo' ('he is living, he is living'). The old man was referring to Parnell and emphasising his argument by saying that none had ever actually seen the great man dead.

> The rising again of Ireland, of her old speech, of her lost leader, dreams all, as we are told. But here, on the edge of the world, dreams are real things, and every heart is watching for the opening of one or another grave.

Yeats's obsession with Maud Gonne was undermining his health, and believing it might help to restore him, Lady Gregory brought Yeats round with her from cottage to cottage when she was collecting folklore. Yeats later wrote that she collected 200,000 words for her book *Visions and Beliefs in the West of Ireland*. As he entered the door of a peasant's cottage, Yeats would tell her that they were passing out of Europe as that word is understood. She said to him one day as they left a cottage: 'I've longed to turn Catholic that I might be closer to the people, but you have taught me that paganism brings me nearer still.' He in his turn was touched when an old man said to him one day: 'She has been like a serving maid among us. She is plain and simple like the mother of God and that was the greatest lady that ever lived.'

Augusta would listen and then write her account afterwards. Later she maintained that she had trained her memory till she could hardly make a mistake; as always, she took a professional attitude towards any work she undertook. She also used to say it was studying Irish history for the purpose of editing *Mr Gregory's Letter Box* that made her an Irish nationalist and in support of her belief she would quote Sir Frederick Burton agreeing with her when she said: 'I defy anyone to study Irish history without getting a dislike and distrust of England.' After Parnell's death she had framed the last photograph taken of him and written under it:

Oh, I hae dream'd a dreary dream
Beyond the Isle of Skye:
I saw a dead man win a fight
And I think that man was I.

She had shown nationalist tendencies as early in 1897 at the time of the Jubilee of Queen Victoria. Lord Gough of Lough Cutra Castle had ordered a bonfire for his estate in honour of the occasion and had asked his neighbours to do likewise. Lady Gregory replied to him that she would not celebrate the Jubilee on account of the Queen's neglect of the country. She remembered that the Prince had told her husband when he was Governor of Ceylon that he had wanted to go Ireland and the Queen had prevented him.

'We are not working for Home Rule, we are preparing for it,' Augusta said, but as she came closer to the people through her work, she began to understand the nationalist point of view more and more. We get a glimpse of her sympathies during the Boer War from her collecting of a number of anti-English ballads that were current at the time, and quoting in her diary with approval the words of an old Galway miller who had said to her:

> Look now, though I don't like to be saying it, look at the English, the way they went against those poor Boers to take their living from them and their land, and they with plenty of their own before. Covetousness led them to it, and curiosity. They thought to go shooting them just as if they were snipe or woodcocks. And it wasn't long before they were stretched in the field, and the Royalty of England along with them, and not a knocker in London town without a bit of crêpe on it.

Later she would approve of the stand made by the rebels in 1916 and write a stirring ballad about them. Like Yeats she had been captivated by John O'Leary's brand of aristocratic nationalism. When Yeats told her that O'Leary had said to him one day, 'I think it is probable that the English national character is finer than ours but that does not make me want to be an Englishman', she asked Yeats would he bring her to meet the old rebel. She thought when she met him that he was like an ancient prophet understanding his people's doom, with his massive head and 'eyes full of smouldering fire'. Gradually the link between her and the county began to weaken. It was 'the return to the people, the reunion after rejection, the taking and the giving, is it not the perfect circle, the way of nature, the eternal wedding ring'. One day, coming back from collecting folklore in the cottages, she found herself in the middle of the County Galway fox hunt, coming back from cub hunting. As the English MFH and his wife rode by, she wondered if they had ever heard of Raftery whose last road this had been. She decided that they had not.

Yeats went back to Dublin after this interlude but at the end of July he came to Coole to stay for two months, a recuperative process for him, with nerves wrecked by his failure to persuade Maud Gonne to respond to his love.

He would have arrived at Coole through a long avenue of arching ilex which gave the impression of a green tunnel out of which he would have emerged on the front lawn of a small Georgian house, somewhat plain with a porch and two sombre wings. At the side there were orchards and pleasure gardens, one with a large catalpa tree where Lady Gregory liked to sit and write her letters and plays. He was to discover there the many woods, all with different names, where a visitor could be buried in a vast cathedral-like atmosphere of green light, before coming out on the silent and mysterious lake where many swans had made their nesting place.

Inside the house there were the accumulations of three generations of Gregorys ('Balzac would have given twenty pages to the stairs,' someone had said). The walls were hung with Persian helmets, Indian shields, swords in jewelled scabbards, stuffed birds, signed photographs of Tennyson, Mark Twain, Thackeray, Browning. In the drawing rooms and sitting rooms were Persian or Mogul paintings, great earthenware urns and silver bowls, with paintings by Canaletto, engravings and mezzotints of friends of the Gregory family, Pitt, Wellesley, Fox, Palmerston, Gladstone. On one wall hung a framed letter from Burke to the Gregory who had been Chairman of the East India Company, saying that in his old age 'he committed to his care the people of India.'

It was in such an atmosphere that Yeats's troubled temperament found itself at rest. The continuity, the sense of order, the decorum, steadied the side of him which might have gone askew with his magical practices and his preoccupation with fairy lore. Lady Gregory was a constant strength to him. Every day she had soup sent up to his rooms at intervals to make sure that his strength was kept at a certain level. Nobody was allowed to disturb the poet. His whole day was organised. When he came down for meals she respected his wish if he seemed too exhausted to converse and remained silent, an heroic gesture in someone as anxious as she must have been for literary talk. He spent much of his time walking by the woods and the lake. 'I was to know later,' Yeats said, 'the edges of that lake better than any spot on earth, to know it in all the changes of the seasons, to find there always some new beauty.' Here he first saw the nine-and-fifty swans,

> Unwearied still, lover by lover,
> They paddle in the cold
> Companionable streams or climb the air;
> Their hearts have not grown old;
> Passion or conquest, wander where they will,
> Attend upon them still.
>
> But now they drift on the still water,
> Mysterious, beautiful;
> Among what rushes will they build,
> By what lake's edge or pool
> Delight men's eyes when I awake some day
> To find they have flown away?

He conveyed some of the peace he found at Coole in 'In the Seven Woods':

> I have heard the pigeons of the Seven Woods
> Make their faint thunder, and the garden bees
> Hum in the lime tree flowers; and put away
> The unavailing outcries and old bitterness
> That empty the heart. I have forgot awhile
> Tara uprooted, and new commonness
> Upon the throne and crying about the streets
> And hanging its paper flowers from post to post,
> Because it is alone of all things happy.
> I am contented, for I know that Quiet
> Wanders laughing and eating her wild heart
> Among pigeons and bees, while that Great Archer,
> Who but awaits His hour to shoot, still hangs
> A cloudy quiver over Pairc-na-lee.

When his nervous system had become more adjusted he confided his infatuation with Maud Gonne to Lady Gregory: 'I might as well have offered devotion to an

image in a milliner's window or to a statue in a museum.'
He may well have shown Augusta a certain poem he had
written cautioning lovers not to let their beloved know
the certainty of their affection.

> Never give all the heart, for love
> Will hardly seem worth thinking of
> To passionate women if it seem
> Certain, and they never dream
> That it fades out from kiss to kiss;
> For everything that's lovely is
> But a brief, dreamy, kind delight.
> O never give the heart outright,
> For they, for all smooth lips can say,
> Have given their hearts up to the play.
> And who could play it well enough
> If deaf and dumb and blind with love?
> He that made this knows all the cost,
> For he gave all his heart and lost.

To these confidences Lady Gregory, thirteen years older
than the poet, responded with sympathy. She was the
rock to which he would cling during the storms of his life
during the next nineteen years until he married, and
even that was partially arranged by Lady Gregory. 'I
cannot realise the world without her,' he wrote later.

> She had been to me mother, friend, sister and brother.
> She brought to my wavering thoughts steadfast
> nobility – all day the thought of losing her is a
> conflagration in the rafters.

3   Life at Coole II

When Horace Plunkett was a cowboy in Wyoming one of his friends said about him that 'that guy can't keep his mind on anything long enough to boil an egg'. Plunkett's leaping mind seemed to reflect itself in his walking, which was a sort of scurrying along, as if he were determined to do as much as he could in a short life. On the Rocky Mountain ranges he rode shirtless, believing this was the best way to cure the tuberculosis which was the reason for his coming to America from Dunsany Castle, County Meath at the age of twenty-five. He was remarkably successful, running ranching companies and doing much of the physical work of a cow-puncher at the same time. But his family, one of the oldest in Ireland, needed him back after his father's death and Horace returned to Dunsany in 1891 to manage the affairs of his nephew, the sixteenth Lord, till he came of age. Back in Ireland his restless energy expressed itself in the founding of a co-operative movement for farmers. He recognised that the Irish peasant, coming into proprietorship of land for the first time in centuries, had no concept of how to sell his produce. This was more often exchanged at the local publican's or grocer's, for flour or porter or stamps, than sold for financial profit. Plunkett wanted the people to combine for business purposes to help themselves. He took off on a massive tour of Ireland in 1893, selecting with an unerring eye those whom he knew would be useful in organising his movement. He then achieved what amounted to a miracle in the context of the Ireland of the nineties, by getting representatives of all parties and religions to unite, in 1894, on a single platform to form an organisation for the improvement of rural life. This was called the Irish Agricultural Organisation Society. Believing that it would help if he had himself elected to Parliament, Plunkett ran for South Dublin in 1896 and won the seat. By 1898 he had established a department of agricultural and technical education (the first department to be created outside the inefficient Castle administration) which he presided over in the guise of vice-president.

Plunkett was to become one of the most remarkable figures in Irish public life. Though he seemed to be in perpetual ill-health, and seldom in a condition where he was not recovering from an operation, he would work up to fifteen hours a day. He had the gift of getting the best out of those who worked with him and, though not an orator, he invented splendid slogans like 'Anglo-Irish history is for Englishmen to remember, for Irishmen to forget'; and 'The more business in politics and the less politics in business, the better for both'.

In the summer of 1896 Horace Plunkett got wind that something was happening at Lady Gregory's Coole that he ought to be in on, and hurried down immediately so as not to miss an opportunity.

Drove to Coole Park [he wrote in his diary] to spy out the land for the IAOS. Lady Gregory had a meeting of influential farmers and I gave them a discourse (dull) . . . W.B. Yeats the young poet, a rebel and mystic and an ass, but really a genius in a queer way, I believe, and Edward Martyn a clever writer of a more imaginative kind, were fellow guests. It was interesting and not by any means a waste of time. Galway is a great surprise to me.

Lady Gregory was full of praise for Horace Plunkett's helping 'the unloosed imagination to practical uses' and organised a co-operative meeting for him while he was at Coole, where he won the hearts of the local farmers. Unaware that Yeats had perfected his oratory at political meetings, Plunkett was surprised at the poet's ability to hold an audience when he spoke at the co-operative:

A real talent; like a rose leaf falling among a lot of agricultural implements.

Augusta was delighted to have Horace in her circle, as she rightly sensed he could be useful in helping her to overcome some of the difficulties she envisaged in her work for Ireland in the imaginative field. She could not have foreseen, however, a most unlikely result of Plunkett's visit to Coole – that AE would join the co-operative movement. An organiser was required to tour the congested parts of the west of Ireland on behalf of Plunkett's organisation. It was Yeats, now in Plunkett's good books, who brought up AE's name. On the surface no one looked less like organising the rural farmers. But Yeats recognised that years of work in the accounts department of Pim's had given AE a firm grasp of financial matters and a head for figures. Also, Yeats was coming into the period when one of his fundamental beliefs was that the truth the artist seeks 'must come from the earth' and he probably felt that contact with the primitive peasantry of the west would further aid AE's development as a poet.

Whatever his reasons, Plunkett acted on this suggestion of Yeats and, after consultation with one of his assistants Patrick Hannon (later Sir Patrick Hannon), approached AE. To his surprise the poet accepted the post and was soon off on his travels, his bicycle stowed in the luggage van of the train so that he could reach the remote villages he had to visit many miles from railway stations. AE wrote to Lady Gregory from Ballina in January 1898, a month after he had started his organising, telling her with some satisfaction that he had founded three Raffiesen banks already in rural villages. He was reading Tolstoy and Henley and Thoreau for inspiration, he told her, but the poverty depressed him:

The soul in me has never spoken since I started. I am devoid of anything mystical at present and know more of the price of eggs than of what is going on behind the veil.

But on his travels he met people whom he could not know of from his experiences of city life. There was a handsome farmer in Crossmolina who had seen fairies fighting under the Nephin Mountains – and the mountains themselves were

a miracle of pure light and dreamy colour. The snow is glittering on the hills round the world and the mighty Nephin half purple and half white over the pale green of the fields is really not of this earth at all.

One night a little boy came and led him over a mountain to a meeting and when the meeting was over the little hand was there to take him back again. Another day he was half-frozen going forty miles to Belmullet in an outside car, and a young girl beside him kept him entertained and warm with Irish stories and quoting bits of poetry. A beggar said to him one day: 'The white sun of Heaven does not look down on poorer people than this man and myself.' And he heard another say to a lady he knew: 'Ah, sure your shadow is only a light at the door.'

Knowing perhaps that Lady Gregory would not approve of faint-heartedness, AE kept his complaints for Yeats, to whom he wrote in the second month of his tour saying he had enough of 'cold bed and bad bacon'. Lady Gregory continued to encourage him, however, and in 1898 AE became Assistant Secretary to the IAOS and in 1901 was allowed home from his travels to edit the co-operative weekly magazine *The Irish Homestead*.

Later Lady Gregory would glory in the fact that AE had been summoned to America and England to lecture on co-operation and loved to tell how when he dined out at 10 Downing Street he talked to the Prime Minister of the day 'like a father'.

* * *

Hyde now spent to good deal of time at Coole collecting folklore and translating. Believing that he had weak lungs Augusta mothered him as she had Yeats. She would lure him from his desk after she felt he had worked hard enough, with the promise of sport on the lake. The gamekeeper would be instructed to have boat and guns ready. Soon Hyde would be on the water, the cobwebs in his mind swept away in the pursuit of wild duck. One day she left him with a bundle of blank paper and came back in the evening to find that he already had completed a play and was out shooting on the lake. After dinner he read her what he had written that afternoon, a piece entitled *The Lost Saint*, and she was left with the feeling 'as if some beautiful blossom had fallen at my feet'.

The respect with which the local farmers treated Hyde thrilled her. One day she noticed him looking up to a man on a haystack who was discussing with him in Irish an ancient manuscript poem. She was amused, too, when certain elderly ladies who had heard that there had been someone out at Coole cover shooting, who talked Irish to the beaters, had remarked 'he cannot be a gentleman if he speaks Irish'. Another day, walking through her garden naming again and again this flower and that, Hyde remarked that if she just wrote down the names it would provide a sonnet ready made for Yeats.

John Quinn, an American visitor and a great patron of Yeats, Synge, Hyde and Lady Gregory, has given an account which captures the atmosphere of Coole in the changing years.

Yeats, Hyde, and I used to sit up every night until one or two in the morning, talking, it seems to me, about everything and everybody under the sky of Ireland, but chiefly about the Theatre of which Yeats's mind was full. These were wonderful nights, long nights filled with good talk, Yeats full of plans for the development of the Theatre. The mornings were devoted to work, the afternoons to out-of-doors, and the evenings to the reading of scenarios for plays, the reading of short plays in English by Lady Gregory and in Irish by Hyde. Lady Gregory and Hyde read out to us from time to time their translations of Irish songs and ballads, in the beautiful English of her books and of Hyde's *Love Songs of Connacht*. Yeats and Lady Gregory made a scenario of a play and Hyde spent three afternoons 'putting the Irish on it'.

It was Quinn who commissioned John Butler Yeats to paint a portrait of Douglas Hyde at Coole. The painter came down for some weeks and before he left was given the honour by Lady Gregory of being asked to carve his name on her tree. But she was not all that taken by his tendency to keep uncertain hours and his insistence on 'going his own way'. Socks were dropped here, articles of laundry there (as Lily Yeats later told her father's biographer). We can imagine that Augusta, having achieved a measure of control over Willie, was not at all pleased to discover in the father an iron resistance to any attempt to 'improve' him.

John Masefield and Bernard Shaw were others who came down to Coole once Augusta began to establish it as an imaginative centre. But her greatest pleasure, no matter how famous her visitors, would be to watch her first two poets, Yeats and AE, together.

June 20th 1900: AE is doing wonderful pictures, he has begun oils which have not the same charm as his pastels but are of course more lasting. The deep pools delight him. He has painted two figures raising a cup, and seven figures holding a sword (at the deep hole) and a Queen and some landscapes – I asked him what he thought these spirits are that he so certainly sees, and he said they are earth spirits that have not yet taken animal forms, but will probably, when our race is extinct, become a new race. He thinks them inferior to us, chiefly because, though more beautiful, they have not the look of being capable of complex emotions or of understanding the nature of sacrifice.

211

Anyone could see them, he says, who can detach the mind from the ordinary business of life and wait for them. He is surprised I cannot see them by the shadowy pools, but I say I am like Martha, careful and cumbered with much serving.

His idea of our life is that we are making a daily sacrifice consciously, but that the consciousness only comes in sleep, and cannot be remembered afterwards; and that the verse 'He giveth his beloved sleep' is really 'He gives to his beloved in sleep'. Even a drunkard is making a sacrifice in having consciously taken the nature of a drunkard to work off the evil of the race (but this I don't follow quite clearly).

Russell and Yeats drew the big tree at Raheen. Yeats made a charming sketch. Russell a charming one also, but with a rather dreadful figure with long ears under the tree. He says it was not very nice, but he would like to stroke it. When a man passed it shrank up, as if it would climb the tree backwards. I showed it to Maurteen who says his own brother-in-law had work to get his horse past that tree, one night, but he is surprised that Mr Russell can see these things in the daytime.

June 26th: All sketching. Evening AE and Yeats tease each other. AE tells how Yeats found a 'clairvoyant' in Miss S. and put her to look in a crystal, and invoke the Angel Gabriel. She looked and saw a Golden Palace. This was puzzling but she looked again, and saw a white-armed figure at the palace window. W.B.Y. was delighted, and prepared questions to put to the Archangel. But a rationalist who stood by observed that the shop opposite had had a lot of gilding about it which was reflected in the crystal and that there was a man in white shirt-sleeves cleaning the window, who was the archangel. W.B.Y. says then in return that he once said that one of AE's group dropped his Hs, AE replied that 'he functioned in a higher sphere'.

August 1st: They had a fiery argument in the woods

212

yesterday on the sword, whether it was the symbol of fire or air, and 'called each other all the names'; but were good friends in the evening. Y. has finished his lyric on the Withering of the Boughs. (At Chevy a woman had said to me, 'If you tell your dream to the trees, fasting, they will all wither.') AE has done, besides his spirit and landscape drawings, a charming little picture of Baby Brian for me. He says if he had money, he would go all over Ireland to look for the two men who are ruling its destinies at present. He has seen them and others have seen them in vision. One lives in a cottage beside a single line railway, a log of wood in front. He is oldish, with a golden beard. The other, young and dark, lives in a park alone. There is a third but he is vague; perhaps not in a physical body. The first time he saw them he was filled with energy and life, so that he worked without effort and with joy for a long time after. I suggest they were symbolic of the new spirit in people and landed gentry, but he declares they were real.

Yeats by now was in a sort of ectasy of discovery. Hyde had made him aware of how old men on the side of the road or in a cottage could celebrate a Galway beauty of fifty years before, 'as old men on the wall spoke of Helen of Troy'. He would hear them singing songs in their cabins which, after Hyde had translated them, he recognised as being written out of symbols that he himself was trying to capture in literature. Un-Romanised, God and nature in the perfection of the human soul seemed one to these people, so that when they sang of their lost nationhood it was in the idealised form of a woman:

Soft, soft Little Rose of the round white breasts,
'Tis thou has left a thousand pains in the centre of my
    heart:
Fly with me my thousand loves and leave the land,
And if I could would I not make a queen of thee, my
    Little Dark Rose,

Were it not that the rhythmic line is over-long, this could be from the court of Aquitaine; or that its sentiment is a trifle extravagant, the address of a Cavalier. Least of all does one think of it as a poet's address to his country in one of the traditional names which were used for Ireland in the seventeenth century, and that this was perfectly understood by the people when it was sung for them round their firesides or in the fields. 'It seemed,' wrote Yeats of this time,

> as if the ancient world lay all about us with its freedom of imagination, its delight in good stories, in man's face and woman's beauty, and that all we had to do was to make the town think as the country felt.

But though the poetic activity continued at Coole it did not interfere with the normal life of the country house:

> On Monday we went to Athenry for a cricket match, and beat the county again. Our men immensely proud [Lady Gregory's diary reads]. Cricket went on all the time. In the match at Athenry, Kiltartan beat the County by three runs, a great triumph. Robert made top score, twenty seven. Robert dreamed that Yeats wanted him to go with him and AE and see visions and he was going, and then he thought 'if I see visions it will spoil my eyesight, and I won't be able to play cricket' so he turned back.

The Robert referred to is Lady Gregory's son, who was now nineteen years of age. He had grown into a handsome young man who had boxed for Oxford and played cricket for Ireland and he was a fearless horseman whose feats on the hunting field Yeats celebrated in verse.

> At Mooneen he leaped a place
> So perilous that half the astonished meet
> Had shut their eyes: and where was it
> He rode a race without a bit?

Robert's ambition was to be an artist and, after studying

at the Slade and in Paris under Jacques Emile-Blanche, he would design numerous sets for the theatre movement as well as becoming a painter in his own right.

Yeats's visits with her to collect poetry from the people, and Hyde teaching her Irish encouraged Lady Gregory to try her hand at translation. She showed she had a gift for rendering Gaelic into English and retaining the original metre and the quality of the language. Yeats would later include five of her translations in the *Oxford Book of Modern Verse*, but there were many other fine pieces as well, 'The Song of Grainne over Diarmuid', 'The Lament for Fair-haired Donough', Raftery's 'Mary Hynes', 'A Poem Written in Time of Trouble By An Irish Priest Who Had Taken Orders In France', and 'Emer's Lament for Cuchulainn'. She knew, however, the limitations of translation and once lamented, after she had put English on a poem of Hyde's, that the sound of the sobbing wind which had filled the verse had vanished when it left the Irish. Her most beautiful translation is 'The Grief of a Girl's Heart' which was sung throughout Galway and which has that elemental sorrow which she felt she had failed to render in her attempt at Hyde's poem.

> O Donall og, if you go across the sea,
> Bring myself with you and do not forget it;
> And you will have a sweetheart for fair days and
>   market days,
> And the daughter of the King of Greece beside you at
>   night.
>
> You promised me, and you said a lie to me,
> That you would be before me where the sheep are
>   flocked;
> I gave a whistle and three hundred cries to you,
> And I found nothing there but a bleating lamb. . . .
>
> It was on that Sunday I gave my love to you;
> The Sunday that is last before Easter Sunday.
> And myself on my knees reading the Passion;
> And my two eyes giving love to you for ever. . . .

You have taken the east from me, you have taken the
  west from me;
You have taken what is before me and what is behind
  me;
You have taken the moon, you have taken the sun from
  me;
And my fear is great that you have taken God from me!

As her knowledge of Irish grew she found herself
enraged by those who looked down on Irish culture.
When she read in the autumn of 1899 that Dr Atkinson
of Trinity had told the Commission of Intermediate
Education that Gaelic literature was almost always
'intolerably low in tone with little idealism' she was
furious. This statement was followed up by Mahaffy
(who had not a word of Irish) telling the same Commission that 'all Irish literature is silly, indecent or
obscene'.

It was typical of Augusta that she would decide that
the best way to channel her anger was to do something
practical about the matter. She knew that in the Royal
Irish Academy were the transcripts of the saga tales
copied down by Eugene O'Curry. She had enough Irish
to translate these. The commentaries by German
scholars would not be a barrier to her as she had an
excellent knowledge of that language. For two years she
spent many hours writing down sagas and tales in the
Academy Library and checking her research against
other manuscripts that were preserved in the British
Museum. The result was *Cuchulainn of Muirthemne*,
and updating of O'Grady's *History of Ireland*, but told in
a style which was much closer to the Gaelic original
than his had been. She was now trying to evolve a style
of her own which derived from the English she had
heard spoken in the cottages and her knowledge of Irish
syntax. There is a certain element of artificiality in Lady
Gregory's 'Kiltartanese', as it is called (after Kiltartan
the neighbourhood around Coole), but it is hard to see
how better rendering of folk speech could have been
given without losing much of the poetry and natural

rhythm. The book was an instant success. Yeats wrote:

> If we will but tell these stories to our children, the land
> will begin again to be a holy land, as it was before men
> gave their hearts to Greece and Rome and Judea.

Eoin MacNeill, one of the founders of the Gaelic League, thought that they were the truest representation of the Irish heroic age ever seen in English, and his only regret was that she was 'investing the Anglo-Irish language with a literary dignity it has never hitherto possessed'. John Masefield wrote a touching letter in which he underlined the difference between the rural community that he had known in England and the one that Lady Gregory was in touch with in Ireland:

> All my boyhood I was near the earth and water among
> folks who held some old-world beliefs and a few thread-
> bare stories, so for an Englishman I was given a large
> measure of the best things the earth has. But I cannot
> tell you how I envy the ragged Irish boy with his wits
> unspoiled by school, and the green earth beautiful
> about him and such tales as those you have gathered to
> tell him of the grand folk who once trod those hills he
> sees, and lie buried beneath the grey cairn where his
> goats go browsing.

President Theodore Roosevelt, after he had read *Cuchulainn of Muirthemne*, became a great fan of Augusta's and told John Redmond that he wanted very much to meet her and hoped that she would come to America.

Cuchulainn of Muirthemne is a seminal book for the writers of the literary renaissance. It showed how the folk speech first put on paper by Douglas Hyde could be used to create a literary style. From this book came the plots for plays later written by Synge and Yeats about the heroic figures of the sagas. Yeats's *On Baile's Strand, The Only Jealousy of Emer, At the Hawk's Well* and *Deirdre* were written on scenarios from Lady Gregory's book from which Synge also took the scheme of his *Deirdre*.

Its style caught the music of Irish syntax and gave it an English equivalent. It was a prose bridge between the two languages. Synge would later perfect, in the compressed space of a play, what she had loosely flung into prose narrative. To city ears it seemed at first unwieldy, because Irish had been lost earlier in the urban areas and the echoes of its inflections were no longer in the urban ear. But when they became accustomed to it, this blend of words was to awaken memories in audiences of the spring time of local life and remind them that 'straw has been turned into bricks'.

A visitor to Coole in the summer of 1898 was John Synge. He had been on the Aran Islands again that summer. Yeats, with his antennae out, heard about his visit and wrote to him while he was on the Islands, asking him to come and stay with Lady Gregory at Coole on the way back. It was clear at this juncture that Yeats had Synge in mind as someone who would work for the movement, for he promised him in the letter to get him a publisher for his book on the Aran Islands. He also told him to try to find out what the islanders knew about the mythological Irish race, the Tuatha de Danann, whom he says they call 'the Dundonians'.

Synge accepted Yeats's invitation and Lady Gregory had him met by a car at Gort station when he arrived on 27 August. She herself had actually been on Inishmaan some time before, collecting folklore, and had felt quite angry when she had passed another person engaged on the same task as she was. She had not realised, until Yeats told her on her return, that it was the same person to whom he had spoken in Paris and told to go to the islands. 'I was jealous of not being alone on the island among the fishers and seaweed gatherers,' she said. Now she felt excited at the prospect of meeting Synge and discussing their mutual experiences. She found him pleasant and quiet and felt an immediate sympathy towards him. The only occasion on which he showed any temperament was when he came in contact with an aggressive Englishwoman who was staying at Coole at the time, and whom he referred to as 'civilisation in its most violent form'.

Lady Gregory noticed that he did not read the newspapers and seemed to have no interest in politics. He made an impression on her when he told her he had given up the black clothes he liked to wear, thinking them not in harmony with nature. She observed that he would slip out into the woods, liking to be alone among the shy animals, the martens, squirrels, badgers. Augusta was the perfect confidante for persons of shy temperament and Synge and she became friends at once. He confessed to her how he never had a conversation with anyone who shared his views until he was twenty-three. She heard of his boyhood, of how, as children, he and his brothers had been forbidden to exaggerate in conversation as it was regarded as sinful. The imagination had been looked on with suspicion as it weakened cultivation of the will. Once he had been reproved for shaking hands with a girl cousin on the grounds that it was an unnecessary display of emotion. Reading Darwin had convinced him early on that religion, as he was taught it, was without meaning. The similarity between the anatomy of the human hand and a bat's wing seemed to him irrefutable evidence that man and the animal world had evolved from a single source. From then on, he had thrown himself into the pursuit of nature, collecting birds' eggs, butterflies, roaming the hills. After that, he had begun to take an interest in the 'other Ireland'.

Augusta, with her own tenacious spirit, would have sensed that here was someone who would not easily abandon a project once he had set his mind to it. She would not have guessed that Synge's métier would turn out to be the theatre, but she recognised that she, Yeats and Synge had the same end in view: articulating in some way the sunken Gaelic culture that they had come across among the people. If Synge could be assimilated into the movement, he could be of the greatest possible use. She knew only too well of the tendency of the Irish to divide on matters of abstract principle, or on a clash of personality. It was a national disease. But here was someone who would not indulge this appetite for division. When the inevitable split did come in the theatre movement, it would be she, Yeats and Synge who would rescue it until it began to make itself important to the art of the twentieth century.

4 The Countess Cathleen

Now that the Irish Literary Theatre was established, the problem was to find actors. The best person to advise them on the matter was George Moore. So Edward Martyn and Yeats hurried over to London to ask Moore if he would take a hand in the new enterprise. Moore had written an enthusiastic introduction to Martyn's play *The Heather Field* when it was published two years before, although he does not hint at this in his account of the visit.

> With the light behind them, my visitors appeared a twain as fantastic as anything ever seen in Japanese prints. Edward great in girth as an owl (he is nearly as feckless) blinking behind his glasses, and Yeats lank as a rook – a dream in black silhouette on the flowered wallpaper.
>
> But rooks and owls do not roost together, nor have they a habit or an instinct in common. A mere doorstep casualty, I said, and began to prepare a conversation suitable to both, which was, however, checked by the fateful appearance they presented, sitting side by side, anxious to speak yet afraid. They had clearly come to me on some great business! But about what, about what? I waited for the servant to leave the room, and as soon as the door was closed they broke forth, telling together that they had decided to found a Literary Theatre in Dublin; so I sat like one confounded, saying to myself: of course they know nothing of Independent Theatres, and, in view of my own difficulties in gathering sufficient audience for

two or three performances, pity began to stir in me for their forlorn project. A forlorn thing it was surely to bring literary plays to Dublin! . . . Dublin of all cities in the world!

It is Yeats, I said, who has persuaded dear Edward, and looking from one to the other, I thought how the cunning rook had enticed the owl from his belfry – an owl that has stayed out too late, and is nervous lest he should not be able to find his way back; perplexed, too, by other considerations lest the Dean and Chapter, having heard of the strange company he is keeping, may have, during his absence, bricked up the entrance to his roost.

As I was thinking these things, Yeats tilted his chair in such dangerous fashion that I had to ask him to desist, and I was sorry to have to do that, so much like a rook did he seem when the chair was on its hind legs. But if ever there was a moment for seriousness, this was one, so I treated them to a full account of the Independent Theatre, begging them not to waste their plays upon Dublin.

'It would give me no pleasure whatever to produce my plays in London,' Edward said, 'I have done with London.'

'Martyn would prefer the applause of our own people,' murmured Yeats, and he began to speak of the by-streets, and the lanes, and the alleys, and how one feels at home when one is among one's own people.

'Ninety-nine is the beginning of the Celtic Renaissance,' said Edward.

Moore was not inclined to come to Dublin, but three weeks later Edward was on his doorstep complaining that Yeats had not been successful in finding someone to play the part of Carden Tyrrell, the hero in *The Heather Field*, and that Yeats was using Florence Farr as stage director. When Moore heard this he was horrified. He thought she was quite the wrong person for Edward's play, with the result that he himself decided to come in

222

and cast the plays. In a few days he had hired May Whitty to play the lead in Yeats's play *The Countess Cathleen* and Thomas Kingston to play Carden Tyrrell in *The Heather Field*. The rehearsals took place in London.

Inevitably, with Moore at the helm there were ferocious rows. One of the actors threw a chair at him after being told he was unsuitable for the part. When Edward whispered that it was important that the play should go on, no matter how inferior the cast might be, Moore replied loudly in the hearing of the cast, 'One can go hunting on bad horses, my dear Edward, but one can't go hunting on goats.'

Over Florence Farr there was a running battle between Yeats and Moore. Yeats, who had known her from his days in the Order of the Golden Dawn, had spent much time working out methods with her by which poetry might be spoken to a psaltery, and this production seemed an ideal opportunity to put their ideas into practice. As a result much time at rehearsal had been spent listening to what Moore described as Florence 'plucking her wires'. After enduring this for some time Moore took Yeats aside one day and said rudely, 'One can hear that kind of thing, my dear fellow, on Sunday in any Methodist Chapel.' Matters came to a climax when Florence Farr asked May Whitty to lie down on the floor in the scene where the Countess Cathleen invokes hell, at which Moore shouted from the stalls: 'the audience will think you are trying to catch cockroaches.'

Meanwhile in Dublin another crisis had arisen. A former Member of Parliament, Frank Hugh O'Donnell (whom Yeats and Maud Gonne had once suspected of being an English spy and had reported to John O'Leary as such) had decided to get his own back by attacking *The Countess Cathleen* on religious grounds. He circulated a pamphlet called 'Souls for Gold' in which he referred to 'the blasphemies of the Countess Cathleen' and accused Yeats of depicting the ancient Irish as 'an impious and renegade people crouched in degraded awe before demons and goblins, like a crowd of black devil worshippers'. Cardinal Logue, having read the pamphlet but not the play, sent a carefully worded letter to the newspapers which suggested that interruptions at the performance would not be out of place. Edward Martyn's scruples were immediately activated. He ran round like a hen in a farmyard seeking for a way out of his predicament – the necessity of choosing between his desire to be a dramatist and his fear of hellfire. Yeats, who saw the whole Irish Literary Theatre movement foundering on the rock of Edward's scruples, unearthed two theologians who read the play and found it impeccable. One of them, a Jesuit, Father Finlay, advised Edward that he need not take the Cardinal's prohibition seriously as his Eminence had not bothered to read the play, and therefore his views were not morally binding. Edward, who had talked of refusing to allow his play to be performed, now agreed to let it go on. For the present the danger was averted. The difficulty now was that the theme of *The Countess Cathleen* was such that it could be interpreted by unscrupulous enemies as having an anti-Catholic bias. The play dealt with a time of famine in Ireland when demons visit the land and buy the peasants' souls for gold. To save her people the Countess Cathleen agrees to sell her own soul (which, as a pearl of great price, the demon merchants are determined to acquire) in order to redeem those of her people who have sold theirs to avoid starving to death. Just as Cathleen appears about to be carried off by the demons, Yeats had arranged an ingenious evasion of the Faustian dénouement which is explained by Aleel, Cathleen's lover, in the beautiful passage which ends the play.

ALEEL

I shatter you in fragments, for the face
That brimmed you up with beauty is no more:
And die, dull heart, for she whose mournful words
Made you a living spirit has passed away.
And left you but a ball of passionate dust.

The 'Cheshire Cheese', once frequented by Burke, Goldsmith and Johnson, and the home of the Rhymers' Club founded by Yeats, Rolleston and Ernest Rhys

George Bernard Shaw in his thirties

The Aran Islands off the coast of Galway. As the last piece of land between Ireland and America, Yeats, Lady Gregory and Synge saw them as an outpost of Irish culture in its purest form

An islander collects seaweed

An Aran fisherman, wearing 'pampooties' and the typical bainin jersey

A young islander using a scythe

The avenue of arching ilex trees leading to Coole

George Moore and W. B. Yeats outside Coole

Isabella Augusta Gregory

Maud Gonne. When Yeats's love for her began to undermine his health, it was to Lady Gregory and Coole that he turned for consolation

Horace Plunkett

The Shelbourne Hotel on St Stephen's Green, where the banquet given by Plunkett took place, and where the young ladies described in *A Drama in Muslin* used to stay during the season

University College, which provided the first university education for native Irishmen under Catholic auspices

G. Clancy, J. F. Byrne and James Joyce at University College. Clancy later became Mayor of Limerick and was murdered by the Black and Tans. He was the model for Madden in *Stephen Hero*

Joyce at graduation

AE in 1901

And you, proud earth and plumy sea, fade out!
For you may hear no more her faltering feet,
But are left lonely amid the clamorous war
Of angels upon devils.

(He stands up, almost everyone is kneeling, but it has
grown so dark that only confused forms can be seen.)

And I who weep
Calls curses on you, Time and Fate and Change,
And have no excellent hope but the great hour
When you shall plunge headlong through bottomless
   space.

(A flash of lightning followed by immediate thunder.)

A PEASANT WOMAN

Pull him upon his knees before his curses
Have plucked thunder and lightning on our heads.

ALEEL

Angels and devils clash in the middle air,
And brazen swords clang upon brazen helms.

(A flash of lightning followed by immediate thunder.)

Yonder a bright spear, cast out of a sling,
Has torn through Balor's eye, and the dark clans
Fly screaming as they fled Moytura of old.

(Everything is lost in darkness.)

AN OLD MAN

The almighty wrath at our great weakness and sin
Has blotted out the world and we must die.

(The darkness is broken by a visionary light. The peasants seem to be kneeling upon the rocky slope of a mountain, and vapour full of storm and ever-changing light is
sweeping above them and behind them. Half in the light,
half in the shadow, stand armed angels. Their armour is
old and worn, and their drawn swords dim and dinted.
They stand as if upon the air in formation of battle and

look downwards with stern faces. The peasants cast
themselves on the ground.)

ALEEL

Look no more on the half-closed gates of Hell,
But speak to me, whose mind is smitten of God,
That it may be no more with mortal things,
And tell of her who lies there.

(He seizes one of the angels.)

Till you speak you shall not drift into eternity.

THE ANGEL

The light beats down; the gates of pearl are wide;
And she is passing to the floor of peace.
And Mary of the seven times wounded heart
Has kissed her lips, and the long blessed hair
Has fallen on her face; The Light of Lights
Looks always on the motive, not the deed,
The Shadow of Shadows on the deed alone.

(Aleel releases the Angel and kneels).

OONA

Tell them who walk upon the floor of peace
That I would die and go to her I love;
The years like great black oxen tread the world,
And God the herdsman goads them on behind,
And I am broken by their passing feet.

(A sound of far-off horns seems to come from the heart of
the light. The vision melts away, and the forms of the
kneeling peasant appear faintly in the darkness.)

There was of course nothing at all in this to justify
Frank Hugh O'Donnell's ferocious attack. But there was
a feeling amongst certain Catholics at the time that Protestants ought not to try to present their version of the
Catholic faith. A fanatical Jesuit in University College
took up O'Donnell's cry for action and succeeded in
persuading his students to organise a protest against the

play. The prospect of a student group present in the theatre on the first night of the production with the intention of stopping the play would have deterred a weaker man than Yeats. But he showed an iron determination when it came to fighting the public on a matter of artistic principle. It was a right he would continue to fight for during the next thirty years with a ferocity which surprised those who only knew the poetic side of his character.

Moore, with his love of a row and an eye for a story, had been in great glee at Edward's religious dilemma and was greatly disappointed when he heard the news that his cousin had rejected the Cardinal's advice. He told Yeats that he had meant to write a pamphlet called 'Edward Martyn and his Soul'. 'What a sensation it would have made,' he said, 'nobody has ever written that way about his most intimate friend. What a chance. It would have been heard everywhere.'

Despite the hold-ups the cast were finally ready to go to Dublin. Moore came along to Euston Station to see them off. Yeats was running up and down the platform supervising the actors' luggage and making sure that they had their seats. But next morning when he got to Dublin Yeats found himself in the middle of a new crisis. Moore, instead of writing the pamphlet 'Edward Martyn and his Soul', had sent it to Martyn in the form of a letter. Martyn was livid; he burst in on Yeats and Florence Farr in the Nassau Hotel where they were having their breakfast after coming off the boat and, waving the letter, told Yeats he would not stand Moore's offensive talk, was withdrawing his play and resigning from the Irish Literary Theatre. Yeats and Florence Farr, who by this time had had their fill of Moore's goings-on, pleaded with Martyn and managed to pacify him. But it took till twelve midday before that perspiring man would agree once more to have his play produced.

The atmosphere in Dublin was charged because of the controversy surrounding the plays, and an attack on the actors was feared. Yeats decided to call in the police for

227

the first night. They were a little sceptical when they met him, as he had made himself well-known in police circles for his anti-Castle activities and his association with the Irish Republican Brotherhood. Yeats was well aware that he was leaving himself open to criticism by asking help from the disliked constabulary. But when an artistic principle was at stake he was above such considerations.

The Antient Concert Rooms – the same hall where Shaw's mother had once sung in opera, now temporarily converted to a theatre – was packed for the opening night of *The Countess Cathleen* on 8 May 1899. Joseph Holloway, an architect who was to be a faithful diarist of Abbey Theatre plays for the next fifty years, noted that 'a pretty little miniature stage, perfectly appointed, had been erected in the hall' and that there were about 500 people present. Holloway watched, 'enraptured as if in fairyland'. But there were interruptions from students in the gallery who created a storm of booing and shouting at the fall of the curtain. Some of the jeers were recalled afterwards by one of the audience: 'a libel on Ireland', 'made in Germany', 'blasphemy', 'we never sold our faith', 'no Irish women ever did it', 'we want no amateur atheist', 'we want no budding buddhist.' However, the cries were all but drowned by the enthusiastic response and rapturous applause from the rest of the audience. Holloway noted with satisfaction that 'Yeats must have felt very proud at the complete triumphing of his enemies'. Yeats, in fact, was so overwhelmed by the reception that he stood on the stage as the actors took their call, not knowing what to do. Then Trevor Lowe, who had played the part of the Second Demon, prompted him to shake May Whitty's hand and after that Florence Farr's. Thus the poet had his first lesson in how an author should behave at the end of his play. Max Beerbohm did not come over till the second night of the play, but he reviewed it well in the *Saturday Review*. The *Irish Times*, hostile to Yeats's nationalist views, rather deviously chose this occasion to attack the play on religious grounds, noting:

In as much as it offends against the tenor of Irish history, in regard to theological connection and against the position of a parish peasant in the face of physical pain, it cannot be considered an Irish play.

But the *Evening Mail* noted

the great poetical beauty of the play

and the *Freeman's Journal*, the nationalist paper, said that

the audience, representative of every section of educated opinion in Dublin, was most enthusiastic, recalling the actors and the author again and again and cheering loudly.

The continued enthusiasm of the audiences delighted Yeats. It was an indication that he had found a medium through which he could communicate with the people. In an age before radio and television, the theatre was the only way in which he could reach a popular audience. If he wanted to further his dream of 'unity of being' here was a means by which he could implant ideas and images in the popular imagination, which could lead to a consensus, 'prince and ploughman, sharing one thought and feeling'.

The following night, Martyn's *The Heather Field* had an equally enthusiastic reception. Holloway seems to have been bowled over.

One cannot give any idea of the amount of pathos and tenderness the dramatist has worked round the incidents leading up to the tragedy of this dreamer whose mind gives way on hearing that his dream has turned out nought but a dream, after all. His love for his brother, son and friend were beautifully indicated, and his utter hopelessness in trying to make his wife understand him one little bit was also admirably hit off. Beyond a doubt, the Literary Theatre is an unmistakeably established fact, and an institution which all Irish people of culture and refinement ought to be justly proud of.

The *Evening Mail* called *The Heather Field* a 'splendid acting play as well as a literary one'. Only the grudging *Irish Times* refused to throw its cap in the air, using the sort of critical approach which one would have thought was out of date.

> The truth is that despite Ibsen and his realism one can scarcely make a drama out of a conversation on a drainage loan advanced by the Board of Works, a wholesale reduction of lands by the Land Commission and similar topics.

Despite this review Edward was delighted with the reception. Generously he made up all losses for the performances so that Lady Gregory was able to inform the guarantors that she would not have to call on them.

Though he was under great tension, Yeats had remained admirably restrained throughout the production. The only time he nearly lost his temper was during a performance of *The Countess Cathleen* when the Second Merchant appeared without a strangled hen, which he had been ordered to produce for a sacrifice. Absolutely livid because he thought that, despite his refusal to remove a line, someone had interfered with the action of his play, Yeats left his seat and rushed round to the back of the stage. There the Chief Demon told him that he had been given charge of the hen and had hung it under the window on a piece of string. When he had pulled up the string that night there was nothing on it. The poet, recognising that thievery and not theology had been at work, was pacified.

Moore had not come over for the first night. But he had received a telegram from Edward saying, 'The sceptre of intelligence has passed from London to Dublin.' Moore described the effect this had on him:

> A vision rose up before me of argosies floating up the Liffey, laden with merchandise from all the ports of Phoenicia, and poets singing in all the bowers of Merrion Square; and all in a new language that the

poets had learned, the English language having been discovered by them, as it had been discovered by me, to be a declining language, a language that was losing its verbs.

Urged by the inflaming telegram Moore hurried over on the evening boat in time for the second production of *The Countess Cathleen*. As he entered the theatre he noted disapprovingly the improvised drop curtain and what he thought were crude sets. But he was quite unprepared for the changes that had taken place in the play since he had rehearsed it in London.

The play seemed to be going quite well. In the middle of the last act some people came on to the stage whom I did not recognise as part of the cast, and immediately the hall was filled with a strange wailing, intermingled with screams, and now, being really frightened, I scrambled over the benches, and laying my hand upon Yeats's shoulder, begged him to tell me what was happening. He answered, 'The caoine – the caoine.' A true caoine and its singers had been brought from Galway. 'From Galway!' I exclaimed. 'You miserable man! and you promised me that the play should be performed as it was rehearsed. Instead of attending to your business you have been wandering about from cabin to cabin seeking these women.' Immediately afterwards the gallery began to howl, and that night the Antient Concert Rooms reminded me of a cats' and dogs' home suddenly merged into one. 'You see what you have brought upon yourself, miserable man!' I cried in Yeats's ear. 'It is not,' he said, 'the caoine they are howling at, but the play itself.'

Though Moore describes this event with humour, it brought to the surface a serious area of disagreement between him and Yeats. Yeats had fixed ideas about dramatic speech and folk participation which were radically different from Moore's approach; this conflict

231

was never resolved, and proved a serious stumbling-block when the two would collaborate in the writing of a play two years later. Nevertheless, without Moore's help the first night of the Irish Literary Theatre could not have got off the ground as it did. As Yeats acknowleged, Moore had an experience of the theatre, a knowledge of play construction, an acquaintanceship with the London acting world that none of the other directors of the Irish Literary Theatre had. It was because of Moore's position in the London literary world that critics like A.B. Walkley, Max Beerbohm and C.E. Montague came over to Dublin to give the productions of the Irish Literary Theatre notice in their newspapers. It should also be said that, while not approving of Yeats's ideas on the production of verse drama, Moore had the highest admiration for his plays. A letter which he wrote to Yeats during the period of the production of *The Countess Cathleen* makes this clear.

Perhaps when I have said that you are the one person since Shakespeare who has succeeded in an actable blank verse play, I have said enough. . . . I was at the Leeds Festival and there I met Fauré – I half read, half told him the story of your *Countess Cathleen*. He thought the play most beautiful and I gave him the copy so that he might have a word for word translation of it. The play is finer even than I thought it was . . . I am your best advertiser, in all the houses I frequent I say, 'I am not the Lord. There is one greater than I, the latchet of whose shoes I am not worthy to unloose.'

Yeats had been attacked by ultra-nationalists for betraying the cause in his production of *The Countess Cathleen*. He had, in fact, made his nationalist stance in relation to the play absolutely clear four months before the presentation at the Antient Concert Rooms. The previous January the Chief Secretary's wife, Lady Betty Balfour, had staged a tableau of *The Countess Cathleen* at the Chief Secretary's lodge in the Phoenix Park. Lady

232

Betty had sent a message to Lady Gregory, asking her to bring Yeats to lunch and mentioning that her husband would so like to meet him. But Yeats made his position clear in a letter to his sister Lily, telling her he could not possibly go near the Chief Secretary's lodge because of his nationalist convictions. Then Lady Betty had asked permission to stage *The Countess Cathleen* in tableau; and Yeats agreed, provided he could meet her on neutral ground. The Countess of Fingal's town house was chosen and there he advised on costumes and consoled Lady Fingal (who was to play Cathleen) when she told him she was not well, with the words, 'you cannot look too well or miserable for this part'. But it was in keeping with Yeats's political outlook that he should have refused to involve himself with social events at the Chief Secretary's lodge. This would have been, for him, collaboration and would not have been looked on with favour by the Irish Republican Brotherhood. In fact, he never forgave T.W. Rolleston for accepting the part of First Demon in the performance there, and alleged that this concession on Rolleston's part resulted in him securing the position of organiser for the Department of Agriculture some months later.

> His nationalist convictions have never been anything more than those of a child . . . put away when the bell rang for meals . . . and I once thought him a possible leader of the Irish race.

This was a bit hard, as Rolleston had only taken up a position with the new body formed to improve Irish agriculture – even if it was employment under the Crown. But Yeats was fanatical in his attitude towards what he regarded as collaboration, and would have felt his view of his former friend borne out when twelve years later Rolleston would obtain work as a translator in the Secret Service in London.

It seems, too, a pity that the exigencies of politics should have kept Yeats and Gerald Balfour from meeting. Balfour was the finest Chief Secretary to serve

233

in Ireland and was largely responsible for putting through the Local Government Act of 1898 which gave autonomy to local councils for the first time (a form of Home Rule) and in getting the important Land Acts of 1903 under way. He was also a member of the Society of Psychical Research (later he became president) and one can imagine how he and Yeats might have talked into the small hours about the Order of the Golden Dawn, Madam's theosophy, and Celtic doings. But they never met and Gerald Balfour was dead before the political atmosphere had changed sufficiently to allow Yeats to socialise with a member of the English ruling caste in Ireland.

5 Celebrations

Horace Plunkett had decided to give a banquet to celebrate the first venture of the Irish Literary Theatre. He told Gill, his editor on the Dublin *Daily Express* which he had recently purchased, to take the dining room of the Shelbourne on an evening following the opening night and entertain a number of selected guests there. Alas, taking a spin on his bicycle in Battersea Park, Horace fell off and fractured his thigh. The banquet had to go on without him, though as he said in his letter to Gill, he longed

> to be there chiefly because as one who has chosen the humbler service of promoting the development of material resources, I am always glad to emphasise the paramount importance from the purely economic standpoint of simultaneously developing our national life in the higher reaches of literature and art.

George Moore later wrote that he came over forthwith to Dublin as a result of the telegram from Edward Martyn, but his arrival does not seem to have been quite as simple as that. On 30 April Plunkett wrote to Gill to say:

> George Moore has just been with me. You know how anti-Irish he has been or at any rate how pessimistic about Ireland. He sees in our economic movement the only hope of regenerating Ireland and he is clever. He won't go over for the Celtic Theatre next week for he suffers terribly from *mal de mer*, but if my idea of a

banquet on the Thursday when there is no performance, could yet come off, he would go and make a
speech which I am sure would be a renunciation of his
former heresies and announcing an allegiance to the
new movement.

By 6 May Plunkett had won his battle; Moore informed
him that he would go over and make a speech at the
dinner.

The Shelbourne Hotel was familiar to Moore. It had
formed the *mise en scène* of *A Drama in Muslin* as the
stately Georgian mansion in St Stephen's Green where
the young ladies would stay during the season, flirting
with the military and hoping to catch husbands at the
Castle balls. The hotel dominates one corner of St Stephen's Green with its red-brick façade, banded with cream
stucco. In 1899 one entered through a frontal glass
awning flanked by two statues of slave girls. Inside on
the left was the great dining-room with its centrepiece
ottoman and walls on which there were paintings of
chalets, lakes and chamois. Here the gentry took their
afternoon tea as the slatted blinds gave a shadow-like
appearance to the streets outside.

Moore arrived early at the banquet to observe the
guests. (He would complain later that there was not a
single opera hat among the guests, though Yeats denied
this.) To Moore's annoyance, one of the first to arrive
was John O'Leary whom he remembered in Paris as
boring him by wanting to talk about Irish affairs when
Moore wanted to talk about Ingres and Cabanel. Now,
perversely, when Moore wanted to talk about the Irish
literary movement, O'Leary would insist on discussing
Lewis Hawkins, Moore's painter friend in Paris. Moore
noticed Edward 'chewing his cud of happiness, a twig
from *The Heather Field*' and 'Yeats's head drooping on
his shirt front like a crane, uncertain whether he should
fold himself up for the night'. John F. Taylor, the barrister, was also there, 'his beard like a horse's collar',
and Hyde, Rolleston and O'Grady. AE had said he

would come afterwards, as he didn't wish to put on evening clothes.

Once the guests were seated Moore's roving eye began its quest, always ready to photograph pictures for inclusion in his portrait gallery. In profile Hyde's head seemed to him 'like a walrus, and the drooping black moustache seemed to bear out the likeness'. Moore was not to get on with Hyde in the next five years. That astute man recognised that the novelist's enthusiasm for the Irish 'scene' was a passing phase, perhaps just a reaction from a mode he was escaping from, and, always careful to steer the boat of his Gaelic League over steady waters, he was resolved not to risk a storm by inviting Moore on board. Moore perhaps resented being upstaged by another Connacht gentleman, which could explain his subsequent savagery towards Hyde. Rolleston, too, made little impression on Moore, the opposite to Hyde, 'very little back to his head', though he did admit that he had a handsome profile. When Moore's neighbour told him that Rolleston had been regarded as Parnell's successor, Moore was incredulous and, perhaps irritated that so many seemed to have acquired reputations in his absence, he dismissed him as 'a Messiah that punctured while the others were going by on inflated tyres'.

Yeats, full of fire after his fight for his play, made the outstanding speech of the night. As reported in the daily newspapers it reads perhaps indifferently by the standards of an orator of his calibre. He defended his play with vigour, denying that he had slandered his country and maintaining that the utterances of the demons and lost souls in the play should not be attributed to himself but to the characters themselves. Literature, he continued, was the expression of universal truths by the medium of particular symbols, and those who were working in the national movement were simply trying to give to truth the visual expression which would most move the people about them. But either the reporting must have been inadequate or Yeats's delivery must

237

have heightened the effect of his words, for the extraordinary impression he made on his listeners does not come over on the printed page. Max Beerbohm who was there as a guest remembered that he made 'Moore gasp' and Moore himself has left an unforgettable picture of the poet in full oratorical flight.

Yeats rose, and a beautiful commanding figure he seemed at the end of the table, pale and in profile, with long nervous hands and a voice resonant and clear as a silver trumpet. He drew himself up and spoke against Trinity College, saying that it had always taught the ideas of the stranger, and the songs of the stranger, and the literature of the stranger, and that was why Ireland had never listened and Trinity College had been a sterile influence. The influences that had moved Ireland deeply were the old influences that had come down from generation to generation, handed on by the story-tellers that collected in the evenings round the fire, creating for learned and unlearned a communion of heroes. But my memory fails me; I am disfiguring and blotting the beautiful thoughts that I heard that night clothed in lovely language. He spoke of Cherubim and Seraphim, and the hierarchies and the clouds of angels that the Church had set against the ancient culture, and then he tolds us that gods had been brought vainly from Rome and Greece and Judea. In the imaginations of the people only the heroes had survived, and from the places where they had walked their shadows fell often across the doorways; and then there was something wonderfully beautiful about the blue ragged mountains and the mystery that lay behind them, ragged mountains flowing southward. But that speech has gone for ever. I have searched the newspapers, but the journalist's report is feebler even than my partial memory. It seemed to me that while Yeats spoke I was lifted up and floated in mid-air. . . .

Hyde spoke briefly in Irish. There is no record of what

he said, but whatever it was made Moore bristle, and provoked this description:

[Hyde's] volubility was as extreme as a peasant's come to ask for a reduction of rent. It was interrupted, however, by Edward calling on him to speak in Irish, and then a torrent of dark muddied stuff flowed from him, much like the porter which used to come up from Carnacun to be drunk by the peasants on midsummer nights when a bonfire was lighted.

Moore then proposed the toast of 'the new movement in Ireland'. He began with a clever piece of intellectual gymnastics to explain his precipitate return to his native land.

I feel conscious that I must seem like a man who, having deserted his mother for a long time, returns to her with effusion when he has learned that she has become rich and powerful. It is for me to forget and Ireland to forgive. Ireland when I knew her was engaged in a struggle for mere existence, with politics her sole distraction. I had no heart for politics. My heart was given from the very first to art. I went to Paris and I lived there till the great artistic movement of the 1880s died at the end of the decade. Then I returned to Ireland, but finding the country in the throes of a great political revolution which I was not qualified to take part in, I went to England. Now art is beginning to fade from the English as from the French horizon. But I notice there is a glimmer in the western air. The beautiful plays that we witnessed this evening are proof that art has once again visited Ireland after many centuries.

He went on to say that 'the agrarian road for the peasants under Parnell has been succeeded by an artistic movement'. Had not the arts of ancient Greece been preceded by an intense outburst of national energy? The conquest of the Adriatic had crystallised in the art of Veronese, Titian and Tintoretto, while Franz

Hals and Rembrandt had flowered after the Hollanders had driven the Spanish out of Holland. Marlborough's victories he then used to complete his theory, maintaining that these had articulated Reynolds and Gainsborough 'and the thirty great painters that flowered from the movement'. He praised Yeats's plays, saying that none except he and Shakespeare had succeeded in verse drama, but when he attacked Kipling, comparing him unfavourably with Yeats, this drew cries of 'no, no' from the audience:

> Kipling will be forgotten in ten years. England's delight in a rhymer who expresses the lust of an African millionaire and the artistic taste of the drunken soldier returning from Hampstead, and England's neglect of *The Countess Cathleen*, could only have happened at the same moment.

He finished by prophesying that in ten years' time the Irish literary movement would have made its impact on world art:

> The Saxon will have recovered from his bout of blackguardism and recognise with sorrow that while he was celebrating Mr Kipling, Marie Corelli, Mrs Humphrey Ward and Mr Pinero, the Celt was celebrating at the poor wayside house the ideals of Mr Yeats.

The speech would have been a triumph had Moore not spoilt it by politics. Yeats is unfair in his account when he says that Moore delivered a purely political document, but it is true that he came out with a vicious attack on William O'Brien, the Irish parliamentary leader. Moore accused O'Brien of being trapped in a web of outworn ideas and alleged that he had no constructive policy. This was just what John F. Taylor was waiting for. He rose to his feet with the words:

> 'Mr Moore has been kind enough to return to Ireland like Bran.'

Moore turned to Yeats.

'Who is he?'
'Bran is one of our greatest legends.'
'Yes, I know that. But the man who is speaking?'
'A great lawyer who has never quite come into his inheritance.'

Taylor continued:

'They have heard from a distinguished son of a distinguished father, Mr George Moore, the reasons which have prompted him to return to Ireland, and his shareholders in Irish glory must feel pleased that at last they have reached the level which Mr Moore considered adequate to induce him to come among them again.'

Taylor was only warming up. Yeats, who knew that he hated William O'Brien and had felt the lash of Taylor's tongue so often in the past, sensed what was coming. No one else was allowed to attack Taylor's favourite butt: 'how dared anyone touch his partridge, his pheasant, his snipe?' Yeats never forgot how that night Taylor described Moore's life in phrases influenced by Carlyle's description of the 'scarlet woman' Dubarry.

While Moore had been memorising the scene for his literary portraits, Yeats had been at the same game and must have watched Moore's reaction to Taylor with a certain amount of pleasure.

Taylor's angular body rigid with suppressed rage, his gaze fixed upon some object, his clothes badly made, his erect attitude suggesting a firm base. Moore's body was insinuating, up-flowing, circulative, curvicular, pop-eyed.

Standish O'Grady, now drunk, staggered to his feet and made an impassioned address. He stood between two tables, leaning on one or the other to balance himself. Yes, he said: there was now a remarkable literary movement. This would be followed by a political movement. And then, his voice rising, he told the guests there would be a military movement, because Ireland had had to pay for English volunteers and had not been allowed to have her own while the country bled to death through emigration and the land was let out to American and British millionaires. He urged the landlords to avail themselves of the new Boy Scout Movement and, pointing to where he believed England to be, said, 'We must train our sons to march on the conquest of a decadent nation.' This was his constant theme, that democracy was decadent and that the Irish landlords had been used by Parliament and deserted in the end: but never had he presented it in public and with such vehemence before. His despairing cry rang in Yeats's ears. 'Drunk or sober,' Yeats wrote, 'idling or toiling, this man had style. Sweetness of voice, nobility of gesture. The torch of others smoked, their wine had dregs: his element burned and ran pure.'

When the speeches were over AE arrived. He had not dined because he refused to put on evening clothes; now he came in in his grey tweeds with his wild beard and shaggy mane of hair. Moore remembered the pleasure that AE's writing and painting had given him:

It had been just as if somebody had suddenly put his hand into mine, and had led be away into a young world which I recognised at once as the fabled Arcady that had flourished before man discovered gold, and forged the gold into a ring which gave him power to enslave. White mist curled along the edge of the woods, and the trees were all in blossom. There were tall flowers in the grass, and gossamer threads glittered in the rays of the rising sun. Under the trees every youth and maiden was engaged in some effusive moment of personal love, or in groups they wove garlands for the pleasure of the children, or for the honour of some God or Goddess. Suddenly the songs of the birds were silenced by the sound of a lyre; Apollo and his Muses appeared on the hillside; for in these stories the Gods and mortals mixed in delightful comradeship, the mortals not having lost all trace of their divine origin, and the Gods themselves being the kind, beneficent Gods that live in Arcady. The paper had dropped from my hands, and I said: Here is the mind of Corot in verse and prose; the happiness of immemorial moments under blossoming boughs, when the soul rises to the lips and the feet are moved to dance. Here is the inspired hour of sunset, and it seemed to me that this man must live always in this hour, and that he not only believed in Arcady, but that Arcady was always in him. While we strive after happiness he holds it in his hand, I said, and it was to meet this man that I had come to Ireland as much as to see the plays.

Horace Plunkett had hoped that AE would meet Moore and had suggested that the two should talk before the dinner, thinking perhaps that AE's influence would restrain Moore from going too far in his speech. Always the businessman, Plunkett had looked for one hundred per cent return for his investment. He was a little disappointed when he heard that Moore had introduced politics. 'If only George Moore's speech had been less extravagant, the *Daily Express* report would have formed an epoch-making document.'

6 Enter the Artist as a Young Man

On the first night of *The Countess Cathleen* Joseph Holloway, the Abbey diarist, noted that 'an organised claque of about twenty brainless, beardless youths did all they knew to interfere with the progress of the play by their meaningless automatic hissings and senseless comments'. These were from University College, a Jesuit-run institution in St Stephen's Green. University College was not a university in the strict sense as it only prepared students for the exams of the Royal University (which was itself merely an examining body). But it had evolved from John Henry Newman's short-lived Catholic University founded in 1854 and had housed itself in the same premises, 86 St Stephen's Green, a granite building with a handsome front and fine spacious rooms inside designed by Robert West and decorated with some of the best plasterwork in the city.

The leader of the students was almost certainly Thomas Kettle, later a well known essayist, poet and professor. In his inaugural address to the University Debating Society earlier on that year, he had referred to the 'Anglo-Celtic revival' as 'dead sea fruit' and asked the people to repudiate it. Now, after the demonstration at the first performance, he and a group of students signed a letter of protest and sent it to the newspapers. 'The subject is not Irish,' the letter began.

It has been shown, that the plot is founded on a German legend. The characters are ludicrous travesties of the Irish Catholic Celt. The purpose of Mr Yeats's drama is apparently to show the sublimity of self-sacrifice. The questionable nature of that self-sacrifice forced Mr Yeats to adopt still more questionable means to produce an occasion for it. He represents the Irish peasant as a crooning barbarian crazed with morbid superstition who, having added the Catholic faith to his store of superstition, sells that faith for gold or bread in the proving of famine. Is Mr Yeats prepared to justify this view of our national character . . .? Has Mr Yeats thoroughly considered the probable effect of presenting this slanderous caricature of the Irish peasant . . .?

The young men at University College represented the first generation of native Irish to avail themselves of a university education under Catholic auspices. They came mainly from the professional classes, sons of doctors, lawyers, engineers, as well as farmers and merchants. One of them who had refused to sign the letter of protest against *The Countess Cathleen* was from the landed gentry and a close neighbour of George Moore's. But no matter how secure their social backgrounds were, they would have felt a sense of inferiority to the sons of the Anglo-Irish ruling class who went to Trinity College a quarter of a mile away at the other end of Grafton Street. The smartly dressed Trinity men, parading in the most fashionable street of the city, could lord it over the University College students with their air of bohemianism and their inbred sense of inferiority. Trinity produced the ruling class – University College were the ruled. But this class recognised that with the prospect of Home Rule they would at some time or another gain control of affairs in the country. John Eglinton, a librarian from the National Library and literary critic, saw the ribald wit and reckless manner of life in some of the University College set as giving them a certain distinction and thought that their interest in everything new in literature and philosophy far surpassed that of Trinity College.

Despite the fact that it was without academic standing, University College had the atmosphere of a university about it. Among the professors were Thomas Arnold (brother of Matthew), and Gerard Manley Hopkins, nursing a gentle imperialism in an alien atmosphere, had taught there up to his death in 1889. Under Newman's rectorship, which began in 1854, a high standard of scholarship had been established and it was he who had appointed Eugene O'Curry to the chair of Irish history and archaeology and commissioned the lectures that were to provide the background for the popularising of the Irish sagas. But Newman had been unable to withstand the pressure of Archbishops Cullen and McHale ('two old country fiddlers playing on the delicate Stradivarius of his temperament') and had soon returned to England, leaving behind him only an exquisite Byzantine church which he had built next to 86 St Stephen's Green.

When Newman's university had failed, the Jesuits took over the running of the beautiful mansion and ran it as a quasi-college of the Royal University. Many of the students were from Jesuit-run schools, Clongowes, Belvedere, Mungret. Others had been educated in priest-dominated seminaries. It is not hard, then, to understand why they should have taken offence at *The Countess Cathleen*. These young men had been brought up to regard the Church as the sole interpreter of faith and morals. Now here was a poet (and a Protestant as well) suggesting that an Irishwoman who had sold her soul to Satan could get into heaven simply because God would look on her motive, not her deed. This was not Catholic theology. How dare a Protestant pretend it was, and wrap the whole thing up in Gaelic mythology to lend it authenticity?

Yet some students did refuse to sign the protest. One of them had entered the college the previous September. His name was James Augustine Joyce and he was studying for an arts degree. He was seventeen years of age and had been at the first night of *The Countess Cathleen* where he had clapped loudly in an attempt to drown the shouts and boos of his fellow students. He, on his father's side, came from a merchant family which had had substantial means for a generation or two but which, by the time James entered college, had fallen on difficult times. His father, a genial sportsman with a vast repertoire of operatic arias and drawing room songs and *Lieder*, had idled, drunk and sung his way through numerous properties as he fathered a family of ten children. James, as the eldest, had known the good days – governesses, boarding schools, nursemaids. Now as a student at University College he was keenly conscious of the gap between the poverty of his home life and the comfortable circumstances which the majority of the student body enjoyed. He had been a scholarship boy right through his schooldays as his father's affairs had taken a bad turn before his eldest son had reached his teens.

His life as a schoolboy at the fashionable Jesuit school, Belvedere, could not have been more different from the schooldays of Yeats, Synge or AE. Joyce had been the captain of the school, the winner of a number of scholarships and one of the most popular boys in the school because of his wit, his clever acting ability, his beautiful singing voice and good looks. He was also intensely religious. As prefect of the sodality of the Blessed Virgin Mary he had had a special prie-dieu reserved for him at the head of the College Chapel where he would kneel in front of the rest of the school, a model of sanctity, before receiving the Blessed Sacrament.

Occasionally driven by powerful sexual urges, he would relieve himself in the brothels that lay among the festering tenements which line the streets he passed through on the way to school. Then this dalliance would be followed by months of ferocious penance during which he would torture his body in reparation for sins which the Jesuit fathers had convinced him would lead to an eternity of hell fire. His great devotion was to the Blessed Virgin. She satisfied the primitive need for a goddess in him and became as Isis and Venus were to the Egyptian and the Roman, or Etain to the Gael. It was to her he offered up his most severely conceived penances, and if he could find a deserted street he would take out a rosary and repeat over and over again his obeisances to her. At incense-filled services he would recite lovingly phrases of extravagant adoration in her praise: Tower of Ivory, House of God, Star of the Sea, Virgin Most Pure.

At College in his first year Joyce had remained in the thrall of religion. But there were other forces beating at the gates of his imagination. He had discovered the writings of Ibsen, who seemed to offer the alternative of an existence lived in pursuit of the truth of self, in which the same self-denial and devotion would be demanded of an artist who adopted this creed as the Church demanded of those who would seek the Kingdom of Heaven. Gradually, with the swing away from the forces of religion, Ibsen, with his determination 'to wrest the secret from life', began to replace in Joyce's mind the authority of the Church. He read voraciously in German, Italian and French as well as Norwegian which he taught himself, and by his second year at University had decided that the role of the artist was the one he wanted to devote his life to. The paper on Ibsen which he read to the University Debating Society demanded that society face up to the new ideas that had blown away the cobwebs of nineteenth-century religious and national superstition.

> The sooner we understand our true position the better; and the sooner then will we be up and going on our way. In the meantime art, and chiefly drama, may help us to make our resting places with greater insight and a greater foresight that the stones of them may be bravely builded and the windows goodly and fair. 'What will you do in our society, Miss Hassel?' asked Rorlund. 'I will let in fresh air, Pastor,' answered Lona.

The close friends Joyce chose for himself in college shared his desire to let in 'fresh air'. Two of them had been to Belvedere with him, John Francis Byrne and Vincent Cosgrave, while the other, Oliver St John

Gogarty, was a student at Trinity. Byrne was knowledgeable and well read, qualities which enabled Joyce to use him as a whetstone on which to sharpen his brain. The subjects varied from transubstantiation to chess and handball. In their marathon walks around the city Joyce would explain his latest position on religion or sex to Byrne and listen attentively to his comments. Sometimes they discussed the possibility of taking communion while in a state of mortal sin – Joyce now believed that sin was an invention of the clergy; at other times the connection between the sacerdotal and the artistic vocation, Joyce maintaining that his writing would convert the bread of life into something that would have an artistic life of its own, as the priest claimed to do in the Mass. They often conversed in a sort of dog Latin – *'jocabimus manum ballum'* ('let us play handball'), *'credo vos mandax in sanguinarium'* ('I think you are a bloody liar') – and they seemed more like a pair of medieval goliards under the shadow of Notre Dame than students in the second city of the empire. A revealing passage in *A Portrait of the Artist* records an incident which shows how the two in their conversation often fused the modern and the medieval in their reaction to an immediate event. As they are walking along the avenues of a suburb they hear a servant sharpening her knives and singing 'Rosie O'Grady' (Byrne appears here as Cranly):

Cranly stopped to listen, saying: mulier cantat.

The soft beauty of the Latin word touched with an enchanting touch the dark of the evening, with a touch fainter and more persuading than the touch of music or of a woman's hand. The strife of their minds was quelled. The figure of woman as she appears in the liturgy of the Church passed silently through the darkness: a white-robed figure, small and slender as a boy, and with a falling girdle. Her voice, frail and high as a boy's, was heard intoning from a distant choir the first words of a woman which pierce the gloom and clamour of the first chanting of the passion:

– Et tu cum Jesu Galilaeo eras.

And all hearts were touched and turned to her voice, shining like a young star, shining clearer as the voice intoned the pro-paroxyton and more faintly as the cadence died.

The singing ceased. They went on together, Cranly repeating in strongly stressed rhythm the end of the refrain:

And when we are married,
     O, how happy we'll be
For I love sweet Rosie O'Grady
And Rosie O'Grady loves me.

– There's real poetry for you, he said. There's real love.

Another goliard-like figure in Joyce's college group was Vincent Cosgrave. Cosgrave was a medical student who was a familiar figure in the city's brothel area known as the Kips. His chief delight in life, aside from the pleasures of the flesh, was church music, Gregorian chant and polyphony. Joyce shared this passion with him and as he could not write music would ask his friend to transcribe any new motet that he might hear in the city churches and bring it to him so that they might sing it together. Going through decaying streets they would often sing Gregorian or a motet from Palestrina together, their clear young voices rising over the noise of the revellers coming out of the pubs. In Holy Week Dublin took on the appearance of Seville or Turin, with gorgeously robed and dramatic liturgical ceremonies taking place in the different churches throughout the city. Joyce and Cosgrave would choose their own particular church each night almost as if going to the theatre and finish up in the Pro-Cathedral on Good Friday where the choir would sing the Passion and death of Christ in the medievally devised Tenebrae.

Joyce's other close friend was Oliver St John Gogarty, whom he·was later to immortalise by putting him in

Ulysses under the name of 'Buck' Mulligan – Malachy St Jesus Mulligan. Gogarty's background was a Catholic Irish one but, after a year studying for the exams of the Royal, he had been sent by his mother to Trinity College to study medicine where he quickly found his feet. There possessing a prodigious memory for Latin and Greek verse, a gift which made him the darling of the dons with their propensity for apt quotation. Mahaffy particularly took to him: with his quick wit and breadth of outlook, he looked on him as a natural successor to Oscar Wilde as his pupil in the art of conversation. Gogarty's lyric poetry, too, was of a high standard for a student of his age (Yeats was later to call him 'one of the great lyric poets of the age') and Dowden had undertaken his tutelage as a poet. Young Gogarty was one of the best known figures in the city, and was generally regarded as the author of most of the Rabelaisian ballads and blasphemous limericks that were in circulation. He dressed elegantly and sported primrose waistcoats, and with his daring as a swimmer and champion cyclist he seemed a descendant of the eighteenth-century bucks who had bestrode the cobblestones of the city of a century before. Joyce and he would meet in Gogarty's country house in Glasnevin where under the yew trees they would write out their verses on single sheets of vellum. They were often seen around the city arm in arm whispering their mockery in one another's ear – engaging in what Padraic Colum has called 'and apostolate of irreverence', satirising Church and State in verse and anecdote.

Joyce had great personal charm and good looks which resulted in his being a popular figure at parties and *soirées* throughout the city. He was tall, with a long face and well-cut features, piercing blue eyes and long chestnut-coloured eyelashes; a slightly protruding lower jaw, indicating stubbornness and determination, was his only inhibiting feature. Despite his poverty he dressed with some style, sporting a tailor-made yachting cap and carrying an ash plant. Like Gogarty he had a prodigious memory, and this had given him a vast repertoire of

251

songs, opera, *Lieder* and ballads: it has been estimated that he knew over two thousand which he could sing at will. His favourite songs were the Elizabethan airs of Dowland and Byrd. But other airs which people remember him singing were von Flotow's 'The Last Rose of Summer' and Balfe's 'When Other Lips and Other Hearts'. He could sing popular songs too, and one of his favourites was 'The Man Who Broke the Bank at Monte Carlo', which he would perform with a monocle in his eye, striding backwards and forwards across a drawing room, his ash plant under his arm. He was an ideal guest for charades at parties with his wit and improvisation and on one occasion played the queen in a take-off of *Hamlet*, greeting Ophelia with a thick Dublin fishwife accent: 'Ah, you poor gerrul.' His friends remember him as someone who was always good for a laugh; he would tell the drill instructor after he had arrived at the gymnasium doubled up, 'I've come in to be cured'; and he once terrified an inoffensive French professor in the College by arranging with a fellow student to stage a ferocious row, and then rushing out to the Phoenix Park to fight a pretended duel.

Joyce had a close relationship with his mother. He was typical of the good-looking charming Irish boy of his time who took the place in a mother's affection of a vagabond, drunken husband. She would do anything for Jim, sometimes even washing his neck before he went out to College in the morning when he was a student. She tried to understand his literary aspirations and they shared a love for music. At Dublin musical evenings he was proud to walk by her side to the piano when she would play Chopin, Schumann and Mendelssohn; sometimes he would accompany her in his splendid tenor voice. Though she suffered both as a wife and mother, she understood Joyce's real affection for his father. John Stanislaus Joyce had held on to his personality through the sort of economic distress and social decline which would have turned most men into shambling nonentities. His glorious voice, vast repertoire of songs and wonderful flow of rich witty conversation he bequeathed to his son, who was to use his father's phrases, similes and astonishing variety of adjectives again and again in his books. That his mother never tried to wean him from his affection for his wayward parent, though she had to slave to keep the family fed and clothed in later years, indicates her strength of character.

With the literary revival Joyce was not in tune, and he regarded it with the intolerance of the young towards the middle-aged. He admired Yeats and had learnt his 'Tables of the Law' and the 'Adoration of the Magi' off by heart. But he considered that the poet was too concerned with the past and not enough with the life that was being lived around him. He sympathised with Edward Martyn's admiration for Ibsen, but felt that Martyn had not gone far enough in fulfilling the master's ideals. It was to Moore's naturalism and European spirit that Joyce was closest, but it was many years before he made contact with that irascible man, and that after both of them had become revered figures in the world of letters. He saw Lady Gregory's possibility as a patron of the arts but had not discerned her function as a catalyst in the revival. He would plough his own furrow, with help from those who would give it, as he set out 'to forge in the smithy of my soul the uncreated conscience of my race'.

7 Getting into their Stride

For the second year of the Irish Literary Theatre it was decided to present three plays, two by Edward Martyn and one by a Belfast poetess Alice Milligan who had been secretary of the Ulster 1798 Centenary Committee and was editor of the nationalist newspaper, *Shan Van Vocht.*

Edward had published his play *Maeve* in the same volume as *The Heather Field.* It has a hint of Ibsen's *Lady from the Sea* and is referred to in the title as a 'psychological drama'. But it is much closer to the mood of the Celtic twilight – with its theme of reincarnated queens and Maeve's choice of voyaging to the Land of Eternal Youth rather than marry a rich Englishman – than it is to the Scandinavian theatre.

Edward's other play, *The Tale of a Town,* was on a contemporary theme. A West of Ireland town derives its prosperity from the fact that it is the nearest port to America. But when the play opens, an English town, Anglebury, has induced the American Steamer Line which has hitherto used the Irish port, to transfer its custom to them. Though it has been agreed that the Irish town should get a percentage of the fee paid by the American line to Anglebury, this fee is being withheld. The hero of the play, a young alderman, Jasper Dean, manages to organise the Corporation into making a serious demand for their rights. But he is vulnerable, for he is engaged to the mayor of Anglebury's niece, who will not marry him unless he leaves Ireland and comes to live in England. In the end Jasper Dean betrays his town

254

and accepts bribes as some of his colleagues, whom he has attacked, have done.

There is Ibsen influence here too as *An Enemy of the People* begins with a threat to the source of the town's prosperity, the Municipal Baths. But Edward draws his allegory beyond the affairs of the town and introduces an analogy between his plot and England's treatment of Ireland. The transfer of the business of the town to Anglebury is a symbol for the Act of Union which transferred the government of Ireland to London, and the refusal to honour the agreed terms presents a parallel for the treatment of Ireland in the nineteenth century when the terms of the Union were broken.

The trouble was that Edward had loaded his play with a gigantic cast; and the personalities of the chief characters in it seemed lost in the welter of action and the interplay of events. 'As it is written,' Moore said to Yeats after reading the play, 'this play could not attract any audience, Irish, English or Esquimaux.' The two of them decided that the best thing to do was to get Moore to rewrite it with Edward during a holiday they intended to take to Bayreuth for the opera season. But Edward, with his usual skill in avoiding what he did not want, managed to survive the Bayreuth trip without having a word of his play altered. The pair, however, did meet Wagner's widow, and his son Siegfried who talked of 'Grandpapa Liszt' and made Moore think of a 'deserted shrine', so like was he to his father in everything except his genius.

Moore could always be trusted to find a pretext for niggling at Edward's susceptibilities; and he did. Even in Bavaria, he pointed out how the south of the country housed the Asiatic gods, and the north the original Rhine gods, Wotan and Loki and the goddesses Frika, Erda and Fria. Edward was about to comment agreeably on this when it occurred to him that the 'Asiatic gods' to whom Moore was referring were the Christian Trinity, which caused him to retort that he was not interested in listening to blasphemy.

255

Back in Ireland it was agreed that Moore would go down and stay in Tulira and work on the revision. But living with Edward demanded disciplines that Moore found unacceptable. He was expected, for instance, to refrain from eating meat on Friday in accordance with Canon Law.

'Why should I, since I'm not a Catholic?'

'If you aren't a Catholic, why don't you become a Protestant?'

'In the first place, one doesn't become a Protestant, one discovers oneself a Protestant; and it seems to me that an agnostic has as much right to eat meat on Friday as a Protestant.'

'Agnosticism isn't a religion. It contains no dogma.'

'It comes to this, then: that you're going to make me dine off a couple of boiled eggs. . . . Two eggs and a potato forced down my throat on a theological fork in a Gothic house that has cost twenty thousand pounds to build.'

Then there was the question of attending Mass on Sundays. Moore had not been for years, and didn't see why he should change his habit to suit his cousin.

'But, Edward, I don't believe in the Mass. My presence will be only –'

'Will you hold your tongue, George . . . and not give scandal?' . . .

'Everybody knows that I don't believe in the Mass.'

'If you aren't a Catholic, why don't you become a Protestant?' . . .

'I have told you before that one may become a Catholic, but one discovers oneself a Protestant. But why am I going to Gort?'

'Because you had the bad taste to describe our church in *A Drama in Muslin*, and to make such remarks about our parish priest that he said, if you showed yourself in Ardrahan again, he'd throw dirty water over you.'

'If you send me to Gort, I shall be able to describe Father –'s church.

'Will you not be delaying?'

'One word more, it isn't on account of my description of Father –'s church that you won't take me to Ardrahan; the real reason is because, at your request, mind you, I asked Father – not to spit upon your carpet when he came to dinner at Tulira. You were afraid to ask a priest to refrain from any of his habits, and left the room.'

'I only asked you to draw his attention to the spittoon.'

'Which I did; but he said that such things were only a botheration, and my admonitions on the virtue of cleanliness angered him so that he never –'

'You'll be late for Mass. And you, Whelan; now, are you listening to me? Do you hear me? . . . You aren't to spare the whip. Away you go; you'll only be just in time. And you, Whelan, you're not to delay putting up the horse. Do you hear me?'

Moore did go to Mass on this occasion but felt ashamed afterwards that he had bowed his head with the congregation and pretended to accept the ceremony as truth. Deciding that it could not be right to do this, even for the sake of the Literary Theatre, the following week (having adroitly discovered that the driver Whelan was a Parnellite and therefore anti-clerical) Moore persuaded Whelan to drop him off at Lady Gregory's place at Coole where he whiled away his Mass time chatting agreeably to Yeats and her ladyship.

Once Moore had decided that he and Yeats would have to rewrite the play between them, he began to spend more time in Coole than he did in Tulira. At Coole he was impressed with the care Lady Gregory took of Yeats – 'clean pens, fresh ink, a spotless blotter' for him each morning. Yeats's mind was currently 'whirling with Formorians' for he was writing his verse play *The Shadowy Waters* about 'a pirate ship laden to the gunwales with Formorians beaked and unbeaked' and

he was not in the proper mood to adapt a work dealing
with the unsound affairs of a shipping line in a modern
seaport.

However, they did a good deal on it together before
Moore finally departed to the Shelbourne Hotel in
Dublin to work on the final draft. When he finished it,
the play had a new title, *The Bending of the Bough*. After
Edward had read it he said he would have nothing to do
with the new version.

'I give you the play. Do with it as you like; turn it inside
out, upside down. I'll make you a present of it!'

'But Edward, if you don't wish me to alter your
play –'

'Ireland has always been divided, and I've preached
unity. Now I'm going to practise it. I give you the play.'

'But what do you mean by giving us the play?' Yeats
said.

'Do with it what you like. I'm not going to break up
the Irish Literary Theatre. Do with my play what you
like.'

Edward had reason to be angry. Moore had transferred
the scene of the play to Scotland. The West of Ireland
town competing with an English one for the attention of
Atlantic steamers had now become a Scottish sea port.
To Edward it seemed the point of his play was lost. Some
of his best lines about the relationship between England
and Ireland had been taken out. Yet despite the
harassing method of its composition, *The Bending of the
Bough* was very well received when it was presented at
the Gaiety Theatre, acted by an English company in
February 1900. The *Daily Express* reported that the
audience numbered among it nearly every man and
woman of intellectual distinction in Dublin and that they
were 'undoubtedly delighted with the performance and
followed the development of the plot with the keenest
sympathy'. The notice of the *Freeman's Journal* critic
seems to show that the substance of Edward's local
allegory had not been lost.

The play is, in fact, a biting and political sabre directed against the influences that have destroyed the Irish gentry's sense of patriotism.

Edward's *Maeve* was also well received:

We have seen nothing so wonderful in an Irish theatre for many years [the *Freeman's Journal* wrote] as the way in which the audience last night in the Gaiety followed the allegory in Mr Martyn's play.

Alice Milligan's one-act play *The Last of the Fianna* gave a Gaelic flavour to the night as it dealt with the dilemma of Oisin, the son of Finn, during the period that Grainne came back to his father's court after she had run away with Diarmuid. The Irish Literary Theatre could feel well satisfied with its second success in ten months. An important factor in this season was that the plays had almost filled the Gaiety Theatre. This held twelve hundred people and was the leading theatre of the city where visiting companies from England and France performed on a regular basis – quite a change from the little Antient Concert Rooms where the Literary Theatre had opened timidly less than a year before.

The trauma which Edward endured at having his play rewritten marks the beginning of his withdrawal from the Irish Literary Theatre. He seems to have lacked a talent for compromise. His complaint would be that the movement was evolving in the direction of 'peasant drama' rather than 'psycholgical drama'. But the peasant drama which Lady Gregory and Synge initiated would later begin to confront social problems similar to those dealt with by the Scandinavian and Russian realists whom Edward admired, though set in a different social milieu. Later Edward would object, too, to the Irish actors who had been brought in to perform plays, believing them incapable of acting 'psychological drama'. Yet the same actors would come to be regarded

259

as among the pioneers of the realistic style of acting in Europe. The trend of Irish drama would evolve so that within a decade the realist play would begin to dominate the repertory of Lady Gregory's and Yeats's theatre.

Unlike Lady Gregory, Yeats, Synge and Hyde, Edward seems to have had little contact with or understanding of peasant life, the Galway peasantry in particular. He could see in their lives no theme for art. It was as if he was in some way word-blind, because the most startling and original language was in constant use among the people who passed his gate daily and worked on his land. He seemed to some of the workers on his estate remote from matters of everyday life. Once he found Murray, the gate lodge keeper, shooting bullfinches which had been eating the strawberries. Edward wanted to know why Murray was doing this and the gate keeper replied, 'They're fierce destructive.' Edward's response was that Murray didn't have to shoot them and why could he not 'just catch the birds and let them go'? His apparent insensitivity to folk dialogue is all the more strange as Edward had a perfect ear for music and was one of the pioneers in the revival of native airs. He could remind readers of his articles in The Leader that if Norwegian native airs had been mutilated as some of the Irish airs had, Grieg might merely have been 'an obscure fumbler in native rubbish ... and not diluted his work with the finest qualities of folk music'. Yet at the same time he could not perceive the usefulness of an oral folk culture as a basis for literary or dramatic art.

Perhaps Edward spread his net too wide. In Bayreuth he had expressed to George Moore his view that the revival of drama must be accompanied by a renaissance of all the arts, painting, sculpture and music. He had plans for this – a stained-glass studio so that ecclesiastical art would flourish again, the endowment of a cathedral choir which would sing Vittoria, Palestrina, Orlando di Lasso, a club where Irish music would be performed.

Edward was to achieve his ambition in these three

spheres. The stained-glass movement which he helped to create did indeed revive ecclesiastical art in Ireland and produced some of the finest stained glass artists of the century: Harry Clarke, Evie Hone, Michael Healy. His Palestrina choir was to give pleasure every Sunday in Dublin's Pro-Cathedral to generations of Dubliners and would have among its members one tenor who would achieve world fame, John McCormack. Edward founded the Pipers' Club in Dublin which would prove a vital force in preserving native music in the interim between folk memory and the coming of the gramophone. His enthusiasm for his various campaigns overcame his natural timidity towards Church authority; he attacked what he called 'the wretched Italian sculptures' which the parish priests imported for their newly built edifices, and 'mosaic schemes in a dominant taste of dirty yellow that make me feel as if a plate of stirabout were thrown in my face'. The current taste in stained glass he dismissed as 'crudely painted window blinds'. Ruskin would have approved of his polemic against the change in class structure which had contributed to much of contemporary bad taste.

> Sham furniture, sham decoration, sham jewellery, sham wine, sham literature of the lowest type were poured out upon the mediocre masses who eagerly swallowed all the rubbish because it was cheap and, to them, undistinguishable from the real and good. By degrees they were joined by the stupid rich to whom good and bad were naturally undistinguishable. Thus there grew to be an immense public in the world who, soon, so got to prefer the cheap and sham that with the distortion which familiarity with inferior things produces on the intellect, they actually ended by viewing with detestation anything truly great in literature or art.

But by breaking away from the Irish Literary Theatre, Edward did himself a disservice. His talent dissipated itself. Later he would form the Theatre of Ireland to present Chekhov, Strindberg, Ibsen and his own plays, as well as those of such dramatists he thought were writing in the 'modern milieu'. But he was not a good organiser and he lacked the stamina of Yeats and Lady Gregory to keep an artistic movement going at full tilt. Though the Irish theatre movement could not have been formed without his help, it was to make its real impact after Edward had broken with it, so that today his association with it is often forgotten, and his achievements unremembered.

8 Royal Visit

The Irish Literary Theatre seemed on the way to success with its second season. This however did not deter Yeats from defying the establishment by joining in a protest against the visit of Queen Victoria to Ireland in April 1900, just two months after the production at the Gaiety. His involvement in revolutionary activity had made him enemies amongst his own class and he would reflect somewhat ruefully on

> the pleasant homes that would never ask me to dine – the still pleasanter homes with trout streams near at hand that never would ask me on a visit.

But he was prepared to suffer ostracism rather than surrender the principles he had learned from O'Leary. Indeed he seemed to select Royal visits especially for demonstrations of disloyalty, and had on occasions rolled up red carpets spread to welcome visiting vice-royalty.

In 1898 he had been elected President for Britain and France of the Executive Council of the Centenary Committee which had been set up to commemorate the rebellion against English rule which had taken place in 1798. Branches had been established in London at Chancery Lane, Soho, Drury Lane, Clerkenwell, Plumstead. He had spoken at numerous meetings throughout the north of England before being one of the principal speakers at a final rally held in Dublin to honour Wolfe Tone in St Stephen's Green. Seated in a wagonette at the ceremony were John O'Leary, Emilio

Cipriani (veteran of Garabaldi's army), Yeats and Maud Gonne. Yeats concluded the meeting with a warning to the Government:

> This immense demonstration has been held at a momentous time in Irish history. England has persuaded herself that she could settle the Irish question by a handful of arms. We have answered England by this great demonstration. She is no longer deceived. She now knows that Ireland cherishes the same spirit still.

He had kept up his nationalist activities when he, Maud Gonne and Edward Martyn became members of the Transvaal Committee which was set up to protest against England's treatment of the Boers during the war. They were joined by a journalist newly returned from South Africa, Arthur Griffith. Griffith, originally a compositor by trade, had gone out to South Africa in 1896 for his health but had returned in the autumn of 1898. A convinced separatist with a brilliant flair for journalism, he had started in March 1899 a weekly paper called the *United Irishman* which was to have a profound effect on future events in Ireland. Griffith's political philosophy was based on the principle that if Ireland wanted separate government the Irish must rely on themselves, and not wait for England to grant it. The formula by which he suggested self-government would be obtained was the withdrawal of the Irish representatives from Westminister and the setting-up of a Parliament at home. He was later to expand this doctrine into the Sinn Fein political organisation ('ourselves alone') which would provide the structure for the armed rebellion in Ireland between 1916 and 1921, at the conclusion of which Griffith would be elected first President of the Executive Council of the new Irish State.

The man Yeats and Maud Gonne found themselves working alongside was small, well-set, with a strong jaw and piercing blue eyes. He had one characteristic which they both admired, a phenomenal capacity for getting work done. He started on his paper before eight a.m. and seldom finished before eight in the evening. For these labours he allowed himself a salary of twenty-five shillings a week.

Griffith's paper was well written, not only because he himself, in James Stephens' words, was 'a master of the English language', but because he induced poets and artists of the literary movement to write for him. Of Yeats, whom he looked up to more than any other Irish writer of the time, he wrote:

> I walk on the stones and on the glass and I meet between them men and women who have never read Yeats, yet consider themselves intelligent Irish persons. Mr Yeats sings of which he knows and sings more beautifully than any Irish poet sang before.

Griffith, a determined anti-cleric, had brought men from the quays along to the first night of *The Countess Cathleen* to support Yeats's play and instructed them to applaud everything that the church would not like.

Thus two months after the second performance of the Irish Literary Theatre in the early spring of 1900, the association of the Transvaal Committee was renewed when Griffith joined forces with Yeats and Maud Gonne in a protest against the visit of Queen Victoria to Dublin. The *United Irishman* opposed the visit vehemently, and in one way or another Yeats, Lady Gregory, Edward Martyn and Maud Gonne all played their part in the protest movement. The ostensible purpose of the Royal visit was publicly to thank the Irish troops who had fought in the Boer War by presenting them with shamrock at a review in the Phoenix Park. But as a large section of the Irish people were not at all pleased to see another small nation humiliated, and since Queen Victoria during her long reign had paid only two visits to Ireland, the timing of the visit was felt by many to be insensitive.

George Moore had kicked off with a ferocious letter to

The Times on 12 March 1900, suggesting that the visit
was an insult to the Irish in view of the treatment of the
country during her Majesty's reign. Yeats followed up
with a letter in the *Freeman's Journal*. He pointed out
that the Queen proposed to come to Ireland on 2 April
(she actually arrived on the fourth), the exact centenary
to the day of the Act of Union's introduction into the
English Parliament, after having been passed, thanks to
bribery, in the Irish one:

> Let any Irishman, who believes the Queen's visit to
> Ireland to be non-political, buy the current number of
> *Punch*. He will there find a cartoon representing the
> Irish members gazing, in various attitudes of terror,
> at a proclamation announcing this visit, while a
> picture of President Kruger, who is made to look as
> much like a chimpanzee as possible, lies at their feet,
> having fallen from the shaking hands of one of them.
> The Irish members are made as hideous as President
> Kruger is made and the whole is inspired by national
> hatred. The advisers of the Queen have not sent into
> Ireland this woman of eighty-one, to whom all labours
> must be weariness, without good reason, and the
> reason is national hatred – hatred of our individual
> national life, and, as Mr Moore has said, 'to do the
> work her recruiting sergeants have failed to do', 'with
> a shilling between her finger and thumb and a bag of
> shillings at her girdle'; and it is the duty of Irishmen,
> who believe that Ireland has an individual national
> life, to protest with as much courtesy as is compatible
> with vigour.

Lady Gregory must have approved of Yeats's stand, for
he was sending her copies of the letters he was writing
before he forwarded them to the newspapers. He had
written to her in early April saying that he had drafted a
resolution condemning the visit on behalf of the Irish
Party and had proposed at the meeting that Tim
Harrington, MP should resign his seat and have it
contested by John McBride who was at that time leading

a brigade for the Boers against the British in South Africa.

Lady Gregory had refused to join in the sentimental 'Union of Hearts' that was sweeping England at the time. She was over in London on St Patrick's Day and was nauseated at the sight of shamrocks on sale, laced with Union Jacks. 'I must give up the poor shamrock until this calamity of vulgarity it is part of is over', she noted in her diary. Instead that day she wore an ivy leaf in memory of Parnell as she crossed Hyde Park to have lunch with Enid Layard. But Lady Layard was so shocked at her disloyalty that Lady Gregory took it off and concealed it under her cloak with a diamond pin until later on in the evening. Edward Martyn too had the chance to make his gesture when Lord Clonbrock accosted him in the Kildare Street Club in March and asked him abruptly, had he refused to have 'God Save the Queen' played at a charity concert at Tulira? Edward replied that this was so, as he did not want songs that were party cries played in his home. Clonbrock snapped that this was a curious statement for a Deputy Lieutenant of the County and a JP, whereupon Edward took the wind out of his sails by saying that he would resign both offices. Again Lady Gregory came in as an adviser for she induced Edward to put his reasons in writing to stop the chatterboxes in the county from slandering him later on.

When I was made a JP and a DL I was a Unionist [Edward wrote]. I had been brought up one, and in ignorance of the history of my country and of its language. Some years ago my ears were opened by reading Lecky's *History of Ireland in the 18th Century*. Since then I have gone on and developed a dislike of England, I have refused to have 'God Save the Queen' and 'The Absent Minded Beggar' performed at a concert in my house because unfortunately in our country Mr Kipling's name has come to mean the same thing as the Union and the extinction of our distinctive nationality. If I am not free to act on

267

my convictions without being liable to be called to task, in however friendly a manner, by the Lieutenant of my country, I have no alternative but to resign the JP and DL.

Then, on 3 April, the day before the visit, Yeats got in his last shot with a letter to the *Daily Express*:

Sir,
Whoever is urged to pay honour to Queen Victoria tomorrow morning should remember this sentence of Mirabeau's – 'the silence of the people is the lesson of kings'. She is the official head and symbol of an empire that is robbing the South African Republics of their liberty, as it robbed Ireland of hers. Whoever stands by the roadway cheering for Queen Victoria cheers for that empire, dishonours Ireland, and condones a crime. But whoever goes tomorrow night to the meeting of the people and protests within the law against the welcome that Unionists and time-servers will have given to this English Queen, honours Ireland and condemns a crime. Yours sincerely,
W.B. Yeats

When the Queen did arrive there was surprisingly little disturbance. Ritual greetings were gone through while the Royal carriage made its way through muted crowds. James Joyce, who was among them, noted 'a tiny lady, almost a dwarf, tossed and jolted to and fro by the movements of the carriage, dressed in mourning and wearing horn-rimmed glasses on an empty and livid face'.

Later that afternoon, when an exhausted Royal personage had sunk down into her bed at the Viceregal Lodge, a gentleman of the court arrived in the room to congratulate her on the reception. 'Where am I?' was the reply he got from the bewildered old lady.

Maud Gonne was furious that she could not be there to create a protest as she had gone down in London with an attack of enteritis. But she had got over it sufficiently a few weeks later to put on her Patriotic Children's Treat. This was a party for the poor children of Dublin conducted in Clonturk Park as a gesture against the one given at the Queen's visit in Phoenix Park. (One may still meet old women in Dublin today who will say, 'I was at Madam's Party in the Park and I got a bun'.) From her sick bed in London Maud wrote a ferocious article on the Royal visit for her French publicity sheet *L' Irlande Libre*:

> Taking the shamrock in her withered hand this Queen dares to ask Ireland for soldiers – for soldiers to fight for the exterminators of the race. And the reply in Ireland comes sadly but proudly not through the lips of miserable little politicians, who are touched by the English canker, but through the lips of the Irish people: Queen, return to your own land, you will find no more Irishmen ready to wear the red shame of your livery. In the past they have done so from ignorance because it is hard to die of hunger when one is young and strong and the sun shines, but they shall do so no longer. See your recruiting agents return alone and unsuccessful from my green hills and plains, for once more hope is revived and it will be in the ranks of your enemies that my children will find employment and honour.

Griffith republished the article a week later in the *United Irishman* which infuriated the Castle authorities so much that they immediately suppressed the edition. Ramsay Colles, the editor of *Dublin Figaro*, a fashionable weekly paper, tried to minimise the effect of Maud Gonne's letter by suggesting that she was in the pay of the British. This so enraged Griffith (who adored Maud Gonne) that he went along to the editor's office and gave him a thrashing with a sjambok he had brought back from South Africa. As a result Colles brought a prosecution and Griffith was given a fortnight in gaol for assault. On his release he was delighted to be greeted by a group of young girls from Maud Gonne's association

'Inghini na hEireann' (Daughters of Erin). To replace his sjambok which he had broken on Colles's back they presented him with a blackthorn stick with a silver ring engraved with his name in Irish. Perhaps the best comment on this inappropriate Royal visit was from Percy French, the popular singer and entertainer, who wrote a witty account of an imaginary after-dinner speech made by the Queen, 'as overheard and cut into lengths of poetry by James Murphy, Deputy-Assistant Waiter at the Viceregal Lodge':

'And that other wan,' sez she
'That Maud Gonne,' sez she
'Dhressin' in black,' sez she
'To welcome me back,' sez she
'Though I don't care,' sez she
'What they wear,' sez she
'An' all that gammon,' sez she
'About me bringin' the famine,' sez she
'Now Maud'll write,' sez she
'That I brought the blight,' sez she
'Or altered the saysons,'sez she
'For political raysons,' sez she
'An' I think there's a slate,' sez she
'Off Willie Yeats,' sez she
'He should be at home,'sez she
'French polishin' a pome,' sez she
'An' not writin' letters,' sez she
'About his betters,' sez she
'Paradin' me crimes,' sez she
'In the *Irish Times*', sez she.

9   Farewell to the Saxon

The lure of his native land had begun to affect Moore.
His frequent visits to the country on behalf of the Irish
Literary Theatre and the outbreak of jingoism which
accompanied the Boer War combined to make him
consider leaving London and taking up residence in
Dublin. 'I live in a sort of nightmare,' he wrote to his
brother Maurice in 1900, 'when I think of the war. If I
were to allow my mind to ponder on it as others do I
should go off my head.' And later:

> On the subject of the war, I think I'm going a little
> crazy because I refuse to speak to anyone except
> those who are against the war. I met a man the other
> day whom I had known all my life, he told me the war
> was a beautiful thing and that this was an exception-
> ally fine example of war. I said, 'I shall never speak to
> you again.'

Moore's brother Maurice might not have been the ideal
confidant for such ideas, for he was a serving major in
the Connaught Rangers who were at that time engaged
in fighting on the Cape. But like his brother George,
Maurice had his own view of what was right or wrong
and currently he felt that English policy in South Africa
was misplaced. He was an ardent Irish nationalist and
was learning Irish in his tent during lulls in the fighting,
which George admired him for but thought 'lurid'. When
Maurice sent home a letter describing how Kitchener
had issued orders that prisoners were to be shot, George
had it published in the *Freeman's Journal*. It was later

taken up in The Times and when two editors on the Cape reprinted The Times statements they landed in jail (a matter for which the major apologised to them twenty years later when he revisited South Africa).

Moore seems to have undergone a lightning conversion during these few months in Ireland. Fifteen years before he had been bawling about his people as 'degenerate aborigines' and declaring that he had a hatred of his own race 'as fierce as that which closes a ferret's teeth on a rat's throat'. He had scourged the clergy for their part in degrading the people. Now it was the Irish race which had become heroic for resisting the foreigner and the church 'for retaining the distinction of religion'. The germs of this astonishing volte face are contained in a speech he made at a meeting of the promoters of the Irish Literary Theatre in the spring of 1900.

I feel that I must apologise for appearing before you with a manuscript of my speech in my hand [he began]. The sight of a manuscript in a country where oratory flourishes everywhere in all ranks of society and in all conditions of intellect must appear anomalous and absurd.

It will be conceded to me that the three great distinctions of nations are religion, language, law. The distinction of religion, Ireland holds secure; for this distinction she has suffered robbery, violence and contumely but on this point I don't think I need persist. And she struggled no less fiercely on the distinction of law. But for the third distinction, the distinction of language, she has shown less determination and perseverance. Fellow countrymen, the language is slipping into the grave and if a national effort is not made at once to save the language it will be unknown in another generation. We must return to the language. It is not known whence or how; it is a mysterious inheritance in which resides the soul of the Irish people.

For hundreds of years the Saxon has attempted to

assimilate the Celt but the Celt through his religion and his language has retained his individuality. The destruction of the Celtic spirit has always been a definite object of Saxon desire.

You will be told that these are sentimental reasons, transcendental reasons. Ibsen writes in a language which is spoken by very few millions yet his plays are read all over Europe and the old Irish poems written in a form no longer spoken are known to European scholars.

The English language in fifty years will be as corrupt as the Latin in the eighth century, as unfit for literary usage and will become, in my opinion, a sort of Volapük, strictly limited to commercial letters and to journalism.

In my youth, Irish was still spoken everywhere; but the gentry took pride in not understanding their own language. It is our misfortune that such false fashions should have prevailed and kept us in ignorance of our language, but it will be our fault if our children do not learn their own language. I have no children and I am too old to learn the language but I shall at once arrange that my brother's children learn Irish. I have written to my sister-in-law telling her that I will undertake this essential part of her children's education. They shall have a nurse straight from the Aran Islands; for it profits a man nothing if he knows all the languages of the world and knows not his own.

The reference to his nephews learning the Irish language was made by Moore in all seriousness. When his sister-in-law, in the absence of her husband at the war, pressed less than diligently in getting a proper Gaelic nurse for the boys, Moore cut them out of his will and only restored them when adequate tuition had been provided. Perhaps it was from Huysmans that he first got his idea that the English language was worn out. He mentions a conversation on the subject of language in *Confessions of a Young Man*. But Moore, who had mastered prose in the novel as no one in his generation had done, now turned to a language which he did not understand as a means of resuscitating literature. 'The English language has become a dry shank bone on the dusty heap of empire,' he declared to his friends – while spending his free evenings going down to the head-quarters of the Gaelic League in Parnell Square just to watch his sentences turn into Irish as he dictated them to a translator.

How far his conversion to the Irish way of things had gone can be judged by the fact that at this time he actually gave an interview to a newspaper advocating clerical censorship. In the *Freeman's Journal* in November 1901 he criticised the London stage censor-ship because it was a lay one, but asserted that 'an ecclesiastical censorship would be an ideal state of things'. When Yeats, appalled at this statement, rushed over to ask him what he meant, Moore replied airily:

> The intelligent censorship of the church will free the stage from the unintelligent and ignorant censorship of the public. No more letters signed, 'father of a family'.

With such sentiments it was natural for Moore to decide in the spring of 1901 to move to Dublin.

It was AE who found him his house at 4 Ely Place, 'the perfect residence, Moore,' he said, 'for a man of letters, one of five little eighteenth-century houses shut off from the thoroughfare and with an orchard opposite which may be yours for two or three pounds a year'. When they got to the house AE, with his practical bent, started testing the boilers and cisterns while Moore was examining the marble mantelpieces, and listening to the caretaker's complaints about passers by:

> 'One does hear some bad language sometimes,' the caretaker murmured, turning her head away.
> 'I'm sure they blaspheme splendidly. Blasphemy is the literature of Catholic countries. AE, what an inveterate mystic you are, as practical as St Teresa;

whereas I am content if the windows and mantelpieces are eighteenth-century. Don't let the slum trouble you, my good woman. A man of letters never objects to a slum. He sharpens his pen there.'

'The convent garden, sir, on the right –'

'Yes, I see, and a great many night-shirts out drying.'

'No, sir, the nuns' underwear.'

'Better and better. Into what Eden have you led me, AE? Who is the agent of this Paradise?'

The rent was a hundred pounds a year and Moore had his 'grey Manet, exquisite mauve Monet and my sad Pissarro' brought over from London, and his Aubusson carpets laid on the drawing room floor. Ely Place was a cul-de-sac and Moore's house the second last of five houses which formed a terrace at the end of it. The house had been built in 1820 and had the long-paned windows with balconies and soft-coloured brickwork typical of the period. This was to be Moore's residence for the next nine years.

Soon he became a figure in the city. His day's work ended at four. After correcting the draft of his morning's dictation he left it with his secretary and set out on a saunter across the city. Perhaps he would visit Grafton Street first in the hope of meeting Tommy O'Shaughnessy, the dapper little barrister, and gleaning some legal scandal from his eager lips. Then he might visit Longworth in the *Irish Times*, and after that ramble south again towards the National Library where he had made a friend of Richard Best, a clever young Celtic scholar who was a librarian there. Moore, as he had always done, continued to educate himself by conversation and Dubliners of Best's calibre were of the greatest possible use to him with their wide knowledge and their willingness to impart it – though sometimes the extent of his ignorance astonished Best, to whom he often showed his manuscripts. Best recalled to the author that he suggested to Moore on one occasion that the use of the subjunctive would improve a certain sentence. 'But what is a subjunctive, Best?' said Moore. When Best explained, Moore said with wide eyes: 'But, Best, that is beautiful, I shall *always* use the subjunctive.' He wrote to Jacques-Emile Blanche that winter:

I have said farewell to my artificial life, the wind from the sea and fields makes me feel another man. I have no lack of friends who will come in and talk to me after dinner. I shall be able to write in the newspapers and mix actively in politics but I think I am going to teach the Irish what art and painting are.

Though Moore talked constantly of his amours ('when I opened the door a woman threw her arms around my neck. "At last I have found you, there are thirteen George Moores in the London directory" '), there was no evidence at his evenings of a feminine presence with a special attraction for him. This prompted Susan Mitchell, AE's secretary, to revive one of Wilde's remarks: 'Some men kiss and tell, George Moore tells and doesn't kiss.' But Moore, between his fortieth and fiftieth years, had had some notable conquests. Pearl Craigie had been his lover until she was replaced by the delicious Maud Burke from San Francisco. 'George Moore, you have a soul of fire,' Maud had declared after she had listened to his conversation at dinner. She was to remain his friend for thirty years after she married the millionaire ship owner Bache Cunard in 1896. And soon after he lost Maud to shipping, Moore met a London painter Clara Christian who, fascinated by his unpredictable Irish personality, decided to follow him to Dublin. Oliver Gogarty remembered her as 'tall, if not taller than myself. Her complexion was as pink and white as Dresden china. She had high cheekbones and no chin. Back she had of bended yew.' Gogarty was one of the few who had seen Clara Christian, for Moore did not permit her to attend his evenings. He had parked her in a country house, Tymon Lodge, about eight miles from Ely Place at

Templeogue. There he used to visit her in the afternoons and follow her around the garden while she attended to her flowers which she adored. It was an attraction of opposites ... Moore's mercurial Irishness beside her very English saneness. How happy he was with her can be seen from one enchanted passage in *Vale*, which in a sentence or two manages to encompass a perfect summer.

> The rooks were building, and a little while after a great scuffling was heard in one of the chimneys and a young jackdaw came down and soon became tamer than any bird I had ever seen, tamer than a parrot, and at the end of May the corncrake called from the meadow that summer had come again, and the kine wandered in deeper and deeper herbage. The days seemed never to end, and looking through the branches of the chestnut in which the fruit had not begun to show, we caught sight of a strange spectacle. Stella said, a lunar rainbow, and I wondered, never having heard of or seen such a thing before.

Clara Christian had exhibited in the Royal Academy and later would show in the New England Arts Club. A love of art bound the two together. Moore used to say he was never himself when he was far away from the smell of oil paint, but he feared an open involvement, which was why he would only walk with Clara over the deserted country roads of Rathfarnham or the hills above Tallaght. After a while he began to see that her temperament would have to be adjusted to his if they were to live together and with the fairness of one artist to another he did not wish to interfere with her creative life. Clara began to notice that a barrier was growing between them. He seldom saw her alone. One day she told him that if he did not care to see her without a chaperone she would rather not see him at all. Moore knew that he would have to break with her and when she told him she was about to be married and asked his advice, he had to conceal his elation as he tried to counsel her as a friend.

He had what, for him, were pangs of remorse, for he had taken her from her roots in London where she had lived with an intimate friend, the impressionist painter Ethel Walker (later Dame Ethel Walker, OBE), and within a year of her marriage Clara had died in childbirth. Moore calls her 'Stella' in his memoirs, but unlike Swift's Stella, who was as cruelly concealed, she did not become part of the legend of his life.

10 Diarmuid And Grania

It was Lady Gregory who suggested that Moore and Yeats collaborate on a play. When Moore had spoken at the Irish National Literary Society in the Gresham Hotel on 22 February 1900, he had told the audience that it was hoped next year they would present a play based on the Irish saga of Diarmuid and Grania with the help of 'the distinguished poet whose contemporary collaborator I have the honour to be'. Lady Gregory had instigated the idea, and now she invited the two writers down to Coole so that they could work together without interruption. Moore finished his journey by bicycle from Gort railway station to Coole. He recognised that he was going to a literary workshop for he knew that Hyde and Yeats had already been given hospitality at Coole while they got on with their poetry and folklore. When he arrived at the house he decided that 'a horn should be hung on the gatepost and the gate should not open till the visitor had blown forth a motif'. He had arrived in time for dinner, but there was no sign of Yeats. He was upstairs in the throes of composition. Dinner was delayed until the poet came down, explaining that just as the gong went he had found a new metre and, allowing himself be carried away by the sound, he had forgotten the time. He made it clear to the company that writing in prose for the projected play was an effort and that he much preferred verse.

This was a hint to Moore of the difficulties in store when they got down to their collaboration. Moore was to do the construction and Yeats the language – at least that was Lady Gregory's idea. But it is clear in retrospect that the mind of the novelist and the poet were moving in different directions when it came to the interpretation of the theme. Diarmuid and Grania, a primitive tale, tells how Grania leaves the Irish chieftain Finn on the night of her marriage and runs away with one of his lieutenants, Diarmuid. Loyal to his leader, Diarmuid avoids carnal contact until Grania tricks him into it. The remainder of the tale deals with Finn's pursuit of the lovers and his eventual arrangement of Diarmuid's death, after which Grania returns to the marriage bed. An obvious way to treat such a theme in dramatic form would have been to write it in verse, especially as Yeats had already shown himself to have had the gift of being able to compose poetic dialogue that worked on the stage. But Moore, who had simply no gift for poetry whatsoever, would have none of this. So prose it had to be. Yeats then suggested a peasant Grania with Irish dialect, at which Moore, with his head full of Wagnerian notions, threw up his hands in horror. 'Anyone could acquire dialect,' he sneered, 'by lying five in a bed in a hovel, and eating American bacon.' He added that it was alright for Yeats to wait like a jackdaw for Lady Gregory to emerge from a cottage with a folk tale and then put style on it, but this play wasn't going to be written in that fashion. Yeats was to maintain later that Moore wanted 'numb, dumb words' and that his practice as a novelist had made him use descriptive and reminiscent dialogue which held up the action of the play. Moore's experience as a novelist and dramatist had given him a knowledge of construction which was invaluable to the shaping of the play. But his lack of feeling for dramatic language brought him into continual conflict with Yeats. In the scene where Diarmuid is dying Moore wanted him to say to Finn, 'I will kick you down the stairways of the stars'. Fortunately Yeats had control where dialogue was concerned and vetoed this.

Their search for a suitable language in which to explain an ancient theme should, of course, have resolved itself in the play being written in Irish. But with

Moore unable to do this, eventually they became so desperate that they agreed to a haphazard suggestion thrown out by Lady Gregory that Moore write the dialogue first in French. Moore recalled how an extraordinary plan was proposed by Yeats who woke him up in the middle of the night to tell him about it:

'What is it? Who is it? Yeats!'

'I'm sorry to disturb you, but an idea has just occurred to me.'

And sitting on the edge of my bed he explained that the casual suggestion that I preferred to write the play in French rather than in his vocabulary was a better idea than he had thought at the time.

'How is that, Yeats?' I asked, rubbing my eyes.

'Well, you see, through the Irish language we can get a peasant Grania.'

'But Grania is a King's daughter. I don't know what you mean, Yeats; and my French –'

'Lady Gregory will translate your text into English. Taidgh O'Donoghue will translate the English text into Irish and Lady Gregory will translate the Irish text back into English.'

'And then you'll put style upon it? And it was for that you awoke me?'

'But don't you think a peasant Grania –'

'No, Yeats, I don't, but I'll sleep on it and tomorrow morning I may think differently. It is some satisfaction, however, to hear that you can bear my English style at four removes.' And as I turned over in the hope of escaping from further literary discussion, I heard a thin, hollow laugh which Yeats uses on such occasions to disguise his disapproval of a joke if it tells ever so little against himself.

Next morning under the weeping ash tree Lady Gregory renewed the idea proposing that after Moore had written it in French, she would translate it into English and a member of the Gaelic League would then translate it into Irish. Then Lady Gregory could translate it back into English again.

But as I was about to tell Lady Gregory that I declined to descend into the kitchen to don the cap and apron, to turn the spit while the *chef des sauces* prepared his gravies and stirred his saucepans, the adventure of writing a play in French, to be translated three times back and forwards before the last and immortal relish was to be poured upon it, began to appeal to me. Literary adventures have always been my quest, and here was one; and seeing in it a way to escape from the English language, which I had come to hate for political reasons, and from the English country and the English people, I said: 'It is impossible to write this play in French in Galway. A French atmosphere is necessary; I will go to France and send it to you, act by act.'

So it was in Paris that the first part of *Diarmuid and Grania* was written, in French. In *Ave* Moore published Act II Scene 2 of the play in French to show, as he said himself, that 'two such literary lunatics as myself and Yeats existed contemporaneously'.

It is hard to take this extraordinary transmutation of dialogue seriously today. But it was just another step in Moore's belief that language needed to be liberated, and draw its strength from tongues that had not been corrupted by over-use.

Eventually the play was completed and Yeats brought it over to Mrs Patrick Campbell to see if she would play the part of Grania.

The shields are the success of the play with her [he wrote to Lady Gregory]. Moore told her that they were my work and she said almost the moment she saw me, 'Oh Mr Yeats, the opening of Act I is wonderful. Why did you not do the whole play?' I then of course explained how essential Moore had been. She went on, 'I am sure I know what part you have done and what part he has done for sometimes the words are beautiful and sometimes they are like a French novel and spoil everything.' She then quoted the part about

282

'your eyes are grey' as beautiful and said, 'It would make an actress crazy with excitement merely to have such things spoken over her', and she took up the play and read them out to somebody who was there. She has begged me to read the play to her right through that she may point out places where she thinks it needs some verbal improvement. This is a delicate matter – I don't quite know how Moore will like it, but she is right. When one has to give up one's standard as I have had to do in this play, one rather loses the power of judging at all. I told her that I was just a lyric poet and that Moore was a very considerable dramatist and she answered, 'Well, you have made a very great work between you', and quoted Max Beerbohm who had said, 'But where do they begin to come together?' I gave her 'The Shadowy Waters' but her chief interest seemed to be, had I written 'a beautiful inscription' to her, but alas I had only written 'Mrs. Patrick Campbell from W.B. Yeats' and slurred over the word Campbell because I was not sure of the spelling.

She agreed to play the part, but Yeats fell ill and while he was laid up, Moore withdrew the play from her. According to Yeats's account this was because Moore had insisted that her manager call on him, while she wanted Moore to call on the manager. Whatever went on, it was Sir Frank Benson's Company who were finally engaged to come to Dublin in June and present the play at the Gaiety Theatre, Mrs Benson playing the part of Grania. The cast would include Henry Ainley, Matheson Lang, H.O. Nicholson.

Another name was to be included in the programme, for Moore, wanting some music for the play, on an impulse wrote to Edward Elgar and asked him if he could supply a horn call:

Mr Benson is going to produce *Diarmuid and Grania*, a drama written by Mr Yeats and myself on the great Irish legend. Finn's horn is heard in the second act, and all my pleasure in the performance will be spoilt if a cornet-player tootles out whatever comes into his head, perhaps some vulgar phrase the audience has heard already in the streets. Beautiful phrases come into the mind while one is doing odd jobs, and if you do not look upon my request as an impertinence, and if you will provide yourself with a sheet of music-paper before you shave in the morning, and if you do not forget the pencil, you will be able to write down a horn call, before you turn from the right to the left cheek, that will save my play from a moment of vulgarity.

Elgar answered with not one but six horn calls, which prompted Moore to ask: would he write music for the scene in which the dying Diarmuid refuses to drink water brought to him in a helmet by Finn, and for the final act when Diarmuid is carried away on a litter to the funeral pyre. To his delight Elgar sent two more pieces. The funeral march particularly delighted Moore:

Out of the harmony a little melody floats, pathetic as an autumn leaf, and it seemed to me that Elgar must have seen the primeval forest as he wrote, and the tribe moving among the falling leaves – oak leaves, hazel leaves, for the world began with oak and hazel.

The rehearsals went slowly. English actors found it difficult to deal with what was after all a very Irish play. They found the Gaelic names almost impossible to pronounce. Grania (which is properly pronounced as 'Grawneyeh') was at various times in the production rendered as 'Grauniar' or 'Grainyeh'. None of them could get their tongue round Caoilte at all. Someone said it should be pronounced 'Sheelsher'. But even on the night of the first performance the cast was still producing variances such as 'wheel chair', 'cold tea' and 'quilty'. Yeats expressed his apprehension in a letter to Lady Gregory:

Here we are, a lot of intelligent people who might have been doing some sort of decent work that leaves the soul free: yet here we are going through all sorts of trouble and annoyance for a mob that knows neither literature or art. I might have been away in the country, in Italy perhaps, writing poems for my equals and my betters.

He was particularly depressed at the time he wrote the letter, because he had just observed a sheep (which Benson was to carry on in his arms) on the other side of the stage, eating the property ivy. The idea of Benson bringing a live sheep on the stage had appealed to Moore, who thought he could use it for publicity purposes:

Benson is very much taken with the idea of the sheep shearing. He says he will carry in a sheep. I told him a sheep is a difficult animal to carry but he says there will be no difficulty for him. The stage will show fleece hung about, there will be branding irons and crooks; Cormac will watch the shearing and when Diarmuid and the shepherd have carried out the kicking animal Cormac will out with his lament. I cannot tell you how pleased I am; I walk about the streets thinking of the fleeces and the sheep. The shearing will take the audience back to the beginnings of things. Man has shorn sheep since the beginning of the wars and the strive [sic] will break in upon Arcady as they always have done.

It had been intended to present a version of Yeats's *The Land of Heart's Desire*, translated into Irish, as a curtain raiser to *Diarmuid and Grania*. But instead Douglas Hyde had been persuaded to take one of the stories from Yeats's *Celtic Twilight* and adapt it for the stage in Irish. This was called in its new form *The Twisting of the Rope*. It tells of a vagabond poet, Hanrahan from Connaught, who is wooing a young girl at a cottage dance in a Munster village. Despite the fact that she is engaged to a local lad, Hanrahan makes up to her and wins her admiration with his fine words. In the end of the play the angry villagers manage to eject Hanrahan by persuading him to join in the twisting of a hay rope which is required to rescue a coach that has fallen into a ditch nearby. As he twists the rope, he inadvertently steps back out of the door which is slammed on him while his rival shouts, 'where is Connaught now?'

Moore originally undertook to direct the play. The actors were five members of the Gaelic League whom Hyde had collected together. Hyde himself was to play the part of Hanrahan the poet. Rehearsals took place in the hall at the Keating Branch of the Gaelic League in Parnell Square. Moore was rather tart with the players when they told him that they had never acted before but could speak Irish, retorting that he hoped they could at least do this since the play was in Irish. Perhaps this was a bad beginning, for though he rehearsed them for three weeks, in the end he had to hand the play over to a young actor called W.G. Fay who directed an amateur group, the Ormonde Players, and worked with Maud Gonne's Daughters of Erin in presenting tableaux. Immediately Fay took over the rehearsals he had Douglas Hyde do a translation of the play into English. Then he had the players do their parts in English while he gave them their positions. After that they turned the play back into Irish and put it together piece by piece.

Hyde turned out to be an inspired actor in the part of Hanrahan. With a fiddle stuck in an inside jacket pocket like a newspaper, this erudite scholar turned into a swaggering vagabond. It was typical of him that he would only expose the extrovert side of his character in an Irish play where it could not hinder the cause to which he had devoted his life. His diary records his excitement at the event, but also underlines the haphazard fashion in which his play was finally brought to the stage:

In the evening at about 9.30 I collected my group. Benson's men made up our male actors and the make-up woman prepared our girls. I got a costume from a

man named Trevanion, a Jewish man, I believe, for
£4.00; the boys provided bainins and the girls made
their own costumes.

The first night in the Gaiety Theatre, on 21 October
1901, was attended by the Vicereine Lady Cadogan and
the Lord Mayor of Dublin. The Gaiety is an elegant
building with parterre, dress circle, upper circle,
gallery and spacious boxes. It held twelve hundred
people and was packed.

Diarmuid and Grania had been thoroughly rehearsed
and was generally well received by the audience,
though the press next day blamed Mrs Benson in the
part of Grania for the play's failure to succeed as it
might otherwise have done.

Yeats was to say to Lennox Robinson many years
later, 'I think *Diarmuid and Grania* is better than I
remembered it to be.' Reading it today *Diarmuid and
Grania* has the mark of a well-made play, whose weakness lies in a failure by Moore to grasp the dramatic
possibilities of Diarmuid's rivalry with Finn. Moore
made him weak and concentrated instead on the character of Grania. There are a number of archaisms in the
dialogue too – 'flouted', 'broil' ('this is a man's broil', i.e.
fight) – which were ridiculous in the context of the time
and which Yeats had specifically warned Moore to
avoid when they began collaboration.

The great success of the night was *The Twisting of the
Rope* or *Casadh an tSúgáin*. This was the first time that
a play in Irish had been performed on a regular stage
and nationalist Ireland came along to support it. It was
received with rapt attention, and there were thun-
derous cheers at the end with the players dancing a
four-hand reel accompanied by the orchestra. Holloway
wrote in his diary next day:

A few years ago no one could conceive it would be
possible to produce a play in Irish on the Dublin stage
and interest all beholders, yet such was the case
tonight when Dr Douglas Hyde's little Gaelic piece

287

The Twisting of the Rope was produced for the first time by Gaelic-speaking amateurs. Dr Douglas Hyde, the author, as Hanrahan, though villainously made up, made love very persuasively and rated those who would deprive him of the young maiden with delightful glibness and sincerely expressed abuse. I have always been told that Irish is a splendid language to make love in or abuse, and having heard Dr Hyde I call well believe it. His 'soft talk' and 'hard words' flowed with equal freedom and apparent ease from his slippery tongue. There was a simple naturalness about the whole scene that was refreshing. The applause was great at the end, and the curtain was raised several times amid continual approval.

During the interval the Gaelic Leaguers in the gods sang songs in Irish and the audience joined in the choruses. It was an emotional moment. Afterwards a crowd mobbed Yeats and Maud Gonne as they left in a cab for supper, and wanted to take the horse out of the cab and drag it there, but Maud, exhausted with public adulation, would not allow it.

Outside the theatre was a figure 'weeping with vexation'. This was Standish O'Grady. He felt that the main play had degraded Finn and his companions. It had drawn them out of the heroic age and brought them down to the level of the mob. The Ireland O'Grady had envisaged was an aristocratic-based society led by its nobility of all backgrounds, Anglo-Irish and Gaelic, and giving away its gods to the people did not appeal to him in the least.

Next day Frank Fay, Willie Fay's brother, reviewed the evening in the *United Irishman*:

Monday evening was a memorable one for Dublin and for Ireland. The Irish language has been heard on the stage of the principal metropolitan theatre and 'A Nation Once Again' has been sung within its walls, and hope is strong within us once more. The Gaiety Theatre was crowded in all parts, and Ireland's greatest daughter, Miss Maud Gonne, sat beside Ireland's greatest poet Mr W.B. Yeats.

In a very short space of time Frank Fay and his brother Willie were to build a company which would interpret these new Irish plays in an Irish fashion. In doing so, they would create a new style in the theatre and make the name of the Abbey significant in the history of twentieth-century drama.

And there was one figure in the stalls at *Diarmuid and Grania* and *Casadh an tSúgáin* for whom the night was to have a special significance. This was John Synge, at home in Dublin at the time. We may imagine the effect on him of hearing Irish spoken for the first time in a professional theatre – the first Irish play. This was the idiom in which he had sensed the material for a new art. Here now was the form – the drama. It must have seemed as if the images he had brought with him from the Aran Islands were playing themselves out before his eyes. The characters in Hyde's play used the same poetic imagery that the Aran folk did – yet the effect was a realistic one because it was based on the speech of the people. Hanrahan, the chief character in *Casadh an tSúgáin* could have been the prototype of the vagabonds Synge had met in the Wicklow glens. Now, in the theatre, he could recreate these figures that had fascinated and obsessed him. Hyde had shown the way. Synge would draw from Hanrahan's personality a whole series of characters, from the tramp in *In The Shadow of the Glen* to Christy Mahon in *The Playboy of the Western World* who split his father 'to the knob of his gullet' and became the toast of a western village for his deed. It was as if all Synge had been working towards had been drawn together in an hour or two by fate. Within a few months Synge had his first play written. It was without merit; but within a year the first of his five masterpieces was complete. That this night meant something special to him is clear from a report written afterwards in French for *The European*:

One could not help but smile at seeing all round the room the beautiful girls of the Gaelic League, who were chattering away in very bad Irish with pale enthusiastic young clerks. But during an intermission of *Diarmuid and Grania* it happened that the people in the gallery began to sing. They sang the old songs of the people. Until then I had never heard these songs sung in the ancient tongue by so many voices. The auditorium shook and in between notes of incomparable sadness there was something like the death rattle of a nation. I saw one head bend down behind a programme and then another. People were weeping when the curtain rose and the play was resumed in the midst of the lively emotion. One sensed the spirit of a nation had hovered for an instant in the room.

11   James Joyce Gets In Touch

James Joyce, aged twenty, was livid with the production
at the Gaiety. A literary movement had been started
without consulting him. Worse, it had continued for two
years and he had not made contact with it. *Diarmuid and
Grania* seemed to him to be a retrospective experiment,
instead of examining the personal predicament of man
in the wake of the new social and philosophical themes
of the previous fifty years. He hurried into print and
published (after it had been refused by the college magazine) a pamphlet attacking the Irish Literary Theatre.
He named it 'The Day of the Rabblement', suggesting
that the Irish Literary Theatre, by giving in to popular
tastes, had been overwhelmed by the mob.

> Nothing can be done until the forces that dictate
> public judgment are calmly confronted. But of course
> the directors are shy of presenting Ibsen, Tolstoy or
> Hauptmann, where even *Countess Cathleen* is
> pronounced vicious and damnable. Even for a tech-
> nical reason this project was necessary. A nation
> which never advanced so far as a miracle play
> affords no literary model to the artist and he must look
> abroad. Earnest dramatists of the second rank,
> Sudermann, Bjornsen and Giacosa can write very
> much better plays than the Irish Literary Theatre has
> staged. But of course the directors would not like to
> present such improper writers to the uncultivated,
> much less to the cultivated rabblement. Accordingly
> the rabblement, placid and intensely moral, is

enthroned in boxes and galleries amid a hum of approval – *la bestia trionfante*. . . .

With some impudence the young critic questioned the standing of the leaders of the movement. Yeats came off best.

It is unsafe at present to say of Mr Yeats that he has, or has not, genius. Edward Martyn, disabled by an incorrigible style, has none of the fierce hysterical power of Strindberg, whom he suggests at times, while Mr Moore, though he has a wonderful mimetic ability, is beginning to draw upon his literary account.

According to Joyce the Irish Literary Theatre had given in to 'the trolls, the multitude and the rabblement' and could no longer be said to carry on the traditions of 'the old master who is dying in Christiania'. He finished by stating grandly that Ibsen's successor was waiting in the wings, with more than a suggestion that he was referring to himself.

His devotion to Ibsen was at its height. The *Fortnightly Review* had published his essay on *When We Dead Awaken*, Ibsen's last play, unaware perhaps that the writer was only a boy of eighteen. Joyce had even gone to the trouble of learning Dano-Norwegian to write a letter to the old man on his seventieth birthday:

What shall I say more? I have sounded your name defiantly through a college where it was either unknown or known faintly and darkly. I have claimed for you your rightful place in the history of the drama. I have shown what, as it seemed to me, was your highest excellence – your lofty impersonal power. Your minor claims – your satire, your technique and orchestral harmony – these, too, I advanced. Do not think me a hero-worshipper. I am not so. And when I spoke of you in debating societies, and so forth, I enforced attention by no futile ranting. But we always keep the dearest things to ourselves. I did not tell them what bound me closest to you. I did not say how what I could discern dimly of your life was my pride to see, how your battles inspired me – not the obvious material battles but those that were fought and won behind your forehead, how your wilful resolution to wrest the secret from life gave me heart and how in your absolute indifference to public canons of art, friends, and shibboleths you walked in the light of your inward heroism.

That he should have been able to compose such a letter in Dano-Norwegian is not only a tribute to Joyce's extraordinary linguistic ability, but to his industry. When he set out to accomplish a task connected with his artistic mission his energy was phenomenal.

Edward Martyn (though Joyce does not appear to have known this) had already begun to distance himself from the Irish Literary Theatre because of its refusal, as he saw it, to follow in Ibsen's path. One can see, then, why Joyce was unlikely to give his benediction to what he looked on as the self-indulgence of middle-aged writers.

The difference between Joyce and the trio of Yeats and Lady Gregory and Hyde was that they saw native culture as a means of expressing a side of their personality which had been repressed and as a means of strengthening their native identity, while Joyce believed that the part of his psyche which was holding him back from joining the mainstream of European thought was exactly that native one. He wanted to shed it – they wanted to plumb its depths. The rural people and their culture meant nothing to Joyce. He had no interest in the Irish language and knew hardly a word of it. He only once visited the Aran Islands and missed completely the material for creative work that Synge and Lady Gregory had found there. A discussion which takes place in his autobiographical novel *Stephen Hero* between Stephen Dedalus and his friend Madden would have seemed like the worst type of West British cant to Yeats, Lady Gregory or Hyde:

- You want our peasants to ape the gross materialism of the Yorkshire peasant? said Madden.
- One would imagine the country was inhabited by cherubim, replied Stephen. Damme if I see much difference in peasants: they all seem to me as like one another as a peascod is like another peascod. The Yorkshireman is perhaps better fed.
- Of course, you despise the peasant because you live in the city.
- I don't despise his office in the least
- But you despise him – he's not clever enough for you.
- Now you know, Madden, that's nonsense. To begin with he's as cute as a fox – try to pass a false coin on him and you'll see. But his cleverness is all of a low order. I really don't think that the Irish peasant represents a very admirable type of culture.

The sounds and murmurs which had disturbed Yeats's ear and resulted in a new rhythm in English verse meant nothing to Joyce. Even in his admiration for the early nineteenth-century poet James Clarence Mangan, he failed to notice the intrusion into his verse of the Gaelic syntax and stress. Joyce could listen to a countryman tell a tale that would have enchanted Synge or Hyde and would have provided them afterwards with the material for a creative work, and remain merely amused by it. He had grown up in an urban environment which had despised rural life and which had cut itself off from the roots of Gaelic culture, so that the existence of a body of literature which had fascinated the leaders of the literary renaissance when they had come across it was unknown to him. His appetite was towards the world outside, for the Continent, and he had convinced himself that 'the Celt had contributed nothing but a whine to Europe'. His classmate, Tom Kettle, expressed a feeling probably shared by many of Joyce's generation of the rising Catholic middle class when he wrote, in a somewhat awkward phrase, 'if Ireland is to become truly Irish, she must first become European'.

Though he had declared himself against the direction the literary renaissance was taking, Joyce decided that he had better do something to make the acquaintance of his peers as they had not so far made any contact with him. Evidently reading papers to the University debating society and publishing pamphlets had not been sufficient to draw the attention of Yeats and AE to him. One evening in the autumn of 1902, he decided to walk across the city to AE's house in Rathgar. It was typical of Joyce that he should cross the river and undertake a journey of five miles without making an appointment. He knew Rathgar well because he had been born in Brighton Square, just round the corner from AE's house, but there was no one in when he arrived at ten p.m., so Joyce waited until the poet returned at midnight. When Joyce asked if it was too late to have a talk, AE replied kindly, 'It's never too late'. When they got to AE's study the two sat down, facing each other in silence for some time – AE bearded, burly and benevolent, Joyce slim, clean shaven and tense. Since both were short-sighted they must have peered somewhat at each other. When Joyce said nothing AE asked kindly, 'Has it emerged yet?' Joyce then offered to read some poems, after making it clear that he did not care whether AE liked them or not. He admitted to a qualified admiration for some of AE's poems, but condemned Yeats for his involvement with the folk movement. They remained talking until four a.m., discussing theosophy, the theatre, Catholicism and eastern religions. When he was going, Joyce, perhaps slightly wounded by AE's well-meant criticism of his verse, remarked to his host, 'You have not enough chaos in you to make a world.' This does not seem to have offended AE, for shortly afterwards he wrote a letter to Lady Gregory, expressing enthusiasm for his youthful visitor:

Tell Willie that the thing I prophesied to him has already come to pass. A new generation is rising, to whose enlightened vision he and I are too obvious, our intelligence backward and lacking in subtlety. The first of the new race called on me a couple of days ago. He wanted to see whether I was he who was to come or was he to look for another. He is going to look for another but he sat with me up to 4 a.m. telling me of the true inwardness of things from his point of view. He is a young man aged twenty – one whom we shall, I think, hear of later on. He writes well, too well indeed for such a boy, and his reading ranges from the medieval saints and theologians to the sacred books of the East. He seemed to quote with equal fluency from Ibsen in the original and the early Franciscans. His name is Joyce. I will hand him over to Willie as one of his men when he comes to town. He is too superior for me. I belong to a lower order of thought than this spectre of fastidiousness . . . I will hand him over to Willie who may be the Messiah he is looking for. I am not.

Feeling perhaps a little overpowered by the visit, AE confided to the artist Sarah Purser, 'I wouldn't be his Messiah for a thousand million pounds. He would always be criticising the bad taste of his Deity.' This did not stop him writing to Yeats about Joyce, introducing him as 'an extremely clever young boy, the first spectre of the new generation', though he added, 'I have suffered from him and would like you to suffer too.' AE fixed an appointment with Yeats for Joyce which the young man did not keep. Instead he buttonholed the poet in the street one day outside the National Library. Yeats decently did not resent this personal confrontation and suggested a cup of tea in a café in O'Connell Street. As they walked along Joyce remarked, with his usual defensive technique, 'I am not treating you with any deference for, after all, you and I will be forgotten.' Yeats does not seem to have taken offence at being included by this young man as a candidate for oblivion. When, after they had reached the café and sat down, he recommended that Joyce read Balzac, Joyce replied, 'Who reads Balzac today?' with a laugh so loud that everybody in the café looked up at the poet; yet Yeats did not reprove him. Obviously Joyce's personality had impressed him. When he told Joyce that his energy and vitality reminded him of William Morris, Joyce replied sarcastically, 'I don't have his physique.' Joyce then proceeded to read Yeats some of his prose epiphanies, once more taking the precaution of telling Yeats that he did not care whether he liked them or not. Yeats thought them beautiful though immature. Earnestly the young man questioned the poet. Was his inspiration drying up? Why did he have to theorise? Yeats suspected for a moment that he was talking to a pietistic Catholic trapped in a rigid Thomistic framework. But a comment from Joyce that he hoped Wilde's deathbed conversion to Catholicism was not sincere, as this would have meant that he would have been untrue to himself, reassured the poet.

Yeats defended the work he and Lady Gregory were doing to bring writers in touch with the popular imagination. He maintained that the artist living in the city can become individualistic and sterile. In the Irish countryside, there was an abundance of energy. The country stories heeded no moral conventions and are like pictures seen by children in the fire. 'When the idea which comes from the individual life,' Yeats finished up, 'marries the image that is born from the people, one gets great art, the art of Homer and of Shakespeare and of Chartres Cathedral'. This prolonged outburst should have made some impression on the young man, but all the poet got from Joyce was 'generalisations aren't made by poets; they are made by men of letters'. When Yeats got up to leave, Joyce held his arm. 'How old are you?' The poet replied, taking two years off his age, 'thirty-five'. 'I thought as much,' said Joyce calmly, 'I met you too late, you are too old.'

This brash remark did not deter Yeats from writing back a fortnight later to Joyce: 'Your technique in verse is much better than the technique of any young Dublin man I've met in my time.' And later he wrote of Joyce's poem 'I Hear an Army' that it was a technical and emotional masterpiece. Quite different in subject and technique from his other poems, it was almost as if, when he wrote this, Joyce had had the ghost of Hopkins standing at his elbow and Yeats's visionary essays surging through his mind.

I hear an army charging upon the land,
And the thunder of horses plunging, foam about
their knees:
Arrogant, in black armour, behind them stand,
Disdaining the reins, with fluttering whips, the
charioteers.

They cry unto the night their battle-name:
I moan in sleep when I hear afar their whirling
laughter.
They cleave the gloom of dreams, a blinding flame,
Clanging, clanging upon the heart as upon an anvil.

They come shaking in triumph their long green hair:
They come out of the sea and run shouting by the
shore.
My heart, have you no wisdom thus to despair?
My love, my love, my love, why have you left me
alone?

12   George Moore Settles In

Though Joyce admired much of Moore's writing, he had
been offended because the novelist had not asked him to
his Saturday evenings. After dinner the younger writers
were expected to come along and join in the conversation – Padraic Colum, Seumas O'Sullivan, George
Roberts among others. But Moore had heard tell of Joyce
as 'garrulous' and may have thought he would have
upset the balance of the evening. Also, Richard Best had
told him that Joyce used to borrow money, a habit that
did not appeal at all to Moore with his frugal budget.
Besides, he told Best, the young man's poems were reminiscent of Arthur Symons.

What added insult to injury was that young Oliver St
John Gogarty, Joyce's bosom friend, was not only a
welcome guest at Moore's evenings but at the dinner
parties for the elder writers which preceded them as
well. Gogarty, trained in the art of conversation at the
dons' table in Trinity, where he had become the pet due
to his ability to recite Greek and Latin poetry, win
athletic championships and produce lyric verse of his
own, captivated Moore. He loved his Rabelaisian
mockery of Church and State and christened him 'the
author of all the limericks that enable us to live in
Dublin'.

Another friend whom Moore had made in his first
year living in Dublin was W.K. Magee, like Richard Best
a librarian at the National Library. Moore needed some-
where to go after dinner to get the cobwebs out of his
brain and he found the National Library, five minutes

away from Ely Place in Kildare Street, a convenient haven. Magee, like Moore, was a bachelor, wrote criticism, valued style and between them a friendship developed which was based on a mutual acceptance of the necessary selfishness of human beings. For literary purposes Magee used the name 'John Eglinton', a stratagem which puzzled Moore. 'A good spanking little name, why does he change it . . .?'

Eglinton would lead him to a special bay in the Library where Moore could read what he wished. The librarian had a keen eye for the chameleon changes in Moore's character and the way it reflected in his physical appearance. Someone in Dublin had suggested that Moore resembled 'a boiled ghost' and there were other unflattering references to his physical appearance; but as he sat at his table in the National Library, his face lit up by an inquisitive smile, Eglinton noted what only John B. Yeats with his painter's insight had observed before, the pale blue eyes every now and then caught in a side light and merging into 'soft, unfathomable light'.

Eglinton was a constant guest at Moore's Saturday nights at 4 Ely Place. These had become a feature of Dublin life. AE, Yeats, Walter Osborne the painter, Lady Gregory and John B. Yeats were some of those who attended, as well as his friends Tonks and Sickert when they came from London to stay with him. A constant visitor was the German scholar Kuno Meyer, who had come over to found a school of Irish learning for the study of the vernacular literature of ancient Ireland which he would refer to as 'the earliest voice from the dawn of European culture'.

The talk was very Dublin, unpredictable, switching from politics to philosophy to poetry in the space of a minute, with none of the social restraints which might inhibit a similar gathering in London. For Moore it was a replacement for the Paris he had left as a young man, with perhaps more wit and savagery than he had known there: it reawakened in him an interest in his heritage which he would put to excellent use in his classic autobiographies. At his evenings Moore would stand in the middle of the drawing room, his hands flying out like fins as he made a point, then retiring into the background if he had said something outrageous, with the bland unselfconscious smile of a small boy saying to himself delightedly, 'I smashed it.' Max Beerbohm, who was present from time to time, has noted how Moore described an arc in the air with the finger tips of his beautifully-modelled hand, rising from close to his mouth, as if to form a suspension bridge for the passage of his idea to his listeners. He pronounced, Beerbohm recalled, the word idea i-de-a, dividing the syllables of his words in this way, and giving the same emphasis to 'the', 'a', 'of' as to other words. One characteristic of Moore's which Beerbohm observed with the sharp eye of the caricaturist was that though his expression appeared to remain unchanged in conversation, his features were perpetually remoulding themselves: the chin receded and progressed; the contours of nose and brow shifted; the oval cheeks went – only Max could have caught this – 'rippling in capricious hollows and knolls'.

Eglinton has recalled about these evenings that

AE pullulated ideas. Yeats walked with his head in a cloud of ideas. In the little room where we wrangled over abstractions, the air towards midnight would grow dim and overcharged with ideas. Seated stiffly in his chair, his glass beside him though seldom lifted, and smoking his excellent cigar, Moore would often feign ignorance, a favorite device with him for making conversation as when with a look of childish embarrassment, he asked us once for an explanation of a very ordinary line he had seen quoted from Burns.

Gogarty has left an excellent account of an evening at Moore's. First there was a hint of his Paris days. 'Claude Monet', he would say, pointing to the painting on the wall. 'Look how the paint is put on. It is like cream.' Then Moore would pontificate upon the wines:

301

'I got this from an old Frenchman who visits his clients in Dublin once a year. He sends it to me in a barrel directly from Marseilles. It is called St Pierre de Mou. I have it bottled by an expert. Gogarty can tell you how excellent it is. I sent my dealer over to see him. Hyde, whiskey? The decanter is in front of you.' Suddenly Hyde spluttered, 'Moore, this isn't whiskey. What is it?'

'But I ordered it from Sedley especially for you.'

'It may be Sedley, but it certainly is not whiskey.' And in a quieter voice, 'who ever heard of a man ordering his whiskey from a grocer?'

After this contretemps, one of the guests patched matters up by asking AE to recite Hyde's translation of 'The Red Haired Man's Wife' with its splendid last verse (Yeats, AE and Gogarty all had flawless memories and could recite almost any piece of verse they were asked without having to look at a book).

But the Day of Doom shall come,
    And hills and harbours be rent;
A mist shall fall on the sun
    From the dark clouds heavily sent;
The sea shall be dry
    And earth under mourning and ban,
Then loud shall he cry
    For the wife of the Red-haired man.

Moore talked about his love life with 'Stella' and told how she had been down to see him that day; Hyde warned him about being too open with this sort of talk and was only slightly mollified when AE began to discuss temple prostitutes in India whose virtue was subordinated to communion with the Divine. When Gogarty commented, 'They first decant the worshipper, and then leave him to his prayers if he has any energy left with which to pray', Moore was delighted for it had given him a phrase for the night, which he began to murmur between hisses of laughter: 'Divine decanters,

302

divine decanters.' But all was not well yet, for Moore was now on his sixth cook, and he had lifted the lid of the chafing dish under which the omelette lay and decided that he was not satisfied. As Gogarty recalls:

Moore went hurrying into his hall, opened the door and blew a police whistle. He returned with a young constable whose helmet was held respectfully under his arm. Moore again raised the lid of the dish and, pointing to the omelette, said, 'Look at that!' While the lid was coming off, the constable's helmet was being put on. The constable gazed at the omelette, looked at us all, and then at the omelette. Moore said, 'I want you to arrest the perpetrator of that atrocity.' The young policeman stood bewildered.

Douglas Hyde said, 'Oh, serve us some before it gets chilled. How can you tell whether it is good or bad until you have tasted it?' Kuno Meyer looked as if he would have preferred to be back in Berlin with a stein of beer and sauerkraut. On AE's bearded face there was an impatient expression. He wanted dinner to be dispatched with all possible speed so that the talk could begin, unimpaired by mastication.

I wondered if Moore had not gone too far by bringing in the police. It might be a *cause célèbre* for a week if it got into the newspaper. Stoker would hear of it and be duly impressed by the importance Moore attached to good cooking.

The constable at last spoke: 'On what charge, sir?'

For a moment Moore was nonplussed. Then he rallied and, lifting the lid, pointed with it. 'That is no omelette. Go down and arrest her for obtaining money under false pretences.'

The reason for such antics was that Moore had already discovered Dublin's acoustic quality. He knew that the tale of his doings would be round the city next day. The little boy who had once taken off his clothes in St Stephen's Green despite his nurse and run round naked to attract attention was still alive in the middle-aged dilettante.

Moore seemed to suffer almost from an incontinence of tongue, or else if he had thought up something he was unable to prevent himself saying it. One day an acquaintance called to tell him of the death of an old friend. Moore appeared stricken and, walking up and down, delivered an eloquent oration on the virtues of the deceased. After some time the visitor timidly interrupted with, 'But, Moore, I did not say Gosse, I said Ross.' Moore's reply was, 'Well I can't go over all that again.'

Another day, dining with Moore, Richard Best told him a story he had heard from Yeats about Wilde after he had come out of prison and gone to Dieppe. Dowson had taken the poet to a brothel to see if it would tempt him to alter his tastes but Wilde had emerged after a while with a somewhat dissatisfied look on his face, and told the waiting crowd, 'Cold as mutton. But tell them in England that I have been here for it will do my reputation good.' Moore's only reaction was to lay down his knife, look round the table and say with mild astonished eyes, 'But Best, I love cold mutton.' Anything to shock. As he was being helped into his fur-lined Astrakhan-collared coat by a young Irish dramatist he murmured, 'This is the reward of ten years' adultery.' Some times he did realise he had gone too far. Once, walking in the Green with Padraic Colum, the young poet, they were discussing how St Gaudens should complete a statute of Parnell which was being erected at the end of Sackville Street in Dublin. 'They could add a fire escape,' said Moore blandly, alluding to the stratagem Parnell had used to escape from his mistress's bedroom when confronted by her husband. 'That is an unworthy remark, Moore,' Colum said, 'Parnell was a great man.' Moore turned round and looked the young poet straight in the eye. 'You are quite right, Colum, I should not have made it, Parnell *was* a great man.'

Not everybody in Dublin took to Moore's talk. His French manner of talking openly about sex scandalised some people, and men could be heard muttering among

304

themselves what they would like to do to him because of his lack of reticence. Moore would counter them blithely with, 'My thoughts run on women – why not? On what would you have them run. On coppermines?'

His new home had begun to captivate him. 'The truth is that I am in love with Dublin', he wrote to his friend, Virginia Crawford in June 1901. 'I think it is the most beautiful town that I have ever seen, mountains at the back and the sea in front, and long roads winding through decaying suburbs and beautiful woods. Dublin dwindles so beautifully, there is no harsh separation between it and the country, it fades away; whereas London seems to devour the country! An army of buildings come and take away a beautiful park and you never seem to get quite out of sight of a row of houses.'

After a bicycle ride with AE to the three-thousand-year-old passage graves in Dowth and Newgrange he was in raptures, believing he had come in touch with symbols of Lir, the sea god. He sent a description to Virginia Crawford:

> The weather is beautiful and from the hill tops I saw Ireland through a mist of divinities. The rocks that these great people piled together for the celebration of their mysteries fill the heart with awe, and the carvings of the sun symbol carries the thought out into those far times when man stood nearer to nature, and therefore nearer to the gods, by far, than he does now. The central dot is world, the first ring is the ring of the waters, the second of Lir manqué, the third ring that of the Infinite Lir. How much greater these places are to me than Rome can ever be! These places were out of fountains of fire the Druids saw the Everlasting Ones ascend in spirals.

Moore had made a deliberate effort to sever any connection that Unionist Dublin might have thought it would have with him because of his landed gentry background and English connection or, indeed, his previously expressed anti-Irish views in some of his books. He had led off with a ferocious attack on Mahaffy in the Nationalist magazine *The Leader*, calling him a 'Handy Andy', a 'Mickey Free' who put on his act to amuse the English, and summing up the professor's book *The Art of Conversation* as 'the writings of a squireen who has been taught to punctuate in the university'. He dismissed Trinity College 'as a museum where there are stored all sorts of educated eccentrics in a seat of learning'.

Having cut himself off from Unionist Dublin he now set out to ingratiate himself with the opposite camp. This did not turn out to be as easy as he expected. He had been particularly pleased at an early stage to get a telegram in Dublin asking him to come over and speak at a meeting of the Gaelic League in the Rotunda. This seemed like recognition from his countrymen at last. When he got over, however, though the meeting was packed, Moore was upset by the failure of Hyde, who was in the chair, to call him before those whom he regarded as nonentities and was not at all impressed by the chairman's reiterated 'From the bottom of my heart, Moore, I am sorry – from the bottom of my heart, Moore.' Soon after this Moore went down to the Gaelic League headquarters in Parnell Square to offer his services. A man at the desk told him to send in what material he had on hand to the editor and they would let him know about it. 'But, my dear man, I am George Moore. They pay a little more attention than that to me in England.'

Nevertheless, Moore still continued to court Hyde and in April 1902 he produced Hyde's play *The Tinker and the Fairy* in Irish in his garden in Ely Place.

During the rehearsals he wrote letters of the most extravagant kind to the author praising his play and suggesting alterations that might make it a perfect piece. A little platform was erected in the garden and though, according to John B. Yeats who was amongst the

306

audience, Moore was 'softly gesticulating his despair' on the day of the performance as some of the guests were late, the weather held up and the play, with a musical accompaniment written by Moore's composer friend Esposito, was a great success. Some of the neighbours jeered from the nearby windows at the barbaric language being discharged in the garden below, but this can only have pleased Moore for he had written to his brother that he thought 'the play would annoy Dubliners very much and add to my pleasure'.

To assert his nationalism even more amongst his neighbours he had his door painted green, almost a sacrilege in Ely Place. Two elderly ladies a few doors down from him encouraged their cats to make love outside Moore's window as a protest against the Fenian hallway. He in his turn hired a pipe band to play outside their house late at night so for some time no one in the cul-de-sac got much sleep.

From his alliance with the Gaelic League Moore got two of his finest books. This was his way. His instinct drove him towards a movement or a group and, whether he was in tune with it or not, he would always manage to nose out material there. One day John Eglinton suggested to him that he write an Irish version of Turgenev's *A Sportsman's Sketches*. Moore, after some negotiation, obtained a commission from the Gaelic League who said they would have the stories translated in to Irish and publish them in that language if Moore would write them first in English. The result was *AntÚr-Ghort* which was published in 1902 with Moore's name in Irish on the title page: *Sgéalta le Seóirse Ó Mordha*. *The Untilled Field*, as it is known in English, is one of Moore's important books. It begins a new movement in the short story in English in that each tale contributes to the overall atmosphere of the book, as a piece of mosaic contributes to the whole. The paralysis underlying the Irish character and the indolence engendered by the climate and landscape is marvellously evoked. (It was from *The Untilled Field* that the young James Joyce took the genesis of *Dubliners*, just as he took the structure for his most famous story 'The Dead' from the concluding pages of Moore's novel, *Vain Fortune*.)

It was not sufficient for Moore, who was now in a sort of frenzy about the re-invigoration of language, to have *The Untilled Field* undergo only one translation, so he got Rolleston to translate one of the stories, 'The Wedding Gown', back from Irish into English. 'It is much improved,' announced Moore, later, 'after its bath in Irish.'

Out of this experiment was to come what Charles Morgan has called 'George Moore's second recreation of the English novel' when he began the series of tales extending from *The Lake* to *The Brook Kerith* and *Aphrodite in Aulis*. *The Lake* began as a short story for *The Untilled Field* but Moore decided to make it into a full novel. It tells of a priest who orders a young school-teacher to leave his parish because of some minor offence, and then realises he is in love with her. Finally he leaves a suit of clothes at the edge of the lake outside the village and swims to freedom, leaving his people to believe that he had been drowned. As he crosses on the boat to England he says to himself, 'there is a lake in every man's heart and every man must gird his loins for the crossing'. It is the message of the realist conveyed through the images of a symbolist and provides a bridge between the two movements. The presence of the lake pervades the book, its emerald-green waters, the changes of wind across the surfaces, yachts scudding across the waves, the sense of inertia created by the all-pervading green of the lake and trees. (It was, of course, Moore's own Lough Carra that he was writing about.) It was typical of his impishness that he should have called the chief character in the book Father Oliver Gogarty, which caused great scandal among the friends of young Oliver Gogarty's pious mother. When she called to complain Moore said blandly, 'Madam, supply me with two such joyous dactyls and I will gladly change the name.'

His differences with his contemporaries were by no means resolved. Despite the fulsome praise heaped on him by Moore – 'your play is perfect . . . I cannot find words to praise it enough' – that devious man Hyde remained deeply suspicious of Moore. As early as September 1900 he had written to AE: 'What an atrocity Moore is, what an actor, he is making himself impossible as a force here if he ever aspired to be one!' and he predicted that Moore would go back to England, saying he had been hounded out of Ireland because of his religious convictions (which is exactly what Moore did do, though some years later than Hyde had predicted). Hyde was single-minded about his Gaelic League, and he sensed Moore's involvement with the movement was only transient. That Moore later recognised that Hyde had seen through him can be judged by the portrait that appears in *Hail and Farewell* where Hyde at times is sketched almost as a species of ape, 'eyebrows like black bushes growing over the edge of a cliff – without doubt an aboriginal'. And in later life one of the very few people for whom Hyde would confess a hatred was George Moore.

Presently, Moore had his first real quarrel with Yeats. At Coole one day in 1902 during a walk, Yeats had outlined the scenario of a play to Moore, suggesting that they might collaborate on it. Some time later Moore telegrammed Yeats:

I have written a novel on the scenario we composed together. Will get an injunction if you use it.

Yeats who, with his usual firmness, would not be bullied, went straight down to Coole and with Lady Gregory's help dictated and wrote there in a fortnight a five-act play. 'Where There is Nothing'. He published it the following week in Arthur Griffith's *United Irishman* to secure copyright. Moore heard the newsboys shouting out the event as he came out of the Antient Concert Rooms and he asked a friend who had read the play in the paper, 'Has Yeats's hero got a brother?' 'Yes.'

'Then Yeats has stolen the spoons.' Now that he was on course for a quarrel Moore decided to make it a really formidable one. His brother noticed the genesis of his next move one day when they were having a discussion on religion. George, no doubt to stir matters up, threw out the idea of changing his religion, then grew intensely interested as he observed from Maurice's reaction how much of a sensation such a change might cause. According to Maurice, 'a new scent had tickled his nostrils'. George was contemplating with delight the shock his apostasy would give Catholics and indulged his vanity in thinking how much rejoicing there would be in Protestant hearts at the accession of so eminent a citizen. He foresaw the ceremony being performed by the Protestant Archbishop of Dublin while the Catholic bishops in Maynooth fumed in fury. Alas, when he wrote to the Protestant archbishop notifying him of his intentions, that dignitary dispatched a humble little parson to attend to Moore's needs. It is not certain, indeed, if the archbishop had heard of the novelist, though it is probably not true that he did, as a Dublin wit suggested, send him coal and blankets under the impression that his conversion was due to financial necessity.

When Moore discussed the matter with AE, the poet told him that, speaking as a Protestant himself, he felt that Moore's unbridled tongue could easily offend whatever clergyman were deputed to instruct him in his new religion. AE's version is that Moore replied,

'Oh no, AE, you don't understand, these men are men of the world.'

'But I tell you, Moore, that I know many of these men and they are truly sincere and believe what they preach and they will ask you to pray, Moore, to go down on your knees, Moore, things you have never done in your life and you will feel very much out of place.'

'Oh no, AE, you don't understand, these are men of the world, they understand perfectly.'

'Well, I warn you,' I said, and departed.

310

Some time later AE met Moore and asked him what had happened at his conversion.

Well [said Moore] what you said nearly burst up the whole thing. When the clergyman came I did not wish to appear to be taken in too easily and I worked up a few remaining scruples, fenced for a while and finally announced my scruples as conquered, and myself ready to be received into the fold. Then the clergyman said, 'Let us have a prayer', and I remembered your words and saw your face looking at me and I burst out laughing. When I saw the horrified look in the clergyman's face I realised it was all up unless I could convince him that it was hysteria, and I clasped my hands together and said, 'Oh, you don't realise how strange all this appears to me to be. I feel like a little child that has lost its way on a long road and at last sees its father', and I, folding my hands anew, began 'Our Father'. I took the wind out of his sails that way, for he had to join in, but he got in two little prayers on his own account afterwards, and very nice little prayers they were too.

Of course it would not do for Moore to engage in such an enterprise without creating as much of a stir as possible out of it. When his apostasy did not seem to have made such an impact as he had hoped among Catholics he wrote a letter to the *Irish Times* saying that the reason he was leaving the Catholic Church was that the Maynooth priests were wearing the King's racing colours on their vestments and that, as an Irish nationalist, he couldn't accept this. Few people, however, took him seriously by now and his religious gyrations were watched more with amusement than distaste. His brother Maurice, whom George had been extremely fond of was, however, very upset. They had had many arguments on the subject of religion and finally quarrelled irrevocably. As they had been close to each other since youth the breach was a sad one. 'The kindly good-natured George that I have known for fifty years is dead,' Maurice was to write later on:

You see he is constituted in this way. He makes violent friendships and then, when he has been too much with his new friends, he tires of them and gets into a positive distaste. . . . He is then urged on by an insatiable desire for a quarrel which must be quenched at all hazards.

This is a perceptive insight into Moore's temperament. But it does not take into account the fact that from his rows he got his art. Quarrelling was often the chemistry by which he ignited the creative spark. There was always the other George Moore, 'the amico Moorini', looking on and ready to include himself in the pageant with the same detachment as the other figures whose characters he drew. He believed that life could have a better ending to a story than art and was engaged, while in Dublin, on his Rousseau-like book about his life – *Hail and Farewell* – which many consider his masterpiece.

On one subject George Moore was expert – himself; and he dug deep with the scalpel to find the quick. Moore's cousin Edward, on the other hand, laboured under the disadvantage that though many of his encounters passed into the legend of the city, he would never succeed in working material from them into his plays. His dispute, for instance, with the Kildare Street Club is recorded in the sober prose of the Law Reports, but it could have provided material for an admirable drama, had Edward possessed George's gift of being able to incorporate his life into his art. To understand the nature of this dispute, it is necessary to grasp what the Kildare Street Club stood for in Dublin. It had been founded by Irish landlords in 1782, and it was said that if you amalgamated the London Carlton Club and the Atheneum, then stuffed the end product with mothballs, you might get something approaching the Kildare Street Club. As late as August 1938 Claude Cockburn heard the Earl of Wicklow in the members' room mulling over the news that some kind of international conflict might well be brewing. He told those in the room that they could take it from him that the whole idea of war was nonsense:

312

'Austria-Hungary,' said he, 'has learned her lesson from the last war. If Hitler were to attack, Austria-Hungary would take him in the rear, and he knows it.'

With regret, his friends reminded him that Austria-Hungary, as such, no longer existed, and that its disparate portions were, directly or indirectly, under the control of Hitler himself.

The Earl reflected briefly and then said, 'Well, be that as it may, Hitler will still not dare to act. He has to reckon with the Serbs. The Serbs, and mark my words, the Serb is a good fighting man,' said he, 'hate the Boche. Serbia will take Hitler in the rear, and he knows it.'

Sadly they told him the situation regarding Serbia – how it had ceased to exist as a separate nation, been merged into Yugoslavia, and how, for various reasons, Yugoslavia was in no sort of shape to be conducting decisive attacks upon Hitler's rear.

'In that case,' said the Earl of Wicklow, 'the whole thing is reduced to an absolute farce'.

The atmosphere had obviously changed very little from Edward Martyn's period. Members then included Lord Clonmel, who had once responded to a beaming smile from Queen Victoria in Buckingham Palace with, 'Madam, I do know your face but I cannot remember where I have met you;' and Bond-Shelton, the last survivor of the *Birkenhead*, whose legs, members said, had been gobbled by a shark who had found him so sour 'that it spat the rest of him back'.

A reminder of Land League days was evident in the rule that no member could bring a guest beyond the clock in the middle of the room. This space was reserved for members only, as it was felt that conversations dealing with the burning of houses and shooting at landlords should not be overheard. But even the depressing atmosphere of those times had not been allowed to diminish the members' élan. Midnight races would be organised up Kildare Street with the servants holding up lit candles to illuminate the course. Lady Gregory's father, Henry Persse, used to complain that he had been cheated out of first place at one of these races by a competitor who had hid himself in the Duke of Leinster's house half way up the street, and so only run part of the course.

The building itself, redesigned after a fire in 1860, was a splendid edifice built by Woodward and Deane, with its Venetian detail, stilted arches and rich, warm brickwork appropriately decorated by the O'Shea brothers with billiard-playing monkeys, while the main feature inside was a magnificent top-lit stair hall with pierced stone balustrades and the giant gondola-like hoods which rested over the baths attached to the squash courts.

Though as a young man Edward had been as loyal to the Union as any member of the Club, by the 1900s his nationalist views were beginning to get under other members' skin. One of his more extreme statements about the Crown had led them to change the rules, in the hope that they could expel him if he were to make a similar outburst in the future. They believed they had got their chance when, at a Sinn Fein meeting held to discuss 'flogging in the army', Edward perkily remarked that it did not concern him whether Englishmen flogged each other or not but 'any Irishman who enters the army or navy of England deserves to be flogged'. As a majority of the members had been at one time or other members of either the army or the navy, a number of them took umbrage and moved to have him expelled.

The secretary wrote to him on behalf of the committee of the Club asking him to explain his conduct and Edward replied by saying that he had not the slightest intention of doing so. Rule 25 of the amended version of the Rules provided that

> if in the opinion of the Club, declared by a resolution of the general meeting in manner hereinafter stated, the conduct of any member in or out of the Club shall at any time after his selection as a member be

injurious to the character and interest of the Club, he shall cease to be a member of the Club as hereinafter prescribed.

A ballot was organised by the secretary, Mr Bailey, and the proposal to expel Edward was carried. His answer was to challenge the legality of the vote in the courts. On paper his case did not look good. Apart from the Club's association with the army and navy, the Royal Family and the Viceroy were *ex officio* members. For a member to recommend flogging as a punishment for service in His Majesty's army seemed inconsistent with the aims of the club, to say the least of it.

The case opened in front of the Master of the Rolls with an impressive array of counsel on both sides. The most telling point made by Edward's counsel was that Bishop Berkeley had declared in the eighteenth century that 'Irish landlords were vultures with iron bowels', and were the Club suggesting that so eminent a philosopher and churchman as Berkeley would have been an unsuitable member, had it been in existence at the time? Counsel also drew the court's attention to a letter which had been written by the secretary to a member of the Club in which he said that he thought it 'a disgrace that the High Priest of the anti-recruiting crusade should have all the privileges of a loyal gentleman's club while his dupes and tools are imprisoned for promulgating his doctrines'.

The unfortunate secretary was hauled over the coals by both the judge and his own counsel for this letter, which was clearly a breach of privilege. But it turned out that he had made a much more damaging mistake in his eagerness to have Edward expelled. He had indeed organised the actual ballot according to the rules, but a statutory meeting was necessary before this could be done and the secretary had failed to organise this. 'Therefore,' said the Master of the Rolls, 'the particular rules under which they purported to act did not give them the jurisdiction they assumed in this particular case and the plaintiff must succeed in the action.'

315

After the case finished Edward returned to his rooms; that night he was back in his seat in the Kildare Street Club dining room. A number of the members came up to congratulate him. One of them, however, asked him why he had chosen to return to a club which had expelled him. 'It is the only place in Dublin I can get caviar,' Edward replied, with a ghost of a smile. This was probably an exaggeration, for his meal at the Club every night continued to be a simple one – a plate of oysters, a pint of ale, followed by a beefsteak and a number of pots of strong tea.

Edward took his revenge on the members in a characteristic way. Each evening now he would kneel in the window of the Kildare Street Club which looked out on the heavily thronged Nassau Street, and at angelus time, six p.m., he would proceed to say the rosary, holding in his hands a prominently displayed circle of beads. A crowd would gather outside and answer the responses while apoplectic members passed behind Edward's back on their way to the bar. Edward was a man of regular habits and he continued saying the rosary at the same time each evening in the Club till the end of his life. As he grew older there were two main events of his day. At ten a.m. he could be seen coming into the Pro-Cathedral for Mass with his servant in front of him carrying a prie-dieu for his master to kneel on. Later, at six o'clock, the same servant could be seen helping Edward hoist his arthritic limbs up the steps of the Kildare Street Club.

He will pass out of the story now, so let us have a last glimpse of him through the eyes of his cousin George Moore as he visits him in his rooms in Lincoln Place, Dublin. To attract Edward's attention Moore had whistled, as of old, a few bars of Siegfried's motif from *The Ring*.

A few minutes afterwards a light appeared on the staircase and the door slowly opened.

'Come in, Siegfried, though you were off key.'

'Well, my dear friend, it is a difficult matter to

whistle above two trams passing simultaneously and six people jabbering round a public-house, to say nothing of a jarvey or two, and you perhaps dozing in your armchair, as your habit often is. You won't open to anything else except a motif from *The Ring*.'

'Wait a moment; let me go first and I'll turn up the gas.'

'You aren't sitting in the dark, are you?'

'No, but I read better by candle-light,' and he blew out the candles in the tin candelabrum that he had made for himself. He is original even in his candelabrum; no one before him had ever thought of a candelabrum in tin, and I fell to admiring his appearance more carefully than perhaps I had ever done before, so monumental did he seem lying on the little sofa sheltered from draughts by a screen, a shawl about his shoulders. His churchwarden was drawing famously, and I noticed his great square hands with strong fingers and square nails pared closely away, and as heretofore I admired the curve of the great belly, the thickness of the thighs, the length and breadth and width of his foot hanging over the edge of the sofa, the apoplectic neck falling into great rolls of flesh, the humid eyes, the skull covered with short stubby hair. I looked round the rooms and they seemed part of himself; the old green wallpaper on which he pins reproductions of the Italian masters. And I longed to peep once more into the bare bedroom into which he goes to fetch bottles of Apollinaris. Always original! Is there another man in this world whose income is two thousand a year, and who sleeps in a bare bedroom, without dressing-room, or bathroom, or servant in the house to brush his clothes, and who has to go to the baker's for his breakfast?

Though Moore was incapable of expressing such a feeling, he almost certainly felt an affinity towards Edward which he did not have for any of the other members of the literary movement, even AE. Edward would never admit the accuracy of the portrait Moore drew of him later on, but it was one done from genuine, almost obsessional affection. There is, to prove it, Moore's pathetic comment about his cousin at the end of his autobiography:

It is a terrible thing to understand Edward better than he understands himself and be unable to help him.

13   Actors And Players

The Abbey Theatre acting style would leave its mark on the acting tradition of the twentieth century. Yet it began with two stagestruck brothers, Frank and Willey Fay, one a secretary to an accountant and the other an electrician. The achievement of the Fays was yet another example of how the chemistry of the period they lived in transferred itself to their work. They had felt the winds of change coming from the European theatre, Ibsen, Strindberg, Ohle Bull in Norway, Antoine and Lugné Poe in Paris, J.T. Grein in London. But they had no means of articulating their enthusiasm in a Dublin dominated by the commercial theatre. Visits of companies led by Edward Compton, Godfrey Tearle, Edward Terry, Henry Irving, Beerbohm Tree, the Kendalls, gave them little insight into what was new in the drama.

Frank wrote critiques in the evening papers and Willie spent eight months of the year acting with fit-up companies which toured Ireland and the north of England. Both brothers were lying in wait for an opportunity to work in the way they wanted. Perhaps it was for this reason Willie was persuaded by Frank to settle down in Dublin instead of spending so much time on the road touring. This way they might have a chance of creating a company that would be in touch with new ideas. Electricity seemed the coming thing, so at Frank's suggestion Willie became an electrician. But at night he continued to direct his little amateur group, the Ormonde Players, and help Maud Gonne with patriotic tableaux which her Daughters of Erin presented.

How they talked about the theatre that could be. Frank's idols were Coquelin and Réjane. To him it was the 'life-like' technique of French actors, their lack of excessive movement on the stage developed by skilful training, which distinguished them from what he saw as the artificiality of the English stage. Arthur Symons, writing in the *Daily Post* and William Archer in the *Morning Leader*, gave Frank further insights into the French style. He drew Willie's attention to Symons's description of Guitry and Brasseur standing facing each other for some minutes, looking at their watches without saying a word and yet conveying a range of emotions to the audience: or Coquelin in *Tartuffe* at the end of the play turning his back on the audience and only giving them a glimpse of the hatred and fury on his face as he was led off to prison. Frank emphasised to Willie that in a similar situation Tree would have taken five minutes to get off the stage, gesticulating like a windmill. Frank wanted actors to speak as naturally as people do when they are talking in conversation. This, of course, was in contrast to the artificial stage speech practised by most of the leading English companies who visited Dublin at the time. But what really opened the two brothers' eyes was a production of *Little Eyolf* in Dublin. After seeing Ibsen's play they realised that the sort of delivery they objected to in English actors could not be used for his dialogue. A new technique would have to be found to suit drama which was based on ordinary people's lives. Rhetoric would not work here.

Frank Fay was a fanatical elocutionist. He had studied with the actress Maud Randford at her school in Westland Row. While initially he had a light voice, at his peak he could fill the Coliseum in London. (Yeats was later to dedicate *The King's Threshold* to Frank Fay for his beautiful speaking in the character of Shanahan.) Frank was also in reaction against the current English habit of breaking up dramatic verse as if it were prose and, having ascertained from his poet friends 'that poetry comes first to them as music', created a form of

320

CELTADES AMBO: MR. YEATS AND MR. MARTYN.

[By Max Beerbohm.]

Two of the protagonists of the 'Celtic movement', viewed by Max Beerbohm

The Kildare Street Club from Trinity College. Founded by Irish landlords, it provided a natural home for reactionary politics and wild Irish eccentricity

Gunsmoke and flags behind the Royal St George Yacht Club — a salute from the fleet during the Royal visit of 1900

The Queen's visit to Ireland — children's day in Phoenix Park

Her Majesty's visit to the Lord Lieutenant and Countess Cadogan at Dublin Castle

George Moore by Max Beerbohm

THE OLD AND
THE YOUNG SELF

Mr. George Moore

YOUNG SELF: 'And have there been any painters since Manet?'

OLD SELF : 'None.'

YOUNG SELF: 'Have there been any composers since Wagner?'

OLD SELF : 'None.'

YOUNG SELF: 'Any novelists since Balzac?'

OLD SELF : 'One.'

George Moore, painted by Tonks in 1920

The heart of Dublin: O'Connell Bridge, previously Carlisle Bridge, in the first decade of the century

A rare photograph of St Theresa's Hall in Clarendon Street, as it was at the first performance of *Deirdre*

Maud Gonne by J. B. Yeats as the Countess Cathleen

John Synge with his mother, Rosie Calthrop (centre) and Annie Harmar in the summer of 1900, outside Castle Kevin in County Wicklow, where Synge spent many holidays

Synge in the grounds of his mother's villa in County Wicklow

The Devil's Glen in the Wicklow hills only a few miles from Dublin, where Synge spent many days out walking

Anne Horniman, Yeats's other
benefactress, who one day said to him,
'I will give you a theatre' — the Abbey
Theatre

The first Abbey Theatre's foyer, by Raymond McGrath. This sketch now hangs
in the new Abbey theatre

The stage of the first Abbey Theatre

Frank Fay as Cuchulain,
by J. B. Yeats

Sinead Flanagan, subsequently the wife of
Eamonn de Valera, and Douglas Hyde in
The Tinker and the Fairy. This was taken in
George Moore's garden at 3 Ely Place.
Note the fiddle shoved into Hyde's jacket
in the manner of a travelling musician.

The Plough and the Stars by Sean O'Casey; cartoon by Grace Plunkett

Sean O'Casey at a rehearsal for *The Plough and the Stars* in 1926. His inscription reads, 'Be clever . . . and let who will be good'

stressed recitative which was based on expressing the meaning of the words as well as bringing up the rhythm. The style the two brothers evolved was to be essentially a realistic one with overtones of poetic speech which they would always lift to the surface if it was in the writing, but anchored in a detailed observation of character.

The critic A.B. Walkley of *The Times* noted some of these characteristics when the Fay brothers first presented their work in London a few years later:

> These Irish people sing our language – and always in a minor key. It becomes in very fact 'most musical, most melancholy'. Rarely, very rarely, the chant degenerates into a whine. But, for the most part, the English ear is mildly surprised and entirely charmed. Talk of 'lingua Toscana in bocca Romana!' The English tongue on Irish lips is every whit as melodious.

They 'ennobled our mother tongue,' Walkley noted, but observes 'as a rule they stand stock still'.

> The speaker of the moment is the only one who is allowed a little gesture – just as in the familiar convention of the Italian marionette theatre the figure supposed to be speaking is distinguished from the others by a slight vibration. The listeners do not distract one's attention by fussy 'stage business', they just stay where they are and listen. When they do move it is without premeditation, at haphazard, even with a little natural clumsiness, as of people who are not conscious of being stared at in public. Hence a delightful effect of spontaneity.

C.E. Montague wrote in the *Manchester Guardian* of a later performance:

> The Irish actors keep still and white and tragic consequences enfold them; set on their ground of grave or simple composure, the slightest gesture carries you far in divination of what prompts it.

What Fay and his brother were primarily concerned with was the same as what would occupy Stanislavsky a

321

decade later in Moscow – how to explore the inner personality of a character. But because they were to form their movement with Yeats, who was concerned with the poetic as well as the realistic theatre, there was always to be a blend of poetry in their technique, which would later become known as the 'Abbey style'.

It was at the first night of *Diarmuid and Grania* that Frank Fay had his moment of truth. He recognised that Yeats and Moore had written a play

> in which English actors are intolerable – the English voice grated on one's ears and the stolid English temperament was equally at variance with what was wanted. The actors did not act the play as if they believed in it: the fact is, they could not for that is not in their nature.

But where could the brothers get Irish plays to produce with Irish players, in the way they wanted to? Greatly daring one night, Willie presented himself on AE's doorstep in Coulson Avenue, Rathgar. He had read two acts of a play, *Deirdre*, which AE had published in the *All Ireland Review*. Would the poet write a third act, and let the Ormonde Players present the finished play?

AE was flattered but puzzled. He told the young man who had delivered himself of this speech on the doorstep to come in. Once he had him sitting down with a cup of tea, AE confessed that *Deirdre* had not been written for production but as a literary exercise. He had no knowledge of stage technique at all. Willie argued in his quiet persistent way. He and his brother thought it was an actable drama. Why not finish it? They wanted plays to produce. Finally, after much persuasion, AE agreed.

Willie went back across the river to the north side where the Fays lived and told Frank they had a play on their hands and a designer too, for AE had consented to do the scenery. When Frank pointed out after looking at the cast list that the Ormonde Players had not enough players to stage *Deirdre* Willie said he could recruit some from his other protégées, the Daughters of Erin.

The Fays had, of course, no theatre. But they had done many charity shows for St Teresa's Temperance Hall run by the Carmelite Fathers in Clarendon Street, just off Grafton Street, and they felt that this was an ideal site in which to present a play if they could get permission to use the hall. It was arranged that they could use it for three nights in April 1902.

The cast was composed of electricians, book-keepers, shop assistants, typists; but Frank and Willie demanded from them a professional attitude to detail. Willie was director, but constantly consulted with 'the brother' as the play proceeded. Halfway through it became clear that AE's play would not be long enough for a full night. Yeats was approached to see if he would help them by letting the company do his *Land of Heart's Desire*. No, he wouldn't, he told them, but he had a little play which he would give them, *Cathleen Ni Houlihan*, and he thought he could persuade Maud Gonne to play the leading part in it. The Fays were enchanted. They had captured two of the leading figures in the Dublin literary world for their first major production. But Maud Gonne – good God! – all Dublin would want for see her.

At first the Fays were a little depressed when Yeats told them that the theme for *Cathleen Ni Houlihan* had come to him in a dream. But they cheered up when he assured them that it was the traditional name for Ireland which the people used to personify the nation in the form of a woman who requires young men to sacrifice themselves of her.

His play opens on the day of the landing of the French army at Killala in May 1798, to liberate Ireland from the English. The first scene takes place in the interior of a cottage where the audience sees a young farmer, about to be married, discussing his prospects with his parents and future bride. Into this family scene comes an old woman who has escaped from the turmoil outside. It is clear to the audience that she is the 'Sean Bhean Bhocht', or the 'Poor Old Woman', the symbol of Ireland bowed down with centuries of suffering. But the characters on

323

stage are not to know this. When the young man finally follows the old woman out of the cottage the audience know that he has gone to fight for Ireland and that the old woman will be made young again by his sacrifice. The dialogue is a blend of poetry and peasant speech which is effective dramatically, and since it was the first time it would have been heard on a stage in a national drama, could be expected to have a thrilling effect on an audience. Yeats had been helped by Lady Gregory in this aspect of the play, for as he said, he found it difficult 'to come down from the high window of dramatic verse'.

AE's play *Deirdre* is based on one of the oldest tales in western Europe. Tristan and Isolde derives from it. Deirdre is born a child of doom in the court of Conor, King of Ulster. At the birth the druids prophesy that she will bring death and destruction to the men of Ulster. But Conor forbids them to put her to the sword and she is brought up to be his ward. Sure enough, when she reaches womanhood she deserts him and elopes to Scotland with the chief of Conor's warriors, Naoise. There she lives with Naoise and his brothers the sons of Usna for seven years, till Conor lures them home by a trick. Naoise is killed along with his brothers by Conor's army, and Deirdre goes to live with the king. After a year, unable to forget Naoise, she dashes her brains out on a stone. The Deirdre theme was to be a key one for writers in the literary renaissance, and later Yeats, Synge and James Stephens would all write their versions of it for the stage.

On the whole AE's interpretation is faithful to the original saga, but he softens the narrative somewhat by having Deirdre and Naoise come back to Ireland through the urging of her nurse rather than through Conor's treachery, and having her die at the same time as Naoise rather than live with Conor after her lover's death. As well as watering down the cruelty of the pagan version, AE occasionally resorts to phrases like 'dear foster mother', 'say on, dear Naoise' and 'ruddy dew'. But as an ancient Irish tale transferred to the stage it is considerably better than *Diarmuid and Grania* and the Fays had found themselves a prize piece.

At the rehearsals AE would sit muffled up in a large tweed coat, peering through a tangle of spectacles and beard. His kindly nature rejoiced in the company of the young actors and he would always sit round after the rehearsal discussing questions about the play with them. Yeats, on the other hand, one of the players Maire nic Shiubhlaigh remembers, seemed to be always in the shadows from which his voice would emerge during lulls in the hammering that was going on on the stage. She said she got the impression that Yeats dressed in loose clothes, with a flowing cravat and his long jet black hair brushed back from his high forehead, looked through her and beyond to another world.

Maud Gonne had agreed to playing Cathleen, but on her own terms. She would only be free for a fortnight, she said. Her work for Ireland came first. She would learn the part before she came from England to save rehearsal periods. But almost as soon as she arrived she was away again. She must, she told them, try out her voice against the Wicklow waterfalls. It was only a day or two before the dress rehearsal that she turned up again, but word perfect and with a sound in her voice that brought tears to the eyes of some of the cast.

Moore had been turning up at intervals to tell the cast what he thought. He wrote to Yeats to say that '*Deirdre* was the silliest play I ever saw' and, as for Cathleen, shouldn't Maud Gonne walk up and down in front of the stage to dominate the audience and convey to them the excitement of the French landing instead of 'crooning by the fire'? Yeats pointed out that she is looking both into the past and the future, and refused to alter the interpretation. He had had enough of Moore's shenanigans in the theatre after three years of the Irish Literary Theatre and was glad to be free of him this time.

It was only possible to use the Temperance Hall for the last three days before the performance. The cast discovered when they got there that the nature of the hall meant that there would be difficulties on the opening night. They would be under some disadvantage when it came to getting themselves on stage. St Teresa's Hall had a high ceiling with good acoustics and a reasonable stage, but there were no dressing facilities and the actors had to put on their costumes upstairs and come down on stage an hour before the curtain went up, where they remained squeezed to the wall, afraid to breathe for fear they would upset the scenery, until the play began. When they did go on stage, they had to sidle on sideways, crablike, because of the lack of space.

The production had been much talked of in Dublin and on the opening night, 2 April 1902, there was a full house. The hall held 300 but by the time the overflow had been accommodated, another hundred or so were standing at the walls on either side of the stage. Among the audience could be seen a mixture of glittering starched shirts and working class clothes. Yeats's Irish Literary Theatre had attracted mainly an upper-class following, the Fays' audiences were more democratic.

Maud Gonne arrived late and had to make a sensational entrance in costume walking up through the audience on to the stage where she concealed herself from the rest of the cast behind the thin canvas scenery until the time came for the second play. 'Unprofessional,' hissed Frank Fay, who was in an understandably nervous mood, at the moment of launching what had been his ambition for years – a full-length play by an Irish playwright with Irish actors.

He need not have worried. *Deirdre* was rapturously received. A thrill ran through the audience as they heard the name of the Irish heroic figure Cuchulain spoken for the first time on the stage. One of the features of the last act was the appearance of AE himself in the part of Cathbad the Druid which he intoned in a deep, chanting voice. Later, a lady member of the audience accused him of being a sorcerer, claiming that she felt three black waves of darkness rolling down over the stage on top of her after he had spoken.

Yeats's play had the audience in an intense stage of excitement from the beginning. There was almost continual applause as they saw the national predicament told through the medium of a peasant tale. It was a new language – 'the English of people who speak in Irish'. The part of the old woman is a finely constructed one. The audience is given continued hints as to who she is, but the characters on the stage show no sign of recognition:

MICHAEL: Have you no one to care you in your age, ma'am?

OLD WOMAN: I have not. With all the lovers that brought me their love, I never set out the bed for any.

MICHAEL: Are you lonely going the roads, ma'am?

OLD WOMAN: I have my thoughts and I have my hopes.

MICHAEL: What hopes have you to hold to?

OLD WOMAN: The hope of getting my beautiful fields back again; the hope of putting the strangers out of my house.

At the mention of the 'beautiful fields' (the four provinces of Ireland), the audience stood and cheered. Now there was a breathtaking hush as Maud Gonne turned towards them:

It is a hard service they take that help me. Many that are red cheeked now will be pale cheeked: many that have been free to walk the hills and the bogs and the rushes will be sent to walk hard streets in far countries: many a good plan will be broken: many that have gathered money will not stay to spend it: many a child will be born and there will be no father at its christening to give it a name. They that have red cheeks will have pale cheeks for my sake and for all that they will think they are well paid.

The old woman leaves the house followed, as in a dream, by the son who is about to get married. Presently his brother comes in. 'Did you see an old woman going down the path?' the father asks him. 'I did not, but I saw a young

327

girl and she had the walk of a queen.'

As the curtain fell the audience came on their feet cheering. The young poet Seumas O'Sullivan wrote that he would remember it as long as he lived, and would recall later in life Arthur Griffith's face 'as he stood up at the fall of the final curtain to join in the singing of what was then our national anthem, "A Nation Once Again" '. Yeats was overwhelmed by Maud Gonne's performance. 'She made Cathleen seem like a divine being fallen into our mortal infinity' was how he described the effect it had on him. Maire nic Shiubhlaigh wrote, too, that she would never forget Maud Gonne's 'willow-like figure, pale sensitive face, burning eyes, as she spoke the final lines'.

Lady Gregory was in the audience that night – a short figure in a long Victorian veil. 'You were very good,' she told the players when she went backstage, 'I hope to see more of you.' Afterwards she could be seen with the Fays and AE discussing the acting and the set. No doubt schemes were stirring in that busy little head.

For three nights the theatre was packed. The reviews on the whole were good. The *Freeman's Journal* thought that the language of *Deirdre* was of 'the loftiest beauty' but felt that, having made Conor into a Celtic Moses, it was not easy afterwards to attribute ordinary human emotions such as jealousy to him. The *Daily Express* thought that 'the sentiments had the true heroic ring . . . but the play was faulty in construction'. The extreme nationalist paper *The Leader* called it 'literary perfume'. But this was offset by Griffith's *United Irishman* which saw the whole night as the beginning of a new national theatre.

Cathleen Ni Houlihan was well received and the *Freeman's Journal* thought 'it would be difficult to speak too highly of a singularly beautiful little piece'. Yeats had initially disliked *Deirdre* and had had to leave the theatre when it was rehearsed. But he had come to like it during the performances. He now saw it 'as if some painting on a wall, some rhythmic procession on the walls of the temple, had begun to move before me with a dim magical light'. The statuesque gestures of the Fays' company had particularly attracted him.

Yeats recognised that he and AE had succeeded in getting on the stage images and symbols that were part of the people's life – the cabin image of Ireland as a beautiful young woman, and a royal drama that took place 500 years before the birth of Christ. It was the culmination of a journey that had started thirty years before when as young men they had set out from the city at weekends to the hills above, to seek in the druids' piles and cairns the secret of life. Now some of their visions had been loosed upon the stage which Yeats looked on as a means of enlarging the national imagination. Synge was to catch the passion of the country folk in wild and exotic form that had not appeared in literature before, and Sean O'Casey twenty-two years later would do the same for the proletarian culture of Dublin.

Yeats and AE had worked deliberately to this end – many streams flowing in one river of life, the ancestral Gaelic imagination binding all who lived on the island in a new identity. The recognition of this could be hastened through the creation of imaginative works which would influence the national psyche.

On this opening night of *Deirdre* and *Cathleen Ni Houlihan* the two poets must have sensed that the forces they had garnered carefully and with much sacrifice throughout the years were now releasing themselves into the national being.

Is there nation-wide multiform reverie [Yeats wrote], every mind passing through a stream of suggestion, and all streams acting and reacting upon one another, no matter how distant the minds, how dumb the lips. . . . Was not a nation, as distinguished from a crowd of chance comers, bound together by this interchange among streams or shadows; that Unity of Image, which I sought in national literature, being but an originating symbol?'

329

14   That Inquiring Man John Synge

'Where, but for the conversation at Florimond de Basterot's had been the genius of Synge?' Yeats was to say later, pondering how the dramatist's talent would have expressed itself had there been no theatre movement. Would he have been a folklorist, a minor poet, an essayist? But the stage was Synge's element. Though his first play was banal, his next three were masterpieces and within three years of this he had written one of the greatest works in the history of theatre, *The Playboy of the Western World*.

Synge wanted to join the richness of the sonnet to his depiction of rural life and he castigated Ibsen and Zola for dealing with the reality of life in 'joyless and pallid words'. But the reality that Ibsen and Zola were dealing with derived from a society from which richness of language had been dredged, and which could not compare with the popular imagination Synge had discovered which still retained the elements of poetry. He found himself in a unique position where he could write about reality and at the same time attain a poetic effect because of the heightened dialogue of the people he portrayed.

The two plays he worked on in the summer of 1902, in a Wicklow villa which his mother had rented, were *Riders to the Sea* and *In the Shadow of the Glen*. Lady Gregory and Yeats were enchanted when they read the two plays. It was obvious that Synge had invented a new form of dramatic dialogue based on Douglas Hyde's prose translations in *Love Songs of Connacht* and strengthened by his own observations of peasant life. They arranged readings for him in London in both their places, and Arthur Symons, G.K. Chesterton and John Masefield were among those who attended. The readings made an instant impression and it was decided to present *In the Shadow of the Glen* in Dublin in October. The Irish National Theatre Society had come into being after the production of *Deirdre* and *Cathleen Ni Houlihan*, with Yeats as President and AE and Hyde as vice-presidents, so there was no difficulty in getting the play included in the Society's autumn programme. Synge had learnt the story of *In the Shadow of the Glen* from his friend Pat Dirane on the Aran Islands, who told it to him one night around the fire. The dramatist simply transferred the milieu to County Wicklow. The play tells of an elderly husband who feigns death to test his young wife's fidelity. When he 'comes alive' she rejects him and goes off walking the roads with a travelling man.

In June 1903, Lady Gregory held a reading for the cast at the Nassau Hotel. Maire nic Shiughlaigh, who was to play the lead, remembers how Synge sat unobtrusively in the background while Lady Gregory read his plays:

He was a gentle fellow, shy, with that deep sense of humour that is found in the quietest people. His bulky figure and heavy black moustache gave him a rather austere appearance – an impression quickly dispelled when he spoke. His voice was mellow, low, he seldom raised it. But for his quiet personality, he might have passed unnoticed at any gathering.

The rehearsals were held in the Camden Hall, a ramshackle structure owned by the Fays. Water was leaking in through the roof and it was bitterly cold during rehearsals. Oliver Gogarty remembers Synge sitting each night during rehearsals, his hand resting on a blackthorn stick held between his legs, silent except for a few sentences which he spoke in a rush as if he wished to get them over quickly.

He had a face like a blacking brush. But for his humorous mouth, the kindling in the eyes and something not robust in his build, he would have been more like a Scotsman than an Irishman. I remember wondering if he were Irish. His voice, very guttural and quick with a kind of lively bitterness in it, was a kind of Irish voice new to me at the time. I've known a good many Irish people but they'd all been vivacious and picturesque, rapid in intellectual argument and vague about life. There was nothing vivacious, picturesque, rapid or vague about Synge. The rush-bottomed chair next to him was filled by talker after talker; but Synge was not talking, he was answering.

Maire nic Shiubhlaigh remembers how Synge used to roll cigarettes constantly and then come up with one in each hand and give them to members of the cast, while Willie Fay recalls Synge as 'a thorny thick-set fellow with the head of a lion and a terrifying moustache'. Synge himself, though he exhibited no sign of discomfort, did not relish the rain coming in at nights in 'the little ramshackle hall' and complained that drunken revellers were to be found in the passages when it was time to go home. One of those was James Joyce who came along to see his friend Gogarty but 'fell the third time' in the passage (an event which he later claimed gave him an opportunity to indulge his predilection for inspecting ladies' lingerie, as female visitors to the theatre stepped over his recumbent form).

During rehearsals, Willie Fay had encountered great difficulty in teaching the cast to speak this new form of dialogue. However, Synge and he got together and experimented and after much hard practice, the director got an idea how the speeches were built up. Once Fay had got the 'tunes' into his head, he was all right and the play went along merrily. Later, when he used to take part in direction himself, Synge would say to his actors, 'Speak the lines for the meaning and the melody will come up.' He had a perfect visual image of the set and could tell Fay exactly where a character was meant to be standing during a particular piece of dialogue. Maire nic Shiubhlaigh had the greatest difficulty at first with this new verbal music; but she broke the sentences up and then joined them together and noticed the fine harmony coming up through the lines.

As the rehearsals progressed, it became clear that there was trouble on the horizon. It was, after all, a daring theme for those days to depict a wife leaving a husband, however aged, for a tramp travelling the roads. The fact that it was based on an Irish folk tale told around the firesides of the west would not make it any more palatable when it would be acted out in front of an urban audience who would lack the Rabelaisian acceptance of farmyard life. Two of the cast, Dudley Digges and Maire Quinn, alleged that the play held Irish womanhood up to ridicule. When Synge refused to change the sections of the play that they objected to, they resigned from the National Theatre Society and Maud Gonne went with them. The other members of the cast remained enthusiastic about the play and rehearsed vigorously under Fay's direction. But news of the quarrel got around and it was rumoured that the Irish National Theatre Society was about to produce a play which presented Irish people in a bad light. The day of the performance, someone (perhaps Dudley Digges) leaked the plot to the *Irish Independent*, the newspaper which at that time had the leading circulation and which catered to a pious readership. 'Synge knows more about the boulevards of Paris than the fishing folk of the Aran Islands,' the paper said, and advised the Irish National Theatre Society to reject 'this perversion of its aims'.

The play opened in October in the Molesworth Hall, a handsome building designed by Benjamin Woodward, just round the corner from his other masterpiece, the Kildare Street Club. It was quite a social occasion, for the theatre movement was coming into vogue. The Chief Secretary, George Wyndham, had asked for six tickets. Frank Fay was chagrined as he felt that the hardback chairs of the hall would not be comfortable enough for Wyndham. He managed to secure an upholstered chair for him which was placed in the front row of the audience.

In the Shadow of the Glen was presented after Yeats's *The King's Threshold* and before *Cathleen Ni Houlihan*. There were some protests from the audience, mainly from Dudley Digges, Maud Gonne and Maire Quinn who, somewhat unsportingly, showed up. Most unfairly, they used the fact that the Chief Secretary had a red chair as a sign that England's 'cruel colour' had been honoured, rather than that George Wyndham's elegant posterior had been accommodated. However, Yeats finished the night's performance with a characteristically stern speech to the audience so that the protesters did not have much of a hearing. The next day, the critics lacerated the play. 'A foul libel on Irish womanhood,' the *Irish Independent* screamed. 'One of the nastiest little plays ever seen.' The *Irish Times*, from which one could have expected something better, complained that 'the play was excessively distasteful and cast slurs on Irish womanhood'. But all this was nothing to the attack that came from Griffith's *United Irishman*:

> Synge is pandering to the enemies of Ireland [wrote Griffith]. The play is a corrupt version of an old tale that derives its imagination from the decadence that passes current in the Latin Quarter and the London Salon. Synge, who is utterly a stranger to the Irish character as any Englishman, has yet denigrated us for the enlightenment of his countrymen.

James Connolly (later a leader in the 1916 rebellion) joined in to say that the theatre should support 'the forces of virile nationalism in their fight against the widespread spirit of decadence, instead of undermining them'. Maud Gonne, in another letter, backed Connolly up.

John B. Yeats was the first to reply in Synge's favour. He pointed out that Ireland was no longer in the dark, and that now was the time for self-examination and self-accusation:

> I do not know whether Mr Synge is as great as Shakespeare but he has begun well. I cannot conceive any event more important in Irish history for some time to come than a few more plays by him.

The young Yeats sprang to Synge's defence too, saying that the Irish National Literary Theatre had three ignorances to contend with:

> First, the Gaelic propagandists that would have nothing thought or said that is not country Gaelic. Second, priests who would deny old ideas that might perplex ignorant farmers, and third, the politician who would reject every idea that is not of immediate service to his cause.

It was no good presenting this sort of argument to Griffith, who despite his respect for Yeats, accused him in his editorial of representing 'adultery as a feature of Irish moral life'. Synge refused to comment on the matter, except to say in a letter to Stephen McKenna, 'On the French stage you get sex without the balancing elements. On the Irish stage you get the other elements without sex. I restored sex. The people were so surprised they saw sex only.'

Today it is not easy to see what all the fuss was about. Synge had to some extent changed the story he had heard from Pat Dirane, which ends with the wife staying with her husband, whereas Nora in his play goes off with a tramp, lured by the promise of a wandering life.

> TRAMP: Come along with me now, lady of the house, and it's not my blather you'll be hearing only, but you'll be hearing the herons crying out over the black lakes, and you'll be hearing the grouse, and the owls with them, and the larks and the big thrushes when the days are warm, and it's not from the like of them you'll

be hearing a talk of getting old like Peggy
Cavanagh, and losing the hair off you, and
the light of your eyes, but it's fine songs you'll
be hearing when the sun goes up, and there'll
be no old fellow wheezing the like of a sick
sheep close to your ear.

NORA: I'm thinking it's myself will be wheezing that
time with lying down under the Heavens
when the night is cold, but you've a fine bit of
talk, stranger, and it's with yourself I'll go.
[she goes towards the door, then turns to
DAN.] You think it's a grand thing you're after
doing with your letting on to be dead, but
what is it at all? What way would a woman
live in a lonesome place the like of this place,
and she not making a talk with the men
passing? And what way will yourself live
from this day, with none to care you? What is
it you'll have now but a black life, Daniel
Burke, and it's not long, I'm telling you, till
you'll be lying again under that sheet, and
you dead surely.

This, of course, is Nora in *A Doll's House*, except that
this Nora seeks to discover herself through the uncertain life of a vagabond, in the company of a tramp. Today
both conflicts appear genuine and moving, but in 1903
Synge's theme was as unacceptable to an Irish audience
as Ibsen's had been to Norwegian audiences two
decades before.

The Irish Ireland movement, led by the Gaelic League
and Sinn Fein, had set out to improve the image of rural
Ireland which they felt had been degraded by the
English press and stage-Irish novelists who presented a
false version of the Irish characer. They missed the
inherent poetry of Synge's play, and concluded that it
was just another attempt by Anglo-Irish Protestants to
hold the nation up to ridicule. Synge could have become
dispirited by this misinterpretation of his artistic vision
but it does not seem to have affected him. Later, when

336

his finest play would cause riots in the theatre, he told a reporter who had asked him about his reaction to the popular feeling, 'I don't care a rap', and snapped his fingers.

Riders to the Sea was not to be presented till later but it had had numerous readings before that which convinced his listeners that Synge had written a work with the elements of genius in it. For the stage production, which took place the following year, he insisted on realism in the costumes and had Aran flannel sent up, dyed red 'madder' and cut to fit the leading actors. Pampooties were made from a cowhide that had been secured when a customer at a tan yard decided not to have a waistcoat made from it on account of his girl-friend's objections to cowskin, and the tanner sold it cheaply to the prop manager for the Fays. An old peasant woman was discovered living with a married daughter in a city tenement who could teach the actresses the 'caoine' or death chant that the islanders sing round their dead. As if in a trance, beside a crumbling marble fireplace that had once warmed the posteriors of aristocrats, she sang her astonishing lament with thin piping notes while the actresses who were learning from her tried to ignore the noise of passing vehicles outside. She was so successful in training the cast that one of them remembered after-wards how it made 'a scene very terrible and yet beautiful to look on'. A spinning wheel was needed which Lady Gregory provided by buying it from a woman in a cottage who had had it for over a hundred years. It was to remain a prop in the company for many years.

Riders to the Sea, which had its first staged performance in February 1904, has been called the finest one-act play in any language. It lasts barely twenty minutes and has none of the movement of classic tragedy. Its effect is obtained through the stoical acceptance of fate by the main characters. Perhaps in this, his first successful completed play, Synge achieved the ambition of which he spoke to Yeats – to bring three hitherto unrelated emotions together; for in *Riders to the Sea*, besides the stoicism of the central characters, there is the ecstasy of the elements they defy and the asceticism of people's daily lives divorced from material ambition.

The audience becomes gradually aware during the play that a mother has lost three sons by drowning (one dashed from a pony into the sea by a wave); and her last speech, as she finds out that her third son has been taken from her, is drenched in the fatalism that Synge found in the character of his island companions.

> May the Almighty God have mercy on Bartley's soul, and on Michael's soul, and on the souls of Sheamus and Patch, and Stephen and Shawn . . . and may He have mercy on my soul, Nora, and on the soul of everyone is left living in the world. Michael has a clean burial in the far north, by the grace of the Almighty God. Bartley will have a fine coffin out of the white boards, and a deep grave surely. . . . What more can we want than that? . . . No man at all can be living for ever, and we must be satisfied.

The play was not well received by the Press though audiences were much moved by it. Joyce's classmate at University College, Arthur Clery, now a drama critic, described it as 'the most ghastly production I have seen on the stage'.

However, a month later, when the play was presented at the Royalty Theatre in London, it was praised by William Archer and Max Beerbohm, and the *Westminster Gazette* described it as 'singularly beautiful, a pathetic piece of hopeless fatalism'. Synge as usual seemed unperturbed by the critics and was more amused than hurt when he heard that George Moore had dismissed the play with a sneer, 'an experiment in language rather than a work of art, a painful rather than a dramatic story'.

15   Joyce Makes An Exit

John Synge had met Joyce in Paris in the spring of 1903, but the encounter was not a particular success. Both shared a total dedication to the artist's role, but neither perceived as yet, in the other's work, artistic merit. Joyce had gone out to Paris before Christmas, ostensibly to study medicine. He had convinced himself that he needed a profession to help him subsidise his writing ambitions. What is more likely is that he used his studies at the Ecole de Médecine as an excuse to savour the literary life of a great metropolis. He had written to Lady Gregory and she had sent him financial help for the trip. She had also written to Synge to ask him to help Joyce find lodgings in Paris. Yeats had been commandeered to help the young poet overcome the terrors of Euston Station in the early morning as the boat train came in. Peering short-sightedly and sleepily down the platform at six o'clock in the morning he had picked out Joyce and brought him to an early breakfast. Later he took him to see Arthur Symons, who was to be of the greatest use to Joyce when he ensured the publication of his first collection of verse, *Chamber Music*.

In Paris, on Synge's advice, Joyce stayed at the Hôtel Corneille. The dramatist found the young man somewhat indolent and unbrushed. But he advised Joyce not to go without food for too long as it had cost him an expensive operation. Joyce told him that he was reading Ben Jonson in the Bibliothèque Nationale and managed to conceal his extensive knowledge of French literature from Synge, who thus got the impression that this was beneath him. Synge concluded that Joyce had a keen intellect which could make him an excellent essay writer, but that he would never be a poet of importance. His mind seemed too full of rules and although Joyce was flattered when Synge told him he had a mind like Spinoza, it is not certain that Synge meant it as a compliment. Synge was unwise enough to lend Joyce the manuscript of *Riders to the Sea* and must have been taken aback when Joyce returned it and told him that 'Ireland requires less small talk and more irrefutable art. No dwarf play, no one-act drama, can be a knock down argument.' Joyce felt quite pleased with himself at having deflated Synge, as he believed, and wrote to his brother Stanislaus: 'I'm glad to say that ever since I read it, I've been riddling it mentally till it has not a sound spot. It is tragic, about all the men who are drowned in the islands – but thanks be to God, Synge isn't an Aristotelian.'

However, he reckoned without Synge's sang-froid. Next time they met, he showed Synge his daybook which the dramatist refused to comment on, except to say that it contained solecisms. When Joyce suggested going out to St Cloud for the Mardi Gras festival, Synge upstaged him by saying, 'Now you want to behave like any bourgeois.'

Joyce would later change his mind about Synge's work and translate *Riders to the Sea* into Italian, as well as selecting it for performance at a play festival in Zurich in 1917. Even at the time he handed the manuscript of *Riders to the Sea* back to Synge, he knew the famous last speech, in which Maurya laments her two drowned sons, off by heart.

Joyce seems to have taken to imitating Rimbaud while he was in Paris, sending back photographs of himself dressed like the French poet and cultivating the habit of deliberate ingratitude towards his friends. (Later in Dublin people would notice similar behaviour.) Lady Gregory was his first target. She had been good enough to get him reviewing work with the *Daily Express* so that he might earn a little money during his Paris stay. Now he turned on her with a savage review of her collection of essays, poems and folk stories, *Poets and Dreamers*, commenting sarcastically, 'If Lady Gregory has truly set forth the old age of her country . . . perhaps in the future little boys with long beards will stand aside and applaud while old men in short trousers play handball against the side of a house.' The work of the Irish Theatre he dismissed as 'dwarf drama' and remarked that 'it is easy to understand why it finds favour with an age which has pictures that are "nocturnes" and writers like Mallarmé.'

Raftery, the vagabond poet whom Hyde, Lady Gregory and Yeats had been so impressed by, he dismissed with a sneer: 'Raftery took shelter once from the rain under a bush. At first the bush kept out the rain and he made verses praising it; then, after a while, it let the rain through and he made a verse dispraising it.' As if to compound his ingratitude he made up a limerick about Augusta which he circulated to his friends in Dublin:

> There was an old Lady called Gregory.
> Who said, 'Come to me all poets in beggary.'
> But she rued her imprudence
> When thousands of students
> Cried, 'We are all in that catégory.'

Joyce was not to remain long in Paris. At the end of April he received a telegram from his father to say that he must return as his mother was seriously ill. In a panic Joyce borrowed money from a pupil he was teaching English to, and hurried back to Dublin. For the next few months, as his mother's life ebbed away, he went through agonies of conscience. Her greatest desire was that her eldest son would take Communion and be reconciled to the Church before she died. He declared himself unable to do so, giving as his reason that he feared the chemical action which would be set up in his soul by false homage to a system which had centuries of veneration behind it. This refusal to compromise what he

341

regarded as his artistic soul was to gnaw at the root of his conscience for the rest of his life. A poem written in the summer of 1903 gives a glimpse of the ravages caused by his mother's death:

> He travels after a winter sun,
> Urging the cattle along a cold red road,
> Calling to them, a voice they know,
> He drives his beasts above Cabra.
>
> The voice tells them home is warm.
> They moo and make brute music with their hoofs,
> He drives them with a flowering branch before him,
> Smoke pluming their foreheads.
>
> Boor, bond of the herd,
> Tonight stretch full by the fire!
> I bleed by the black stream
> For my torn bough!

Around this period Joyce's younger brother Stanislaus, whom he had made privy to his determination to 'wrest the secret from life', wrote in his diary that 'Jim sits on the hearthrug, his arms embracing his knees, his head thrown a little back, his hair brushed straight off his forehead, his long face red as an Indian's with the reflection of the fire. There is a look of cruelty on his face.'

His mother's death and his refusal to allow 'the chemistry' of the Church to affect him seems to have unleashed another chemistry in Joyce – the ruthlessness of the artist who will put his art above family and country. He had dedicated himself to the Blessed Virgin as a boy, and when she had been put aside his mother had been a substitute. Now there was nothing but himself. He could talk of this to nobody until, a year after his mother's death, he was able to break his silence to a new acquaintance:

> My mind rejects the whole present social order and Christianity – home, the recognised virtues, classes of life and religious doctrines. How could I like the

idea of home? My home was simply a middle-class affair, ruined by spendthrift habits which I have inherited. My mother was slowly killed, I think, by my father's ill-treatment, by years of trouble and by my cynical frankness of conduct. When I looked on her face as she lay in her coffin – a face grey and wasted with cancer – I understood that I was looking on the face of a victim and I cursed the system which made her a victim.

In the person to whom he had written this he believed he had found someone who would renew the feminine principle for him and not deter him in his artist's vocation. She was a young Galway girl, Nora Barnacle, who had run away to Dublin to escape the treatment of a brutal uncle and who, like Ibsen's Lorna Hassell, believed in letting in 'fresh air'. She had a joyous acceptance of sex which for the first years of her relationship with Joyce would enable him to fulfil his own sensual nature and at the same time protect him from the dangers of casual sexual encounters outside the family bed. She was to be his strength throughout his life and without her help he might not have survived. From her he took much of the character of Molly Bloom who would personify a special energy he wished to direct into literature. Later he would embody it in the persona of a river whom he named Anna Livia, a fertilising mother rushing out to the ocean, to renew the parched plains and deserts of the earth.

It did not take him long to make up his mind to leave Dublin again. Within four months of meeting Nora he set out with her for Switzerland, in October 1904. Lady Gregory gave him his fare after he had proved to her he had a job to go (in fact the job in Zurich did not materialise, but he moved soon after to Pola where, thanks to his skill in languages, he was employed in a Berlitz school).

Dublin, according to Joyce, was suffering from 'hemiplegia of the will'. He could accomplish nothing there. He had grown up under two imperial powers, the

British Empire and the Roman Catholic Church. He wanted to be free of both. Even the language he spoke was not his own, certainly not that of his forebears. He recognised its strangeness when he heard it spoken on the tongue of an Englishman. The chains that prevented him from expressing himself as he wished could only be broken in the Europe that he had so often dreamed of as he tramped the empty beaches of his native city – the great Continent that lay out beyond, 'of entrenched and marshalled races'.

Joyce would take his roots with him and create his artistic conscience in exile, away from the world that had bred him. He only returned twice to Dublin; and after 1912 never visited the place again. Yet throughout his life there was scarcely a line in any of his books that did not relate, in some way or another, to his native city.

16 The World Their Forum

By helping James Joyce, Lady Gregory was to hasten the young man's fulfilment of his genius. Now she was herself finding another outlet for her energies. She had become a playwright. Her first play, *Twenty Five*, was presented at the Molesworth Hall in March 1903 by Fay's actors. It was well received and this encouraged her to set her mind to writing more works for the theatre. She enjoyed great success in her lifetime, and in later years, whenever audiences were dropping off, it became the thing to put on a Lady Gregory play to restore box office receipts.

She was fifty-one when she had her first play presented. Yet she was eventually to write over a hundred plays, some of which were to have a national influence. It used to be said that Lady Gregory's *The Rising of the Moon* had made more rebels in Ireland than a thousand political speeches or a hundred reasoned books. Lennox Robinson attributed his beginnings as a dramatist to seeing *Cathleen Ni Houlihan* and *The Rising of the Moon* performed in Cork, where he recognised for the first time that play material could be found at his own doorstep.

Where did she get her gift for the theatre, a much rarer one than that of the novelist? Perhaps her awareness of people and her passion for contact with those outside her social circle had quickened her understanding of popular response without which no playwright can be a success. As the years went on, she became more and more skilled in technique. Shaw consulted her on one occasion when he was writing *Saint Joan*. He wanted to suggest the changing of the wind before the relief of Orléans by the waving of a pennant. Lady Gregory, when he read the passage to her, suggested that he have a boy sneeze instead, and the delighted playwright accepted her advice.

She also did a good deal of directing over the years, and once even played the part of Cathleen Ni Houlihan with some success during a crisis in the theatre when no one else was available. *The Workhouse Ward* is perhaps her masterpiece, illustrating her ability to use heightened dialogue on the stage against a realistic background, and at the same time to provide an insight into social conditions under the guise of high comedy. She first wrote the play as a scenario after a visit to Gort workhouse. There she heard of a wife who had become an inmate of the same workhouse in which her husband was already installed. She had been maimed sometime previously as a result of a knife thrown at her by the same husband. Lady Gregory wondered how both of them would get on when they met. 'Would he be glad to meet her for old time's sake?' This gave her an idea for a scenario which she wrote out about two old men in a workhouse ward side by side in bed. She was intending to put dialogue on it, when Yeats maintained they needed another play in Irish. Loyally Augusta turned it over to Douglas Hyde to dramatise in Irish. His version turned out to be unpopular with theatre audiences. Lady Gregory spotted the flaw. The old men in their beds were speaking to an imaginary audience of workhouse inmates. She now rewrote the play from her own scenario and had the characters speak to each other so that the theatre audience was immediately drawn into the quarrel. The two old men are sniping at each other when the play begins:

MICHAEL MISKELL: And you didn't bring away my own eels, I suppose, I was after spearing in the Turlough? Selling them to the nuns in the convent you did, and letting on they to be your own. For you were always a cheater and a

346

	schemer, grabbing every earthly thing for your own profit.
MIKE MCINERNEY:	And you were no grabber yourself, I suppose, till your land and all you had grabbed wore away from you!
MICHAEL MISKELL:	If I lost itself, it was through the crosses I met with and I going through the world. I never was a rambler and a cardplayer like yourself, Mike McInerney, that ran through all and lavished it unknown to your mother!
MIKE MCINERNEY:	Lavished it, is it? And if I did was it you yourself led me to lavish it or some other one? It is on my own floor I would be to-day and in the face of my family, but for the misfortune I had to be put with a bad next door neighbour that was yourself. What way did my means go from me is it? Spending on fencing, spending on walls, making up gates, putting up doors, that would keep your hens and your ducks from coming in through starvation on my floor, and every four footed beast you had from preying and trespassing on my oats and my mangolds and my little lock of hay.

A sister of McInerney comes to visit him. She had been left a legacy and wants to take her brother home to her farmhouse. But as she talks to him he begins to wonder what life would be like without his old workhouse companion to quarrel with. He begs her to take the two of them to live with her.

MIKE MCINERNEY:	It is what I often heard said, two to be better than one. . . . Sure if you had an old trouser was full of holes

347

> . . . or a skirt . . . wouldn't you put
> another in under it that might be as
> tattered as itself, and the two of
> them together would make some
> sort of a decent show?

But she refuses to have Michael Miskell, so Michael McInerney elects to stay in the workhouse rather than leave his chum. After the sister leaves the two begin quarrelling again and they are throwing pillows at each other as the curtain comes down.

MICHAEL MISKELL: Tricky is it! Oh, my curse and the curse of the four and twenty men upon you!

MIKE MCINERNEY: That the worm may chew you from skin to marrow bone! (Seizes the pillow.)

MICHAEL MISKELL: (Seizing his own pillow.) I'll leave my death on you, you scheming vagabond!

MIKE MCINERNEY: By cripes! I'll pull out your pin feathers! (Throwing pillow.)

MICHAEL MISKELL: (Throwing pillow.) You tyrant! You big bully you!

MIKE MCINERNEY: (Throwing pillow and seizing mug.) Take this so, you stobbing ruffian you! (They throw all within their reach at one another, mugs, prayer books, pipes, etc.)

A play like The Workhouse Ward established a genre. It was seeing Lady Gregory's works, and others that had grown out of them, on the Abbey's first American tour that inspired Eugene O'Neill to write for the theatre. Lennox Robinson has gone so far as to suggest that the whole direction of the American theatre – the emergence of the black as a subject, the Kentucky mountainy man, the lonely farmer's wife in the mid-west, the North Carolina school of plays – was inspired by Lady Gregory and the playwrights who followed in her footsteps.

Her absorption with the theatre movement was by now complete. It was she who singlehandedly fought Dublin Castle and the Viceroy for the right to put on Shaw's *The Shewing up of Blanco Posnet* after it had been banned in London by the Lord Chamberlain. This demand was tantamount to establishing a sort of Home Rule for the arts in Dublin, yet she won. When the finances of the theatre were becoming impossible in the twenties, it was Augusta who visited the newly established Irish Government and succeeded in obtaining an annual grant with the result that the Abbey became the first theatre in the English-speaking world to receive a state subsidy. In the theatre Green Room she used to quote her proverb, 'Grip is a good dog, but Hold Fast is a better one.' When anyone would suggest that it might be prudent to avoid controversy, she would reply, 'I'm a lover of peace as long as it is not the peace of a dead body.' This sturdy little woman would mother the players like a brood of hens. She made the Green Room the centre of the cast's activities. Here they could meet in the evenings, brew tea and cut slices of Lady Gregory's specially made Gort barmbrack which she brought up on opening night for her 'chicks'. This brack was a monumental affair, a huge cartwheel of a fruit cake made especially by her own bakers at Gort which was so heavy that it took two to carry it. It was packed with good things, including candied peel and glacé cherries, and of itself could make a meal for some of the hungry players after the night's performance. And even when she toured with the players, she would insist on a Green Room for them. When they were performing for six weeks in the Maxine Elliott theatre in New York in 1911 and she found there were no facilities of this kind, she gave up her own room offstage, installed some books there, made regular arrangements for tea and saw to it that the actors could have a place to socialise. She was always aware of them as a company, not a touring group put together on an *ad hoc* basis.

Indomitable she proved in the face of opposition to her theatre. Once in New York, J.M. Kerrigan, a member of the cast of *The Playboy of the Western World*, became apprehensive as potatoes, cigar boxes, rosaries were hurled at the actors from the audience. But he got the 'fright of his life' when he heard a voice from behind one of the flats: 'Don't use up your voice, we're going to start all over again.' Augusta had crept on the stage to issue instructions so that the mob might be put in their place. Sure enough, the curtain was lowered and the play recommenced from the first scene, this time without interruption from a surprised audience. The following night, to make absolutely sure that there wouldn't be a repeat of the interruptions, Augusta had her friend and admirer, Theodore Roosevelt, former President of the United States, attend the performance, accompanied by Colonel Emmet, a grand nephew of Robert Emmet. All three sat in prominent seats in the front box. When the crowd saw them, they began to clap. Roosevelt stood up to acknowledge their cheers and as he did so took Lady Gregory by the hand so that she was cheered as well.

In Dublin, with Yeats to support her, she was just as tigerish when it came to standing up to opposition as she had been in New York. Yet with her practical sense, she never forgot that the theatre could not survive without public support. Her diary is everywhere sprinkled with notes referring to the attendance at plays:

> The sight of the Abbey audience tonight makes me feel glad to have been born.

> At the theatre tonight, splendid audiences – a joy.

If the audience was poor, she would go out by the stage door when the curtain was up and come round to the front hall to enter the auditorium in the dark and pass as a new arrival, thus encouraging a thin attendance. She knew every aspect of her theatre – the charwomen, the attendants, the stage managers, down to the bit of worn carpet leading to the stalls, the bit that must be cut out and have another sewn in because there wasn't enough money to buy a new carpet. The Abbey was the centre of her life, and because of her, and her partnership with Yeats, it survived.

To Yeats the theatre had now become of paramount importance. It was a vehicle through which he believed he could best achieve that unity of being where prince and ploughman might share a common thought, partaking in a collective unconscious aroused by the use of myth. Wagner's music dramas were doing for Germany what the Greek tragedies had done for Greece and Yeats believed that Ireland, with legends as beautiful as the Norse or German, could become once again a holy land to her own people.

It was through the personality of Cuchulain, whom he had first come across in O'Grady's histories, and who is to the Irish cycle what Ulysses and Siegfried are to the Greek and German tales, that Yeats felt he could explore the theatre as a unifying force. Cuchulain seemed a symbol, a force reaching from the elements, through which a people might aspire to a better understanding of their relationship with the heavenly flux. In the context of himself as a magus Yeats felt he could create changes in the national psyche if he could bring this heroic figure to life on the stage. He was to write five plays in his Cuchulain cycle, much the same as the structure of *Der Ring des Nibelungen*, except that Yeats's dramas were written at various periods of his life and reflect the different influences which affected his work as he matured. He completed his last Cuchulain play in the cycle in 1939, just a few weeks before his death.

As he progressed from his first presentation of the character in 1904, Cuchulain's personality seems to evolve into a sort of universal primitive figure as much Oriental as European. Dance, music and mask are all used in the later plays as, with that characteristic instinct of his, Yeats nosed out the Japanese Noh form to help him unify different arts on the stage. His initial concept of the character which he worked on in 1903 was straightforward enough. The story of how Cuchulain inadvertently kills his own son whom he had had (unknown to him) by a Scottish princess, Aoife, was still told around the country firesides in the west. A hundred-year-old man had set it down for Lady Gregory and told her how the son, as he lay dying, had said to his stricken father:

> Did you not see how I threw every spear fair and easy at you and you threw your spear hard and wicked at me? And I did not come out to tell my name to one or two, but if I told it to anyone in the whole world, I would soonest tell it to your pale face.

What is clear in *On Baile's Strand* is how much Yeats had progressed in his mastery of verse written for the stage since his first play eight years before. When he has Cuchulain argue with King Conor about the advantages of parenthood, the lines are muscular and effective.

CUCHULAIN: It's well that we should speak our minds
     out plainly,
    For when we die we shall be spoken of
    In many countries. We in our young days
    Have seen the heavens like a burning
     cloud
    Brooding upon the world, and being more
    Than men can be now that cloud's lifted
     up,
    We should be the more truthful.
     Conchubar,
    I do not like your children – they have no
     pith,
    No marrow in their bones, and will lie
     soft
    When you and I lie hard.

CONCHUBAR: You rail at them
    Because you have no children of your
     own.

CUCHULAIN: I think myself most lucky that I leave
    No pallid ghost or mockery of a man
    To drift and mutter in the corridors
    Where I have laughed and sung.

Faced with the difficulties of enacting heroic clashes on the stage, Yeats invented an ingenious device – he had them narrated by a fool to a blind man. These two characters foreshadow his use of chorus in later plays. Cuchulain, in despair at what he has done when he realizes that the unnamed warrior from Scotland who has challenged him is his son, dashes into the sea and dies fighting the waves.

BLIND MAN: Where are the kings? What are the kings doing?

FOOL: They are shouting and running down to the shore, and the people are running out of the houses. They are all running.

BLIND MAN: You say they are running out of the houses? There will be nobody left in the houses. Listen, Fool!

FOOL: There, he is down! He is up again. He is going out in the deep water. There is a big wave. It has gone over him. I cannot see him now. He has killed kings and giants, but the waves have mastered him, the waves have mastered him!

BLIND MAN: Come here, Fool!

FOOL: The waves have mastered him.

BLIND MAN: Come here!

FOOL: The waves have mastered him.

BLIND MAN: Come here, I say.

FOOL: (Coming towards him, but looking backwards towards the door.) What is it?

BLIND MAN: There will be nobody in the houses. Come this way, come quickly! The ovens will be full. We will put our hands into the ovens. (They go out.)

Yeats imposed some of the ideas on this production which he was later to develop in his concept of the theatre as a place where the mind would be liberated. The setting was made of curtains of unpainted jute, and he had these floodlit with amber lights to give the effects of 'cloths of gold'. When the upstage doors were opened to Cuchulain's son, he stood 'silhouetted against a background of topaz blue, given an effect of sea and sky with an atmosphere that could never be obtained by paint'.

This is typical of Yeats's longing for simplicity on the stage, suggestion rather than realism. In a letter to Lady Gregory he had referred to an over-elaborate set in a production by Beerbohm Tree as 'thrice vomited flesh'. His ideal was Maeterlinck's concept of 'an old man seated in his armchair with his lamp beside him' and he hoped to rid the stage of everything that is restless, everything that draws away from the sound of the human voice. The convention of the contemporary English stage which demanded movement for its own sake, and which often resulted in beautiful speech being chopped up to accommodate stage business, he regarded with horror. At one time to combat this influence he had thought of putting his players in barrels and having them wheeled around.

As a painter himself, friend of painters and coming from a painting family, he had advanced ideas on set design. He very much believed in bringing artists into the theatre and would write instructions for them to suit the mood of his plays; blues and greens for sailing into the sunrise in *The Shadowy Waters*, orange, red and black for the sexuality of *The King of the Great Clock Tower*. Ricketts, Shannon, Sturge Moore were some of the artists he used and it was Beardsley he had chosen to design the programme for his first play.

It was, however, in Gordon Craig, the creator of modern set design, that he found the artist most suited to his ideas. Craig held Yeats in the highest regard and once told the author that, after Yeats's praise for his sets for *Acis and Galatea*, nothing else mattered for him. Craig's great purple-blue cloth as a backcloth for Purcell's *Dido and Aeneas* would have seemed perfect to Yeats, especially as with clever lighting in the last act, it softened into shimmering blue and brought the blues and greens of the costumes into a perfectly blended harmony. Later, when Craig designed the setting for Yeats's *The Hour Glass*, the poet wrote to him that the play seemed to be performed in the heart of a great pearl throughout which darted the sunlit shadows falling through a meridian sea.

They worked together on a series of screens for the stage which anticipated the trend of modern set design. From the very beginning of his association with the drama, Yeats had shown tendencies towards total theatre – chorus, dance, music allied to drama. Wagner, of course, believed in a similar union but, for him, music was paramount; while for Yeats the spoken word came first, music second.

He had an instinct for seeking out those who could flesh out his images in arts where he had little experience. He would have Loie Fuller dance for him, discover Michio Ito for his oriental plays, and after the war recruit a young dancer into his theatre for his Cuchulain play *Fighting the Waves* – Ninette de Valois.

Even in music he could scent the new, though he was quite tone deaf. George Antheil's *Aeroplane Sonata* (which had caused a riot at its first performance in Paris) appealed to him, and it was to him he went for the music for *Fighting the Waves*.

It would become fashionable to criticise Yeats as a dramatist, while conceding his greatness as a poet. Practical men of the theatre who worked with him held a different view. He was simply too far in advance of his time for his conception of total theatre, simplicity of design and use of lighting to be accepted as it should have been. Lennox Robinson has commented that anyone who can read the last passage in *The Countess Cathleen* and say that Yeats is not a dramatist is 'a fool'; while Katherine Worth, the English critic, has gone so far as to say that Yeats 'conjured out of nothing the form the theatre at large would not see for almost fifty years'.

17 Miss Horniman's Present

It was Yeats's friend of the 'Golden Dawn' days, Miss Horniman, who had designed and made the costumes for *On Baile's Strand*. She had entered Yeats's life again about 1902. He had asked her to design costumes for an earlier play, *The King's Threshold* (about a poet who threatens to starve himself to death at the gate of the King's palace unless his wishes are acceded to), and she had thanked him for giving her the opportunity 'to work as an artist'. The determination and eccentricity she had shown as a young woman when she had cycled, worn bloomers, smoked and crossed the Alps alone were now at their height. She dressed in gowns of heavy tapestry material and always wore a piece of jewellery made in oxidised silver, carved in the shape of a dragon. She liked to begin her letters to Yeats with 'Dear Demon'.

Anne Horniman's desire to help the new theatre movement was genuine. Her heroes were Ibsen, Sudermann, Hauptmann. In *Samhain*, the occasional magazine of the Irish National Theatre Society, she read Yeats's statement that the plays of the new movement 'will make the theatre a place of intellectual excitement, a place where the mind goes to be liberated as it was liberated by the theatres of Greece and England and France at certain great moments of their history and as it is liberated in Scandinavia to-day'. This sufficiently impressed her to decide to help her friend in a practical way. One evening, after a performance of *The Shadowy Waters* when Yeats had come before the audience and made an impassioned speech in favour of freedom of ideas in the theatre, Miss

Horniman came up afterwards and said with a smile, 'I will give you a theatre.' She made good her promise, hiring the architect and theatre-lover Joseph Holloway to convert the Mechanics' Institute, a former music hall in Abbey Street, into a theatre – the Abbey Theatre – with a full proscenium stage, pit and balcony which would hold nearly six hundred people.

Miss Horniman's personal relationship with Yeats was not an easy one. She was almost certainly in love with him, and resented Lady Gregory's protective attitude towards him, especially the way in which the older woman had the poet down to Coole for long periods of recuperation and work.

> You are ceaselessly victimised by Lady Gregory [she wrote to him], on the score of your gratitude for her kindness. You are being made a slave, your genius is put under a net in that precious 'garden' and you are only let out when you are wanted to get something out of me.

This was manifestly unfair, for Lady Gregory was as much concerned with Yeats's artistic progress as was Miss Horniman. The difference between the two women was that, while both shared a gift for getting things done, Lady Gregory was an artist and Miss Horniman was not. 'You know,' Yeats confided in a moment of unusual indiscretion to an English director of the Abbey a few years later, 'Miss Horniman is a vulgarian.' He still retained a great affection for her and, indeed, was deeply in her debt, for she was to pay for the publication of the collected edition of his poems. But in matters relating to acting and design, it seems that Miss Horniman had poor taste. Her costumes were over-ornate and heavy, even garish, her sense of colour poor. During rehearsals for *On Baile's Strand* she and Yeats had got into much argument. He compared the red cloaks she had designed for the kings to 'fire extinguishers' and commented in front of the cast that they looked 'like Father Christmases'. When Miss Horniman insisted that red was the correct colour in archaeological terms, Yeats replied testily, 'Hang archaeology, it's the effect we want', and made the actors carry their red robes on their arms.

Miss Horniman liked her friends to address her as 'Tabby' and had an inordinate affection for cats. When anything pleased her, she would say it made her purr. But if she got angry she held her hands stretched out like claws and would emit low hisses. She took this obsession to the length of appearing unannounced on the stage during rehearsals to tell stories about cats: if the cast showed any resentment about this extraordinary conduct, she would observe that actors were jealous of cats because they could not compete with them for an audience's attention.

The Irish theatre could not have succeeded as it did without Anne Horniman, for all her peculiarities. She contributed, as a private individual, vast sums towards the Abbey – the equivalent of a quarter of a million pounds today – and in addition to providing the directors with a theatre would continue to subsidise the actors' salaries, thus enabling the Abbey to have a full-time repertory company, even after she had fallen out of sympathy with the theatre's policy.

Meanwhile Synge was busy in the autumn of 1903 working on two new plays, *The Tinker's Wedding* and *The Well of the Saints*. He was living a good deal now with his family in Crosthwaite Park in Kingstown, about nine miles from the city, and in a villa which his mother had taken in County Wicklow. It may have been financial dependence which necessitated Synge staying with his mother, but there was probably an element of maternal dependence as well. In some ways this woman, who differed from him in every way as far as his artistic ambitions were concerned, seems to have been essential to him to maintain his equilibrium. Her care for his spiritual welfare was unremitting. Because of his indifference to religion she believed he would be damned and constantly prayed for him: 'I do ask God to reveal himself to my poor boy.'

To add to the atmosphere of religious suffocation in the

Synge household, John's elder brother Sam had come from the missions in China to stay with the family for a few months in 1903. So narrow-minded that he refused to wear a clerical collar in public for fear of being mistaken for a Catholic priest, he forced the younger members of the Synge household to learn the names of the lesser prophets on Sunday, maintaining that it was not a day for acquiring secular knowledge. When a nephew put sugar on his stewed rhubarb, the Reverend Sam remarked that if sugar had been necessary in rhubarb, God would have put it there, a comment which drew an approving smile from Mrs Synge.

His mother's attitude towards John's connection with the theatre remained constant. She greeted with grim satisfaction the publisher's rejection of his essays on the Aran Islands. Poor John. She could have told him, all along, that this would happen. But 'men like Yeats and the rest of them' fooled him into thinking that Irish literature and the Celtic language 'and all those things they are trying to revive' were of any importance. She did hope his eyes had been opened. Mrs Synge looked on the stage as sinful and, in his lifetime, none of his family was permitted to attend a play of Synge's. She would argue that it was permissible to read Shakespeare but held that putting his plays on the stage created temptation for the people who acted. Later, after her death, Synge would go through agonies of remorse for having left Ireland to work on a play while his mother was seriously ill (she died while he was away) and would rage against those 'who go on as if art and literature were the first things', maintaining that there was nothing nobler 'than a single-hearted wife or mother'. But by that time he himself had the shadow of death on him. Now, though deeply attached to his mother, he continued to pursue his craft with absolute dedication, despite her constant disapproval.

The two plays he was working at both dealt with the revolt of the individual against authority. Synge chose tinkers and vagabonds to represent the individual stance, while using the Church as a symbol of authority.

The Tinker's Wedding would have proved so offensive to audiences at the time (in it a priest is tied up in a sack to be drowned in a bog because he refuses to marry a pair of tinkers who can't provide sufficient money for the wedding ceremony) that it would not be performed until after Synge's death. The Well of the Saints received less than a warm welcome when it was eventually produced. As usual Synge did not seem to be aware of popular reaction when writing his plays. Yeats's phrase that Synge 'was incapable of political thought' has a good deal of truth. Synge could sit all day watching a white cloud twist through the ragged peaks of Carrintwohil Mountain like a piece of lace, with no other idea than to make 'Irish plays as beautiful as Ireland'. But Yeats tended to romanticise Synge's character, especially in those diaries written shortly after Synge's death. The playwright was not as remote or withdrawn in his private life as he is depicted by many with whom he came in contact. His family involvement, his dependence on his mother, the knowledge that his brother slept with a revolver under his pillow to protect him from tenants that he had evicted, had left Synge with an ambivalent and insecure element in his personality. When he did eventually fall in love with a working-class actress from the theatre movement who reciprocated his affection, the dependent, neurotic side of his character came to the surface. This supposedly shy, contemplative man used every device from bullying to cajolery and abject humiliation to exact her acquiescence. It was on his hills, his glens, his roads, that she must walk with him and develop her life, alongside his so that, as the creature of his making, she would fit the role he had laid out for her. This side of him Yeats certainly was not aware of. But when it came to his art Yeats was right when he believed Synge's sole purpose was the perfection of his work: 'Those who accuse Synge of some base motive are . . . of such as those that Goethe thought when he said, "The Irish always seem to me like a pack of hounds dragging down some noble stag." '

Moore had turned by now and was on the rampage

against the theatre movement. Yeats considered that he was jealous and wanted to be stage director, a role in which he had always fancied himself. Whatever the reason, the novelist composed a diatribe against the Fays which he sent to the literary Magazine *Dana* signed under the pseudonym 'Paul Rutledge'. He tried to get young Gogarty to sign it but the poet, though he was a friend and admirer of Moore's, wanted no part in this internecine quarrel. In the letter Moore literally flayed Fay's stage management, interweaving somewhat pedantic comments to show his own knowledge of the art of stage direction. With typical sarcasm, Moore played down the success which the players had had on a recent London visit with the critics there:

> We hope that Mr Fay will not be beguiled, deluded, destroyed by the praise of these journalists who would have praised any little bushman who came over to London with a boomerang. The same little bushman would be praised in Paris. It is the custom of journalists to praise strangers for, who knows, the boomerang may make a hit.

It was too late for Moore to get back in with Yeats and Lady Gregory and Synge, either by ingratiating himself or by attack. They had realised that, like his cousin Edward, he lacked staying power and organisation. They knew they had the makings of an important movement and were not going to let it be upset by any individual, however brilliant an artist he might be in another sphere. His fury at his exclusion became Neronic. He would brood over it for half a decade. Then, as was his wont, he converted his anger into art. It was the ancient bard of the Irish Court lashing out at the enemy with his pen. Moore sensed, with his eye for satire, Yeats' soft underbelly, his connections with trade through his mother's shipping and milling relations in Sligo, and this could plausibly be set off against the landed gentry of Moore Hall. This he did in his autobiography, describing Yeats as dressed in 'an immense fur coat . . . with a paunch and

361

a stride', and providing a wicked account of a speech made to raise money for the Dublin Art Gallery:

> Yeats began to thunder like Ben Tillett against the middle classes, stamping his feet, working himself into a great temper. And we asked ourselves why should Yeats feel himself called upon to denounce his own class; millers and shipowners on one side and on the other a portrait painter of distinction: and we laughed, remembering AE's story that one day, while Yeats was crooning over his fire, Yeats had said that if he had his rights he would be Duke of Ormond. AE's answer was 'I'm afraid, Willie, you were overlooking your father' – a detestable remark to make to a poet in search of an ancestry; and the addition: 'we both belong to the lower middle class' was in equally bad taste. AE knew there were spoons in the Yeats family bearing the Butler crest, and he should have remembered that certain passages in 'The Countess Cathleen' are clearly derivative from the spoons.

In the serialisation of Moore's autobiography it turned out that there was a libel against Lady Gregory, implying that as a young girl she had engaged in proselytising. Yeats persuaded her to take action so that the libel was removed. Old fox that he was, Yeats himself waited till Moore died to reply in kind to the attacks on himself, which he did when he published his autobiography. These were some of the darts which he unleashed on his former colleague in *Dramatis Personae*:

> It was Moore's own fault that everybody hated him except a few London painters.

> He was Milton's lion rising up, pawing out of the earth, but unlike that lion stuck halfway.

> Moore had gone to Paris straight from his father's racing tables, from a house where there was no culture, as Symons and I understand that word, acquired copious and inaccurate French, sat among art stu-

dents, young writers about to become famous, in some café; a man carved out of a turnip looking out of astonished eyes.

Moore was from one of those Catholic families beaten down by the Penal Laws, despised by Irish Protestants, by the few English Catholics they met, and had but little choice as to where they picked up their brides. Boys on one side of old family grew up squireens, half-sirs, peasants, who had lost their tradition, gentlemen who had lost theirs. Lady Gregory once told me what marriage coarsened the Moore blood but I have forgotten.

But this would be in the future for Yeats. He had, like Moore, the savagery of the Gael but he could bottle it up for years if it would not help his purpose to unleash it at a certain time. What he was concerned with at this time was the movement. He knew Moore could upset it and, as with Hyde and the Gaelic League, he was determined to keep him away from anything to do with the theatre.

Another drop-out from the movement was AE. He looked on the theatre as a diversion for a poet of Yeats's talents. He told his friend that he could never influence the same number of people as a dramatist as he could as a poet and pointed out that the audiences at the Abbey could never compare with the thousands who would read his poetry. He also resented Yeats's autocratic attitude to the movement and his often savage dismissals of people involved in it, such as '– should go back to his office stool'. For the serene AE, such comments were unacceptable. When Yeats, questioned as to the merits of one of AE's young poets, replied, 'Why should a wise dog praise his fleas?', AE felt deeply hurt and was further offended when Yeats referred to AE's group as 'Russell's canary birds' and suggested he was getting 'groundsel' for them through his connection with the agricultural movement. It was no good AE trying to argue with Yeats either. As soon as he would make his point AE was liable to say, 'Yes, Russell, but that was before the peacock screamed,' or some other such dismissive phrase. That

Yeats was AE's hero there is no doubt. He felt he had to some extent helped to invent him, in those early years in Dublin while they explored the mystery of the unseen, and the sciences and the philosophies of the East together. There was, however, too much of the saint in AE, and too much of the driving selfishness of the artist towards perfection in Yeats, for their paths not to diverge in later years. Yeats kept his eyes fixed on a single goal, while AE branched off into politics, journalism and agricultural economy. Yet when he lay dying in Bournemouth, the one thing that was uppermost in AE's mind was that he had not heard from the friend of his youth, and he was only satisfied when at last a telegram arrived to tell him that Yeats knew what was happening and had expressed concern.

AE believed in democracy in a movement, volunteers. Yeats wanted a select few, and told Russell firmly that he had 'gathered the strong and capable about me, and all who love work better than idle talk will support me. It is a long fight but that is the sport of it'. Later he wrote to his American patron, John Quinn, to tell him that Russell's idea of democracy in the theatre was at an end and that if all went well, Synge, Lady Gregory and himself would have everything in their hands. It turned out as he had anticipated. Yeats was a master at gaining control. He had shed Moore, he had shed AE. The blood of merchants and sea captains had left him a gift for authority. He knew how to get his way. He would create a triumvirate, and it was they who would rule. After Synge's death, others were appointed to the board, but the power always remained with two persons, Yeats and Lady Gregory.

18 Curtain Up

As the day approached for the opening of the Abbey
Theatre, Tuesday 27 December, 1904, the excitement
mounted. The former music hall was now a compact
little theatre which held five hundred and sixty-two
people. It had been intended that the stage would extend
out into the pit in an Elizabethan fashion but limitations
of space prevented this. Above the pit was a balcony.
The whole auditorium had been constructed to give an
intimacy between the actors on the stage and the audience that was not possible in any of the other Dublin
theatres. Visitors entered the theatre through glass
doors leading from Marlborough Street. On either side
were stained glass windows of a tree in leaf by Sarah
Purser. On the walls hung copper-framed mirrors made
at a home industry in Youghal, and embroidered
tapestries worked by Lily Yeats. To the left was the
actors' Green Room. Paintings by John B. Yeats on the
walls included portraits of Lady Gregory, AE, Miss
Horniman, Maire nic Shiubhlaigh and the Fay brothers.

Yeats noted that the stars were quiet and favourable.
In the theatre that afternoon there had been much chaos
as the cast prepared. They had not eaten since breakfast. Shortly before the curtain went up Willie Fay was
seen swinging from a baton in the flies, wig askew,
trying to fix a last-minute defect. Synge, as he sat upon
an upturned property basket rolling a cigarette, said to
one of the actresses: 'God bless you, I hope you are as
happy as I am. I am so honoured that my little play
should be chosen for the first week.'

365

On the first night Yeats's *Cathleen Ni Houlihan* and *On Baile's Strand* – as well as Lady Gregory's *Spreading the News* – were to be presented, and on the second night Synge's *In the Shadow of the Glen* would replace Lady Gregory's play.

W.B., looking splendid in evening dress, kept bobbing in behind the scenes to see that everything was all right. Lady Gregory was ill and could not come up till later in the week. Out in front was an audience so varied that one of the actresses felt it must be 'one of the most fashionable events of the year'. John Dillon, MP, who had been Parnell's second-in-command as well as one of the founders of the Land League with Michael Davitt, was there, Stephen Gwynn, AE, Edward Martyn, John B. Yeats, Hugh Lane the art collector who was just beginning his distinguished career. The evening began with an overture from the Abbey 'orchestra' which was composed of one violinist, Arthur Darley, who had known Synge in Paris and had been a fellow member of an orchestra with him there. Darley appeared in front of the curtain at the side and played Irish airs with a shy but delicate touch. Just before the curtain went up Yeats made his entrance and was delighted when the pit clapped him as soon as he appeared.

The evening opened with *Spreading the News*, Lady Gregory's light comedy about how rumour can give currency to what never has happened. The Fays got the 'pace of a football match' into it and, according to Yeats, writing to Lady Gregory shortly afterwards, 'at times it was hard to hear the lines there was so much applause and laughter'. Then came Yeats's *Cathleen Ni Houlihan*, in which Holloway considered that Maire nic Shiubhlaigh, who played the part of the old woman, exceeded Maud Gonne's original performance. The evening ended with *On Baile's Strand*, Yeats's Cuchulain play. 'This is,' the *Freeman's Journal* commented, 'one of the best acting plays Yeats has written' and concluded that 'the poet has emerged from the shadows'. Maire nic Shiubhlaigh never forgot Frank

Fay's playing of Cuchulain, 'fondling his lines, his little figure gaining power through the beauty of his words'.

Yeats appeared in front of the curtain at the end and paid a special tribute to Miss Horniman who was not present as she had had to return to England during the rehearsals. 'Authors must be free to choose their own way,' he said,

> but in the pilgrimage towards beauty and truth they require companions by the way. Because of this subsidy the Abbey will be able to say 'Does it please us?' and then have the question answered, 'Does it please you?'

The *Irish Times* thought the night might be 'an epoch maker'. The following night Synge's play also received excellent notices. John Masefield wrote in the *Manchester Guardian* of the actors.

> With an art of gesture admirably disciplined and a strange delicacy of enunciation they performed the best drama of our time in the method of a lovely ritual. Their art is unlike any to be seen in England. It is never common, it is never derivative. One thinks of it as a thing of beauty, as a part of life, as the only modern dramatic art springing from the life of a people.

Lady Gregory was well enough to come to Dublin at the end of the week and she, Yeats and Synge met together one afternoon at the theatre. One can imagine the three, as they talked in animated fashion about their plans, wandering on and off the stage to savour their new building from the vantage point from which their plays would be presented. They had now a theatre, a company of actors and a group of playwrights. This would be a place where the imagination would have free rein. The theatre could help to fuse the national image so that the people might find an identity. It would be the centre around which a renaissance of writing and poetry could grow up. As they stood on the stage in the gloom of a winter's afternoon, looking out into the dark of the pit beyond the gleam of the brass rail around the orchestra stalls, and the slender cast iron poles supporting the curve of the balcony, they could not have foreseen the difficulty they would face – the interminable quarrels with the players and managers, near-bankruptcies, even riots. But they had a common bond. The class they had come from did not give in easily and had achieved much as organisers and administrators in many countries of the world. They would use these gifts now for the benefit of the people amongst whom their ancestors had come centuries before, to articulate a sunken culture into the literature of the world.

> John Synge, I and Augusta Gregory, thought
> All that we did, all that we said or sang
> Must come from contact with the soil, from that
> Contact everything Antaeus-like grew strong.
> We three alone in modern times had brought
> Everything down to that sole test again.

19 The Perfect Circle

Twenty-four years after the opening of the Abbey the circle was complete. The founders had gone to the people for inspiration for their work. Now the people were writing dramas out of their own lives – and one of them, a labourer, Sean O'Casey, had achieved a masterpiece.

'I felt at the end of it,' Lady Gregory said after she had seen *The Plough and the Stars*, 'as if I should never care to look at another; all others had seemed so shadowy to the mind after this.' O'Casey's work was to be of world importance. He invested his characters of the slum world with the same sort of wild wit and imaginative derision that Synge had captured in his rural dramas. James Agate, the *Sunday Times* critic, described the last act of one of O'Casey's plays as 'amongst the greatest pieces of tragedy since Shakespeare'. In the United States George Jean Nathan and Brooks Atkinson hailed his genius and Eugene O'Neill, when he was at the height of his fame, wrote to O'Casey saying, 'I wish to God I could write like you.'

He had made many attempts at literary work before finally trying his hand, in 1902 at the age of forty, at drama. When he sent his first plays to Lady Gregory she told him that 'your strength is characterisation' and said he should rewrite them. It was this which had encouraged him to create *The Plough and the Stars*.

Riots accompanied the first performance in February 1926, when members of the audience objected to a prostitute on the stage in a play which had as its background the Irish rebellion of 1916. It was also said that the national flag should not have been brought into a public house. On the fourth night of the opening week there were serious disturbances. At the point when the prostitute, Rosie Redmond, comes into the pub after a political meeting, there was pandemonium and cries of: 'Get her off the stage. It's a disgrace in a Catholic country. There are no women like that in Dublin.' As the garbage flew the curtain was brought down. Yeats had stood white-faced in the wings. He had asked the playwright's permission to call the police, and said with some satisfaction, 'This time it will be their *own* police, O'Casey.'

Now he walked on stage standing behind the curtain which was down. The stage manager had been instructed not to raise it until Yeats gave the signal. The poet listened intently through the curtain, like a black-bird poised to take wing. Then precisely at the moment he sensed a lull in the noise, he snapped, 'Now, Barlow.' Up went the curtain. At the sight of the tall, splendid figure with the shock of now white hair thrown back from the great bronze forehead, there was a sudden silence.

I thought you had got tired of this which commenced about fifteen years ago,

Yeats began. There was not a murmur, the audience was mesmerised.

But you have disgraced yourselves again. Is this going to be a recurring celebration of Irish genius; Synge first, then O'Casey! The news of the happenings in the last few minutes here will flash from country to country. Dublin has again rocked the cradle of a reputation. From such a theatre as this went forth the fame of Synge. Equally, the fame of O'Casey is born here tonight. This is his apotheosis.

O'Casey was to say afterwards to Barry Fitzgerald that he had to go home and look up the word 'apotheosis' in the dictionary to find out whether Yeats thought he was a success or a failure, but the meaning of the poet's coura-geous address was clear to the crowd. 'Yeats was like a

370

lion that night,' one of the actors told the author. 'No one could have withstood him, the lower lip sticking out like a fighter, his body trembling with suppressed rage.'

Lady Gregory was in Coole on the opening night but she came up the following day to back her playwright to the hilt. The play went on with police in the house every night.

Augusta had found a new chick to mother. Sean christened her Blessed Brigid O'Coole for the friendship and hospitality she extended to him in her country house where he enjoyed congenial company and calm and peace for his work. Later he would quarrel with Yeats but Lady Gregory would always remain his close friend.

As Yeats had said, O'Casey's play had not been the first to create a riot in the theatre. Only three years after the opening of the Abbey in 1907 there had been a series of demonstrations at Synge's *The Playboy of the Western World* when some of the actors had been assaulted on the stage despite the fact that Yeats had called in the police to protect them. Then the objectors centred their opposition on the use of the word 'shift' – which was nothing more prurient than a description of a woman's nightdress. What was really behind the protest was that the play described a young man being made a hero by girls of a Western village because he had slain his father in a fit of temper. This was showing Irishmen up in a bad light before the world, the objectors felt, ignoring the fact that Synge had created a peasant Don Juan in a surrealist play full of wild humour and laughter that has made it a classic.

Poor Synge did not live to complete another play, for he died in 1909 of Hodgkin's disease. In the last year shortly before his death he had at last conquered his shyness to become engaged to the most beautiful actress in the Abbey company – who was to play the lead part in his play *Deirdre* when it was produced in an unfinished version after his death.

By the time Synge died the literary renaissance was flourishing. From the beginning of the century to the mid-twenties Dublin overflowed with literary talent

371

– writers, poets, dramatists. Among the younger generation were poets of the quality of Padraic Colum, Oliver St John Gogarty, Seumas O'Sullivan and Francis Ledwidge. Then James Stephens emerged with his marvellous tale of philosophical leprechauns, *The Crock of Gold*. Lord Dunsany, Horace Plunkett's nephew, achieved a wide reputation as a novelist and at one time had his plays running in London, New York, Paris and Moscow. A whole school of Abbey actors emerged who were to make their mark on world theatre – Barry Fitzgerald, Sarah Allgood, Arthur Sinclair, Fred O'Donovan, Sydney Morgan, Maureen Delaney, F.J. McCormick.

Dublin's literary evenings became celebrated outside Ireland. Yeats held his on Tuesday, AE on Sunday and Moore on Saturday. To these evenings, in search of imaginative excitement and good talk, came writers and artists from England, America and the Continent – Augustus John, Bernard Shaw, Gabriele d'Annunzio, John Singer Sargent, Mancini, William Rothenstein. Their reports of the wit and flow of conversation that characterised Dublin salons at this period, helped to establish the reputation of the city as a centre of a literary renaissance.

Alongside the literary achievement a school of painting was developing. Yeats's brother, Jack, was capturing in paint the world his friend Synge had written about in prose and drama. William Orpen and Walter Osborne, along with John Butler Yeats, caught the physiognomy of their time on their canvases. Sarah Purser and Celia Harrison were two notable women painters. Hugh Lane, Lady Gregory's nephew and an outstanding collector, offered his collection of impressionist paintings (the finest outside Paris) to the Dublin Municipal Gallery on condition that they would construct a satisfactory building to house the collection. When they failed to do this Lane left the collection to the Tate but changed his mind in favour of Dublin just before he drowned on the *Lusitania* in 1915. Owing to a technicality the codicil was unenforceable and it was not until 1959 that the Dublin gallery (now named the Hugh Lane Municipal Gallery) was given the right to share the bequest with the Tate.

This was also the period when Ireland seemed about to win self-government. In Britain the Liberal Party in power were committed to a policy of self-rule for Ireland though for some the process seemed too slow. The energy of two decades before seemed to renew itself – and when no outlets could be found through constitutional channels, the national desire for independence asserted itself in an armed rebellion which achieved partial success when the new Irish State was established in 1922. Yeats, though he sided with the rebels, worried that his plays might have sent some of them to their death. Had Cuchulain departed the stage to stalk through the General Post Office where the rebellion had commenced? Had his play about the poet hunger striker in ancient Ireland inspired the leaders of the rebellion to starve themselves to death for political ends?

> Did that play of mine send out
> Certain men the English shot?

In 'the troubles' Augusta had been firmly on the Irish side against England and wrote poetry and prose that was used in Nationalist pamphlets and recited throughout the country. As indomitable as ever, even during the worst period of the Black and Tan war, she refused to close the Abbey. One day, coming out of the theatre with Lennox Robinson, while she was being escorted to her tram, there was an ambush and a volley of shots. People fled in all directions, and Augusta was beseeched to lie down. But she stamped her elegant little foot in the direction of the English soldiers and said with her slight lisp, 'Up the rebelth.'

Edward Martyn was the first of the founders of the Irish Literary Theatre to die, in 1924. After his break with Yeats and Lady Gregory in the Irish Literary Theatre, he never returned to the movement. When it became obvious to him that he would not recover from his illness, he arranged his death with as much eccentricity as he had shown in his life. His body, as directed in his will, was taken to Cecilia Street Medical School to be dissected. When this order had been carried out the corpse was conveyed in a mortuary van, along with the bodies of six other paupers, in a plain deal box to be interred by the public authorities in an unknown grave.

As for his cousin George Moore, he severed his connections with Ireland in 1912 after a period of uneasy relationship with the country of his birth. He had fought with almost everybody in the movement, and now reverted to a firm dislike of his native land. 'No country is so foreign to me as Ireland but I am not sure if this last sentence represents you, I think it does,' he wrote to John Eglinton. In England he resumed his friendship with his painter friends Tonks, Steer, Sickert. He produced five more novels before his death in 1933, none of them the equal of the work he had done before he left Ireland, though all written in the same perfect prose. He had always considered that James Joyce had plagiarised his *Confessions of a Young Man* with a *A Portrait of the Artist as a Young Man* and the end of his novel *Vain Fortune* with his story *The Dead*. Thus he must have been pleased when, at the height of his fame in August 1929 on a visit to London, Joyce took the opportunity of going to see him. They got on surprisingly well, Joyce, according to Moore, seemed anxious to accord him the first place, but Moore modestly demurred and declared the younger man first in Europe. They talked about Dujardin who had been a close friend of Moore and from whom Joyce was said to have taken his idea of the *monologue intérieur*. They both agreed that Paris had played an equal part in their lives and Moore completed his surprisingly agreeable reception of Joyce by telling him, 'I have been only a revolutionary while you have been a heroic revolutionary for you had no money.'

When Moore died in January 1933, Joyce sent a funeral wreath, inscribed 'To George Moore from James Joyce', and created a great deal of trouble with the executors when he found that it had not been acknowledged in the newspapers. But it would not have been Moore if he had not managed to cause some trouble even at his own funeral. He had asked for his ashes to be scattered over Lough Carra, a request that embarrassed the pious element in the family who were burdened with the task of arranging what amounted to a 'pagan' ceremony. The funeral oration, written by AE (who was too ill to attend), was read over the grave. It ended with the words, 'If any would condemn him for creed of theirs he had assailed, let them be certain first that they laboured for their ideals as faithfully as he did for his.' These sentiments were echoed in the inscription devised for his gravestone:

He forsook his family and friends
For his art
Because he was faithful to his art
His family and his friends
Reclaimed his ashes for Ireland

James Joyce was of course by this time the most controversial writer writing in any language. *Ulysses* had set a course which many considered made the novel outdated. Painters, composers, sculptors all claimed to have derived inspiration from Joyce's writing, especially his 'Work in Progress' which finally emerged as *Finnegans Wake*, a study of the sub-conscious mind written in what amounted to a new language. He would almost certainly have received the Nobel Prize for Literature, had he not died in Zurich in 1941 when no award was being made owing to the war.

Although she stopped writing plays in the 1920s Lady Gregory continued for years to make her weekly journeys to Dublin for directors' meetings at the Abbey where she ruled with a firm hand. The Government grant to the theatre in 1925 brought her much pleasure. It would ensure the continuance of the Abbey after her death. Dubliners now recognised her as a familiar figure in the streets with a black mantilla over her beautiful grey hair and a single jewel hanging on her breast. Gogarty's remark that she was like a 'permanent understudy for Queen Victoria' was pleasantly malicious but she reminded Frank Fay so much of the queen that he used to feel an almost overwhelming desire to address her as 'your Majesty'.

Augusta never stopped trying to build bridges between people of opposite views, and would invite people from both sides who had fought in the Civil War to the theatre so that they might meet one another there and forget some of their differences. By 1930 she had survived a serious operation for four years but was getting increasingly arthritic and deaf. She still hobbled around Coole with a small hatchet in her gloved hands cutting down thistles and chopping down ivy, muttering with satisfaction as she worked, 'So perish all the King's enemies.' Her son Robert's death in 1918 as an airman with the Royal Flying Corps had been a dreadful loss. It grieved her that Coole had had to be sold before her death to the Land Commission by her daughter-in-law; she had longed in vain for 'someone of our blood to keep it open as a home'. Knowing its fate, she had the Gregory vault sealed up and arranged her own burial place in Galway city beside the grave of her favourite sister, Arabella, many miles from the pigeons of the seven woods, the swans rising from the lake and her autograph tree with the names of Yeats, AE, O'Casey and others carved upon it. She died on 22 May 1932. The following day a grief-stricken Yeats wrote: 'I have lost one who has been to me for nearly forty years my strength and conscience.'

By this time Yeats had become recognised as the finest poet writing in English. He had been awarded the Nobel Prize for Literature in 1924. He was a Senator of the new Free State and he devoted a great deal of time to help design the new coinage and the robes of the lawyers (who, ultimately, refused to wear them). His health was uneven but his output did not diminish, and he entered a new period of creativity in 1928 with the publication of *The Tower* which contained what many critics consider his best verse. His death took place at Cap Martin in January 1939, shortly after he had written the stage directions for *The Death of Cuchulain* in which the hero's severed head is represented by a parallelogram. It was said that he murmured verse as he died. He was buried in the cemetery of Roquebrune which looks down on the sea. Yeats's wish that he be buried in Drumcliffe, County Sligo, was left unfulfilled with the outbreak of war. But in 1948 the Minister for Foreign Affairs in the Irish Government was Maud Gonne's son, and he arranged for the poet's body to be brought back to Ireland on an Irish naval corvette and reinterred in Drumcliffe. After lying in state in the town square of Roquebrune, the coffin was taken to Nice by road and then transferred to the corvette. Twelve days later, Yeats's body was piped ashore in Galway by an army band.

An immense crowd attended the funeral at Drumcliffe churchyard where Yeats's ancestor had been rector. Many had come from Dublin, among them, it was said, those who were so carried away by the congenial atmosphere which accompanied the obsequies that they did not return to the capital city for months, even years. Now the poet lay, at last, where he had wished, under the shadow of Ben Bulben's whale-like form, where once Diarmuid and Grania had sheltered, over which clouds from the Atlantic tumbled and wrestled like warriors of old.

A last note, a fanfare of trumpets in Saint Patrick's Hall, Dublin Castle, in June 1938. The floating banners of the Knights of Saint Patrick with their dim gold and silver adorned the walls as they had when Prince Albert Edward had been invested in the Order in June 1887. Exactly fifty-one years later an old man with white hair and full moustache was coming up the aisle beneath the ceiling with its oval picture of Saint Patrick converting the Irish, past the white painted walls, the gold listed panels, towards the pillars at the end of the immense room. Douglas Hyde was about to be inaugurated as the first President of Ireland.

On his journey to the Castle, he had travelled through the streets with the clip-clop of the mounted escort that led the cavalcade mingling with the cheers of the crowd, just as the Viceroys used to come from Westland Row on their arrival in Ireland. Representatives of all the Irish Churches were in Saint Patrick's Hall as well as the Diplomatic Corps, the University dons, Lord Mayors of the principal cities and members of the Irish Parliament. But the red coats of the Guards, and the black corded jackets of the Rifles who used to attend the fashionable Castle balls in St Patrick's Hall, had been replaced by the green uniforms of the Irish National Army; and where Liddell's orchestra used to pour down waltzes on the gay viceregal throng, there was now an Irish military band to play the new anthem.

After the fanfare of trumpets was over Mr de Valera, the Prime Minister, began an address in Irish:

We are glad to pay you honour as one worthy of the office to which you have been called. Your foresight in saving from death our own sweet language, which your work and that of your colleagues of half a century ago have made it possible for us now to restore, merits for you the gratitude of all the generations of the Irish that are to come. Thanks to you we can, if we will, be once more a complete nation ranking high amongst the oldest of the nations of the world.

A scholar, a *chraoibhin dhilis*, you symbolise for us the things by which our people set most store, in your person you hold up to us the ancient glory of our people and beckon to us to make the future rival the past, urging us to be ever worthy of our inheritance as a great spiritual nation, whose empire is of the soul.

As Douglas Hyde emerged from Dublin Castle as President of Ireland he bowed and spoke to the Irish-speaking battalion who formed the guard of honour for him. The guns in nearby Collins barracks fired a salute and, simultaneously, the Irish flag was hoisted over the Viceregal Lodge in Phoenix Park where once the Union Jack had floated each summer to signify that the King's representative was in residence. At five o'clock that afternoon President Hyde entered the Viceregal Lodge, now, renamed Aras an Uachtarain.

One wonders what thoughts were in Hyde's mind on that June day. Did he think of those years when as a young man he had been a member of the class whose lives had revolved around viceregal life and how he had kept hidden in his heart his secret passion for the culture of the people whose cabins lay in the environs of the great estates? He had spent a large part of his life poring over manuscripts and setting down poems and stories from the people's lips so that the culture of the Gael might not perish.

The literary renaissance which had used the culture he had brought to the surface as the basis for its success had left him behind when it came into its own. His beloved Gaelic League had abandoned him when he refused to allow political decisions on its executive in 1915. Hyde had drifted out of public life and was seventy-eight when he was asked out of retirement to receive the highest honour of the State in 1938. But it is hard to imagine him now feeling any bitterness. He believed in achievement and getting things done. Irish, the official language of the new State, had been used at his inauguration. He would only have rejoiced at the success of his former colleagues in the literary renaissance.

The year following his inauguration fuel became scarce, a result of war conditions. The President immediately opened his coal cellars and donated the contents to the people of Dublin. Turf from the bogs became the chief heating element in the Aras; where once princes and kings had been in residence, emperors who held sway over a quarter of the globe, now the homely smell of turf smoke permeated the massive rooms with their rococo plasterwork and the great halls with their coffered, barrel-vaulted ceilings and screens of fluted Doric columns.

THE END

Select Bibliography

Where there is material in the text which I felt required specific identification, I have appended the number of the page on which it appears to the relevant book in the bibliography.

ABELS, Jules: *The Parnell Tragedy* (The Bodley Head, London 1966)

Allingham, William: *Poems* (The Dolmen Press, Dublin 1967)

Alspach, Russell K.: *Irish Poetry from the English Invasion to 1798* (The University of Pennsylvania Press, 1943)

Anderson, R.A.: *With Horace Plunkett in Ireland* (Macmillan, London)

Arnold, Bruce: *Orpen, Mirror to an Age* (Jonathan Cape, London 1981)

Arnold, Matthew: *The Study of Celtic Literature* (Dent, London 1867)

BAILEY, Kenneth C.: *Trinity College, Dublin* (Hodges Figgis, Dublin 1947)

Bax, Arnold: *Farewell My Youth* (Longmans Green, London 1943)

Bax, Clifford: *Some I Knew Well* (Phoenix, London 1951)

Beerbohm, Max: *And Even Now* (Heinemann, London 1920)

——*Around Theatres*, Vols I & II (Knopf, New York 1930)

——*Mainly on the Air* [p. 212] (Heinemann, London 1946)

Behrman, S.N.: *Conversation with Max* (Hamish Hamilton, London 1960)

Bence-Jones, Mark: *Burke's Guide to Country Houses*, Vol I-Ireland (Burke's Peerage, London 1978)

Benson, Eugene: *J.M. Synge* (Macmillan, London 1982)

Bernard, Marc: *Zola* (Grove Press, New York 1960)

Bjersley, Brigit: *The Interpretation of the Cuchulain Legend in* the works of W.B. Yeats (Lundequist, Upsala 1950)

Blavatsky, Helen P.B.: *The Secret Doctrine: The Synthesis of Science, Religion and Philosophy*; 2nd edition (2 vols) (Theosophical Publishing, London 1888)

Blunt, Wilfrid S.: *My Diaries*; foreword by Lady Gregory (2 vols) (Martin & Secker, London 1919–20)

Boldick, Robert (ed.): *Pages from The Goncourt Journal* (Oxford University Press, Oxford 1978)

Bolger, Patrick: *The Irish Co-operative Movement, Its History and Development* (Institute of Public Administration, Dublin 1977)

Bourgeois, Maurice: *John Millington Synge and The Irish Theatre* (Constable, London 1913)

Bourke, Marcus: *John O'Leary* [p. 68] (Anvil Press, Dublin)

Bowen, Elizabeth: *The Shelbourne* (Harrap, London 1951)

——*Collected Impressions* (Longmans, London 1950)

Bowen, Zack: *Padraig Colum* (South Illinois University, Carbondale 1971)

Boyd, Ernest: *Appreciations and Depreciations: Irish Literary Studies* (The Talbot Press, Dublin 1917)

——*Ireland's Literary Renaissance* (Figgis, Dublin 1915)

Boylan, Henry: *A Dictionary of Irish Biography* (Gill & Macmillan, Dublin 1978)

Bradley, Bruce: *James Joyce's Schooldays* (Gill & Macmillan, Dublin 1982)

Brooke, Raymond: *The Brimming River* (Allen Figgis, Dublin 1961)

Brown, Malcolm: *The Politics of Irish Literature: From Thomas Davis to W.B. Yeats* (Allen & Unwin, London 1972)

——*Sir Samuel Ferguson* (Bucknell University Press, Lewisburg 1973)

——*George Moore: A Reconsideration* (University of Washington Press, Seattle 1955)

Bushrui, S.B. (ed.): *Sunshine and Moon's Delight: A Centenary Tribute to J.M. Synge, 1871–1909* (Colin Smythe, Gerrards Cross, 1972)

Byrne, Donn: *Blind Raftery* (Sampson Low, London n.d.)

CARDOZO, Nancy: *Maud Gonne–Lucky Eyes and a High Heart* (Gollancz, London 1979)

Carney, James: *Early Irish Poetry* (Mercier Press, Cork 1965)

Castiglione (trans. Singleton): *The Book of the Courtier* (Anchor Books, New York 1959)

Cave, Richard: *A Study of the Novels of George Moore* (Colin Smythe, Gerrards Cross 1978)

Chadwick, Nora: *The Celts* (Penguin Books, Harmondsworth 1970)

Chart, D.A.: *The Story of Dublin* (Dent, London 1932)

Chesterton, G.K.: *Autobiography* [p. 76] (Hutchinson, London 1936)

Chisholm, Anne: *Nancy Cunard* (Penguin Books, Harmondsworth 1981)

Clarke, Austin: *Twice Around the Black Church: Early Memories of Ireland and England* (Routledge & Kegan Paul, London 1962)

Clery, Arthur: *Dublin Essays* (Maunsel, Dublin 1919)

Cockburn, Claud: *I Claud* [p. 221] (Penguin Books, Harmondsworth 1967)

Coffey, Diarmid: *Douglas Hyde: President of Ireland* (The Talbot Press, Dublin 1938)

Colum, Mary: *Life and the Dream* (Macmillan, London 1947)

Colum, Mary & Padraig: *Our Friend, James Joyce* (Gollancz, London 1939)

Colum, Padraig: *Arthur Griffith* (Browne & Nolan, Dublin 1959)

——*The Road Round Ireland* (Macmillan, New York 1926)

——*Three Plays* (Allen Figgis, Dublin 1963)

Cooper-Prichard, A.H.: *Conversations with Oscar Wilde* (Philip Allan, London 1931)

Cork, Tom: *The Phoenix Park Murders* (Hodder and Stoughton, London 1968)

Corish, Patrick J.: *The Catholic Community in the 17th and 18th Centuries* (Helicon, Dublin 1981)

Corkery, Daniel: *Synge and Anglo-Irish Literature* (Cork University Press, Cork 1931)

Courtney, Sister Marie-Therese: *Edward Martyn and the Irish Theatre* (Vantage Press, New York 1957)

Cousins, James H. & Margaret E.: *We Two Together* (Ganesh, Madras 1950)

Coxhead, Elizabeth: *Daughters of Erin* (Secker & Warburg, London 1965)

——*Lady Gregory: A Literary Portrait* (Macmillan, London 1961)

Craig, Edward Gordon: *The Art of the Theatre* (T. Foulis, London 1905)

——*Designs for the Theatre* (Penguin Books, Harmondsworth 1948)

Craig, Maurice: *Dublin 1660–1860* (Figgis, Dublin 1969)

Croft-Cooke, Rupert: *Feasting with Panthers* (W.H. Allen, London 1967)

Cross, Colin: *The Fall of the British Empire* (Hodder & Stoughton, London 1968)

Cunard, Nancy G.M.: *Memories of George Moore* [p. 48] (Rupert Hart Davis, London 1956)

Curran, C.P.: *Under the Receding Wave* (Gill & Macmillan, Dublin 1970)

Czira, Mme Sydney: *The Years Flew By* [p. 56] (Gifford & Craven, Dublin 1974)

DALY, Dominic: *The Young Douglas Hyde* [p.11] (Rowman & Littlefield, Totowa, N.J. 1974)

Daly, John: *Irish Jacobite Poetry* (Cumming, Dublin 1844)

Darroch, Sandra: *Ottoline – The Life of Lady Ottoline Morrell* (Coward, McCann & Geoghegan, New York 1975)

Delaney, Frank: *James Joyce's Odyssey* (Hodder & Stoughton, London 1981)

Denson, Alan (ed.): *Letters from AE* (Abelard & Stoughton, London 1981)

Devoy, John: *Recollections of an Irish Rebel* (Young, New York 1929)

Dickinson, P.L.: *The Dublin of Yesterday* (Methuen, London 1929)

Digby, Margaret: *Horace Plunkett: An Anglo-American Irishman* (Basil Blackwell, Oxford 1949)

Donoghue, Denis: *The Third Voice* (Oxford University Press, 1959)

Dowden, Elizabeth & Hilda: *Letters of Edward Dowden and his Correspondents* (Dutton, New York 1914)

Dufferin, Helen Lady: *Poems and Verses* (John Murray, London 1894)

Duffy, Sir Charles: *Young Ireland, A Fragment of Irish History 1840–1845* (Fisher Unwin, London 1896)

Dunleavy, Gareth: *Douglas Hyde* (Bucknell University Press, Lewisburg 1974)

Dunsany, Lord: *Patches of Sunlight* (Heinemann, London 1938)

EGLINTON, John: *Anglo-Irish Essays* (The Talbot Press, Dublin 1917)
——*A Memoir of AE* [p. 62] (Macmillan, London 1937)
——*Irish Literary Portraits* (Macmillan, London 1935)
——*Literary Ideals in Ireland* (T. Fisher Unwin, London 1899)
Ellmann, Richard: *Eminent Domain: Yeats among Wilde, Joyce, Pound, Eliot and Auden* (Oxford University Press, New York 1967)
——*James Joyce* (Oxford University Press, New York 1959 (revised ed. 1982))
——*The Identity of Yeats* (Macmillan, London 1954)
——*Yeats: The Man and the Mask* (Faber & Faber, London 1961)

FALLIS, Richard: *The Irish Renaissance* (Gill & Macmillan, Dublin 1928)
Farr, Florence: *A Short Inquiry Concerning The Hermetic Art* (Theosophical Publishing, London 1894)
Fay, W.G. & Carswell, Catherine: *The Fays of the Abbey Theatre* [p.235] (Rich & Cowan, London 1935)
Fay, Gerard: *The Abbey Theatre: Cradle of Genius* (Hollis & Carter, London 1958)
Fay, Frank: *Towards a National Theatre* [pp. 225–227] (Dolmen Press, Dublin 1970)
Figgis, Darrell: *AE: A Study of a Man and a Nation* (Maunsel, Dublin 1916)
Fingal, Elizabeth, Countess of: *Seventy Years Young* [p. 162] (Collins, London 1937)
Fitzpatrick, W.J.: *'The Sham Squire' and the Informers of 1798* (Gill, Dublin 1865)
——*The Life of Charles Lever* (Downey, London 1901)
Flannery, James W.: *W.B. Yeats and the Idea of a Theatre* (The University Press, New Haven 1976)
——*Miss Annie Horniman and the Abbey Theatre* (Dolmen Press, Dublin 1970)
Fleming, Lionel: *Head or Harp* (Barrie & Rockliff, London 1965)
Flower, Robin: *The Irish Tradition* (Clarendon, Oxford 1947)
——*The Western Island* (Clarendon, Oxford 1944)
Foster, R.F.: *C.S. Parnell: The Man and His Family* (Humanities Press, Atlantic Highlands, N.J. 1976)
Fraser, G.S.: *W.B. Yeats* (Longmans, London 1954)

GARNETT, David: *Great Friends* (Macmillan, London 1979)

Gaunt, William: *The Aesthetic Adventure* (Jonathan Cape, London 1945)

Gerber, Helmut E (ed.): *George Moore in Transition* (Wayne State University Press, Detroit 1968)

Gibbon, Monk: *The Masterpiece and the Man – Yeats as I knew him* (Rupert Hart-Davis, London 1959)

Gogarty, Oliver St John: *As I was Going Down Sackville Street* (Rich & Cowan, London 1932)

——*Many Lines to Thee – Letters to G.K.A. Bell* (Dolmen Press, Dublin 1971)

——*Tumbling in the Hay* (Constable, London 1939)

——*It Isn't This Time of Year At All* [pp. 194, 213–214] (McGibbon & Kee, London 1954)

Greene, David H. (with Edward Stephens): *J.M. Synge, 1871–1909* (Macmillan, New York 1961)

Greene, David H. (with Dan H. Lawrence): *The Matter with Ireland* (Rupert Hart-Davis, London 1962)

Gregory, Anne: *Me and Nu* (Colin Smythe, Gerrards Cross 1970)

Gregory, Isabella Augusta, Lady: *Collected Plays* (ed. Anne Saddlemyer) (Colin Smythe, Gerrards Cross 1970)

——*Coole* (Cuala Press, Dublin 1931)

——*Cuchulain of Muirthemne: The Story of the Men of The Red Branch of Ulster*; preface by W.B. Yeats (Murray, London 1904)

——*Gods and Fighting Men: The Story of the Tuatha de Danaan and of the Fianna of Ireland*; preface by W.B. Yeats (Murray, London 1904)

——*Ideals in Ireland* (ed.) (Unicorn Press, London 1901)

——*Journals 1916–30* (ed. Lennox Robinson) (Putnam, London 1946)

——*The Kiltartan History Book* (Maunsel, Dublin 1909)

——*The Kiltartan Poetry Book – Translations from the Irish* (Putnam, London 1919)

——*Mr Gregory's Letter Box* (Colin Smythe, Gerrards Cross 1981)

——*Our Irish Theatre* (Putnam, London 1913)

——*Poets and Dreamers* [p. 138] (Hodges Figgis, Dublin 1903)

——*Seventy Years: Being an Autobiography of Lady Gregory* [pp. 20–30] (Macmillan, New York 1974)

——*Visions and Beliefs in the West of Ireland*; with Two

Essays and Notes by W.B. Yeats (2 vols.) (Putnam, London 1920)

——*Collected Works: The Coole Edition of Lady Gregory's writings in progress* (Colin Smythe, Gerrards Cross 1970)

Grein, J.T.: *Dramatic Criticism* (J. Long, London 1899)

Gwynn, Denis: *Edward Martyn and the Irish Revival* (Jonathan Cape, London 1930)

Gwynn, Stephen: *Essays of Today and Yesterday: Experiences of a Literary Man* [p. 67] (Thornton Butterworth, London 1926)

——*Oliver Goldsmith* (Thornton Butterworth, London 1935)

——*Saints and Scholars* (Thornton Butterworth, London 1929)

——*Scattering Branches: Tributes to the Memory of W.B. Yeats* (Macmillan, London 1940)

HALL, J.B.: *Random Records of a Reporter* (Simpkin Marshall, London n.d.)

Hall, Wayne E.: Shadowy Heroes (Irish literature in the 1890s) (Syracuse University Press, 1980)

Harpur, Geo. M.: *W.B. Yeats and W.T. Horton – Record of an Occult Friendship* (Macmillan, London 1980)

——*Yeats's Golden Dawn* (Macmillan, London 1974)

Haslip, Joan: *Parnell* (Stokes, New York 1937)

Headlam, Maurice: *Irish Reminiscences* (Robert Hale, London 1947)

Hogan, Robert (with James Kilroy): *The Modern Irish Drama:* (i) *The Irish Literary Theatre 1899–1901;* (ii) *Laying the Foundations 1902–1904;* (iii) *The Abbey Theatre 1905–1909* (Dolmen Press, Dublin 1975–78)

Holland, Vyvyan: *Son of Oscar Wilde* [p. 77] (Penguin Books, Harmondsworth 1957)

Holloway, Joseph: *Joseph Holloway's Abbey Theatre* (ed. Robert Hogan & Michael J. O'Neill) (South Illinois University Press, Carbondale 1967)

Holroyd, Michael: *The Genius of Shaw* (Hodder & Stoughton, London 1979)

Honan, Park: *Matthew Arnold: A Life* (Weidenfeld & Nicolson, London 1981)

Hone, Joseph: *The Life of George Moore* (Gollancz, London 1936)

——*W.B. Yeats, 1865–1939* (Macmillan, London 1965)

Howarth, Herbert: *The Irish Writers 1880–1940: Literature Under Parnell's Star* (Rockliff, London 1958)

Hunt, Hugh: *The Abbey Theatre, 1904–79* (Gill & Macmillan, Dublin 1979)

Hunter Blair, Sir David: *In Victorian Days* (Longmans, London 1939)

Hutchins, Patrick: *James Joyce's World* (Methuen, London 1957)

Hyde, Douglas: *Beside The Fire* (Nutt, London 1890)

——*Casadh An tSugain* (in Samhain No. 1) (T. Fisher Unwin, London 1901)

——*Love Songs of Connacht* (T. Fisher Unwin, London 1893)

——*Poems From The Irish* (Allen Figgis, Dublin 1963)

——*Songs Ascribed to Raftery* (Gill, Dublin 1963)

——*The Literary History of Ireland* (T. Fisher Unwin, London 1899)

——*The Religious Songs of Connacht Vols I & II* (T. Fisher Unwin, 1905)

——*The Revival of Irish Literature* (with Sir Charles Gavan Duffy and George Sigerson) (T. Fisher Unwin, London 1894)

——*The Stone of Truth* (Irish Academic Press, Dublin 1979)

Hyde, H. Montgomery: *The Life Of Oscar Wilde* [p. 77] (Eyre Methuen, London 1976)

Hyde, Mary: *Bernard Shaw and Alfred Douglas – A Correspondence* (John Murray, London 1982)

INGLIS, Brian: *The Story of Ireland* (Faber & Faber, London 1956)

——*West Briton* (Faber & Faber, London 1962)

Irwin, Wilmot: *Betrayal in Ireland* (The Northern Whig, Belfast)

JACKSON, HOLBROOK: *The Eighteen Nineties* (Grant Richards, London 1913)

Jeffares, A. Norman (with K.G.W. Cross): *A Centenary Tribute to W.B. Yeats* (Macmillan, London 1965)

——*Yeats, Man and Poet* (Routledge & Kegan Paul, London 1962)

Johnson, Josephine: *Bernard Shaw's New Woman, Florence Farr* (Colin Smythe, Gerrards Cross 1975)

Johnston, Charles: *From The Upanishads* [p. 60] (Whaley, Dublin 1896)

Jordan, R. Furneaux: *A Medieval Vision of William Morris* (The William Morris Society, London 1960)

Joyce, James: *A Portrait of the Artist As a Young Man* [p. 159] (W.B. Huebsch, New York 1916)

——*Chamber Music* (Elkin Matthews, London 1907)

——*Dubliners* (Grant Richards, London 1914)

——*Pomes Penyeach* (Shakespeare & Co., Paris 1927)

——*Selected Letters* (ed. Richard Ellmann) (Faber & Faber, London 1975)

——*Stephen Hero* (Jonathan Cape, London 1944)

——*The Critical Writings* (ed. Richard Ellmann & Ellsworth Mason) (Faber & Faber, London 1959)

——*Ulysses* (Shakespeare & Co., Paris 1922)

Joyce, P.W.: *English As We Speak It In Ireland* (Wolfhound Press, Dublin 1979)

Joyce, Stanislaus: *Dublin Diary* (Cornell University Press, Ithaca 1962)

Judge, W.M.Q.: *Notes on the Bhagavad Gita* (Theosophy Company, Bombay 1965)

Jullian, Philippe: *Oscar Wilde* (Constable, London 1969)

Jung, Carl: *Memories, Dreams, Reflections* (Vintage Books, New York 1963)

KAIN, RICHARD M.: *Dublin In the Age of W.B. Yeats and James Joyce* (Norman University Press, Oklahama 1962)

——*Susan Mitchell* (Bucknell University Press, Lewisburg 1970)

Kavanagh, Peter: *The Story of the Abbey Theatre* (Devin-Adair, New York 1950)

Kelleher, John V.: *Matthew Arnold & The Celtic Revival In 'Perspectives of Criticism'* (ed. Harry Levin) (Harvard University Press, Cambridge, Mass. 1950)

Kennedy, Tom (ed.): *Victorian Dublin* (Kennedy, Dublin 1980)

Kennelly, Brendan (ed.): *The Penguin Book of Irish Verse* (Penguin Books, Harmondsworth 1970)

Kettle, Thomas M.: *An Irishman's Calendar* (Browne & Nolan, Dublin n.d.)

——*The Day's Burden* (Browne & Nolan, Dublin 1937)

Kiberd, Dealan: *Synge And The Irish Language* (Macmillan, London 1979)

Kiely, Benedict: *Poor Scholar – A Study of the Works and Days of William Carleton* (Sheed & Ward, New York 1947)

Kilroy, James: *The Playboy Riots* (Dolmen Press, Dublin 1971)

LAWRENCE, W.J.: *Old Theatre Days and Ways* (Harrap, London 1935)

Le Fanu, W.R.: *Seventy Years of Irish Life* (Edward Arnold, London 1914)

Leslie, Anita: *The Marlborough House Set* (Doubleday, New York 1973)

Leslie, Shane: *Doomsland* (Chatto & Windus, London 1923)

——*The Film of Memory* (Michael Joseph, London 1938)

Lhombreaud, Roger: *Arthur Symons* [pp. 106–107] (The Unicorn Press, London 1963)

Lindsay, T.S.: *Gay to Grave* (Church of Ireland Publishing, Dublin 1932)

Longaker, Mark: *Ernest Dowson* [p. 105] (Oxford University Press, London 1945)

Longford, Christine: *Biography of Dublin* (Methuen, London 1936)

Longford, Elizabeth: *A Pilgrimage of Passion* [p. 25] (Weidenfeld and Nicolson, London 1979)

Lydon, James: *Ireland in the Middle Ages* (Gill & Macmillan, Dublin 1973)

Lynham, Shevaun: *Humanity Dick* (Hamish Hamilton, London 1975)

Lyons, F.S.L.: *Charles Stewart Parnell* (Collins, London 1977)

Lyons, J.B.: *Brief Lives of Irish Doctors 1600–1965* (Blackwater, Dublin 1978)

Lytton, Constance: *Letters, Selected and Arranged by Betty Balfour* (Heinemann, London 1925)

MCBRIDE, Maud Gonne: *A Servant of the Queen* [pp. 79–81] (Gollancz, London 1935)

McDonagh, Thomas: *Literature in Ireland* (The Talbot Press, Dublin 1916)

McLysaght, Edward: *Irish Life in the 17th Century* (Blackwell, London 1950)

——*Changing Times* (Colin Smythe, Gerrards Cross 1978)

McManus, M.J.: *Adventures of an Irish Bookman* (The Talbot Press, Dublin 1952)

McNeill, J.G. Swift: *What I have Seen and Heard* (Arrowsmith, London 1925)

Madden, Daniel O. (ed.): *Grattan's Speeches* (Duffy, Dublin 1867)

Manganiello, Dominic: *Joyce's Politics* (Routledge & Kegan Paul, London 1980)

Mannin, Ethel: *Two Studies in Integrity* (Jarrolds, London 1954)

Martin, Augustine: *James Stephens* (Gill & MacMillan, Dublin 1977)

——*W.B. Yeats* (Gill & MacMillan, Dublin 1983)

Martyn, Edward: *The Dream Physician* (Talbot Press, Dublin 1914)

——*Grangecolman* (Maunsel, Dublin 1912)

——*Ireland's Battle for her Language* (Gaelic League, Dublin n.d.)

——*Morgante The Lessor, His Notorious Life and Wonderful Deeds* (Swan Sonnenschein, London 1890)

——*'The Heather Field' and 'Maeve'*; with an introduction by George Moore (Duckworth, London 1899)

——*'The Tale of a Town' and 'An Enchanted Sea'* (T. Fisher Unwin, London 1902)

Masefield, John: *Some Memories of W.B. Yeats* [p. 117] (Cuala Press, Dublin 1940)

Maxwell, W.H.: *Wild Sports of the West* (Gresham, London n.d.)

Mercier, Vivian: *The Irish Comic Tradition* (Clarendon, Oxford 1962)

Meyer, Dorothy M.: *Memories of AE* (Colin Smythe, Gerrards Cross 1978)

Meyer, Michael: *Ibsen* (Penguin Books, Harmondsworth 1974)

Mitchell, Susan: *George Moore* [p. 219] (Maunsel, Dublin 1913)

Moody, T.W.: *Davitt and the Irish Revolution* (Oxford University Press, New York 1981)

Moore, George Augustus: *A Drama in Muslin* (Vizetelly, London 1886)

——*A Mummer's Wife* (Vizetelly, London 1885 & Heinemann, London 1918)

——*Celibates* (Walter Scott, London 1895)

——*Confessions of a Young Man* (Heinemann, London 1916)

——*Conversations in Ebury Street* (Heinemann, London 1930)

——*Diarmuid and Grania* (in *Dublin Magazine*, April–June 1951)

——*Esther Waters* (Walter Scott, London 1894)

——*Evelyn Innes* (T. Fisher Unwin, London 1898)

——*Hail and Farewell: Ave, Salve & Vale* (ed. Richard Cave) [pp. 153–55, 161–2, 166–69, 179–81, 192–94, 197–200, 223–24, 256] (Colin Smythe, Gerrards Cross 1976)

——*Impressions and Opinions* (Werner Laurie, London 1913)

——*Letters from George Moore to Edouard Dujardin, 1886-1922* (ed. John Eglinton) (Crosby Craige, New York 1929)

——*Letters of George Moore with an introduction by John Eglinton, to whom they were written* (Sydenham, Bournemouth 1942)

——*Letters to Lady Cunard, 1895–1933* (Rupert Hart Davis, London 1957)

——*Memoirs of My Dead Life* (Heinemann, London 1921)

——*Modern Painting* [pp. 34–35] (Walter Scott, London 1893)

——*Parnell and His Island* [p. 37] (Swan Sonnenschein, London 1887)

——*The Bending of the Bough* (T. Fisher Unwin, London 1900)

——*The Lake* (Heinemann, London 1921)

——*The Untilled Field* (T. Fisher Unwin, London 1903)

——*Vain Fortune* (Henry, London 1891)

——*Ebury Collected edition* (20 vols) (Heinemann, London 1937)

Morgan, Charles: *Epitaph on George Moore* (Macmillan, London 1935)

Morris, W. O'Connor: *Memories & Thoughts of a Life* (George Allen, London 1895)

Murphy, Gerard: *Saga and Myth in Ancient Ireland* (Sign of the Three Candles, Dublin 1971)

Murphy, William M.: *Prodigal Father, The Life of John Butler Yeats* [p. 57–58, 64–67] (Cornell Univ., Ithaca 1978)

Murray, Rev Robert: *Archbishop Bernard* (Hodges Figgis, Dublin 1931)

NIC SHIUBHLAIGH, Maire: *The Splendid Years* [p. 229–30, 234, 238] (James Duffy, Dublin 1955)

O H-AODHA, Michéal: *Theatre in Ireland* (Basil Blackwell, Oxford 1974)

O'Brien, Conor Cruise: *The Shaping of Modern Ireland* (Routledge & Kegan Paul, London 1960)

O'Broin, Leon: *The Prime Reformer* (Sidgwick & Jackson, London 1971)

O'Brien, Wm.: *The Parnell of Real Life* [p. 18] (T. Fisher Unwin, London 1926)

O'Casey, Sean: *Autobiographies* (Macmillan, London 1963)

——*Letters: Vol I, 1910–41, vol II, 1942–54* (Macmillan, New York 1980)

O'Connor, T.P.: *The Parnell Movement* (Bastable, London 1887)

O'Driscoll, Robert ed.: *Theatre and Nationalism in 20th Century Ireland* (University of Toronto Press, Toronto 1971)

O'Fearáil, Pádraig: *The Story of Conradh na Gaelige* (Clodhanna Teo, Dublin 1971)

O'Grady, Hugh Art: *Standish James O'Grady, The Man and the Writer* (Talbot Press, Dublin 1929)

O'Grady, Standish James: *Early Bardic Literature* (Rivington, London 1879)

——*Fionn and His Companions* (Talbot Press, Dublin 1921)

O'Kelly, Claire: *Illustrated Guide to Newgrange* (O'Kelly, Cork 1967)

O'Sullivan, Seumas: *Poems* (Maunsel, Dublin 1912)

——*The Rose and Bottle and Other Essays* (The Talbot Press, Dublin 1946)

O'Sullivan, Seumas (with Estella Solomons): *Retrospect* (The Dolmen Press, Dublin 1973)

O'Sullivan, Vincent: *Aspects of Wilde* [p. 48] (Constable, London 1936)

O'Tuama, Sean: *The Gaelic League Idea* (Mercier Press, Cork 1972)

Owens, Graham ed.: *George Moore's Mind & Art* (Oliver & Boyd, London 1968)

PACKENHAM, Thomas: *The Boer War* (Weidenfeld & Nicolson, London 1979)

Paige, D.D.: *Ezra Pound, Selected Letters, 1907–41* (New Directions, New York 1950)

Payne, Ben Iden: *A Life in a Wooden O.* [p. 253] (Yale University Press, New Haven 1977)

Pearl Cyril: *The Three Lives of Gavan Duffy* (New South Wales University Press, Kensington 1979)

Pearson, Hesketh: *Bernard Shaw* (Collins, London 1942)

Plunkett, Horace: *Ireland in the New Century* (Murray, London 1905)

Pogson, Rex: *Miss Horniman and the Gaiety Theatre, Manchester* (Rockliff, London 1952)

Postgate, Robert: *Robert Emmet* (Martin Secker, London 1931)

Power, Arthur: *Conversations with James Joyce* (Millington, London 1974)

——*From the Old Waterford House* (The Carthage Press, Dublin 1940)

RAFTERY, Joseph: *The Celts* (Mercier Press, Cork 1964)

Raitt, A.W.: *The Life of Villiers de l'Isle Adam* [p. 34] (Clarendon, Oxford 1981)

Ransome, Arthur: *Oscar Wilde* (Methuen, London 1913)

Reid, B.L.: *The Man from New York (John Quinn and his Friends)* (Oxford University Press, New York 1968)

Renan, J. Ernest: *The Poetry of the Celtic Races* (Kennikat Press, Port Washington, New York, 1970)

Richardson, Joanna: *Théophile Gautier* (Max Reinhardt, London 1958)

Robinson, Sir Henry: *Memories Wise and Otherwise* (Cassell & Co., London 1923)

Robinson, Hilary: *Somerville and Ross* (Gill & Macmillan, Dublin 1980)

Robinson, Lennox: *Bryan Cooper* (Constable, London 1931)

——*Curtain Up* (Michael Joseph, London 1942)

——*Dark Days* (The Talbot Press and T. Fisher Unwin, 1918)

——*Ireland's Abbey Theatre – A History, 1899–1951* (Sidgwick & Jackson, London 1951)

——*I Sometimes Think* (Talbot Press, Dublin 1956)

Rodgers, Wm.: *Irish Literary Portraits* [p. 234] (BBC Publications, London 1972)

Rolleston, C.H.: *Portrait of an Irishman* [p. 70] (Methuen, London 1939)

Rolleston, T.W.: *Sea Spray, Verses and Translations* (Maunsel, Dublin 1909)

Rose, Marilyn G.: *Katherine Tynan* (Bucknell University, Lewisburg 1974)

Rosset, B.C.: *Shaw of Dublin* (The Pennsylvania State University Press, 1964)

Rothenstein, Wm.: *Men and Memories* (3 vols) (Faber & Faber, London 1931–39)

Russell, Leonard (ed.): *English Wits* (Hutchinson, London 1940)

Russell, George William (AE): *Collected Poems* (Macmillan, London 1935)
——*Co-operation and Nationality* (Maunsel, Dublin 1912)
——*Deirdre* (Maunsel, Dublin 1907)
——*Letters From AE* (ed. Alan Denson) (Abelard Schuman, London 1961)
——*The Candle of Vision* [p. 60] (Macmillan, Dublin 1918)
——*The Inner and the Outer Ireland* (The Talbot Press, Dublin 1921)
——*The Living Torch* (ed. Monk Gibbon) (Macmillan, London 1938)
——*The National Being* (Maunsel, Dublin 1916)
Ryan, Desmond: *The Sword of Light: From the Four Masters to Douglas Hyde* (Arthur Barker, London 1939)
Ryan, Dr. Mark F.: *Fenian Memories* [pp. 104, 184] (Gill, Dublin 1945)
Ryan, W.P.: *The Irish Literary Revival* (privately printed, London 1894)

SADDLEMYER, Ann: *Theatre Business* (Colin Smythe, Gerrards Cross 1982)
Setterquist, Jan: *Ibsen and the Beginnings of Anglo-Irish Drama: 1. John Millington Synge* (Lundequist, Upsala 1951)
——*2. Edward Martyn* (Lundequist, Upsala 1960)
Shaw, George Bernard: *Autobiography* (Max Reinhardt, 1971)
——*Collected Letters* (ed. D.H. Lawrence) Vols. I. 1874–1897, & II, 1898–1910 (Max Reinhardt, London 1965 & 1972)
——*John Bull's Other Island* (Constable, London 1907)
——*Shaw and Ibsen* (ed. J.L. Wiesenthal) (University of Toronto Press 1979)
Sheehy, Jeanne: *The Rediscovery of Ireland's Past* (Thames & Hudson, London 1980)
Sheridan, John D.: *Mangan* (Talbot Press, Dublin 1937)
Short, K.R.M.: *The Dynamite War* (Gill & Macmillan, London 1979)
Sinnett, A.P.: *Esoteric Buddhism* (Chapman & Hall, London 1892)
Skelton, Robin (with David Clarke): *Irish Renaissance* (Dolmen Press, Dublin 1965)
Smythe, Colin: *A Guide to Coole Park* (Colin Smythe, Gerrards Cross 1973)
——*Robert Gregory* (Colin Smythe, Gerrards Cross 1981)

Somerville-Large, Peter: *Dublin* (Hamish Hamilton, London 1979)

Stanford, W.B.: *Ireland and The Classical Tradition* (Allen & Figgis, Dublin 1976)

Starkie, Enid: *A Lady's Child* (Faber & Faber, London 1941)

Stephens, Edward: *My Uncle John* (ed. Andrew Carpenter) (Oxford University Press, London 1974)

Stachey, Lytton: *Eminent Victorians* (Chatto & Windus, London 1918)

——*Queen Victoria* (Chatto & Windus, London 1921)

Summerfield, Henry: *That Myriad-Minded Man, AE* (Rowman & Littlefield, Totowa, N.J. 1975)

Symons, Arthur: *Cities, Sea Coasts and Islands* (Collins, London 1919)

——*Collected Works* (9 vols) [pp. 123–24] (Secker, London 1929)

——*The Symbolist Movement in Literature* (Heinemann, London 1899)

Synge, John Millington: *Collected Works* (gen. ed. Robin Skelton) (Oxford University Press, London 1962–68)

——*i Poems* (ed. Robin Skelton) (OUP, London 1962)

——*ii Prose* (ed. Alan Price) [pp. 133–134] (OUP, London, 1966)

——*iii Plays I* (ed. Ann Saddlemyer), 2 (ed. Ann Saddlemyer) (OUP, London 1968)

——*Collected Letters* (ed. Ann Saddlemyer) (Clarendon, Oxford 1983)

——*Some letters of John Millington Synge to Lady Gregory and W.B. Yeats* (Cuala Press, Dublin 1971)

TAAFFE, Michael: *Those Days Are Gone Away* (Hutchinson, London 1959)

Tery, Simone: *En Irlande* (Flammarion, Paris 1923)

Thackeray, William Makepeace: *The Irish Sketch Book* (Oxford University Press, London 1908)

Thompson, David: *Woodbrook* (Penguin Books, Harmondsworth 1976)

Tillett, Gregory: *The Elder Brother (Biography of Charles Webster Leadbeater)* (Routledge & Kegan Paul, London 1982)

Tuohy, Frank: *W.B. Yeats* (Macmillan, London 1976)

Tynan, Katherine: *The Wandering Years* (Constable, London 1922)
——*Twenty-five Years* [pp. 78, 83] (Smith, Elder, London 1913)
——*The Middle Years* [p. 60] (Constable, London 1916)
UNTERRECKER, John: *Yeats and Patrick McCartan: A Fenian Friendship* (Dolmen Press, Dublin 1965)
Ussher, Arland P.: *Three Great Irishmen: Shaw, Yeats, Joyce* (Gollancz, London 1952)

WALKLEY, Arthur B.: *Drama and Life* (Methuen, London 1905)
——*Playhouse Impressions* (T. Fisher Unwin, London 1892)
Wilde, Lady: *Ancient Legends of Ireland* (Ward & Downey, London 1888)
Wilde, Sir William: *Irish Popular Superstitions* (Irish Academic Press, 1979)
Wilson, Edmund: *Axel's Castle* (Scribner, New York 1943)
Wolfe, Humbert: *George Moore* (Eyre & Spottswood, London 1931)
Woodham Smith, Cecil: *The Great Hunger* (Harper & Row, New York 1962)
Worth, Katherine: *Irish Drama of Europe: From Yeats to Beckett* (The Athlone Press, London 1978)
Wyndham, George: *Essays in Romantic Literature* (Macmillan, London 1919)
Wyndham, Horace: *Speranza: A Biography of Lady Wilde* (Boardman, London 1951)
Wisenthal, J.L. ed.: *Shaw & Ibsen; with introduction by JLW* (University of Toronto Press, 1979)

YATES, Frances A.: *Giordano Bruno and the Hermetic Tradition* (The University of Chicago Press, 1964)
Yeats, J.B.: *Letters to His Son* (Faber & Faber, London 1934)
Yeats, William Butler: *Autobiographies* [pp. 48, 74, 140, 168-9] (Macmillan, London 1955)
——*A Vision* (Warner Laurie, London 1926)
——*Collected Plays* (Macmillan, London 1952)
——*Collected Poems* (Macmillan, London 1956)
——*Essays and Introductions* (Macmillan, London 1961)
——*Explorations* (Macmillan, London 1962)
——*Irish Fairy Tales* (T. Fisher Unwin, London 1892)
——*John Sherman & Dhoya* (T. Fisher Unwin, London 1891)
——*Memoirs: Autobiography – First Draft, Journal* (ed. Denis

Donoghue) (Macmillan, London 1972)

——*Mythologies* (Macmillan, London 1962)

——*Representative Irish Tales* (Putnam, London 1891)

——*The Letters of W.B. Yeats* (ed. Allan Wade) (Macmillan, New York 1955)

——*The Secret Rose* (Lawrence and Bullen, London 1897)

——*The Celtic Twilight* (Lawrence and Bullen, London 1893)

——*The Senate Speeches of W.B. Yeats* (ed. Donald R. Pearce) (Faber and Faber, 1960)

——*The Wanderings of Oisin* (Kegan, Paul, Trench, London 1889)

——*Uncollected Prose* (2 vols) (Columbia University, New York, 1970 and 1975)

Young, Ella: *Flowering Dusk* (Longmans, New York 1945)

Index

411